ON THE EIGHTH DAY

PRAYING THROUGH THE LITURGICAL YEAR

Breedlove, Kane, Perry, and West

WESTBOW
PRESS®
A DIVISION OF THOMAS NELSON
& ZONDERVAN

WestBow Press books may be ordered through booksellers or by contacting:

WestBow Press
A Division of Thomas Nelson & Zondervan
1663 Liberty Drive
Bloomington, IN 47403
www.westbowpress.com
844-714-3454

ISBN: 978-1-6642-5477-0 (sc)
ISBN: 978-1-6642-5478-7 (hc)
ISBN: 978-1-6642-5476-3 (e)

Library of Congress Control Number: 2022901473

Printed in the United States of America.

WestBow Press rev. date: 2/21/2022

With every blessing in Christ —

Willa Kane

Sally Breedlove

DEDICATION

With gratitude to
Lekita Essa,
who heard the Holy Spirit's call to prayer
and shared it with a waiting world.

Contents

Foreword

Do nothing, and the world will define you by default. Your habits shape you and can alter the way you think, which is why following Jesus closely requires consistent training. You will only get to know Jesus more intimately as you spend time with him—and the main means he has given us by which to spend time with him are the central disciplines of prayer and reading his Word.

Even though most followers of Christ know the importance of these central disciplines, many find their times of praying and reading scripture to be shallow, boring, or even overwhelming. Instead of allowing them to experience deeper intimacy with Jesus, their hit-or-miss approaches can lead to frustration. Although they want to grow, they do not know how to cultivate a flourishing devotional time with God.

On the Eighth Day recognizes the need for followers of Jesus to practice their faith through spending consistent time in scripture and in prayer. In the introduction, Madison Perry notes that "the default ordering of our age revolves around habits of work and breaks from work." Our lives have become so inundated with *doing* that we forget what it is like simply to *know* Christ and *be* with him.

On the Eighth Day addresses our deep need to dwell with Jesus. The structure of *On the Eighth Day* is oriented around the liturgical church calendar, a rich heritage of faith based on a different rhythm of life—one not centered on work schedules but on the Great Story that God has been writing. As Perry writes, these liturgical rhythms "give you the opportunity to connect your daily exposure to God's Word with the large story of God's redeeming work." The resulting devotionals sanctify space and time, using each day to draw you through the movement of the year.

Each day in this guide to prayer opens with a passage from scripture, continues with a call to prayer based on that passage, and finishes with a recommended closing prayer. This structure is similar to two of my own resources—*Handbook to Prayer* and *Handbook to Renewal*—that help readers pray scripture back to God through a balance between form and freedom in their prayer lives. I have found that using these devotional tools at the beginning and again at the end of the day for even five minutes at a time can help you cultivate a deeper intimacy with Jesus. In addition, using *On the Eighth Day* provides you with an opportunity to encounter Christ through a consistent structure that gives you the freedom to respond to what you read.

Numerous writers, each bringing their own unique voices, have come together to contribute to this devotional out of their diversity. Their voices are unified through and driven by their dependence and reflection on scripture. You too have the opportunity to experience this unity and diversity as you meditate on what is written and respond in your own words in prayer. *On the Eighth Day*, then, exemplifies the beauty of the unity and diversity of the body of Christ. God has given each of us insights and spiritual gifts to encourage and equip one another, "speaking the truth in love" (Ephesians 4:15 NASB).

As you reflect on the words of this work, I pray that you will move into a deeper relationship with the one who created you, trusting in the Father, abiding in the Son, and walking by the Holy Spirit.

Kenneth Boa
President and Founder of Trinity House Publishers, Reflections Ministries, and Omnibus Media Ministries
Author of *Handbook to Prayer, Handbook to Renewal,* and *Conformed to His Image*

Introduction

MADISON PERRY

You hold in your hands a reminder of an invitation you received long ago. When you first heard this invitation, you may have felt excited. At this point, though, perhaps it is more like a relic of a past enthusiasm. You may have overlooked it, set it aside, or covered it up in embarrassment. Perhaps it now lurks on the fringes of your life.

But *On the Eighth Day* is a reminder of that invitation to know and be known by Christ. You have been invited to a banquet, to feast in the halls of Zion and dwell forever in the kingdom of God. Before you lies nothing less than everything, no matter what you have lost or suffered, or even inflicted on the world around you.

The invitation to step into that reality and to love and be loved by God is present on every page of the Bible. However, left to our own devices, we do not have eyes to see God's glory or ears to hear God's call. Adrift in the imagination of our hearts, we wander far. The outcome is that scripture's gloss becomes familiar and dull. Yet this need not be the case. God's Word is living and active, capable of piercing even to the dividing of soul and spirit, and his mercies are new every morning. Guided by the Holy Spirit, scripture presents you with a feast to take in and offer back to God in prayer.

There is another name for the day you are living today: the eighth day. Jesus Christ was resurrected the day after the last day of the week. If the first day was a day of creation, the eighth day was one of new creation, life in Christ on the far side of the grave. By the power of the Holy Spirit, you can live in this new day in the midst of the old order. Today you can be reconciled to God and live into the day of resurrection as you respond to God in faith.

Within *On the Eighth Day* you will find daily *calls to prayer*, opportunities to be guided by scripture into prayer. Each day you will find passages of scripture that pull you into the world of God's Word, new landscapes of fresh truth where the Holy Spirit will equip you for friendship with God. Rather than hoping to provide "meditations," whose main purpose would be to relate to you our thoughts or devotional ideas, we hope that as you engage with what is present within these pages, our words will recede, leaving you open to God's Word and its power. We cannot set the terms of your engagement with God, but we can hope to guide you into what may feel like new terrain and prepare you for real life—life with Christ.

These calls to prayer were written during the onset of the global COVID-19 crisis of 2020–21, a time when our best attempts to order our own lives were exposed as gravely wanting and founded on shifting sand. Our routines instantly evaporated, and our institutions seemed helpless. How were we to draw near to the Lord during a shutdown? The Spirit worked in our group of friends to develop new rhythms of prayer that began and ended with scripture. We shared this idea with others and began crafting nightly invitations to prayer. Before long, thousands of believers around the world had begun to engage in prayer with us.

The dilemma that faced us so obviously during that time period remains with us now. What will quicken our hearts, shatter and rebuild our imaginations, and pull us back toward our God on a daily basis? Surely God's Word is up to the challenge.

Speaking of rhythms, while the default ordering of our age revolves around habits of work and breaks from work, there is another pattern of living that *On the Eighth Day* highlights. In the Old Testament, the Lord sets annual patterns of feasting, reflection, sacrifice, and action for Israel in the form of the annual calendar. The early church carried on with these patterns, reconfiguring them to make plain their reference to Christ. Guided by the Holy Spirit, the church attempted to integrate the life of Jesus Christ into its yearly path of seasons and feasts. The church's annual circuit orbited the person of Christ, every day bringing a fresh opportunity to draw real life from the one who is life.

We have ordered *On the Eighth Day* to follow the church's calendar in the following order: Advent to Christmas; Christmas to Epiphany; Epiphany to Lent; Lent to Holy Week; Holy Week to Easter; Easter to Ordinary Time. Each section begins with a brief introduction to the season. Following the church's calendar will give you the opportunity to connect your daily exposure to God's Word with the large story of God's redeeming work. In contrast to the moment-to-moment life of quiet desperation set by modern culture, here we find an older, truer way of living, one that draws its momentum from the arc of salvation and discovers deep wells of rest and strength in Christ.

As you immerse yourself in the Word of God, open yourself to his Spirit, and orient yourself within the life of Jesus, we pray that you will move into a new reality. The kingdom of God is near. Repent, believe, and find your life in the gospel!

Introduction to the Christian Year

STEVEN E. BREEDLOVE

It requires no profound insight to see that people in the modern digital and economic world have no framework for how to think well about time. We have a progression of school years and, within them, the progression of material learned and exams taken. We also have a series of purchasing days tied to certain festivals—Halloween, Black Friday, Christmas. But we have lost the sense that each season is connected both to the preceding one and the one that follows.

Perhaps this loss results from the movement away from an agricultural world, where land was left fallow for a season before it was sown and where sowing necessarily preceded growing, which resulted in harvest. It was impossible in the agricultural world to divorce one season from another, and each season contributed its own gift and preparation to the next. But this loss of connection between the seasons is also the result of trading the church calendar for the economic calendar, where every season is "harvest" and none is "planting."

The church calendar is not a series of discrete seasons, yet our discipleship under the tyranny of the economic calendar makes it initially difficult to see this. As the 2019 Book of Common Prayer says, "The Christian Year consists of two cycles" (687). In other words, we don't have Advent, Christmas, and Epiphany. Instead, we have the Incarnation Cycle, which consists of Advent, Christmas, and Epiphany. And we don't have Lent, Easter, and Pentecost. Instead, we have the Paschal Cycle, which consists of Lent, Easter, and Pentecost. In each of these cycles, the seasons are intricately connected to and dependent on one another, and in each, the pattern is the same—preparation, celebration, and growth. In a previous age, we might have simply said that mortification and repentance must precede rejoicing, because they sow the seeds for it, and that rejoicing is the foundation for growth, discipleship, and mission, because we reap a harvest from the object of our rejoicing. We cannot divorce Lent from Easter, and we cannot divorce Easter from Pentecost. Each season prepares for the next, and trying to live the spiritual life in only one season is like trying to have only harvest without sowing. We need to be planted anew each year. The Christian year offers us the framework for this.

As you let *On the Eighth Day* help shape your day-by-day prayers, notice how your response to scripture and your prayers change as you hold in mind what season it is. Is it a time for preparation? for rejoicing? for a rekindled awareness of God's presence and his call to us?

God himself has given us the gift of agricultural seasons and the gift of the rhythm of the Christian year. Let them both draw you more deeply into a prayer-filled life with God.

Introduction to Advent

Advent is a season of hopeful waiting for the coming of Christ. We fast in Advent, but it is a fast motivated by expectation, not penitence. It is like anticipating a wedding banquet, which we would hardly prepare for by eating too much cheap food. Instead, we wait with modest fasting, with joy and expectation, because a rich and lavish feast is coming. The certainty of Christmas offers us the ability to wait patiently and steadfastly.

It is ultimately the return of Christ, not Christmas, that we await in Advent. The First Coming is proof that the Second will also arrive, and our joyful waiting for Christmas should prepare us for Christ's return. More than anything, this is the season of the year when we should cultivate longing and hope for the Second Coming of Christ.

Prayer in Advent is marked by this expectation and grounded in the truth that Christ will come again and restore all things. Every reading of scripture should be considered from the standpoint, "What will this mean when Christ returns?" The season offers us a particular form of discipleship—training in expectancy as we wait within the tension of Christ's First and Second Coming. It is the season when, even as we learn hopeful patience, our hearts fill with the prayer, "Lord, I long for your return! Please prepare me to celebrate your arrival!"

Advent Day 1

NATHAN BAXTER

Reflect on Isaiah 48:12–22

Call to Prayer

The passage opens with God's calling his covenant people to listen. The earth and the heavens listen to God when he summons them. Will God's people act worse than soil and stone? "Listen to me," covenant people (Isaiah 48:12 NIV).

God summons all people—and all powers—to gather and listen: "Come together, *all of you*, and listen" (Isaiah 48:14 NIV; emphasis added). God addresses all people: the favored and the marginal, the covenant-embraced and the covenant outsiders. God addresses all powers: the spiritual and the social, the rising and the falling. Whoever and however you may be, God summons you.

God invites all people to listen closely to him at all times: "*Come near me* and listen to this" (Isaiah 48:16a NIV). Listening closely is not only a matter of paying attention but also a matter of drawing near. And drawing near is more than a matter of proximity; it's a matter of posture, of attitude, of disposition. God is speaking openly: "From the first announcement I have not spoken in secret" (Isaiah 48:16b NIV). God is present to us wherever and whenever we may be: "At the time it happens, I am there" (Isaiah 48:16c NIV). Will you not only come near to God where you are but also have a willingness to attend?

The same God who made all things (Isaiah 48:13) and who directs all circumstances and powers (Isaiah 48:14–15) is ever willing and able to redeem, teach, and direct (Isaiah 48:17). "If only you had paid attention" (Isaiah 48:18 NIV). The words are less an indictment and more a lament from God's loyal-love heart.

What are you hearing in Isaiah 48:18–22?

As you go to prayer, listening to God's voice, how are you being drawn near to hear and trust the God who is with you?

Recommended Closing Prayer

> Speak, Lord, your servant is listening.
> *(1 Samuel 3:9 NIV)*

Advent Day 2

ART GOING

Reflect on Isaiah 49:1-6

Call to Prayer

Isaiah 49 is the second of the towering servant songs of Isaiah. There at the beginning is that Advent word: *listen!*

The promise of the Servant's coming is not for captive Israel only. God's Servant will be "a light for the nations" (Isaiah 49:6 ESV). God's salvation is going global!

In the face of uncertainty and polarization, at the beginning of a possibly dark winter season, is there light for the nations? Is there a message of hope?

This passage in Isaiah gives us a resounding yes! We will have a new beginning and an everlasting Savior. We will see salvation stretching to the ends of the earth. There is no better news for our weary world.

Isaiah beckons us to let God have the last word and to listen to his promise to reconnect the people with himself and to put the land in order.

As you pray, are you able to imagine yourself being called to be a part of God's servant people, the ones he will use to bring light to the nations? As you hear that promise, pray for God to kindle in you a holy imagination, and ask how you might be a light-bringer this season.

Recommended Closing Prayer

> Lighten our darkness, we beseech you, O lord; and by your great mercy defend us from all perils and dangers of this night; for the love of your only Son, our Savior Jesus Christ. Amen.
>
> *(Anglican Church in North America Book of Common Prayer)*

Advent Day 3
ART GOING

Reflect on Isaiah 50:4–5

Call to Prayer

Does God waken your ear to hear? Does the Lord speak to you through his Word? The prophet's vivid imagery describes an everyday experience of listening with anticipation of hearing a word.

> The Lord has given me the tongue of those who are taught,
> that I may know how to sustain with a word him who is
> weary. (Isaiah 50:4 ESV)

Of course, Isaiah 50—before it is a word to and about us—is first a picture of Jesus, the Servant. Can you picture the Lord beginning each day having his ear opened to hear as those who are taught? Jesus's decisive response was obedience rooted in listening.

We also read so that we may hear as obedient servants. We hear so that we may be comforters. Our comforting sends us back each day for a fresh word. Isaiah 50 invites us into this rhythmic vocation.

The driving impulse for our listening is so that we will know how to sustain with a word someone who is weary. You likely won't have to look far to find a weary friend or family member. Do you have a word for them?

As you pray, remember that everything depends on your becoming a hearer before God. Take time each day—at best, a regular fixed time— to read the Bible and to listen quietly for a word spoken to you. Ask for your heart to be stirred for a living conversation with the Father in prayer. And ask for a word that you may share with someone in need.

Recommended Closing Prayer

> Blessed Lord, who caused all Holy Scriptures to be written
> for our learning: Grant us so to hear them, read, mark, learn,
> and inwardly digest them, that by patience and the comfort
> of your holy Word we may embrace and ever hold fast the

blessed hope of everlasting life, which you have given us in our Savior Jesus Christ; who lives and reigns with you and the Holy Spirit, one God, for ever and ever. Amen.
(Anglican Church in North America Book of Common Prayer)

Advent Day 4

ART GOING

Reflect on Isaiah 51:1–8

Call to Prayer

Throughout Advent, God desires to keep us in an attentive frame of mind. "Ponder the rock from which you were cut," reads another version of Isaiah 51:1 (MSG). The Lord invites you to ponder, to look back, and to reflect on *the rock from which you were hewn*. Look back to Abraham and the call to go out, not knowing anything except God's promise and assured companionship. That's one of the fruits of listening and pondering; we get reacquainted with the promise-giver, and he transforms our perspective.

Isaiah 51 is packed with incentives to keep listening to God. The first incentive is that God is a life-giver. If he could bless old Abraham and barren Sarah with new life, and out of that unpromising beginning create a nation to bless the nations, then why wouldn't he do something new with you and me? What blessing and multiplication can you imagine in your life?

Not only that, but also God is a world-changer. Do you like the way the world is now? Neither does God. The difference between you and him is that he can change it—through his life-transforming gospel. Maybe it's time to turn off the news of the day for a moment and tune in to the good news of God's redeeming work.

Finally, our God is a courage-inspirer. Don't be afraid. He made you. He will be your Comforter, your Keeper, your Friend.

As you pray, think about Abraham and Sarah, and celebrate that you were hewn from the same rock. Pray filled with hopeful anticipation of God's unremitting new creation. The apostle Paul loved reminding his fellow believers that God had promised to send the Holy Spirit, who would *come alongside to build them up*. Pray for that!

Recommended Closing Prayer

O, Father, fill our hearts with faith. Come alongside us, Holy Spirit, and lead us in the way everlasting. Be our Comforter, our Keeper, our Friend. In the precious name of Jesus. Amen.

Advent Day 5

ART GOING

Reflect on Isaiah 52:7–10

Call to Prayer

Can you hear it? In the din of our noisy world, through the relentless voices inside our heads, amid the onslaught of social media, can you hear the steps of the runner?

Who is racing into your life these days to bring good news? Who are the messengers announcing to you and reminding you that "your God reigns" (Isaiah 52:7 ESV)?

It's easy to lose sight of God's reign in the commotion of our lives. Where are you hearing a counter message of sovereign order and a promise of flourishing?

Whose voice is cutting through the noise to incite your hope? Are you paying attention to the God-appointed promise-bringers? And are you giving thanks for those who are working nimbly and tirelessly to penetrate the cacophony of despair?

Maybe these days you're feeling the nudge of the Spirit calling you to strap on your gospel shoes and to publish peace, to bring good news of happiness.

Maybe he is calling you to bring good news—the good news of Jesus—to fearful and discouraged family, friends, and neighbors. Maybe you are called to build up those around you by speaking these beautiful and true things about God. Wouldn't that be a delightful focus as you pray?

Invite the Holy Spirit to *come* alongside you and encourage you to be a road-racing messenger of good news. And keep praying for all the messengers out there.

> How beautiful … are the feet of those who bring good news. (Isaiah 52:7 NIV)

Recommended Closing Prayer

> Almighty God, you sent your Son Jesus Christ to reconcile the world to yourself: We praise and bless you for those whom you have sent in the power of the Spirit to preach the Gospel to all nations. We thank you that in all parts of the earth a community of love has been gathered together by their prayers and labors, and that in every place your servants call upon your Name; for the kingdom and the power and the glory are yours, for ever and ever. Amen.
>
> *(Anglican Church in North America Book of Common Prayer)*

Advent Day 6

ART GOING

Reflect on Isaiah 53:3–6

Call to Prayer

Many of us have a hard time with silence and solitude and the thoughts that surface in those moments. We don't always like what comes to mind when we lie awake in the quiet of the night.

It's hard to silence the accusing internal voice as we're pressed into self-appraisal. How to still those thoughts? What will make the unbearable guilt and shame go away? Who can bear it for us? Do we have to just live with it?

The season of Advent restarts the wondrous cycle of the church's year of redemption; it begins afresh the story of our coming King. Hearing Isaiah 53 now reminds us that we need to hear and meet again and again, not just the baby in the manger, but also the sin-bearer, Jesus—our substitute.

As you reflect on Isaiah 53, trace the life-giving progression of our guilt being met by Christ, our substitute, who counters our shame with his healing grace. The cycle begins with our owning who we are. "If we say that we have no sin, we deceive ourselves, and the truth is not in us. If we confess our sins, he who is faithful and just will forgive us our sins and cleanse us from all unrighteousness" (1 John 1:8–9 ESV).

As you pray, pray your way slowly into this ancient prayer of confession, and give thanks that you get to live in the life-giving rhythm of grace.

Recommended Closing Prayer

> Almighty God, Father of our Lord Jesus Christ,
> maker and judge of us all:
> We acknowledge and lament our many sins and offenses,
> which we have committed by thought, word, and deed
> against your divine majesty,
> provoking most justly your righteous anger against us.
> We am deeply sorry for these our transgressions;
> the burden of them is more than we can bear.
> Have mercy upon us,
> Have mercy upon us, most merciful Father;
> for your Son my Lord Jesus Christ's sake,
> forgive us all that is past;
> and grant that we may evermore serve and please you in
> newness of life,
> to the honor and glory of your Name;

through Jesus Christ our Lord.

Amen.

(Anglican Church in North America Book of Common Prayer)

Advent Day 7

ART GOING

Reflect on Isaiah 54:1–10

Call to Prayer

Isaiah takes a long, loving look at the sin-bearing servant of the Lord and has one thing to say: "Sing" (Isaiah 54:1 ESV).

Perhaps singing is a hard prospect for you. Perhaps life feels too arduous or painful, and singing is the last activity you want to engage in.

But there is that urgent appeal in Isaiah 54:1: "Sing, O barren one, who did not bear; break forth into singing and cry aloud, you who have not been in labor!" (ESV).

Let joyful song explode out of you—you who see your emptiness filled, your wilderness blooming!

If we've been listening to Isaiah, and through him to the Lord, then we've been called again and again to remember God's mercy, to be refreshed by his promises, to have our hope rekindled, and to be sent forth as messengers ourselves, fueled by the Spirit of the God who loves.

And now we're urged to sing!

The people of God sing. Moses sings. Miriam sings. Deborah sings. David sings. Mary sings. Angels sing. Jesus and his disciples sing. Paul and Silas sing. When people of faith remember who God is and what God does, they sing. The songs are irrepressible.

Singing is an expression of defiant joy in the face of overwhelming sadness. Suffer we do, but sing we must!

As you pray, why not let your voice sound forth? Sing!

Recommended Closing Prayer

> Oh sing to the Lord a new song;
> sing to the Lord, all the earth!
> Sing to the Lord, bless his name;
> tell of his salvation from day to day.
> Declare his glory among the nations,
> his marvelous works among all the peoples!
> For great is the Lord, and greatly to be praised.
> Amen.
> *(Psalm 96:1–4a, ESV)*

Advent Day 8

TAMARA HILL MURPHY

Reflect on Isaiah 55:1–3, 55:7–9, 55:12–13

Call to Prayer

Over and over again throughout Israel's history, we find that God's people can't discern between what satisfies and what destroys. The lack of discernment that led them to give their most valuable offerings to idols could be rooted in a willful forgetfulness of all that had come before them and all that was promised for the future. Forgetting God's rescue meant forgetting their exile.

Forgetting their disobedience in the desert meant forgetting their propensity toward idolatry, discontent, and rebellion. Having lost their taste for what truly satisfies, they could no longer imagine the pleasant land God had promised as something worth believing.

Nevertheless, God remembered his covenant. His wrath was consumed by his immense love, a love so contagious that it required even the Israelites' captors to show compassion for God's people.

This immense and generous love flows through the exalted invitation in Isaiah 55. In contrast to the unmet cravings from living in an economy of idol worship, Yahweh summons everyone to come for the richest delights. He calls out like a street vendor offering the finest of all food and drink with no price.

This is God's economy. Humanity's habitual fascination with power continually sinks down into idolatrous practices filled with fear, anxiety, and scarcity. In the body and blood of his Son Jesus, God consumes such a system.

As you come to pray, hear Christ's invitation from Luke 14:33: "So then, none of you can be My disciple who does not give up all his own possessions" (NASB). Jesus, the voice of Yahweh, picks up the cry of a holy street vendor. *Come, find a way of life that is free for everyone yet costs everything.*

Those who have not forgotten their own history of rebellion will listen and turn from their inheritance of idolatry. Consider how responding to the call of Jesus brings the richest kind of delights found only in the free, gracious, and immense love of God. Give thanks to the Father, who will never forget his covenant and who will, in fact, bring all exiles home.

Recommended Closing Prayer

Lord, we cannot pretend to be free of guilt for the same sins that our ancestors committed. Forgive us, and welcome us back into the way of Jesus, so that we might delight in your abundant goodness and welcome others into the everlasting promise of your covenant. Amen.

Advent Day 9
TAMARA HILL MURPHY

Reflect on Isaiah 56:1–8

Call to Prayer

Isaiah 55 assures us that Yahweh's economy is free yet costs everything; Isaiah 56 tells us who the beneficiaries of that economy are: "For my house shall be called a house of prayer for all peoples" (Isaiah 56:7 ESV). Those who respond to the voice of Yahweh, spoken through Jesus, are invited in off the street to gather around the table. Everyone is welcome to the Lord's household.

Everyone is welcome, yet Yahweh reveals a certain zeal for the outcast. Not only the outcast in society's terms, but also those who recognize within their own hearts that they are not worthy to be called sons and daughters. Yet they are so drawn to the household of God that they'd be willing to enter as servants of the one true King. To these few, God not only creates space within his household but also offers a "monument and a name better than sons and daughters" (Isaiah 56:5 ESV). For those who do not presume through any sort of human legitimacy to enter this economy except as servants to the just and righteous God, the Father bends over backward to make a place of honor within his house.

It seems that Yahweh, the Creator of all humankind, cannot even imagine a home without a place of honor for the outcast, the foreigner, and the prodigal. It has been said that to confront means to face a person coming toward you until you recognize him as a brother. The Father runs toward the outcast as someone more highly valued than even a daughter or a son.

As you prepare to pray, ask God to increase your imagination about his house of prayer for all people. What does this look like? Where do you need to turn your gaze in order to be one who, like the Father, runs toward the outcast, the foreigner, and the prodigal?

Recommended Closing Prayer

> O God, you have made of one blood all the peoples of the earth, and sent your blessed Son to preach peace to those who are far off and to those who are near: Grant that people everywhere may seek after you and find you; bring the nations into your fold; pour out your Spirit upon all flesh; and hasten the coming of your kingdom; through Jesus Christ our Lord. Amen.
> *(Anglican Church in North America Book of Common Prayer)*

Advent Day 10

Reflect on Luke 16:13–17, 16:19–24

Call to Prayer

When faced with Christ's words on money and possessions, we may be tempted to do exegetical backflips to make the verses mean something other than money and possessions. Whenever scripture focuses on wealth, it may be referring to more than money and possessions, but it never means less.

At the base of biblical justice is the teaching that Jesus gives about money. We learn through teaching after teaching that, in God's generosity, our wealth belongs to us and yet does not.

The Bible says that all our money belongs to God. Jesus makes sure we don't miss this point by coming at the subject from every angle possible. There may not be a starker warning than the story of the rich man and the beggar Lazarus. From the merciful heart of God, Jesus wants all who will listen to recognize exactly what is at stake.

As you pray, allow yourself to read the story of the rich man and Lazarus with an open heart and an open mind. Notice if resistance or defensiveness rises up within you. Ask the merciful God, who "stands at the right hand of the needy" (Psalm 109:31 NIV), to reveal what is underneath the defensiveness. Is it fear or shame or blame? Know that when God brings conviction, the Spirit will make clear to your whole self—body, mind, and spirit—how to repent. Listen for that clear direction from our faithful God.

Where there is clarity, confess your sin, receive the cleansing forgiveness of Christ, and trust the Spirit to help you make restitution. If you're able to sit quietly without distraction, notice your breathing, and occasionally breathe in while saying, "Lord Jesus Christ, Son of God," and exhale saying, "have mercy on me the sinner." Repeat until your heart is settled.

Recommended Closing Prayer

> Conclude this time by reading Isaiah 57:18–19, giving thanks for God's faithful love: "'I have seen their ways, but I will heal them; I will guide them and restore comfort to Israel's mourners, creating praise on their lips,' says the Lord. 'Peace, peace, to those far and near,' says the Lord. 'And I will heal them'" (NIV). Amen.

Advent Day 11

TAMARA HILL MURPHY

Reflect on Isaiah 58:6–12

Call to Prayer

Worshipping God in spirit and truth leads us to ask what we can do to show our devotion. The practice of fasting and repentance is one answer to the question. But God wants to be clear that fasting and the rituals we associate with religious devotion are only the first steps. They are only the beginning.

The fasting God chooses unleashes a vision beyond our private devotion and even our congregational practices of worship. God desires an allegiance that brings about the wide and deep realities of his vision of justice. Worship moves from private prayer to Sunday sanctuary out into the neighborhoods, workplaces, and cities. No piece of rubble is left untended in God's desire for wholeness.

In Psalm 113, we find a bird's-eye view of this majestically enthroned God, higher than anyone or anything, stooping low to rescue the wretched and to pick up the poor from out of the dirt. Once again, we hear the heart of the Father running toward the down-and-out, preparing a place of honor among the brightest and the best.

In God's radical generosity, he makes a way for those who've lived in ruin to become repairers, rebuilders, and restorers of a just and beautiful city. In God's miraculous economy, the rubble of our past lives is the material we're given to work into the new foundations of a glorious, renewed community. Not only that, but also God's radical generosity shares the glory with those who help him rebuild. "You'll be known as those who can fix anything" (Isaiah 58:12 MSG). Have you heard anything more preposterous or more wonderful?

All of it, the radical, justice-forming, and glory-sharing generosity of God, propels us from a beginner's religious practice to a full-throated, embodied hallelujah!

Begin your time of prayer by considering the words of the psalmist: "From dawn to dusk, keep lifting all your praises to God!" (Psalm 113:3 MSG). Ask the Holy Spirit to help you think back over the past year. If that feels overwhelming to you, then focus on one month or just today. When has God picked you up? rescued you? treated you as an honored guest? What ruin or rubble from this time might God be inviting you to offer for rebuilding?

Give thanks and rest in the assurance of our good, restoring God.

Recommended Closing Prayer

Father, thank you for lifting me out of the slimy pit, out of the mud and mire. Thank you for setting my feet on a rock and giving me a firm place to stand. Amen.
(Adapted from Psalm 40:2 NIV)

Advent Day 12
TAMARA HILL MURPHY

Reflect on Isaiah 59:9–10, 59:14–21 and Luke 17:20–21

Call to Prayer

At first look, a building seems to be defined by the solid materials forming its walls, ceilings, roof, and floors. However, anyone who enters the building will soon begin to interact with the emptiness and openness of the space. The size, arrangement, and beauty of the rooms, closets, and invisible spaces of a building become as important as anything visible.

Today's passages move between the visible and invisible realities of a world in desperate need of rescue. In Isaiah, we see what's missing. The prophet laments that within the places where humankind lives, there's no room for justice, righteousness, or truth. In this cramped, dark abode, humans grope along the walls, blindly searching for a bright and lighted space.

The Lord looks into human structures we have built, but he finds only self-serving spaces; he finds no justice. Offended and incredulous, the Lord intervenes. Is there a better description of a savior than one who puts "on righteousness as body armor, and a helmet of salvation on his head...garments of vengeance for clothing, and wraps himself in zeal as in a cloak" (Isaiah 59:17 CSB)?

In Jesus, God breaks open the cramped, dark spaces built by human blindness and hubris. The invisible God takes on visible flesh, embodying all the immutable attributes of God within skin, blood, and bones. The Redeemer keeps God's covenant and comes to restore a beautiful Zion.

Still, many choose to grope along blindly. Still, the space of God's kingdom must be entered to be truly seen.

In prayer, ask God to open the eyes of your heart to discern both the visible and invisible work of the Spirit in you, amid you, and through you. Consider the spaces within and without where Christ is bringing God's kingdom to earth, as it is in heaven. Give thanks for the invitation to stride freely in the spacious place Christ has opened to us.

Recommended Closing Prayer

> Sovereign Lord, as you have promised,
> you may now dismiss your servant in peace.
> For my eyes have seen your salvation,
> which you have prepared in the sight of all nations:
> light for revelation to the Gentiles,
> and the glory of your people Israel.
> *(Luke 2:28–32 NIV)*

Advent Day 13

NATHAN BAXTER

Reflect on Isaiah 60

Call to Prayer

In this passage, God invites us to open eyes of hope, to see in the light of his glory. God invites—even commands—an extended exercise of holy imagination. It is an exercise rooted in God's promises and faithful power, energized by hope, and illuminated by the presence of the God who makes and keeps promises.

Lift up your eyes and imagine the restoration of broken and scattered families. Let "your heart throb and swell with joy" at the prospect (Isaiah 60:5 NIV).

Let visions of reconciliation among peoples and nations unfold where hostilities have ceased and joyful gift-giving becomes normal. Let hard-to-fathom possibilities unfold before the eyes of your heart.

Look at familiar ruins and imagine restored, grand opening polish. Look at the best architecture and richest decor, then let your imagination make them better still in splendor, stability, accessibility, and safety.

Let memories of danger, distress, or shame become springboards for reversals beyond your best dreams. With safety beyond threats, peace beyond foreboding, honor beyond any degradation, let visions of God's peace pass before your eyes and beyond your understanding.

Allow these holy imaginings to lead you into a time of petition and praise before the Lord.

Recommended Closing Prayer

O God, you are able to do exceedingly abundantly beyond all that we ask or imagine, and you purpose to manifest your glory in Christ Jesus and in your church. Lead me in imagining greatly that I may hope deeply

and be surprised by your joy when you exceed all our hopes with your glory. In Jesus's name. Amen.
(Adapted from Ephesians 3:20-21 ESV)

Advent Day 14
TAMARA HILL MURPHY

Reflect on Isaiah 61

Call to Prayer

Could there be a more astounding climax to the Old and New Testament readings from the past several days than Isaiah 61? God gives Isaiah the script for the first message Jesus will ever preach.

"The Spirit of the Lord God is upon me …. I will greatly rejoice in the Lord; my soul shall exult in my God" (Isaiah 61:1, 61:10 ESV)

Sometimes the Anglican lectionary pairs the powerful prophecy of Isaiah with Mary's prophetic anthem in Luke:

"My soul magnifies the Lord, and my spirit rejoices in God my Savior" (Luke 1:46 ESV).

The same spirit proclaiming through time and space from Isaiah's vision in the temple through the womb of Mary is the one carrying the holy of holies within, leaping from the synagogue scroll unfurled in the human hands of the Son of God. From Jerusalem to Nazareth to the present, we hear the echo for our time:

"The year of God's favor" (Isaiah 61:2 ESV).

The same spirit anoints us all to bring good news to the poor, bind up the brokenhearted, proclaim liberty to the captives, open up the prisons, comfort all who mourn, build up the ancient ruins, and repair the ruined cities, the devastations of many generations.

"But you shall be called the priests of the Lord" (Isaiah 61:6 ESV).

As part or all of your prayer tonight, take some time to be silent, without any noise or distraction, and to pause and meditate on these words. There's no need to strive for a profound insight during this time. Just be still.

If you begin to sense thoughts or feelings bubbling up in the quiet, notice them without trying to analyze. You might breathe out one phrase each time you're tempted to become distracted: "My soul magnifies the Lord" (Luke 1:46 ESV) or "The Spirit of the Lord is upon me" (Isaiah 61:1 ESV).

Trust God as your heavenly Father to be present with you through Christ and by his Spirit. End your time with a simple prayer or chorus. Go in peace.

Recommended Closing Prayer

Silence.

Advent Day 15

A B I G A I L   H U L L   W H I T E H O U S E

Reflect on Isaiah 62

Call to Prayer

Names have the power to define us and to shape our destinies. We know this from personal experience and also from God's Word. Throughout scripture, God changes a name in order to indicate a new season or calling. Often, it's an invitation to step into a deeper, truer identity that the individual cannot yet fully comprehend: Abram becomes *Abraham*, the father of many; Saul becomes *Paul*, the humble servant of the gospel; and Simon Peter becomes *Cephas*, the rock on which the church is built.

We see something similar in this passage. Rather than be termed "forsaken" or "desolate," Zion shall be called "married," the object of God's "delight" (Isaiah 62:4 ESV), a people "sought out" and "a city not forsaken" (Isaiah 62:12 ESV). The prophet wants the people of God to know that their current circumstances do not define them and are not the final word. Rather, God has a destiny for his people, and he is calling them to step into it by embracing their identity as his beloved.

What names are you wearing today? As God's covenant ones, purchased by the blood of the Lamb, we can and should appropriate the names we find in Isaiah 62:12 (ESV): we are the Holy People, the Redeemed of the Lord, the ones who are sought out and not forsaken.

Regardless of our circumstances or the raggedness we might feel, God says that we are a "crown of beauty" and like royal diadems sparkling in his hands (Isaiah 62:3 ESV). Do you believe this to be true? Or is there something in the way—some stone you need to clear—in order for you hear the Lord speak these loving words over you?

Take a moment now to invite the Lord to be present with you and to bring anything to mind that you need to confess. Turn it all over to him. Then reread the passage for this day and ask the Holy Spirit to highlight if there is a name he wants to give you for this season ahead.

Recommended Closing Prayer

Father, thank you that the truest thing about us is not what we see or experience but what you say about us in your Word. Give us the grace to believe that we are your beloved and that we have been made radiant by Christ's dying and rising. Help us to shed our false selves and to live as your sought-out and redeemed people. In your Son's precious and powerful name, and by your Spirit. Amen.

Advent Day 16

NATHAN BAXTER

Reflect on Isaiah 63

Call to Prayer

Unfair odds in an undeserved battle on an uneven playing field— it's a scenario that stirs both outrage at injustice and support for the underdog. This scenario is evoked in the first six verses of our reading, and perhaps we don't quite notice it because we're squeamish about the notion of wrath.

Yet notice Isaiah 63:5 and let it hold your imagination: "I looked, but there was no one to help, I was appalled that no one gave support" (NIV). Attend again to Isaiah 63:3: "I have trodden the winepress alone; from the nations no one was with me" (NIV).

No one would stand on the side of divine justice and righteousness. No spiritual powers or principalities, no other "gods," would join to help. No kings, or rulers, or armies, or heroic warriors rose to the occasion to side with those fighting for an embattled yet just cause. "I looked, but there was no one to help" (Isaiah 63:5 NIV).

No one would rally in support of divine intervention that would bring true peace, wholeness, safety, and abundance. God laments: "From the nations no one was with me" (Isaiah 63:3 NIV).

Profound disdain for righteousness and pervasive cowardice to commit fully to justice rightly evokes anger—even our feeble and often misguided anger. "I was appalled that no one gave support" (Isaiah 63:5 NIV).

God ultimately must act alone and forsaken, against sin and evil, to deal with the injustice and corruption that not only wrecks societies but also wrecks the hearts of God's covenant people. Though alone and forsaken, God arises not merely in wrath, but especially in kindness and compassion, and love and mercy—the paradoxical themes of verses 7–19.

God alone can be trusted to act for justice and to do so in mercy.

As you go to prayer with this passage, begin by praising the one who, alone, won victory.

Recommended Closing Prayer

Lord Jesus, Lamb of God, you alone won victory over evil—even mine—and you alone are worthy because you were slain and, with your blood, you purchased for God persons from every tribe and language and people and nation, even those who abandoned you to fight alone in your kindness for the salvation of the world. I bow to your wisdom and grace. Amen.

Advent Day 17

A B I G A I L   H U L L   W H I T E H O U S E

Reflect on Isaiah 64

Call to Prayer

In our reading from Isaiah 64, the prophet pleads for God to "come down" (Isaiah 64:2 NIV)—to intervene in the life of his people like fire kindling brush or boiling water. He reminds the people of how God did "awesome things that [they] did not look for" (Isaiah 64:3 NIV) in the past, and then he goes on to say these words:

"From of old no one has heard or perceived by the ear, no eye has seen a God besides you, *who acts for those who wait for him*" (Isaiah 64:4 NIV; emphasis added).

The prophet reminds us that God acts on behalf of his people. He does not sit idly by; he does not slumber or sleep. Rather, he *intervenes* in the life of his people in very active ways to protect and provide. Like the guard at a castle gate, God keeps us, watching our very going out and coming in. Nothing escapes his notice; there is a deep security in the knowledge of his providential protection and care.

But the prophet also reminds us that God acts for those *who wait for him*. Waiting involves ceding control, surrendering time lines, actively resisting the impulse to move on our own, and instead looking to the God who moves on our behalf. Waiting involves hope, trust, and persistent prayer.

As you sit with difficult situations in your own life and the life of our world—with all that is unfinished, uncertain, and waiting to be resolved—invite God to become present to you and to all that you are carrying. Where do you need God to act this Advent? Where does the waiting feel especially hard? Ask God for the courage and grace to wait and to trust that he will provide in due season. Remember the times in your life when God did awesome things that you did not look for, and expect him to be faithful, again. Submit your requests in faith, knowing that your keeper is watching over you, your loved ones, and our world in the waiting.

Recommended Closing Prayer

> Heavenly Father, you have promised to hear what we ask in the Name of your Son: Accept and fulfill our petitions, we pray, not as we ask in our ignorance, nor as we deserve in our sinfulness, but as you know and love us in your Son Jesus Christ our Lord. Amen.
> *(Anglican Church in North America Book of Common Prayer)*

Advent Day 18

SALLY BREEDLOVE

Reflect on Lamentations 3:19–30

Call to Prayer

"The 'worst' is never the worst" (Lamentations 3:30 MSG).

"Wait for hope to appear" (Lamentations 3:29 MSG).

"God's loyal love couldn't have run out" (Lamentations 3:22 MSG).

The prophet Jeremiah is likely the one who offered these promises to the Jewish people as their world fell apart. Jerusalem was razed and the nation obliterated. Every educated and wealthy person had been hauled off to captivity in Babylon. All appeared to be lost. Five poems of heartbreaking lament fill this book of the Bible.

But Lamentations is not a book of despair. Rather, it's an honest speaking of agony, confusion, and anger. It was true that the pain Jerusalem was suffering was the result of a shattering loss. Things would never be the same, but Lamentations proclaims that the Lord is mightier and more beautiful than every loss.

Are you in a season with much to lament? The Bible takes the lead in teaching you how to speak honestly. Name your sorrows and your losses.

In the midst of your lament, remember that you are talking to the one who is more real than your grief or your fears. The mighty eternal God, who is Father, Son, and Holy Spirit, will never walk out on you and refuse to return. He is here as Immanuel in the midst of it all. He will one day make "all things new" as Revelation 21:5 (ESV) promises.

When you sense you have spoken your heart, be still for a moment. God accepts you as you are. As best you can, pray that your hope grows and that your courage grows. Who do you know who is lost in sadness or fear? Pray for that person to know the loyal love of God in new ways. Pray you become the kind of person who offers a calm, fixed hope to others.

Recommended Closing Prayer

> Lord Jesus Christ, you stretched out your arms of love on the hard wood of the cross that everyone might come within the reach of your saving embrace: So clothe us in your Spirit that we, reaching forth our hands in love, may bring those who do not know you to the knowledge and love of you; for the honor of your Name. Amen.
> *(Anglican Church in North America Book of Common Prayer)*

Advent Day 19

NATHAN BAXTER

Reflect on Isaiah 65

Call to Prayer

This passage weaves contrasts between two stories of call-and-response.

On one hand is the story of willful ignorance and studied silence despite God's constant voice. God has been calling "all day long" (Isaiah 65:2 NIV), day by week by month by year, across generations. So many with every advantage of access to God's gracious call have given back neither glad nor even reluctantly fitting responses. Instead, obstinate and imaginative avoidance of God's saving and guiding voice, alongside haughty and hypocritical self-justification, unfolds, persistent as the smoke of a smoldering fire. Intentionally oblivious to the realities God has written clearly, caught up in echo chamber stories of good fortune coming their way, and with destiny as their guest, those with every opportunity to listen and to answer remain silent to God's call and deaf to God's voice. The story's end for these people is distressingly predictable: hunger, thirst, distress, grief, shame, anguish, oblivion.

On the other hand, this is the story of unlikely attendants and surprising respondents who've caught echoes of God's calling. A whole mass of unseeking finders and a few servants preserved through crushing circumstances—these answer the voice of God and enter into conversation with their Creator and Redeemer. They find God far quicker to respond than they themselves have ever been to their dearest friends or family. "Before they call I will answer; while they are still speaking I will hear" (Isaiah 65:24 NIV). And they find God more creative than they could have ever imagined as they settle into an astonishing new heaven and new earth.

At the crux of both stories is the Caller. On the cross, for both kinds of listeners, was the Listener who said, "Here I am, I have come to do your will" (Hebrews 10:9 NIV).

As you go to prayer, ask for the God-given grace to attend to his words and respond in obedience.

Recommended Closing Prayer

Lord, open my ears and soften my heart to respond to the ways you call to me. Amen.

Advent Day 20

SALLY BREEDLOVE

Reflect on Malachi 3:13–18

Call to Prayer

Malachi 3 overflows with tension. God's people have become his detractors. What's happened? They're angry because it seems as though keeping God's rules hasn't done them any good. Their lives are just as hard as the lives of those who ignore God. Furthermore, the very definitions of faith, morality, and ethics are under attack, undermined by the scorn of the unbelieving world. God's people are on the defensive.

We too live in a world where God is being charged with crime after crime and where Christians are seen as the problem. Who hasn't struggled with holding onto the teachings that used to be accepted by the majority but are now scorned by many? Who hasn't questioned God's ways in this world?

Doubt and struggle are normal for people who live by faith, but how do we resist putting God on the witness stand? What do we do instead?

Let Malachi 3:16 teach us: "Then those who feared the Lord spoke with one another" (NIV).

Our world is upside down with violence, side-taking, blaming, and contempt. More than ever, those who love God need to talk with each other.

As you pray, ask yourself, "Who could I call?" Who needs the encouragement of your friendship and your faith (no matter how weak it seems to you)? Is there something God has taught you that you sense you are to share with another person? Pray for that person and that conversation. Make that call. We need each other.

In this season of Advent, hold your own heart close to God's promises. "Then those who feared the Lord spoke with one another. The Lord paid attention and heard them, and a book of remembrance was written before him of those who feared the Lord and esteemed his name" (Malachi 3:16 NIV). These people who encourage each other in the faith, Malachi says, are God's treasure. They are children of the heavenly Father. They will be spared on the day of God's wrath.

Let your heart be at peace.

Recommended Closing Prayer

Gracious God and most merciful Father, you have granted us the rich and precious jewel of your holy Word: Assist us with your Spirit, that the same Word may be written in our hearts to our everlasting comfort, to reform us, to renew us according to your own image, to build us up and edify us into the perfect dwelling place of your Christ, sanctifying

and increasing in us all heavenly virtues; grant this, O
heavenly Father, for Jesus Christ's sake. Amen.
(Anglican Church in North America Book of Common Prayer)

Advent Day 21
SALLY BREEDLOVE

Reflect on Malachi 4

Call to Prayer

Pause a moment and allow yourself to imagine these realities:

- Pride and evil done away with, until no darkness at all remains.
- All wrong vanished to less than ashes like the powdery dust that remains from a fiercely hot oven.
- Your health and energy restored so you feel eighteen years old again, ready to tackle anything.
- A true north orientation for your whole life because the ancient words God gave Moses make sense to you.
- Families restored, so fathers love their children and sacrifice for them and children are filled to the brim by the attention of their fathers.

Could all these good things possibly come true?

Malachi isn't daydreaming. He's declaring God's promises to us. A day is coming when one good thing will overtake the next. This coming day will be more than a new era. It will be life itself.

Wonderfully, Malachi doesn't say, "Work to make these things happen." That ought to relieve us. The complexity and brokenness of our world is everywhere. We know we can't manufacture a societal change of this magnitude or legislate it into being.

So, what's our response to the problems we live with as we seek to hold onto the promises of God? Do we do nothing until God sets things right?

Not at all. Today matters. As the apostle Peter puts it, "Since everything here today might well be gone tomorrow, do you see how essential it is to live a holy life? Daily expect the Day of God, eager for its arrival" (2 Peter 3:10–11 MSG).

As you pray, thank your heavenly Father that one day all will be utterly made right. In this season of active waiting, ask him to show you how to live a holy life that anticipates his coming. Ask him to show you just one thing that you can repent of and do differently.

Recommended Closing Prayer

O Lord, help me to live this day for that day. For Jesus's sake. Amen.

Advent Day 22

ELIZABETH GATEWOOD

Reflect on Isaiah 24

Call to Prayer

Isaiah's prophecy of judgment and destruction seems to flip between different explanations for and responses to this coming judgment.

Is it God who causes calamity? Or is it the sin of the people—their lawlessness and breaking of the covenant—that has defiled the earth?

And what is the proper response? To sing for joy, giving glory to God, or to lament, as Isaiah does in Isaiah 24:16?

In the middle of these questions is a stark description of the earth's defilement and bitterness. The cities—beacons of civilization and places of refuge and protection—are ruined. The music and dancing—manifestations of the beauty of human culture and imagination—have ceased. The fertility of the earth—necessary for the survival of all life—has been stripped and exhausted. The land is withered.

Who is responsible? Is God? Is Israel? Should they mourn and lament? Should they praise God anyway? The chapter ends not with answers but with a stark affirmation of God's presence and power. God reigns in great glory and power.

As you pray, hold these tensions and ambiguities—in this passage and in your own life—before the Lord.

Recommended Closing Prayer

God, ours is a world where joy often turns to gloom with the grief of lives lost, disease, natural disasters, and fractured relationships. Are we responsible? Are you, God? Should we lament, or should we keep praising you anyway? Fill our mouths and hearts with both words of lament and words of praise. Give us courage to do the work that is ours to do for the healing of the world. Amen.

Advent Day 23

ELIZABETH GATEWOOD

Reflect on Isaiah 25

Call to Prayer

Isaiah 25:8 declares, "He will swallow up death forever. The Sovereign Lord will wipe away the tears from all faces; he will remove his people's disgrace from all the earth. The Lord has spoken" (NIV).

Isaiah describes the redemption of the world as a rich banquet, one with the best wine and the best meat. But this is no stiff corporate dinner with fine food but dull conversation. The best part of this feast are the guests. All people will gather at this banquet table. And there will be no tears. The world will be healed and made new.

We live in the tension between these vibrant promises and our difficult daily existence. Perhaps the redemption that Isaiah describes feels like a far-off dream to you. As we move deeper into this Advent season, we sense more and more the tension between hope in the Lord and longing for the fulfillment of his promises, between the felt pain of our world and the desire for its future restoration.

Take a moment and let these words settle in your heart and mind. Ask the Lord how to live well within these realities. As you pray, name your griefs and longings before the Lord. Pray for redemption in specific areas. Thank God for his promise to restore all things.

Recommended Closing Prayer

God, is it true that you are capable of wiping away all tears? the tears of a wife abandoned and disgraced by her husband? the tears of families pressing their hands together against hospital windows? the tears of children in detention facilities who may never see their parents again? the tears of broken relationships, economic hardship, disease? If you can do it, why not now? Lord, we long for your heavenly banquet. We long to feast with all peoples at the table of your abundance. Come quickly, Lord Jesus. Set the banquet table. Wipe our tears. We are ready. Amen.

Advent Day 24

ELIZABETH GATEWOOD

Reflect on Luke 1:26–56

Call to Prayer

Ask any woman who has been pregnant and she will tell you what a strange experience it is to have your body invaded and overcome by new life. It starts invisibly, with fatigue and nausea. It's a strange thing to suddenly have your capacities for productivity drastically diminished. As new life grows, it makes clothes uncomfortable and unwearable. It makes prior activities and indulgences impossible. It is a small grief not to be able to take a long bike ride or enjoy a sushi dinner with friends.

A mother, her body uniquely strong and generative, becomes weak even in the beautiful exhibition of her strength.

We long for the gospel to enter into our lives in scheduled and controlled ways. We try to tame and rationalize its wilder demands and invitations. And yet, Jesus breaks into our lives and our world with explosive new life.

Mary welcomes it—the weakness of motherhood and the explosiveness of the gospel—with humility and joy.

As you pray, consider in what ways you are tempted to package the gospel as a consumer item that fits in with your lifestyle. Pray for God to reveal to you where you may be missing his presence and his invitations to new life.

Recommended Closing Prayer

God, we would prefer to have some control over how you transform our lives and hearts. We have goals and plans. We have busy schedules. We have careers and obligations. We want to tame and contain your presence and your invitations because they are too much for us. In this season of Advent, let us be more like Mary, who welcomed the chaos and inconvenience of Jesus with joy and openness. Let us learn from the women around us who courageously become weak to bring new life into the world. Show us where we need to surrender pieces of ourselves to give room for you and your transformative presence in the world. Give us the strength of Mary to be weak, to be overcome by your new life. Amen.

Advent Day 25

ELIZABETH GATEWOOD

Reflect on Luke 1:57–80

Call to Prayer

After a strange and humbling season of muteness, Zechariah gets his voice back. He meets his infant son John and introduces him to the world. And we read that this strange news—a mute father made to speak again, an angel-promised baby—captures the minds of the people who hear about it. After etching John's name and receiving his voice back, Zechariah perhaps says a few repentant or wry words to his wife, who has just given birth. Then he gives a beautiful prophecy and benediction on the life of his son.

Perhaps he cradled the infant John the Baptist as he turned to him and said, "And you, my child" (Luke 1:76 NIV).

John prepared the way for Jesus, plowing the soil of people's hearts and imaginations so that when they met Jesus, they could see him and accept him; the gospel could take root.

During Advent, we are more aware than ever that we live in the "already but not yet," the time after Jesus's life, death, and resurrection but before his Second Coming to make all things new. And our work is not so different from John's. We too are called to go on before the Lord to prepare the way for him. We all have a different vocation and location, but we are each called to make the world new again. We pursue and embody beauty, justice, and truth. We preach the gospel and let our lives be transformed by it. We work for the renewal of people, places, and institutions. We prepare the way for Jesus.

As you pray, hear Zechariah's words as a benediction over your own life and work.

Recommended Closing Prayer

God, you place us and call us to specific work for your kingdom. Yet so often our work is a source of frustration, shame, longing, and pain. Would you let us see our work as part of your grand redemption of the world? Teach us from the life of John the Baptist about what it looks like for our lives to point to you. Reveal to us specific ways that our work can embody and proclaim your coming kingdom. Give us creativity, patience, and endurance to do the specific work that you have called us to do. Amen.

Advent Day 26

Reflect on Isaiah 7:14 and Micah 5:2–5a

Call to Prayer

Through unlikely means and unpromising servants, God brings forth signs of his goodwill and emblems of his kingdom purposes.

Our two texts were recalled by those who knew Christ best and had seen God's promises realized in his life, death, resurrection, and ascension. Gospel writers Matthew and Luke both draw upon these passages to illuminate how a son born in Bethlehem to a young virgin from Nazareth grew up to fulfill the deepest hopes of God's people and the deepest gifts of God's promises.

With such signs of God's love and mercy given in the birth, life, death, resurrection, and ascension of Jesus, we have been assured of God's goodwill and have been given emblems of his kingdom purposes. With Jesus's mother, Mary, we have great reason to sing:

> His mercy extends to those who fear him,
> from generation to generation.
> He has performed mighty deeds with his arm;
> he has scattered those who are proud in their inmost thoughts.
> He has brought down rulers from their thrones
> but has lifted up the humble.
> He has filled the hungry with good things
> but has sent the rich away empty.
> He has helped his servant Israel,
> remembering to be merciful
> to Abraham and his descendants forever,
> just as he promised our ancestors.
> (Luke 1:50–55 NIV)

As you enter prayer, begin with praise. Hope in God's promises for you and for the whole world.

Recommended Closing Prayer

My soul magnifies you, Lord! My spirit rejoices in you, God my Savior. You have been mindful of me and have given me signs of your great goodness through Jesus Christ!

Advent Day 27 (Christmas Eve)

ABIGAIL HULL WHITEHOUSE

Reflect on Psalm 134

Call to Prayer

Our psalm begins with a call to worship. It's as if the psalmist is scurrying around the temple, beckoning all who might hear him to drop what they're doing and engage in worship. In context, the psalmist is summoning the Levitical priests—those servants of the Lord who stood watch in the temple—but this is a perfect summons for us, too, on this Christmas Eve.

Come. Stop what you're doing—all your prepping, planning, and last-minute gift wrapping—and draw near to the God who came close in Christ; dwell with him in these sacred and set-apart moments ahead. Fix your mind, attention, and imagination on him.

And *bless the Lord.* Speak well and wonderfully of our incarnate King. Let your words be bountiful, gracious, and true as you contemplate his character in prayer. Let your praise pour forth uninhibited.

And *lift up your hands.* Don't limit your worship only to your words! Lift up your hands! Lift up your voice! Lift up your heart! Let your whole body respond to the God who came as an infant and as an offering. Posture yourself in such a way that worship flows freely through you.

"Come, bless the Lord, all you servants of the Lord, who stand by night in the house of the Lord! Lift up your hands to the holy place and bless the Lord!" (Psalm 134:1–2 ESV).

As you pray on this Christmas Eve, offer up the very best and brightest sacrifice of praise to our King, who came and is coming again. Delight yourself in the Lord, and dwell richly with him in this last day of Advent.

Recommended Closing Prayer

Our Jesus, root of David, bright morning star, thank you that you dwell with us and dwell in us. Manifest your presence now, our Immanuel. In your most holy name. Amen.

Introduction to Christmastide

STEVEN E. BREEDLOVE

Do we recognize what it means that the Eternal Word of God became man?

This, after all, is what the season of Christmas (all twelve days) is about. *God became man.* This single thought drives a season of pure celebration. We feast during this season not because he died and rose (that comes later), but simply because he became a human being! In the Incarnation, God said yes to his creation, rather than ridding himself of it. What is more, he said yes to our human nature itself! In Jesus Christ, human nature—even its physicality—was drawn into the life of the Trinity.

This should drive our prayers as we feast during the season of Christmas. God has said yes to creation and to us, and our humanity is now a part of God's own life. As we pray during this season, our prayers should be full of joy, not only because we have not been rejected, but also because a way has been made for us to be in the presence of God as what we are—creatures in bodies. Like Mary, we should treasure this in our hearts and let it overflow in peace and joy in our prayers as we feast.

Christmastide Day 1 (Christmas Day)

ABIGAIL HULL WHITEHOUSE

Reflect on Luke 2:1–14

Call to Prayer

What would it have been like to be there on the night the angels appeared to the shepherds?

As you read through these familiar words from Luke 2, place yourself in the scene. Imagine what it would have smelled like, looked like, and sounded like to be keeping watch over the flock. Was it cold? warm? bright? still? What does it look like in your mind? Allow yourself to wonder.

Then ask God to help you inhabit this scene and to find your place within it. Where are you on this night? Are you one of the shepherds, or are you an onlooker in the dark? Are you with Mary and Joseph in the stable, or are you somewhere else? Give yourself permission to engage with scripture in this imaginative way and take some time to locate yourself within this scene. Be open to any of the many ways God might lead or speak.

Now reflect on verses 9–14. What strikes you as you sit with this passage? Can you envision the angels, or the sound or the feel of the glory shining around them? How do you react to their presence and the news they share? What, if anything, comes to mind as you contemplate this heavenly host?

Linger in this scene and take note of any words, images, or impressions that seem significant. Take whatever comes as a gift from God, and turn it back to him in the form of a prayer. Thank him for his incarnation, and invite him to be with you in a special way this Christmas.

Recommended Closing Prayer

> Moonless darkness stands between.
> Past, the Past, no more be seen!
> But the Bethlehem-star may lead me
> To the sight of Him Who freed me
> From the self that I have been.
> Make me pure, Lord: Thou art holy;
> Make me meek, Lord: Thou wert lowly;
> Now beginning, and always:
> Now begin, on Christmas day.
> ("Moonless Darkness" by Gerard Manley Hopkins)

Christmastide Day 2

DREW WILLIAMS

Reflect on Luke 2:29–38

Call to Prayer

Of all the people in the temple that day, why is it that Simeon and Anna were chosen to recognize the long-awaited Messiah in the arms of a young mother? We might imagine it was because they both had attained some extra measure of personal piety. Luke describes Simeon as righteous and devout (Luke 2:25). Anna virtually lives at the temple, worshipping God with fasting and prayer night and day (Luke 2:37). Luke is not suggesting, however, that these individuals were without sin. In the book of Psalms, the righteous were certainly not without sin, as Psalm 32 teaches us. Rather, they were those who did not rest in their sin but repented and trusted God. In the Old Testament, the righteous were those who chose to make following God a way of life.

No doubt that Simeon and Anna were both remarkably faithful people, but something else distinguishes them in their cloistered encounter with the infant Jesus. The clue is in Luke's description of Simeon: "the Holy Spirit was on him" (Luke 2:25 NIV). It is the gift of the Holy Spirit that has stirred in them both such a longing for the fulfillment of the presence and promise of Jesus. We discover that same longing and that same gift in David, a man who was not without fault but who nevertheless was a man after God's own heart. He was a man anointed by God's Spirit who would pray, "As the deer pants for streams of water, so my soul pants for you, my God" (Psalm 42:1 NIV).

Simeon and Anna shared this extraordinary and intimate audience with the infant Messiah because, even in their old age, they had not let the gift of the Spirit grow cold. The Holy Spirit longs to fill and stir up our hearts. He gifts his people in every generation to long for and recognize the presence and promise of Jesus. As you pray, ask God that you might desire more and more to know him, just as Simeon and Anna did.

Recommended Closing Prayer

Holy Spirit, lift my heart and stir in me a longing for the presence and promise of Jesus. Amen.

Christmastide Day 3
DREW WILLIAMS

Reflect on Matthew 2:13–15

Call to Prayer

Leading up to this prophetic vital warning to flee to Egypt, Joseph has found himself being severely tested and challenged. He must have imagined the deepest betrayal of the heart; he has known broken hopes and has experienced the pain of a lost future—all laced with the arsenic of public humiliation. Mary and Joseph's betrothal was a binding agreement, and it gave Joseph legal remedies for Mary's apparent betrayal. He had the prerogative to publicly divorce Mary on the grounds of adultery, claim the dowry, and have her stoned to death.

In this way he could have publicly cleared his name, received a little financial restitution for his trouble, and disposed of the infamy of Mary's continuing presence in the community. Mary's and Jesus's lives lay within Joseph's hands. Yet in the silence of his pain, a different music rises up in Joseph's heart. We read, "And her husband Joseph, being a just man and unwilling to put her to shame, resolved to divorce her quietly" (Matthew 1:19 ESV). Within the spectrum of possibilities open to him, Joseph chose the most compassionate. In all his pain, Joseph chooses mercy. He is not in denial. He does not pretend that these events have not taken place. From within his crucible of pain, he clings to the character of God, and from the heart of Joseph's pain comes not vengeance but the tender mercy of God.

Had Joseph held on to his anger, had he remained fixed on vengeance and the need to clear his own name and to shame Mary, then would he have been able to receive the dream? Would he have had the heart to hear and respond to this new critical prophetic warning to take the infant Jesus and Mary to safety in Egypt? It was the mercy of God that again helped him to recognize God's voice and plan. Mercy will always serve to tune our hearts to the frequency of God's own heart.

As you pray, ponder what you personally know about receiving and offering mercy. In what ways do you long for your Father to make you more like Jesus?

Recommended Closing Prayer

Lord Jesus, in your great mercy, help me to recognize your voice and your plan. Let your mercy retune my heart to the frequency of your love. Amen.

Christmastide Day 4
DREW WILLIAMS

Reflect on Matthew 2:16–23

Call to Prayer

Joseph's life is wildly different from anything he might have imagined when he was first betrothed to Mary. And yet, a series of extraordinary dreams bring Joseph into God's greater plan. In yesterday's passage, Joseph accepted God's plan and took a full and active part in it. Acting upon the instructions from his dream, Joseph took Mary and the infant Jesus to safety in Egypt.

Today's verses involve a dream that lays out a carefully timed set of prophetic instructions plotting the course for Joseph to bring Jesus safely to Nazareth (via Egypt), narrowly avoiding Herod Archelaus.

Immediately, Joseph responds. He shepherds his family back to Nazareth and stands by Mary as a faithful husband and by Jesus as a faithful stepfather.

This sequence of prophetic instructions is not, however, the only thing that Joseph receives from God. Out of this prophetic awakening, Joseph is blessed with a wholehearted trust and confidence that God will supply him with all the strength he needs to walk out his calling.

Sometimes our dilemma is not that we don't know what God is asking of us, but whether or not we have the strength to walk it out. Do we ever have it in us to go through with what God is asking of us? The answer is invariably "Absolutely not!" And yet, as God was faithful to Joseph, so he is faithful to supply us with all the strength we need to wholeheartedly take up our part in his good plans. "The one who calls us is faithful, and he will do it" (1 Thessalonians 5:24 NIV).

Pray for the willingness to receive the Spirit's power and presence so that you can live in obedience to his call on your life.

Recommended Closing Prayer

Father, I thank you that in everything you call me to, you are faithful to supply the strength I need. This day, I ask you to fortify me in your love and mercy so that I may wholeheartedly take up the place that you have made for me in your good plans. Amen.

Christmastide Day 5

DREW WILLIAMS

Reflect on Luke 2:41–52

Call to Prayer

The twelfth year in the life of a Jewish boy was the final year of preparation before he entered fully into the religious life of the synagogue. We can presume that Joseph would have taught the young Jesus the commandments of the law and then, at twelve years of age, Jesus would have gone through a ceremony by which he became a bar mitzvah, or "son of the commandment." And this was the year Jesus chose to stay behind in the temple.

It is worth noting Jesus's strategy for learning. He clearly had made a plan to seek out teachers, and when he had identified them, he sat in their midst, listened to their teaching, asked questions, and gave answers. Do we bring the same wholehearted attention to our heavenly Father's desire that we grow in the grace and knowledge of our Lord and Savior Jesus Christ?

There is profound mystery in our faith. Our ways are not God's ways, and there are matters that are truly beyond our comprehension. There is, however, much that the Lord has blessed us to understand. At just twelve years of age, Jesus demonstrates God's desire that we continually seek to grow in the knowledge and love of God.

Jesus also models for us how theological and spiritual formation is meant to take place in the heart of the community of God's people. Mary and Joseph did not find Jesus sitting alone behind a pillar, poring over ancient scrolls. They found him at the temple, in the very midst of those who could teach. He was listening and actively participating in a shared time of learning.

Pray about your own desires for your community of Christians. Will you ask the Lord to stir in your heart the same quest for understanding? Will you ask the Lord to give you the courage to take Jesus's example and seek to grow in the knowledge and love of God in the community of his people?

Recommended Closing Prayer

Lord Jesus, stir in my heart a desire to grow in deeper knowledge and love of you. I ask that you also supply the courage to allow me to grow in understanding in the community of your people. Amen.

Christmastide Day 6

BILL BOYD

Reflect on Matthew 3:5–17

Call to Prayer

In Matthew, the kickoff for Jesus's ministry is his baptism. His baptism isn't just a step into a river; it is an immersion into humility. This counterintuitive way of doing life and ministry will be Jesus's calling card. Jesus took on flesh in order to come alongside men, women, and children in their actual need. If they are hungry, he identifies with their hunger. If they are spurned, he identifies with their loneliness and shame. If they have eyes of faith, he notices that faith and praises them. He walks with the marginalized and needy.

The questions turn back to us: With whom do we find ourselves walking and talking and living on a daily basis? Who arouses our empathy, our desire to help, our compassion? Do we stand in line with sinners to be baptized, or do we stand on the sideline with the Pharisees?

Jesus humbled himself to be one with sinners so that sinners might be one with God. In Jesus's economy, the haves have faith, and the have-nots have everything else. The heavens part; the Spirit Dove descends; and the voice of God proclaims the pleasure of God with his Son, a have-not in the eyes of the world, so that those who acknowledge their neediness will become true haves—holders of faith, hope, and love.

As you pray, consider how might you repent of living as if you have no deep need. How might you repent of turning a blind eye to those aware of their deep need? Hear and receive, in your need, the words spoken by the Father to all willing to share in Christ's baptism and friendship: "With you I am well pleased" (Mark 1:11 NIV).

Recommended Closing Prayer

Gracious Father, we renounce Satan and all the spiritual forces of wickedness that rebel against you. We renounce the evil powers of this world which corrupt and destroy your creatures. We renounce all sinful desires that draw us away from your love. We turn again to Jesus as our Savior, we trust in his grace and love, and we commit to follow and obey him as our Lord. In his precious name. Amen.

(Anglican Church in North America Book of Common Prayer)

Christmastide Day 7 (New Year's Eve)

SALLY BREEDLOVE

Reflect on Psalm 91

Call to Prayer

For centuries, this psalm has been beloved by the church. It encompasses it all—full protection from everything, and the invitation to sink your life into the shelter and love of God. Perhaps the psalm leaves you comforted yet also with questions. It is deeply reassuring to know you are kept by the mighty and very present God. At the same time, perhaps you sense some resistance and questioning inside your soul. *No plagues? No evil? No pestilence? No fear?*

It's this psalm that the evil one quotes when he tempts Jesus to jump from the pinnacle of the temple so as to prove that God keeps his people from all harm all the time. But Jesus refuses to turn the psalm into a proof text of God's goodness. Jesus, who fully feared, loved, and obeyed God, also endured a great deal of opposition in his life and ultimately died on the cross.

We long to know God as Christ did. We long to dwell beneath the shelter of his wings. We believe he is mighty and loving, but still, there is so much wrong and so many broken and scary things. Especially now.

It is New Year's Eve. A new year begins tomorrow morning. What will it be like? As you pray tonight, pause and tell the truth about your own heart as you sit in this moment. Will you trust yourself to God's sheltering presence like Jesus did? Will you by faith believe that this beloved psalm speaks of the absolute and final outcome of our broken world? One day there will be no evil, no pestilence, no pain, no dying. Will you even now, in the midst of trouble, entrust your soul and the lives of those you love to the eternal God? He is your home and your strong shelter.

Think of people you know who are fearful and struggling. Pray they will know that God is their mighty shelter and that one day all will be made well.

Recommended Closing Prayer

Father, we live in a land of disorder and pain. Yet we run to you for shelter, God Most High. Please grant us your rest. Let us know your Holy Spirit's peace, by which you led Paul and Silas to sing while in prison. Let us hear you singing over us as we sleep. Amen.

Christmastide Day 8 (January 1)

DREW WILLIAMS

Reflect on Luke 4:1–13

Call to Prayer

Jesus's resistance to the enemy in this desert battle has a lot riding on it. Should Jesus succumb to the enemy's stratagem, then he will be proven no better than the first Adam, causing the story of our salvation to end here. Jesus's success in this moment of sustained and fierce combat ultimately leads to his full and final victory for us upon the cross. At the cross, Jesus disarmed the rulers and authorities and put them to open shame by triumphing over them. To fail in this wilderness testing would have been to forfeit that ultimate victory.

In addition to the cosmic implications of this desert battle, the fact that the enemy's present-day strategy remains largely unaltered as he assaults the children of God is also worthy of our attention. To Jesus in the desert and to us today, the enemy makes the same play.

Does this sound remotely familiar: "Surely if you really are a child of the King, then claim your blessings! God has promised to send you all manner of natural and supernatural provisions to make you and keep you healthy, wealthy, and prosperous. Are you sure that you have what is truly owing to you? Why don't you let me make up the shortfall?"

But Jesus did overcome the enemy in the desert, and his victory upon the cross is eternal and irrevocable. This means that while the enemy is stuck with the same old script, we have a new heart and a new spirit. The enemy still insinuates his tired propaganda, but we who wait for the Lord will renew our strength. The enemy remains a present darkness, but he attacks us from a place of defeat.

In Christ's victory we have been given authority over all the power of the enemy. Upon the battlefield, the Holy Spirit will not let us be tempted beyond what we can bear. And Jesus has promised to provide "a way out" (1 Corinthians 10:13 NIV) so that we can endure. The enemy's propaganda might well remain the same (and it is true that we are often susceptible to it), but in Jesus, the fierceness of the spiritual battle we are fighting has been radically changed in our present and eternal favor.

As you pray, pray for yourself in the arenas of your life where it is hard for you to stand firm in Jesus. Pray for God's mercy and help for those you know who are struggling.

Recommended Closing Prayer

Lord Jesus, I stand upon your victory upon the cross. I now take my stand against Satan and all his lying ways and command him to depart from me. I put on the full armor of God so that I may be able to stand firm against all the strategies of the evil one. Amen.

Christmastide Day 9
STEVEN A. BREEDLOVE

Reflect on John 1:1–5, 1:14, 1:16–18

Call to Prayer

John begins his Gospel by pulling back the curtain on the mysteries of the essential identity and nature of God. He invites us into an unfamiliar world to hear words that human faculties are not strong enough to fully understand. We see from afar. This is holy ground.

Don't turn away quickly from mystery. Take off your shoes and stay awhile. At the least, we can absorb this: From before time, the God we never fully understand is communicating. He is the Word, eternally reaching out, making himself known. He is Life, begetting life. He is Light, turning on the lights so that darkness must loosen its grip on us. Life and light will grow if we'll only linger and look.

Not content to dwell in mysteries beyond our kin, the Word became flesh and dwelt among us. Later John writes, "That which was from the beginning, which we have heard, which we have seen with our eyes, which we looked upon and have touched with our hands, concerning the Word of life" (1 John 1:1 NIV).

John's Gospel burden is for us to know that when we see Jesus, we see God. When we learn something from Jesus, the Light that is Life itself is shining. The eternal Word, Creator God, became a person we could see, talk with, touch, handle. Jesus has made the God we can never see understandable and knowable. We can say, "We know God because we see Jesus." Amazing love. How can it be?

Later, Jesus invites two curious disciples of the Baptist to come to his house. His words were simple: "Come and see" (John 1:39 NLT). And they did as he had bid. Indications are that they sat and talked with him for hours through the evening meal. The passion of God to personally connect with people has bridged the gap from the unfathomable mysteries of eternity to the simple homeliness of a kitchen table in ancient Israel.

How much does God want to communicate with you? How much does he want you to know him, to be his familiar friend?

As you pray, ask God to give you the determination to sit with Jesus, to linger with him, to talk with him, and to listen to him. That's what he wants, any and every day and night, for the rest of your life.

Recommended Closing Prayer

Heavenly Father, give me a heart that longs to linger in your presence. Amen.

Christmastide Day 10

STEVEN A. BREEDLOVE

Reflect on John 2:13–22

Call to Prayer

Invariably, the question emerges: "One cleansing of the temple or two?" A good case can be made for either, but surely it is no stretch of the imagination to see that money changers and marketers could have quickly reverted to their greedy ways as soon as the pressure let up. Don't we do the same with our fond sins?

However, as you turn to consider the actual event, keep in mind that Jesus has made the God we can never see understandable and knowable. "No one has ever seen God, but the one and only Son, who is himself God and is in closest relationship with the Father, has made him known" (John 1:18 NIV). When Jesus cleanses the temple of the tools of marketing and banking, God is acting. The Word is speaking. Light is invading darkness. Life is making its presence known.

The message that God declares concerns his priority for dedicated space (and time) when we are not occupied with the cares of this world, when we can focus, listen, reflect, pray, and draw near to him. Silencing distractions is not just for serious followers: this housecleaning occurred in the Court of the Gentiles, space set aside for "outsiders" to approach God in order to listen, learn, and pray in their own quests for truth. Dozens of languages could have theoretically been heard here every day, but God's message is singular and understandable for any ears: "I prioritize devotion and worship! Therefore, you must prioritize devotion and worship." Jesus is righteously angry when he declares this message by his actions, but the Word is turning on a light in our darkness. We are being pushed toward life.

One of the fiercest battles in our lifelong journey of following Christ is accepting the fact that he sets the terms. But he does, and his terms are clear: "I want your attention and your heart!"

As you begin your time of prayer, consider your own soul in this season. Has Jesus forcibly scattered your well-organized, meticulously counted coins in the dirt? Has he gotten your attention? If so, then why go back to the way it was? Why not take his message to heart? How can you maintain God's own priority, a time when distractions are laid aside in favor of focused listening, prayer, and reflection?

Recommended Closing Prayer

> Gracious and holy Father, please give me intellect to understand you, reason to discern you, diligence to seek you, wisdom to find you, a spirit to know you, a heart to meditate upon you, ears to hear you, eyes to see you, a tongue to proclaim you, a way of life pleasing to you, patience to wait for you, and perseverance to look for you. Grant me a perfect end, your holy presence, a blessed resurrection, and life everlasting. Amen. *(Benedict of Nursia)*

Christmastide Day 11

STEVEN A. BREEDLOVE

Reflect on John 3:1–10, 3:14–17

Call to Prayer

Have you been born? Yes or no? Do you know for sure? Have you given birth? Do you know for sure? Ridiculous questions! We know we have been born. We know if we have given birth. Birth and giving birth are definitive markers as obvious as the ground beneath our feet.

Jesus says that the second birth is just as definitive. Unfortunately, many of us struggle at times to know for sure whether we are born again or whether being born again is a certain reality. The apostles Peter and Paul help us here.

"Blessed be the God and Father of our Lord Jesus Christ! According to his great mercy, he has caused us to be born again to a living hope through the resurrection of Jesus Christ from the dead," Peter writes declaratively in 1 Peter 1:3 (ESV). In Christ, we *have been* born again! Peter goes on to declare that this new life breathes the air of hope, acts by tested faith, and grows in love. Hope, faith, and love are the essential nature of the newborn life Jesus names in John 3:1–17.

As we dig deeper, we realize that this declaration of the nature of new life is also an invitation, an aspiration, and a decision. *We live into what we are declared to be, taking on the shape of the life that God has already drawn for us in Christ.*

Paul says it even more pointedly in Philippians 3:12–14: "I press on to make it my own [i.e., a life of knowing Christ], because *Christ Jesus has made me his own*" (ESV; emphasis added). Paul is saying, *Jesus has given me a certain kind of life. I choose this life, pressing on toward the goal, the prize.*

The question, then, is quite simple: Do you want to be born again? Are you hopeful that Christ will give you eternal life? Do you long for that life? If so, then by definition, he has already implanted new life in you. The Spirit is at work. Hold tight to the hand that is already holding you tight!

As you pray, consider one promise you've been given in Christ and receive it as sure hope. Think of the first thing that you know God has told you to do (or not to do), and then do it (or stop doing it). Aspire to love Jesus and others whom he is calling you to love. Write down or speak aloud your hope, faith, and love.

Recommended Closing Prayer

> Grant me, even me, my dearest Lord, to know you, and love you, and rejoice in you. And, if I cannot do these perfectly in this life, let me at least advance to higher degrees every day, until I can come to do them in perfection. Let the knowledge of you increase in me here, that it may be full hereafter. Let the love of you grow every day more and more here, that it may be perfect hereafter; that my joy may be full in you. I know, O God, that you are a God of truth, O make good your gracious promises to me, that my joy may be full; to your honor and glory, with the Father and the Holy Spirit you live and reign, one God, now and forever. Amen.
>
> *(Saint Augustine)*

Christmastide Day 12

STEVEN A. BREEDLOVE

Reflect on John 3:25–36

Call to Prayer

Throughout his Gospel, John makes it crystal clear that Jesus Christ has come from heaven, that he has existed for eternity, that he speaks words that the Father gives and does only the Father's will, and that he is, in fact and fullness, God incarnate. John's goal is to present and promote

Jesus as "the Christ, the Son of God," and to convince us to believe in Christ and "have life in his name" (John 20:30–31 ESV).

Such an emphasis should give us a measure of holy discomfort. We love John 15:15: "No longer do I call you servants ... but I have called you friends" (ESV). We run when he invites, "Come to me, all who labor" (Matthew 11:28 ESV). But this same Jesus who hung out all evening at a table with two disciples in John 1 also cleansed the temple with a whip in John 2. He confronts Nicodemus bluntly: "Unless one is born again he cannot see the kingdom of God" (John 3:3b ESV). Christ pulls no punches.

John the Baptist is an exemplar disciple of the Lord; he establishes a governing GPS signal for the Christian life: "He must increase, but I must decrease. He who comes from above is above all" (John 3:30–31 ESV). In this posture of submissive allegiance, John says, "This joy of mine is complete" (John 3:29 ESV).

In order for Jesus to increase, he must do so in two seemingly discordant directions. He must increase as Commander. Are we willing to welcome Jesus as "above all"? Will we accept the terms he sets, or do we imbibe the spirit of our world, sitting in judgment of Jesus, determining whether or not what he says fits our sensibilities and logic?

But he must also increase as the one who comes from heaven and to earth, to us. He tells us what he has seen and heard about a world infinitely truer and more beautiful than what we can imagine. He offers to us his own first and best gift—his Spirit—without measure.

How do we hold together "Commander" and "Comer"? Be assured, he is always both.

As you pray, consciously consider Jesus the Christ. Do business with him about how he might increase in stature in your soul and imagination, and how you might decrease in your need for recognition and satisfaction. Welcome him to be with you in your prayers. Rest. Rejoice. Receive. Bow. Smile.

Recommended Closing Prayer

> Lord Jesus Christ, I am no longer my own, but thine. Put me to what thou wilt, rank me with whom thou wilt. Put me to doing, put me to suffering, Let me be employed by

thee or laid aside for thee, exalted for thee or brought low for thee. Let me be full, let me be empty. Let me have all things, let me have nothing. I freely and heartily yield all things to thy pleasure and disposal. And now, O glorious and blessed God, Father, Son, and Holy Spirit, thou are mine and I am thine. So be it. And the covenant which I have made on earth, let it be ratified in heaven. Amen. *(John Wesley)*

Introduction to Epiphany

STEVEN E. BREEDLOVE

The word *epiphany* means "manifestation," and the Feast of Epiphany, celebrated on January 6, commemorates the manifestation of Jesus Christ to the Magi, who represent the entire Gentile world.

This is a feast day in the life of the church because it commemorates that God revealed himself not just to the people of Israel, but also to those outside the promise. The Magi were the first, but the Gospels record Jesus's interactions with other Gentiles, and the book of Acts demonstrates God's plan to bring salvation in the name of Jesus to every tribe, tongue, and nation. Most of us are, by God's grace, recipients of this kindness, so we celebrate the fact that the doors of salvation are open wide to those not numbered among the Israelites!

The season of Epiphany, which is regarded as the first of two periods of Ordinary Time in some traditions, follows the feast day. During this season, we are given the chance to focus on who God has revealed himself to be in Jesus Christ. We are encouraged to celebrate not just a general revelation of his existence, but also the specific manifestation of the character of Jesus Christ, who is God in the flesh. The Magi worshipped him as King, though they were kneeling before a humble child. Do we see the nature of Jesus as clearly as they?

Prayer during Epiphany springs from the desire to understand Jesus Christ. Rather than emphasizing application or obedience, our devotional reading focuses on simply seeing Jesus clearly. In this season, we pray that God will reveal himself to us as we read, and we hunger to understand the character of our Lord Jesus Christ because in him, Father, Son, and Holy Spirit are made manifest!

Epiphany Day 1

Reflect on Matthew 2:1–2, 2:11

Call to Prayer

Who attended Jesus's birth? Who witnessed the coming of the Son of God? His mother and stepfather, "blue-collar" shepherds, a host of angels, and the Magi. Political and religious leaders were threatened by rumors of his birth. They did not attend the birth, but they sought to ensure that, if he actually were born, their "rival" would be eliminated.

Who attended the death of Jesus? Again, his mother, plus a different set of blue-collar people, his disciples. There were angels, legions, alert and waiting, while the mystery of redemption unfolded. Again, politicians and religious leaders united to eliminate the threat of a supposed king. And there were two wealthy wise men, Joseph of Arimathea and Nicodemus.

Isn't it fascinating that two marker moments of the human life of the Son of God, his birth and death, were attended by many everyday people plus some unusually wealthy, learned people? Why would the Father guide wealthy men to both the crib and the cross?

Maybe there's a message of comfort. While it may be difficult for a wealthy ("learned") person to enter the kingdom of God, it is not impossible (Mark 10:23–27 and 1 Corinthians 1:26–31). But perhaps another reason is that the Father simply wanted to honor his Son. After the unthinkable injustice, pain, and shame of the cross, perhaps the Father wanted to make a statement. He stirred up Joseph and Nicodemus, two men who had come to hope in Jesus as Messiah, to beautify his brutalized body with a rich man's burial.

Perhaps the same tenderness filters into the story of the Magi. Yes, there are primary messages about epiphany and gospel mission. Also, one of scripture's darkest stories of injustice, murder, and grief is triggered by their worship. The Son was born into a tragic, sinful, often ugly world. Perhaps these birth gifts from wealthy men were, among other things, a statement from a Father to his Son.

We normally mark births with gifts. We mark deaths with eulogies and gratitude, sometimes giving charitable gifts to honor the departed. Would it be so strange if the God of love were to mark both the birth and death of his Son with gifts of love?

As you pray, receive these words from the Beloved: "As the Father has loved me, so have I loved you" (John 15:9 NIV). Receive this assurance from the Holy Spirit: "Nothing in all creation will ever be able to separate us from the love of God that is revealed in Christ Jesus our Lord" (Romans 8:39 NLT).

Recommended Closing Prayer

> Look on us, O Lord, and let all the darkness of our souls vanish before the beams of your brightness. Fill us with holy love, and open to us the treasures of your wisdom. All our desires are known to you, therefore complete what you have begun, and what your Spirit has awakened us to ask in prayer. We seek your face, turn your face to us and show us your glory. Then will our longing be satisfied, and our peace shall be perfect. Amen.
> *(Saint Augustine)*

Epiphany Day 2
FRANCIS CAPITANIO

Reflect on John 4:1–29

Call to Prayer

Have you ever been surprised to find that Jesus is talking with you? If so, then you have come to see the Samaritan woman in yourself. She was looked down upon by God's people and Christ's disciples, and though the Twelve would not admit it, they couldn't grasp why Jesus would condescend to such a level as to talk to a Samaritan, a woman, and a sinner. There are many parts within each of us that think the same thing and raise their voices when we come to the Lord to pray. "But Jesus," they say, "don't you know who it is you're talking to?"

We see our own unworthiness to come before the Son of God, yet this can cause us to see the greatness of his love with even greater clarity. How great a thing this is that the same one who condescended to speak to Moses from the cloud and the pillar of fire speaks to the Samaritan and meets with each and every one of us. It is this that shows the greatness of his humility; there is nothing equal to his lowliness. Even as he began teaching on the mountain, Jesus made lowliness and meekness the foundation of all he had to say with the beatitudes. This humility is perfectly seen in Jesus in the conversation with a simple sinful woman eager to hear about the kingdom of God.

As we pray, let us all remember that we are no better than the Samaritan woman, and yet he longs to be with us. When we consider our weaknesses, the unsteadiness of our will, our inner pride, and the multitude of our sins, this should help us see his greatness, even as it helps us see his love, because he still wants to be right where we are. He knows us and he still wants us. The Samaritan woman is in good company sitting by the well, conversing with the Lord. We can sit there, too.

Recommended Closing Prayer

Lord, I don't know why you want to talk with me, but I know that you do. As the voices within me rise up to condemn me, quiet them with your love, and let them know that you are here to give me living water despite where I've been and who I am. I am thirsty. Thank you for letting that be enough.

Epiphany Day 3

FRANCIS CAPITANIO

Reflect on John 4:43–54

Call to Prayer

"The man took Jesus at his word and departed" (John 4:50 NIV).

When we come to the Lord in prayer, do we ask him for what we need with confidence? Do we believe that he will do what is best for us and that, having asked, we have put our needs in his capable hands? Do we depart in peace?

Or, on the contrary, do we hold on to our anxiety? Do we get angry because we feel he is cheating us of what we deserve? Do we demand a sign so that we know he will do what we ask?

Like the royal official who asked Jesus to heal his son, we should strive to take Jesus at his word and depart to go on with our day with the confidence that it is he who knows our needs and will meet them. It seems that Jesus rebukes the crowd by saying, "Unless you see signs and wonders you will not believe" (John 4:48 ESV). And yet, he performs the sign for this man, who then believed, along with his whole household.

Sometimes, because of our weaknesses, we need a sign to believe and God is willing to give it. Sometimes we don't need a sign or God isn't willing to give one. But at the core of all our requests, we must believe that it is Jesus who knows what we need, whether his answer is a yes or a no to whatever it is we ask.

Prayer meets trust at the moment we depart. It's at this point, when we walk away to continue with our day, that true faith is tested and refined if we take him at his word.

As you pray, ask for the faith to take Jesus at his word.

Recommended Closing Prayer

Lord Jesus Christ, as I leave my prayers and the reading of scripture behind in order to begin my day, I know you don't leave me behind. As I depart from prayer, you do not depart from me. But as I go about my day, give me the faith to know that you have heard my requests, that you love me, and that you know what I need and when I need it. Knowing all this, let me depart in peace to do the work you have given me to do this day. Amen.

Epiphany Day 4

KARI WEST

Reflect on Psalm 70

Call to Prayer

Do you turn to the Lord in desperate times? Do you offer quick prayers—like gasps, like cries for help—to your God? David is assailed on all sides: he's facing enemies who jeer at him and mock him, and who seek his ruin—and some even who seek to take his life. In his terror, poverty, and neediness, he begs the Lord for succor.

How we need God's help to know our own insufficiency in hardships. How quickly we grasp for our false saviors. Maybe we turn inward, assuming that if we just dwell on our problems long enough, we can come up with our own solutions. Maybe we distract ourselves, reaching for comfort, or pleasure, or sleep to dull the difficulty. Maybe we take our rage and exhaustion out on those around us, enjoying the momentary relief and then enduring the lingering guilt.

Perhaps our greatest weakness is our self-deception, our persistence in the lie of self-sufficiency. We must learn to acknowledge, with David, that we are poor and needy and in desperate need of God's rescue.

The Holy Spirit is willing and ready to teach us.

As you pray, ask for what you need, starting with the need to know your own neediness. Ask the Holy Spirit to lead you into deeper humility and deeper peace. Praise Christ for his grace that bears us up.

Recommended Closing Prayer

Almighty and everlasting God, you are always more ready to hear than we are to pray, and to give more than we either desire or deserve: Pour upon us the abundance of your mercy, forgiving us those things of which our conscience is afraid, and giving us those good things for which we are not worthy to ask, except through the merits and mediation of Jesus Christ our Savior; who lives and reigns with you and the Holy Spirit, one God, for ever and ever. Amen. *(Anglican Church in North America Book of Common Prayer)*

Epiphany Day 5

KARI WEST

Reflect on Genesis 1:1–5

Call to Prayer

God draws near to what is formless and empty. He hovers over it like a bird hovering and fluttering her wings over her nest, and he brings about life, newness, order, beauty.

This is the very first thing we ever learn about the Lord from scripture: He is a God who creates. He is for life, for teeming, full-bodied, varied, glorious existence. He pulled light into reality. And what is the very first word that God uses to describe what he has made? It is *good*.

God is still for what he has made by the word of his power. He is still a Creator, still speaking life into his world, though that world has fractured almost beyond recognition. Creation is still held together in Christ—for whom and by whom all things were made—and it will be remade by him.

Christ is that very good light for all humankind, shining in the darkness, never to be overcome.

As you pray, rest in God as the crafter of all that is good. Recall something lovely in the world and thank him for making it. Praise him for his word of power and his firm commitment to the good of his creation. Hope in the coming restoration of all things.

Recommended Closing Prayer

O God, you made all things, and in you all things hold together. You are our Creator, and the world is full of your majesty and love. We praise you, our Father and our King. Your kingdom come and your will be done on earth as it is in heaven, we pray. Amen.

Epiphany Day 6
KARI WEST

Reflect on Genesis 17:3–8, 22:18

Call to Prayer

Our God is a God of covenant who desires deep relationship with the people made in his image. He reaches out; he renames and reforms. He takes an old barren couple and creates a great nation from them. He is not constrained by our limitations. He is faithful throughout all generations. He desires to bring blessing to all nations through his people.

Most important of all, he promises to be our God.

Read these words again and receive these truths as God's gift to you today. He promises to be your God. There is nothing else you need. He is committed to you. He desires your good. He desires to bring about the good of the world through you. He will be with you now and forevermore.

As you pray, hope in these promises of God. Be at peace.

Recommended Closing Prayer

Our Lord of covenant faithfulness, let us rest in you. Thank you that you are our God throughout all generations. Glory be to you forever and ever. Amen.

Epiphany Day 7

KARI WEST

Reflect on Exodus 3:7–12

Call to Prayer

We serve an attentive, compassionate, powerful God. The Lord witnessed the afflictions of his people, was moved by their suffering, and worked to bring them out of slavery and into a good, spacious, abundant land.

Do you believe that God sees you and hears you? Do you know that he is full of compassion for you? We too have been rescued from slavery and are being led to good and spacious land, not through the fearful and uncertain Moses, but by the perfect and obedient Christ.

Your hardships and your tears never go unnoticed by the Lord. He has wrought your greatest rescue, and he will keep you by his power until you are "planted on the mountain of his holy inheritance—the place made for his dwelling" (Exodus 15:17 NIV).

As you pray, confess what is hard in your life. Offer these difficulties up to the Lord. Then read these verses again, and ask for greater faith in our attentive, rescuing God. Know that he will always do you good and will act in his perfect timing. Rest in the saving work of Christ.

Recommended Closing Prayer

> "The Lord is my strength and my defense;
> he has become my salvation.
> He is my God, and I will praise him,
> my father's God, and I will exalt him."
> *(Exodus 15:2 NIV)*

Epiphany Day 8

MADISON PERRY

Reflect on Psalm 1

Call to Prayer

Psalm 1 is about God's prototype for maturity. It speaks of a single righteous person who is like a tree. For Christians, that person is Jesus, who hung on a tree. From his life we receive a life that will look like his life, as will our growth.

The growth of a tree never makes the headlines. A tree's growth is slow and steady, unremarkable, and repeated. Every day, trees draw water. Every evening, they stretch their limbs and shake their leaves.

Regardless of our circumstances, each day presents us with chances for newness and growth.

The life of the Spirit persists. Continue in regular prayer. Seek the Lord. Do the ordinary things you already know to do. Continue in this basic and organic God-given life, every day a resurrection.

It is sometimes said that the righteous person is simply the person who prays Psalm 1 and means it. As you pray, appreciate the life that flows into you from God's Vine, our Lord Jesus Christ. Feel your roots settle. Maybe lift your arms up toward God's light. He is good and intends good for us. He sees farther than where we will be tomorrow. He sees a whole leafy forest of children and blessings He will bring about through our slow and steady submission.

Recommended Closing Prayer

> Blessed is the man
> Who walks not in the counsel of the wicked
> Nor stands in the way of sinners
> Nor sits in the seat of mockers
> But his delight is in the law of the Lord.
> And on His law he meditates day and night.
> He is like a tree,
> Planted by streams of waters

That yields its fruit in its season
And whose leaf does not wither.
In all that he does prospers.
Not so are the ungodly, not so,
They are like the dust
That the wind drives away.
Therefore the wicked shall not stand in the judgment
Nor sinners in the congregation of the righteous
For the Lord knows the way of the righteous
But the way of the wicked shall perish. Amen.
(Psalm 1 ESV)

Epiphany Day 9

KARI WEST

Reflect on 1 Samuel 16:1–13

Call to Prayer

God chose the youngest, the smallest, the one perhaps considered unimportant by his family. God tells Samuel not to be swayed by appearances, by human strength, or by the ability to impress. The Lord knows that what matters is at the heart of a person.

We know from the rest of scripture that David loved God, trusted God, and knew his need for God. He was a man after God's own heart (Acts 13:22). Samuel was still looking for a king similar to Saul, someone impressive and mighty. But God knew David's desire to please him, to follow hard after him—and this is what truly mattered.

Is there an area in your life where you are tempted to judge as Samuel did in this passage? God still works through the humble, the lowly, those who know how very much they need him. As you begin your time of prayer, repent of any ways you are walking in self-sufficiency. Ask for a heart of faith that judges rightly and esteems the same qualities that

God esteems. Thank him for his Spirit that is always at work changing our hearts and renewing our souls so that we might know more and more of our need for God.

Recommended Closing Prayer

Lord, thank you that you create new hearts within us. Give us the grace to be humble and to love what you love. In Christ's holy name. Amen.

Epiphany Day 10

KARI WEST

Reflect on Psalm 65

Call to Prayer

Blessed are those whom God has chosen to bring near to him. Do you often think of your Christian identity in those terms—that you are one chosen to dwell near God? Even more than that now, on this side of the cross, you are the one God chooses to dwell within. That is an immeasurable glory and a deep mystery.

He has brought you near, you who were once so far off. He has brought you near. And what a God to be near! What a God dwells within you! He answers his people with mighty, righteous acts. He stills the roar of the sea and the tumult of the nations. He draws forth songs of joy from the dawn and the setting of the sun. He enriches the soil, directs the rivers, and dresses his world in abundance and gladness.

Creation shouts to its Creator. And we are the ones chosen to be near our Creator God. We are the ones chosen to be indwelt by this abundant, rich, magnificent God.

As you pray, join your voice to the hidden melody of the world and praise God for who he is, what he has done, and how near he is to you.

Recommended Closing Prayer

> Oh Lord, blessed are those you choose
> and bring near to live in your courts!
> We are filled with the good things of your house,
> of your holy temple.
> You answer us with awesome and righteous deeds,
> God our Savior,
> the hope of all the ends of the earth. Amen.
> *(Psalm 65:4–5 NIV)*

Epiphany Day 11
WILLA KANE

Reflect on Psalm 3

Call to Prayer

In Psalm 3, David exposes us to the sadness in his heart as he flees from his own son Absalom, who is trying to kill him and usurp his throne. Many who once followed David are now against him.

David cries out, "O Lord, how many are my foes!" (Psalm 3:1 ESV).

Which foes are you facing today? Name them. Cry out to the Lord with your fear, your sadness, and your need.

"Many are saying of my soul, 'There is no salvation for him in God'" (Psalm 3:2 ESV).

In David's day, Satan used the lie that God would not save his people. It's the lie Satan still whispers today in a worldly chorus that sows seeds of doubt and discouragement in our hearts.

Like David, we have a choice: we can believe the lie of Satan, or we can believe our God will save us.

David is sure that God, his shield, will protect him. God, the lifter of his head, will change his perspective. We can be confident of these things, too. With God's help, because he lifts our heads, we can look up instead of down. We can fix our eyes on Jesus and not on our circumstances.

As we gaze upon our Lord and remember what he died to accomplish, a miraculous thing happens. We see his glory in the gospel, and we are changed. If he has saved us for eternity, how will he not also save us from the challenges we face?

Like David, we can go from despondency to trusting in a sure and certain destiny: our names are written with the blood of Christ in the book of life. We can lie down and sleep without fear because our God never slumbers or sleeps.

As you pray, lay your heaviness at his feet. Then praise him as the one who hears, answers, delivers, and blesses his people.

Recommended Closing Prayer

> O soul, are you weary and troubled?
> No light in the darkness you see?
> There's light for a look at the Savior,
> And life more abundant and free.
> Turn your eyes upon Jesus,
> Look full in His wonderful face,
> And the things of earth will grow strangely dim
> In the light of His glory and grace. Amen.
> ("Turn Your Eyes upon Jesus" by Helen Howarth Lemmel)

Epiphany Day 12
MADISON PERRY

Reflect on Psalm 4:1, 4:6–8

Call to Prayer

In Psalm 4, we find words to inhabit that demonstrate a rightly oriented heart and words in which we can rest. As we pray them and let them do their work, we can enjoy fellowship with our God.

When praying these words, we assume the posture of someone who is in need. "Answer me when I call, O God of my righteousness!" (Psalm 4:4 ESV). This is someone who has had prayers answered before, yet again they find themselves in need of God's provision.

We all know that cycle, and we mustn't feel worn out by it. In this prayer, God gives us words to persevere. He doesn't want us to stop. He gives us the strength to continue to come to Him, and he gives us his love to move us to seek after the good of others. In this life prior to the Second Coming of our King, the problems are never resolved with finality.

But we worship the God revealed in Christ, and even when embattled and weak, we have something precious: "You have put more joy in my heart than they have when their grain and wine abound" (Psalm 4:7 ESV). Even in our fearful days where tomorrow is always up for grabs, we can know the deepest of joys. This isn't a drunken, over-the-top ecstasy. It is a rooted and peaceful appreciation of God's goodness, known in the ordinary meals, prayers, and passing of time with loved ones. This is the joy of a humble heart, a heart broken and restored by Jesus's life-changing death and resurrection.

Pray that you will trust more deeply that God alone can give you a stable and peaceful joy. As you hear news about our world that makes you anxious, pray that you will turn to Jesus. Pray for strength not to be kidnapped by your fears. Who do you know who is filled with anxiety? Pray for that person, asking that God will settle his peace and goodness over his or her soul.

Recommended Closing Prayer

> Most loving Father, you want us to thank you for all things, to fear nothing but the loss of you, and to cast all our cares on you. Protect us from faithless fears and worldly anxieties, and grant that no trials in this life will keep us from seeing the greatness of your everlasting love in Jesus Christ. Amen.
> *(Anglican Church in North America Book of Common Prayer)*

Epiphany Day 13

KARI WEST

Reflect on Psalm 68:19–35

Call to Prayer

God is the one who daily bears us up. God possesses unseen, unending storehouses of power and strength. He promises to act on behalf of his chosen people. In this passage of scripture, he acts to bring about justice, salvation, and deliverance from death.

Too often we forget our God who rides in the ancient heavens, whose power is in the skies, who reigns in his sanctuary, and who delights in giving strength to his people.

The psalmist imagines a dancing procession of Israelites from the tribes at the farthest edges of the land coming together to praise the Lord in his sanctuary. And then even more broadly, the psalmist says the nations of Cush and Egypt will reach out to the Lord, and the kingdoms of the earth will sing to him.

Are you feeling weak and exhausted today? Are there trials and burdens threatening to overwhelm you? Remember, God daily bears you up. Call to mind this great throng of jubilation rejoicing in the just and salvific acts of our God. Hope in the coming global recognition of his great power, holiness, and deep abiding love. With the psalmist, cry out, "Blessed be God!" (Psalm 68:35 ESV).

Recommended Closing Prayer

> Most holy God, the source of all good desires, all right judgements, and all just works: Give to us, your servants, that peace which the world cannot give, so that our minds may be fixed on the doing of your will, and that we, being delivered from the fear of all enemies, may live in peace and quietness; through the mercies of Christ Jesus our Savior. Amen.
> *(Anglican Church in North America Book of Common Prayer)*

Epiphany Day 14

SALLY BREEDLOVE

Reflect on Deuteronomy 33:26–27a

Call to Prayer

As Moses faces his own imminent death, his passion is preparing God's people for a future without his leadership. He urges them to understand that obedience brings blessing and that brokenness and sorrow will follow the choice to turn from God. He reminds them that their time of wandering in the wilderness represents a living picture of the loyal goodness of God and their own stubborn, untrusting hearts.

These verses from Deuteronomy 27 conclude Moses's passionate pleading for the people to trust God. So, how does he sum up it all up?

God is your home, Moses tells them. *You have lived forty years in the wilderness, but the deeper truth is that you have always been at home in God. He is your safety. No matter what it looks like, you will not fall into the abyss.*

We too can bank our lives on Moses's promise. If our trust is in the Lord Jesus Christ, then we are at home. We belong to someone who loves us and keeps us.

Moses's words foreshadow the promise Jesus later makes to all who put their faith in him: "My sheep hear my voice, and I know them, and they follow me. I give them eternal life, and they will never perish, and no one will snatch them out of my hand. My Father, who has given them to me, is greater than all, and no one is able to snatch them out of the Father's hand" (John 10:27–29 ESV).

Pray that you will trust and follow the Lord Jesus Christ and that you will know him as your home.

Recommended Closing Prayer

We praise you, Lord. Let all our acts of service be acts of prayer done in your name, and make all our prayers in your name to be acts of service for this world. Come, Lord Jesus, and bring your kingdom, your peace, and your everlasting life. Amen.

Epiphany Day 15

SALLY BREEDLOVE

Reflect on Hebrews 2:10–18

Call to Prayer

The writer of Hebrews assumes we fear death and the loss that death entails. This fear turns us into slaves. We are shackled, the writer of Hebrews says, by our strategies to avoid the inevitable and our attempts to pretend that death in any of its forms will never come to us.

Our fears echo those that accompanied Adam and Eve as God exiled them from the Garden. They lost the fullness of God's presence, their deep communion with each other, and their life-giving connection with creation. They lost a true sense of themselves. In some sense, death was magnified. Their lives knew the tentacles of death. That fear, almost on a chromosome level, has been passed from generation to generation. We are indeed afraid of death, and that fear makes us slaves.

If someone were to ask you to name your fears or losses, could you make a list? Pause and consider these questions right now: What are you afraid of? How has your fear of death made you a slave?

The death Christ died destroyed death's power. We do not need to be afraid of loss. All will be made whole in the age to come. Even now while we still struggle with our fears, with our circumstances, and with the fact that we struggle, Christ's heart toward us is sympathetic, merciful, and faithful. He understands. He wants to help us. He is not ashamed to call us his brothers and sisters.

As you pray, thank Christ that you are not alone, that he understands, and that he wants to help you. Ask him to reveal your fears and to speak his peace to those fears.

Most loving Father, please strengthen us to give thanks for all things, to fear nothing but the loss of you, and to cast all our care on the One who cares for us. Preserve us from faithless fears and worldly anxieties and grant that no clouds of this mortal life may hide us from the light of the love which is immortal, and which you have manifested unto us in your Son, Jesus Christ our Lord. Amen.

(Anglican Church in North America Book of Common Prayer)

Epiphany Day 16

SALLY BREEDLOVE

Reflect on Job 19:23–27

Call to Prayer

Job's story might confuse you. His friends speak eloquently about seeking God, doing the right thing, and knowing God's blessing. And Job? He speaks like an angry man, insisting that he must be heard, like a man who has no regard for the advice of his friends.

At the end of the book, God declares that Job's friends did not speak accurately about God as his servant Job had. (And in an act of mercy, God directs Job to offer sacrifices for them and to pray for them.)

Back to the puzzle at hand. How does Job speak rightly about God? He is emotional, confused, and dismissive of his friends' desire to help. He despairs. He insists on being heard. He shouts at the heavens. But he never turns his back on God. Everything he says assumes that God really exists, that he listens, and that he hears.

What is the outcome of Job's raw and honest heart? What happens when a person keeps talking to God—rather than about him—in the midst of great pain? In Job's torrent of words, he comes to moments of startling insight, as seen in the words of this passage. Job's Redeemer lives. His life is not over when he dies. One day, in his flesh, he will see his Redeemer taking his stand on this earth.

Is this your hope as well? The only sure things are the crucifixion and resurrection of Jesus Christ and the promise that after we die, we will be raised with him.

If you are in a similar season of wrestling and anger, let Job be your teacher. Keep talking to God. Don't turn away from him in cynicism or indifference. Let him see your anger, your confusion, and your despair. When you have said all you need to say, simply be silent and listen. God has not left you. Know that his presence is greater than whatever churns within you. Let God speak or not speak. Simply know he holds you.

Recommended Closing Prayer

Lord, you know everything about us and about me. Thank you that you never leave us. Thank you that this life is not the final word. Thank you that one day, in a made-new heaven and earth, you will gather to you all those who are redeemed by the blood of Jesus Christ. Thank you that one day in my new body I will see you face-to-face. In the name of Jesus. Amen.

Epiphany Day 17
SALLY BREEDLOVE

Reflect on 1 Kings 19:1–8

Call to Prayer

Elijah's work had been intense and strongly opposed. He felt that even his friends had turned on him. He was afraid of those in power, so he ran.

God in his mercy does not desert us when we are running away, when we are exhausted, when we have lost hope. That message is part of the big story of the Bible. We see it over and over, from Cain, to Hagar, to Jacob, to Jonah, to Peter, to Paul, and to us. God is the same. He pursues us and he comes to us in Christ Jesus.

Elijah's story in 1 Kings 19 is a picture of God's meeting us when we can't go any farther. The angel offers Elijah sleep and food.

It is the same for us. Always God invites us to rest, to trust his provision, even to lie down and sleep in the midst of uncertainty.

As you prepare to pray, consider the angel's words: "The journey is too much for you" (1 Kings 19:7 NIV). Indeed it is. We need God's provision: the bread of his Word, the water of his Spirit, the rest that is offered in Jesus Christ. Thank God that you are not in charge of directing, producing, or protecting your own life.

Recommended Closing Prayer

> Be present O merciful God, and protect us through the hours of this night, so that we who are we wearied by the changes and chances of this life may rest in your eternal changelessness; though Jesus Christ our Lord. Amen.
>
> *(Anglican Church in North America Book of Common Prayer)*

Epiphany Day 18
WILLA KANE

Reflect on Psalm 48:1, 48:3, 48:9–14

Call to Prayer

The psalmist begins by acknowledging the greatness of the Lord. Because he is great, our response is to praise him for the city that is his own. Jerusalem was a majestic city when this psalm was written. God himself dwelt there in a temple protected by towers, ramparts, and citadels.

Now God dwells through his Spirit in the hearts of his people, as Paul reminds us when he writes, "Do you not know that you are God's temple and that God's Spirit dwells in you?" (1 Corinthians 3:16 ESV).

We are his temple, and he is our fortress. Man-made defenses aren't what save God's people. God himself is our Savior and Defender. His steadfast love and his righteousness are our sure defense, our strength, and our glory.

Think about God's steadfast love for you. What has God done for you over the course of your life? Recall the ways he has protected you, led you, and strengthened you. What is God seeking to teach you about his beauty and strength, his power to protect, and his love for you?

Listen to the psalmist's hope: "For this God is our God for ever and ever; he will be our guide even to the end" (Psalm 48:14 NIV). We can be so caught up in our daily routine and in the urgent questions or difficulties we face that we can forget the bigger picture. Whatever testifies to God's love and work is what will stand the test of time. What is it you want to say? What will you be ready to declare about your Father God?

As you pray, remember how far God has brought you. Once you were lost, but now you have been found. Thank God for his trustworthy love. Thank God for the ways he has cared for you, even in the darkness that now faces you. Ask him for ongoing help for yourself and for others. Rejoice, knowing that his victory has already been accomplished in the resurrection of Jesus.

Recommended Closing Prayer

> Increase, O God, the spirit of neighborliness among us, that in peril we will uphold one another, in suffering tend to one another, and in homelessness, loneliness or exile, befriend one another. Grant us brave and enduring hearts that we may strengthen one another, until the disciplines and testing of these days are ended and you again give peace in our time, though Jesus Christ our Lord.
> Amen.
> *(Anglican Church in North America Book of Common Prayer)*

Epiphany Day 19

Reflect on Romans 15:13

Call to Prayer

Here in Romans 15, the apostle Paul prays that the lives of Christians would be characterized by hope, trust (believing), joy, and peace.

Hope is not wishful thinking or finger crossing for some uncertain outcome. Biblical hope is a confident expectation of good things to come, rooted in the character of God. We hope in a God whose promises are certain: "I am God, and there is no other …. My purpose will stand" (Isaiah 46:9, 46:11 NIV). We hope in a God who never changes while ruling over an ever-changing world: he is "the same yesterday and today and forever" (Hebrews 13:8 NIV). We hope in a God whose faithfulness is steadfast: "Let us hold fast the confession of our hope without wavering, for he who promised is faithful" (Hebrews 10:23 ESV).

Confident hope and trust go together. Trust comes from walking hand in hand with the God in whom we have placed our hope. Pause to reflect on where you have been placing your hope of late. Is the Lord Christ your first and best hope, the one your heart trusts?

With hope and trust as the anchor of our souls, joy and peace are God's gifts to us to receive and to cultivate in our lives by the power of the Spirit. Joy is an abiding delight in God that springs from a living, vital relationship with him through our Lord Jesus Christ. Peace comes from knowing whose you are and where your life will ultimately lead. Creation in its present state and everything in it is passing away. Our future hope is in the dawning of a new creation and in eternal life with Christ.

Recentering ourselves on these truths can transform the way that we live out our day-to-day lives. As you come to pray, renew your trust in the God of hope; receive the joy and peace of life in Christ; and ask that God will empower you to exemplify these fruits of the Spirit to those around you.

> Lord Jesus, stay with us, for evening is at hand and the day is past; be our companion in the way, kindle our hearts, and awaken hope, that we may know thee as thou art revealed in scripture and the breaking of bread. Grant this for the sake of thy love. Amen.
>
> *(Anglican Church in North America Book of Common Prayer)*

Epiphany Day 20

SALLY BREEDLOVE

Reflect on Deuteronomy 8:1–16

Call to Prayer

In Deuteronomy, Moses recounts what the past forty years have been like. Those who listened were children born in the wilderness, so they had children's memories and the stories their families had chosen to tell them. Before Moses dies, he sets the record straight by telling them the real story of those wilderness years.

If you were Moses, what would you want the next generation to know? Would you want them to know how badly their parents had gone off course or the dire consequences of choosing disobedience? Perhaps you'd paint a compelling picture of the good and prosperous future that God has planned for them in the new land.

Moses will preach those things in the course of this book. But in Deuteronomy 8, his focus is on the faithful fatherly love of God.

God cared for his wilderness people in miraculous ways. Yes, he trained them by trial, but they were not his boot camp recruits under the heavy hand of a harsh sergeant. They were not world-class spiritual athletes being trained by a coach who always demanded more, more, more.

Moses knows God. He reminds the people that God himself is father and that God's plan has always been to do his people good in the end (Deuteronomy 8:16). Knowing the end is good grows hope and endurance.

When Satan tempts Jesus in the wilderness, Jesus recalls this passage. Jesus trusted his father's care and his father's provision.

As you begin your time of prayer, contemplate a season of past trial in your own life. What can you tell others about that time? Will you see it only as a terrifying wilderness, or will you have a different story? Will you be able to admit to the generations that follow you that such a trial revealed the places where your own heart was broken and misshapen?

And most of all, can you proclaim the things you have come to know by experience—that God is indeed Immanuel? He is God with us, and in the end, he always does us good.

Recommended Closing Prayer

> O God, you are my God; earnestly I seek you;
> my soul thirsts for you;
> my flesh faints for you,
> as in a dry and weary land where there is no water.
> So I have looked upon you in the sanctuary,
> beholding your power and glory.
> Because your steadfast love is better than life,
> my lips will praise you.
> So I will bless you as long as I live;
> in your name I will lift up my hands.
> My soul will be satisfied as with fat and rich food,
> and my mouth will praise you with joyful lips,
> when I remember you upon my bed,
> and meditate on you in the watches of the night;
> for you have been my help,
> and in the shadow of your wings I will sing for joy.
> My soul clings to you;
> your right hand upholds me. Amen.
> *(Psalm 63:1–8 NIV)*

Epiphany Day 21

MADISON PERRY

Reflect on Psalm 5:1–12

Call to Prayer

In this psalm, King David leads us into the throne room of God, the center of heaven and earth. This is not a moment of cozy comfort, but one of respect and splendor that will lead us to immense joy. For even in so grand a place as God's throne room, David tells God, "I, through the abundance of your steadfast love, will enter your house" (Psalm 5:7 ESV). None of us deserves to be here, but we are welcomed by a great love. Despite how out of place we are, how listless and sinful we know ourselves to be, we are beloved, and greeted, and given the chance to address God.

David asks for the righteousness of God, a gift that we know comes through Jesus Christ, who humbled himself under death so that we could be lifted up. Remember how undeserving you feel to be in the throne room of the Most High God. When we are covered in God's righteousness, we are transformed into sons and daughters of this King. Then, we will be moved as David is to encourage others to sing for joy. This is the consequence of that radical love that welcomes us in—it lifts us up, fills us, and gives us peace.

This psalm is not a thought experiment. It is real—more real than any other news or opportunities you have heard of today. If you will submit to God and ask him for the righteousness of Christ, then he will give surely give it.

Be led into God's throne room by the blood of Christ. Take refuge here, and in faith claim it as a resting place of joy. Pray for someone you know who does not know God as his or her refuge. Pray that this person will know that God stands ready to hear his or her cry. Look for a moment at your own heart: where do you turn when you hear more bad news? Ask God to give you a heart that runs to him first.

Recommended Closing Prayer

> Hear my cry, O God,
> listen to my prayer;

from the end of the earth I call to you
when my heart is faint.
Lead me to the rock
that is higher than I,
for you have been my refuge,
a strong tower against the enemy.
Let me dwell in your tent forever!
Let me take refuge under the shelter of your wings!
Amen.
(Psalm 61:1–4 ESV)

Epiphany Day 22
MADISON PERRY

Reflect on Psalm 6

Call to Prayer

No matter where we turn, no matter what we have achieved, no matter what we have earned, lost, or forfeited, the riches of the grace of God are on offer right now. The riches of the world are dust compared to this, the glory of knowing God.

That is why David turns to the Lord every day. His surrounding circumstances are often different, but his goal is the same. He comes seeking life.

While external worries often drive us to the Lord, there is an internal struggle that threatens our relationship with God. And it is this inner battle that we witness as David faces God's wrath at the start of this psalm. "Be gracious to me, O Lord, for I am languishing; heal me, O Lord, for my bones are troubled" (Psalm 6:2 ESV).

We, like David, have welcomed sin into our lives through countless doors. It lives with us now, often out of sight. Come to the Lord and ask him to save you in his steadfast love. Honestly reckon with the powerful vices you carry in reserve.

Our Father wants to make your heart a deep well filled with the Spirit of his Son, a fountain from which love flows to a hurting world. Come and ask him to renovate your heart. For those of us who have approached Jesus before and asked him to take our sin, there remain new depths to which Christ's grace will penetrate if only we will ask. Ask him to forgive you, to cleanse you, and to bring you into a right relationship with him.

As you pray, take a moment to call to mind the great mercy of God. He knows all about you and yet still calls you his beloved son or daughter of Jesus. We have not been abandoned. Thank him for his mercy and forgiveness. Think of someone you love who is burdened by failures and closed in by shame. Pray that this person comes to know how dearly his or her Father in heaven loves him or her.

Recommended Closing Prayer

Lord, you say that if we confess our sins, you are faithful and just to forgive us our sin and to cleanse us from all unrighteousness. Because of your grace and mercy, I confess to you the things I have done wrong this day, the good things I have left undone, and the sinful thoughts and intentions of my heart. Trusting in your great mercy, here is my confession: [Here, mention those things you have to confess]. Amen.

Epiphany Day 23
MADISON PERRY

Reflect on Psalm 8

Call to Prayer

This psalm is an invitation to step into a new world, a world where every square inch of creation testifies to our Creator.

Whether you know it or not, this world is made to be a vessel for God's glory, an intricately arranged diorama where each element is meant to reflect the stunning light that shines from the face of Christ. Stars reflect the glory of God, as do fish, sheep, oxen, and birds.

Have you passed through the day without realizing that this world is a marvel? This psalm challenges us to pause and thank the Lord for the gifts we have been given, from the air we have breathed to the trees we have barely noticed. This is part of our role as priestly stewards of creation—to encounter God's glory in creation and turn that encounter into prayer.

No bird is just a bird. All creation is meant to be a vessel for God's glory. And amid all this intricacy and great intention, we come to God's magnificent achievement in people.

This too can be surprising. We see each other midstream, in the middle of our movement from birth to natural death. It is easy to forget that the people who pester you, baffle you, and otherwise offend your sensibilities are made "a little lower than the angels" and are crowned with "glory and honor" (Psalm 8:5 NIV). God desires that all his children should be saved and become humble bearers of his glory.

Pause now and recall the majesty of God revealed in the created order. Consider the places you have been called to steward this world, to care for plants, animals, land, and people. Thank the Lord for the whole range of people in your life—friends, family, neighbors, enemies. Pray that the Lord will be at work to bring them humility and wisdom, as well as the ability to join you in praise of our God.

Recommended Closing Prayer

O Lord, our Lord, how majestic is your name in all the earth! We praise you for our creation, our preservation, and all the blessings of this life. We ask that all people might be brought within the reach of your saving embrace, that they might serve you in thought, word, and deed and know your eternal life. May your Holy Spirit be at work, drawing more and more people unto you. Amen.

Epiphany Day 24

MADISON PERRY

Reflect on Psalm 13

Call to Prayer

Are you in a long season of waiting on the Lord?

In this psalm, David reports having "sorrow in my heart all the day" (Psalm 13:2 ESV). He has turned to the Lord, and finding little counsel, he has only his own soul for that purpose. He is isolated and feels the approach of death.

But in verses 5 and 6 of this psalm, there is a turning point:

> But I have trusted in your steadfast love;
> my heart shall rejoice in your salvation.
> I will sing to the Lord
> because he has dealt bountifully with me.
> (Psalm 13:5–6 ESV)

Here, in the face of his present sense of abandonment, David remembers the Lord's salvation, an event so great that even the present circumstances can't threaten it. David has been saved, and he remembers it. As he turns to God in praise, he understands his life very differently. The Father's love has never left him, but now he remembers it—and now he will trust it and is moved to singing. This is an eternal love that outlasted whatever circumstances faced David and that will also outlast any crisis that assails us.

As you pray, ask God how long you will have to wait. Let the question hang. Ask how long your suffering or difficulty will continue. Be honest. Now recall your salvation and trust in God. Remember God's love, your betrayal of him in sin, and the salvation and promise of Jesus Christ. Rejoice in that salvation that shines bright even now, in the midst of hardship.

Recommended Closing Prayer

Father, in the midst of great troubles, we rest in your arms. You have given us the greatest salvation and have caused us to be reborn to a living hope through the resurrection of Jesus Christ. We praise you for your victory over death! May the whole world come to know this salvation and restoration. Help us to continue trusting you. Please, Lord, let your kingdom come in all its fullness, and be at work in the present moment. Amen.

Epiphany Day 25

ELIZABETH GATEWOOD

Reflect on Isaiah 28

Call to Prayer

The prophet Isaiah speaks vivid words of woe to the leaders of Israel and Judah. They have settled for cheap beauty. They have settled for pithy morality and spiritual wisdom, distorting God's Words into a list of rules. They have settled for false assurances and protection by making a covenant with death instead of turning to the living God.

The things they have settled for will not last. God's judgment of them will be fierce. Isaiah's rich imagery speaks for itself. God will be like a flooding downpour and a hailstorm that beats down upon the false things. These idols will be thrown to the ground, trampled, consumed, flooded.

But God will set his people free. He will build something more enduring than their idols: the cornerstone. He will build something new, marked by righteousness and justice, something where false beauty, false spirituality, and false hope will have no place.

How often do we mourn when our false gods are destroyed? We have settled for cheap beauty and yet grieve when it fades. We have settled for pithy morality and spiritual wisdom and yet cling to it tightly. We have made a covenant with death, seeking to protect ourselves from it with insurance policies, security systems, and healthy living, yet we are bewildered when death and illness still creep in.

These things we turn to will not last. And still when we experience their failure, we grieve. God invites us away from these idols and to the cornerstone of Jesus Christ. In him, we see true beauty, not the cheap and fading beauty of an image-obsessed culture. In him, we see the true spiritual wisdom of being united with Christ. In baptism, we have been joined to him in his death and have been raised with Christ. We no longer need false assurances and imagined protections against death, because we are sealed to Christ's life.

As you pray, consider where you are settling for false beauty, pithy morality, and empty hope. Imagine the downpour of God's severe mercy washing away your idols and turning you toward the cornerstone that is Jesus Christ.

Recommended Closing Prayer

God, when our idols tumble and crumble and our facades of beauty, truth, and control fade, we grieve. We do not know what else to do. We cannot see in these moments your severe mercy coming to us in the form of cleansing judgment. We cling to our meager substitutions, accustomed to this cheap fare. It feels painful. Yet you offer us nothing less than yourself—true magnificent beauty; righteousness by being joined to your very body and sealed by the Holy Spirit; and everlasting life in Christ. As Isaiah writes, your plan is wonderful and your wisdom magnificent. Would you bring the rain and hail of your cleansing grace and, in your tenderness, walk with us? Amen.

Epiphany Day 26
NATHAN BAXTER

Reflect on Isaiah 29:13–24

Call to Prayer

God's prophets have never been easy to hear, to understand, or to take to heart. Their complex poetry, their blending of accusation and encouragement, their tender vehemence, and their lacerating entreaties—it's all hard to take as a whole. Yet, when we listen long enough and longingly enough, letting their words do their God-given work, our ears hear well enough and our eyes see clearly enough to let our hopes rise from true repentance.

As you pray through the passage from Isaiah, can you savor the words as holy love?

Ask the Holy Spirit to turn the prophetic words into meeting places of humble joy as you ask questions such as the following:

- Lord, are there gaps between my lips and my heart or ways I "turn things upside down" with you (Isaiah 29:16 NIV)?
- As I pray about the waywardness and complaints around me, how are you inviting me to hope humbly in your wisdom and to stand in awe of your holiness?

Recommended Closing Prayer

Grant, Almighty God, that the words we have heard this day from your word may by your grace be grafted in our hearts, that they may bring forth in us the fruit of a righteous life, to the honor and praise of your Name; through Jesus Christ our Lord. Amen.

(Anglican Church in North America Book of Common Prayer)

Epiphany Day 27
NATHAN BAXTER

Reflect on Isaiah 30:8–18

Call to Prayer

Isn't it strange how ancient words can transcend time and place to resonate here and now?

Yet is this not God's gracious design for these and other scriptures?

God instructed Isaiah to write down what he spoke then so that ears in later times would hear. Hundreds of years later, another Spirit-moved writer, Paul, declares, "Everything that was written in the past was written to teach us, so that through the endurance taught in the scriptures and the encouragement they provide we might have hope" (Romans 15:4 NIV).

The "Lord who longs to be gracious" (Isaiah 30:18 NIV), who is also "a God of justice" (Isaiah 30:18 NIV), speaks patiently though earnestly across the centuries to any who will turn again to listen, settle in with his Word, and remain quiet long enough to begin trusting.

As you ponder the scriptures as a way into prayer, take heart from the promised blessing of Isaiah 30:18. Wait with and for God.

Recommended Closing Prayer

> Our God, in whom we trust: Strengthen us not to regard overmuch who is for us or who is against us, but to see to it that we be with you in everything we do. Amen.
> *(Anglican Church in North America Book of Common Prayer)*

Epiphany Day 28
NATHAN BAXTER

Reflect on Isaiah 31

Call to Prayer

Friends and allies are vital to safety in a world that lives and dies by a swordlike strategy.

The prophet Isaiah wrote in a time when Israel and Judah were threatened by the Assyrian empire and sought Egypt as an ally. The people of Yahweh had, however, made a habit of neglecting their Fiery Friend, their covenant Lord.

How easily God's people and their leaders forget that "he too is wise and … does not take back his words" (Isaiah 31:2 NIV). Though we may forget our truest Friend and wisest Ally, God does not forget us. And still, God calls us away from the unstable security of the sword and every other idol that disappoints.

"Return" (Isaiah 31:8 NIV), God says to his fickle friends. Return, not to be shamed but to be saved.

As you turn to prayer, ask God your Friend to sift your alliances so that you can trust him more deeply.

Recommended Closing Prayer

> O God of peace, who has taught us that in returning and rest we shall be saved, in quietness and confidence shall be our strength: By the might of your Spirit lift us, we pray, to your presence, where we may be still and know that you are God; through Jesus Christ our Lord. Amen.
> *(Anglican Church in North America Book of Common Prayer)*

Epiphany Day 29
NATHAN BAXTER

Reflect on Isaiah 32:1–8

Call to Prayer

In the stormy times we often inhabit (perhaps not so different from other times in history), we rightly long for leaders and rulers like Jesus. We rightly long for a clear-sighted, open-eared society where even the fearful-hearted and hesitant can participate with understanding.

The Righteous Ruler has entered our scoundrel-filled world, has set new creation in motion, has ascended to the "right hand of the majesty on high," and waits patiently for his enemies to be confounded (Hebrews 1:3; 2:5–9; 10:13).

We may hear folly and may lament the spread of error. Evil schemes may prevail for a time. Lies may overwhelm the poor and needy. Still, the noble ones who take shelter in King Jesus may still make noble plans and stand even in a storm by noble deeds.

As you pray, bring the stormy parts of your life and the world into the shelter of God's presence. Be still with him and listen. Might he be nudging you to collaborate with him in noble plans or deeds?

Recommended Closing Prayer

> O Rock divine, O Refuge dear
> A shelter in the time of storm;
> Be Thou our helper ever near
> A shelter in the time of storm.
> ("A Shelter in the Time of Storm" by Vernon J. Charlesworth)

Epiphany Day 30
NATHAN BAXTER

Reflect on Isaiah 33:1–6

Call to Prayer

Many value creativity. Destructiveness is all too easy, far too common. Many more value loyalty. Betrayals are all too common, far too easy.

Perhaps unwittingly, the widespread desires for creativity and loyalty signal our longings for their source: the Creator, whose loyal love is fresh every morning.

As you pray, make Isaiah 33:2 the core of your petition: "Lord, be gracious to us; we long for you. Be our strength every morning, our salvation in time of distress" (NIV).

Make Isaiah 33:5 a springboard for adoration and hope: "The Lord is exalted, for he dwells on high; he will fill Zion with his justice and righteousness" (NIV).

Trust Isaiah 33:6 as the key to true treasure and prevailing prayer: "He will be the sure foundation for your times, a rich store of salvation and wisdom and knowledge; the fear of the Lord is the key to this treasure" (NIV).

Recommended Closing Prayer

> Most loving Father, you will us to give thanks for all things, to dread nothing but the loss of you, and to cast all our care on the One who cares for us. Preserve us from faithless fears and worldly anxieties, and grant that no clouds of this mortal life may hide from us the light of that love which is immortal, and which you have manifested unto us in your Son, Jesus Christ our Lord. Amen.
> *(Anglican Church in North America Book of Common Prayer)*

Epiphany Day 31
NATHAN BAXTER

Reflect on Isaiah 34:8–17

Call to Prayer

The prophetic passages that speak of God's judgment upon oppression, violence, and lawlessness make many moderns uncomfortable. But rightly heard, they can be sources of hope and directions for prayer.

Passages such as Isaiah 34 speak of God's decisive and final removal of violence and oppression from the new creation he is preparing to reveal. All wars we have ever witnessed or read about have been, at best, temporary and partial remedies for greater wrongs. Oppression, violence, and lawlessness return again all too soon.

How seldom do we see the predators of nature at rest and nesting or nurturing. How seldom do scavengers rest from their post-carnage work.

More seldom still do the predators and scavengers of human society rest, or change, or meet their ends.

Yet prophetic hope promises a day when all evils will be not slowed but stopped, not curbed but crushed. That hope can only be fulfilled by the God in whom both justice and mercy shine.

As you pray, consider the measuring line of chaos and the plumb line of desolation, and yield your hopes for righteousness and peace to the only One who does all things well.

Recommended Closing Prayer

> Eternal God, in whose perfect kingdom no sword is drawn but the sword of righteousness, no strength known but the strength of love: So mightily spread abroad your Spirit, that all peoples may be gathered under the banner of the Prince of Peace; to whom be dominion and glory, now and for ever. Amen.
> *(Anglican Church in North America Book of Common Prayer)*

Epiphany Day 32

NATHAN BAXTER

Reflect on Isaiah 35:1–10

Call to Prayer

Where God's judgment falls to make a desert into a wasteland and "a haunt for jackals"—as portrayed in Isaiah 34:4 (NIV)—that same place becomes the scene of God's recreation. Where judgment has fallen, mercy and renewal spring up.

It is the way of the cross, where Jesus bore the rage of nations and all judgment for the depredations of rebel humankind. The place where Jesus hung parched now flows with living water. The place where the cry of dereliction went up is now the place where sounds of joy rise up. The place where scavengers cast lots for cast-off clothing is now the place where redeemed people find robes of righteousness and garments of praise.

Where judgment has fallen, mercy and renewal spring up.

As you go to prayer, rejoice in anticipation of the day when gladness and joy will overtake you in all your desolate places.

Recommended Closing Prayer

> O God of unchangeable power and eternal light: Look favorably on your whole Church, that wonderful and sacred mystery; by the effectual working of your providence, carry out in tranquility the plan of salvation; let the whole world see and know that things that were cast down are being raised up, and that things that had grown old are being made new, and that all things are being brought to their perfection by him through whom all things were made, your Son Jesus Christ our Lord. Amen.
> *(Anglican Church in North America Book of Common Prayer)*

Epiphany Day 33

KARI WEST

Reflect on Isaiah 38

Call to Prayer

God hears prayer and responds to it. Somehow, in the mystery of his sovereignty and our human freedom, prayer moves the hand of God. In this passage, we witness God seeing Hezekiah's tears, listening to his words, and then granting his requests—both personal deliverance from his illness and the city's deliverance from the Assyrian king. Not only that, but God also grants a miraculous sign to assure Hezekiah of his promises. He pulls back the sun's shadow.

Illness is beaten, death is cheated, an evil ruler is routed, and the shadow retreats—leaving the sun to shine in all its brightness.

Such is the power of prayer. God delights to answer his people. Will you come before him and trust that he hears you, that he catches each of your tears, and that he bears your burdens? Father to child, friend to friend, husband to wife—these are the barest echoes of what he is to you.

He will rise with healing in his wings. He will trample death again. He will conquer all evil. He will retract all shadows. We won't need the sun's brightness, for the Lord will be our everlasting light.

Recommended Closing Prayer

> Lord Jesus, stay with us, for evening is at hand and the day is past; be our companion in the way, kindle our hearts, and awaken hope, that we may know you as you are revealed in Scripture and the breaking of bread. Grant this for the sake of your love. Amen.
> *(Anglican Church in North America Book of Common Prayer)*

Epiphany Day 34

KARI WEST

Reflect on Isaiah 40

Call to Prayer

What a beautiful juxtaposition we find in these verses between might and tenderness, vast power and personal love, and awe-inspiring majesty and gentle care. God pulls out the starry host; he measures the nations as dust on the scales; he holds the vast oceans in the hollow of his hand; and he sits enthroned in the heavens. And God tends to his people gently; he carries them as lambs, close to his heart. He draws near and empowers the weak and the weary.

This is your God. He is tending to you as the perfect Shepherd to his flock—protecting, guiding and cherishing. He holds you close to his heart. In all his marvelous, unimaginable glory as the great King of heaven and earth, God draws near to you and gives you strength.

Do you feel forgotten? Does your life feel enfolded in difficulty, hidden from all help? Hear God's answer to you in these words. Let your Savior speak to you, and may you know the all-encompassing, ever-near love of God as you pray.

Recommended Closing Prayer

God over all, your presence is undeserved, your peace is unmerited, and your love is unfathomable. Grant us the grace to know you as you are and to follow you all the days of our lives. For our Great Shepherd's sake. Amen.

Epiphany Day 35
STEVEN E. BREEDLOVE

Reflect on Isaiah 41:1–10

Call to Prayer

Isaiah 41 begins with a courtroom scene, a trial where God is both judge and prosecutor. The nations are the audience watching God prove his case. The idols of the world are defendants prosecuted by God. Yet there is also a special group in the audience; the trial is for their benefit: Israel.

God questions and accuses the idols in Israel's presence, challenging them to predict the future or explain the past. But he also addresses Israel directly as a prosecutor might address a jury. Israel needs to listen because they have depended upon the idols of pagan nations many times. They have been humbled and broken by these nations, and they are fearful. Where has the God of Israel been in this dangerous world?

Yet the Lord answers their fears. He says to them, "Fear not, for I am with you; be not dismayed, for I am your God; I will strengthen you, I will help you" (Isaiah 41:10 ESV). Over and over, he tells them not to fear. He has not abandoned his people. He will rescue them from slavery and exile.

God proves that the idols are nothing; they are merely things people build to protect themselves. They cannot do anything; they do not know the past; and they cannot tell the future. God alone can do these things; he alone is Lord over history, and the world is in his hands.

As you pray, consider that we, like Israel, live in a chaotic world. Like Israel, we are tempted to trust in what we build with our hands. Like Israel, we forget that God is actually the King of all nations and we attempt to protect ourselves by our own efforts and power.

Let us pray that God will reveal the places where we trust in our own efforts rather than the King's.

Let us pray that we will return to deep trust that God will be present with us and protect us.

Recommended Closing Prayer

You, O Lord our God, hold us by the right hand. It is you who says to us, "Fear not, for I am the one who helps you!" You are the Holy One of Israel, yet also our Redeemer. You alone know the future, and nothing happens outside your sight. May we live without fear, trusting that you are Lord over history. Amen.

Epiphany Day 36
STEVEN E. BREEDLOVE

Reflect on Isaiah 42:1–4

Call to Prayer

In the midst of God's indictment of the idols of the nations, he pauses to describe his servant. The idols are nothing, unable to save and ignorant of the past and the future. Israel's God alone is the Lord—he alone can deliver, and he alone knows the future. But remarkably, even God's servant can do what the idols cannot; he will actually succeed in bringing justice to all nations! God has proven throughout history—through people such as Moses, Deborah, and David, and even pagans like Cyrus—that when he desires, he can anoint an ordinary person and, through this servant, bring justice and salvation. His lowly servants are more powerful than the gods of the nations simply because the Spirit of God rests upon them.

From our vantage point living in the era of the resurrected and exalted Christ, we know that God the Father is ultimately speaking of his Son, who is the true Servant of God. Anointed by the Spirit at his baptism, he has triumphed and brought justice and the law of salvation to the ends of the earth. He is the true image of God, the living icon, God himself in the flesh, and he can do what false gods cannot. But in Jesus we also see the character of the Father, who declared, "A bruised reed [a servant] will not break, and a faintly burning wick he will not quench" (Isaiah 42:3 ESV). Jesus delivers with tenderness, protecting the wounded as he conquers, enlarging the faith of hearts that are only faintly burning wicks. God's character shines through the life of Jesus as he shields the bruised and fainting and accomplishes justice.

As you pray, remember that God uses his humble servants, anointed by the Spirit, to deliver. Remember that his salvation is tender, protecting those who are bruised and only faintly alive.

Let us pray that God will heal our bruises and brighten our small flames of faith.

Let us pray that we will see where he is anointing ordinary people to deliver others.

Let us pray that he will anoint us to bring justice and the law of salvation to the nations.

Recommended Closing Prayer

O Lord, you have anointed your Son, the true Servant, to bring salvation to the world. Anoint us also with your Spirit so that we might be his messengers of salvation to the bruised reeds and faintly burning wicks who live near us. Amen.
(Adapted from Isaiah 42 NIV)

Epiphany Day 37

STEVEN E. BREEDLOVE

Reflect on Isaiah 43:1–7

Call to Prayer

There are moments in the Bible when we see that God's concerns are not always the same as ours. We want to be free of pain and difficulty, but God cares more that our hearts long for his presence and that we trust him. God allowed his people to be plundered, trapped, and hidden in prisons because they rejected him. Judah had sinned against God and refused to walk in his ways, and so God gave his people to their enemies. They longed to be free of the exile, but God longed more for them to be faithful to him.

But even in delivering his people up to suffering and exile, God did not abandon them. His love for them was far too strong. He promised redemption—not a superficial sentiment, but instead *actual redemption*, where the north and the south, the east and the west, release the prisoners to go home and rebuild their families and lives. God chastised for a season, but he did not abandon. It was because of his love that he purged his people of their idolatry—for idolatry brings death.

Yet even in the dark moments when God's people were driven from home in suffering, God was not far off. When Daniel's three friends were cast into the fiery furnace in Babylon, God walked there with them. Ezekiel, while in the land of Babylon, saw the throne of God on wheels carried by angels so that God would be with the exiles where they were. They were being disciplined, but God was suffering their exile with them! And in Isaiah 43:2, we hear God say to those in exile, "When you pass through the waters, I will be with you" (NIV).

I will be with you.

I will be with you in your suffering. I will be with you in your grief. I will be with you in your exhaustion. And even if I have to discipline you, to purge you of idolatry, I will be with you in the discipline.

As you pray, rejoice that the Lord is with you no matter where you are or what you are enduring.

Let us pray for those Christians who are blind to the presence of God in their lives.

Let us pray for those who have not yet met God and do not know that he would be with them.

Recommended Closing Prayer

You, O Lord, have created and formed us. You have redeemed us, so we need not fear. You have walked through the waters with us; indeed, you have walked through the waters of death for us. The flames will not destroy us, for we are called by your name! You are the Holy One of Israel, our Savior! Amen.
(Adapted from Isaiah 43 NIV)

Epiphany Day 38
STEVEN E. BREEDLOVE

Reflect on Isaiah 44:1–5

Call to Prayer

One of the greatest and most frequent themes of the prophets is God's faithfulness to his people even while they are faithless to him. He is the husband pursuing an adulterous wife or the father stretching out his hands to a rebellious son. His people are perpetually wandering, going astray, and joining themselves to other lovers and masters.

In the midst of this dark night of faithlessness, Isaiah 44:5 gleams like a torch. The people finally begin to understand—they are God's through and through! No more false masters, no more illicit lovers! They write his name on their hands, just as a child with a marker claims toys as her own. No one will ever again forget that he or she belongs to God!

But this doesn't happen because the people are finally enlightened or finally faithful. Isaiah 43 ends, yet again, with the failure of the people.

The people don't reach this point of understanding because of something in and of themselves. They aren't better than the rest. In the words of Isaiah 44:3, they are merely "thirsty land" and "dry ground"

(NIV). But God wasn't content for them to stay that way. He poured out his Spirit, watering their hearts and transforming them, so that they finally realized who they were—God's people through and through! It was the Spirit, undeserved and without measure, poured on the thirsty land of their hearts that caused this transformation.

As you pray, acknowledge the thirsty land of your heart. Acknowledge its dry ground.

Let us pray that God will continually pour out his Spirit on us, watering the cracked and dry ground of our hearts.

Let us pray that God will pour out his Spirit in our families, so that we will believe within the depths of our being that we are the Lord's.

Let us pray that God will pour out his Spirit on our churches, so that the only thing that matters to us is faithfulness to God.

Recommended Closing Prayer

You, O Lord, have chosen us! You have formed us from the womb and helped us. You have poured water on the thirsty land of our hearts and sent streams through the desert places of our lives. Pour out your Spirit yet again so that we might know that we are yours! Amen. *(Adapted from Isaiah 44 NIV)*

Epiphany Day 39
STEVEN E. BREEDLOVE

Reflect on Isaiah 45:1–7

Call to Prayer

It must have been startling to the Israelites that God was going to use Cyrus, the great Persian king, to save the Israelites. He was a pagan who did not know the God of Israel—an idol-worshipper! Was there no new Moses or faithful Israelite that the Lord could raise up to deliver his people? Why use this pagan king?

Yet God anointed him, subdued nations under him, broke the doors of bronze before him, and gave him the treasures of other nations. Given that Israel had suffered under the great kings of pagan nations—Egypt, Assyria, Babylon—the ascent of Cyrus may have filled them with dread. The Israelites did not have a store of good experiences from the hands of idol-worshipping kings.

Yet God raised up Cyrus for the sake of his servant Jacob, for Israel, his chosen one! He exalted a ruler they would never have chosen to deliver them. There are many times when God does not tell his people why he does what he does, but in this instance, he explained himself. His reasoning was simple. He used a pagan king to deliver his people, one they could not control and did not expect, simply so that they might finally understand that God, and God alone, is the Lord!

If the deliverer had been one of their own, someone they could trust, control, and assist, they would always have been tempted to believe that they had played a role in their deliverance. But God desired for his people to finally say, "Only you, O Lord, create light and darkness; only you can raise up or destroy nations. Only you are God!"

As you pray, remember that God uses people we do not expect to accomplish his will. Remember that he, and he alone, can deliver. Remember that he is the Lord over kings and nations and is Lord over the past, present, and future.

Let us pray that we will see where God is at work in our nation.

Let us pray that we will grow to believe that only God can deliver.

Let us pray that we will follow where God leads, rather than trying to do things our way.

Recommended Closing Prayer

You are the Lord, and there is no other. Besides you, there is no God! You equip those you choose to accomplish your will so that people will know, from the rising to the setting of the sun, that there is no one besides you! Amen.

(Adapted from Isaiah 45 NIV)

Epiphany Day 40

STEVEN E. BREEDLOVE

Reflect on Isaiah 46:3–7

Call to Prayer

God's prosecution of the idols is full of holy mockery. He is nothing like the gods of the nations, who are mere statues crafted by goldsmiths for a fee. People cry out to these gods for deliverance from trouble, yet the gods cannot even move themselves, let alone the people who worship them. They are so helpless that they have to be carried on the shoulders of men.

God, on the other hand, is the one carrying his people. He does what the idols cannot, and he has borne his people from cradle to grave for centuries. They rest on his secure shoulders.

Though we are unlikely to cry out to a statue to carry us and deliver us, we still face the temptation of seeking help from the works of our hands. We look to our careers, our bank accounts, or our political parties to assist us, deliver us, and save us. Yet like the idols of nations long destroyed, the works of our hands cannot carry us— we carry and build them. They are less powerful than we are because we created them. It makes no sense that we would trust in their power to protect us.

Only God has the strength to carry us. Only God has the strength to save us. He has held us on his shoulders since before our birth, and he will carry us beyond the grave!

As you pray, remember the times when you have seen God carrying you. Remember the moments when you have seen his deliverance.

Let us pray that we will not trust the works of our hands for salvation.

Let us pray that we will seek refuge in the hands of our Creator.

Let us pray that we will remember that God is carrying us at every moment of every day.

Recommended Closing Prayer

Lord, you have borne us from before our lives began, even from the womb! You will bear us until old age and the grave. You have made us; you will continue to carry us; you will save us! Amen.
(Adapted from Isaiah 46 NIV)

Epiphany Day 41
STEVEN E. BREEDLOVE

Reflect on Isaiah 47:5–7

Call to Prayer

Isaiah 47 is one of those passages that many people struggle to appreciate. God's rebuke of Babylon and his prophecy of judgment seem worlds away from the twenty-first century. Yet even here we hear the heart of God, and even here his voice can speak to us.

As he said to Babylon, he was angry with his people, so he profaned his heritage. They had rejected him, so he sent them into exile and defiled the land. But he was not seeking to destroy them! Even the purpose of the exile was for their salvation because the idols that they worshipped were far more dangerous than losing their homes. Their idols would destroy their souls, stealing the life God had given, so God removed them from their homes to break their enslavement to idols.

But the Babylonians were proud, and they showed no mercy to the Jews. They thought that they would rule forever and showed no regard for the weak and pitiful. So God declared that Babylon, too, would be destroyed.

God's care is for the weak, the aged, and the vulnerable. Those who are poor and humble in spirit are precious to him. The proud, the merciless, and the cruel are rejected by him because they show no regard for those in whom God delights.

As you pray, take great comfort in the fact that God loves you, not because of your successes and strength, but instead simply because he has created you. He does not need you to be powerful and is not ashamed of your weakness. But as you pray, also remember that God rejects those who, in their pride, despise the weak and the humble of the world.

Let us pray that God will root out all pride and cruelty from our hearts.

Let us pray that, like God, we will protect and care for the weak.

Let us pray in thanksgiving that God is near to us as we are poor in spirit and brokenhearted.

Recommended Closing Prayer

O God, you are the Redeemer of the humble, the Savior of the weak. You reject those who arrogantly destroy others. Soften our hearts to the cries of the weak. Keep us from pride and cruelty. Thank you for loving us in our weakness! Amen.
(Adapted from Isaiah 47 NIV)

Epiphany Day 42

ART GOING

Reflect on Isaiah 48:1–6

Call to Prayer

The first word of Isaiah 48:1 (NIV) is the key: *listen.* Isaiah uses the word ten times in this chapter, and it keeps coming back in the ensuing chapters. The Hebrew word is the familiar and essential *Shema*—the first word and name of the Jewish profession of faith (Deuteronomy 6:4 NIV): *Hear, O Israel.* Amid all the various themes of these chapters of Isaiah is the recurring invitation: *Listen.*

And oh how we need to listen. Hearing a clear word from God is the only way we'll escape the prison of self and the allurement of culture. The living God speaks so that we will not listen fruitlessly to cultural idols or only to ourselves. Isaiah calls out Israel for not really listening to him. They confessed faith but failed to live it out.

Not only are they quick to credit idols for their blessings, but also they are not open to the "new things" (Isaiah 48:6 NIV) God has in store. And even though God has told them about his character and his mighty acts, they have never been good listeners.

That's the challenge and invitation to us: to become listeners!

As you pray, ask for focus and attentiveness this season to the God who speaks, who speaks to you. Examine your listening. Take an inventory of the voices that drown out the voice that matters most, namely, that of the God who wants to do a new thing in your life.

Recommended Closing Prayer

> O Almighty God, you pour out on all who desire it the spirit of grace and of supplication: Deliver us, when we draw near to you, from coldness of heart and wanderings of mind, that with steadfast thoughts and kindled affections we may worship you in spirit and in truth; through Jesus Christ our Lord. Amen.
>
> *(Anglican Church in North America Book of Common Prayer)*

Epiphany Day 43

KARI WEST

Reflect on Psalm 46:1–3

Call to Prayer

Perhaps these vivid descriptions of chaos and uncertainty—the earth giving way, water roaring, and mountains quaking—strike a chord of resonance for you. Perhaps your days feel closer to calamity than calm.

What are we to do as the earth trembles and the mountains fall into the heart of the sea?

May we be a people who find fresh courage in the answer this psalm offers us. God is our constant help in every season. God is our strong refuge. God is our Rock and our fortress. God dwells forever in his holy city, and we will all one day gather on those far distant shores of glory. The trials of this present time cannot compare to what lies in wait for those who are the Lord's.

As you pray, take one of the descriptions of God in this passage and meditate on it. Ask the Lord to give you fresh insight into his character. Praise him for his constancy and his care.

Recommended Closing Prayer

> Father, you are our refuge and strength,
> an ever-present help in trouble.
> Therefore we will not fear, though the earth give way
> and the mountains fall into the heart of the sea,
> though its waters roar and foam
> and the mountains quake with their surging.
> Lord Almighty, you are with us.
> God of Jacob, you are our fortress. Amen.
> *(Adapted from Psalm 46:1–3, 46:7 NIV)*

Epiphany Day 44

M A T T   H O E H N

Reflect on 2 Corinthians 9:7–8

Call to Prayer

When paying off monthly credit card debts, you may find it jarring to observe how many of life's expenses are obligatory and bring no sense of pleasure.

We're reminded by Paul in this passage from 2 Corinthians 9 that our tithes and offerings to Christ and his church are to be markedly different. The mark of Christian giving is cheerfulness—a deep pleasure at the opportunity to present our gifts to the Father, who created us out of love; to the Son, who gave up his life to redeem us; and to the Spirit, who resides in us and sanctifies us. Paul writes elsewhere that "it is for freedom that Christ has set us free" from the works of the law (Galatians 5:1 NIV), and these verses in 1 Corinthians remind us that this freedom pertains to giving as well. We are to give not out of reluctant obligation, but out of gratitude for all that God has given to us. We are to give not out of begrudging compulsion, but out of a genuine desire.

While we don't give out of a utilitarian expectation of return, Paul does promise that God gives good gifts to the cheerful giver—namely, God's love, his abounding grace in one's life, all of life's needs being sufficiently met, and being equipped for good works. The Christian gives cheerfully because God is a benevolent God—he has already given us the greatest possible gift of his own Son, and he will not be frugal in giving us these additional good gifts as well.

As you pray, consider your recent heart posture toward giving and tithing. Have you been reluctant? Have you felt under compulsion? Or has giving been an occasion of joy for you?

Recommended Closing Prayer

Almighty God, you are the Maker of all things and Lord over all creation. We ask that you give us cheerful hearts in returning to you a portion of all that you have given to us, so that our hearts may be aligned with your will. We ask this through Jesus Christ your Son, your ultimate gift, given to us out of love. Amen.

Epiphany Day 45
MATT HOEHN

Reflect on 2 Corinthians 10:3–6

Call to Prayer

"Be *in* the world but not *of* the world" is a familiar saying in Christian circles. It means we are people of dual citizenship. We are temporarily residents of this world, and we are called to inhabit it in a faithful way. However, our ultimate home is in the kingdom of God, and this kingdom commands our truest allegiance.

"Being in the world" as a Christian often entails opposition—being on the receiving end of misunderstandings, slights, and sometimes even overt antipathy. Paul reminds us that this battle is spiritual in nature, and not simply according to the flesh. As citizens of the kingdom of God whose allegiance is to Christ, we are not to condescend to the "battle tactics" of this world: insults, slander, incendiary social media retorts, or a "punch back" mentality. We are to fight this battle with entirely different weaponry—the armor of God (Ephesians 6), which includes the belt of truth, the breastplate of righteousness, the shield of faith, and the sword of the Spirit.

Though the world may revile us and throw its worst at us, our fight is not aimed at the destruction of our perceived opponents, but at their salvation. We are to wield our spiritual weapons to "destroy arguments and every lofty opinion raised against the knowledge of God" (2 Corinthians 10:5 ESV). The first subject of our weaponry is ourselves. We are to discipline ourselves in "tak[ing] every thought captive to obey Christ" (2 Corinthians 10:5 ESV).

It can be tempting to lower ourselves to the world's standards of combat when defending the faith—to adopt an "ends justify the means" mentality. Paul will have none of this. We must always keep at the forefront of our minds that "we are not waging war according to the flesh" (2 Corinthians 10:3 ESV) and "the weapons of our warfare are not of the flesh" (2 Corinthians 10:4 ESV).

Prayer is perhaps the leading weapon with "divine power to destroy strongholds" (2 Corinthians 10:4 ESV). As you pray, ask that God would equip you to die to self, live for Christ, and oppose Satan, sin, and temptation in all that you do.

Recommended Closing Prayer

> Almighty God, give us grace to cast away the works of darkness, and put on the armor of light, now in the time of this mortal life in which your Son Jesus Christ came to visit us in great humility; that in the last day, when he shall come again in his glorious majesty to judge both the living

and the dead, we may rise to the life immortal; through
him who lives and reigns with you and the Holy Spirit, one
God, now and forever.
Amen.
(Anglican Church in North America Book of Common Prayer)

Epiphany Day 46
MATT HOEHN

Reflect on 2 Corinthians 11:2–3

Call to Prayer

When we think of the virtues that comprise the Christian life and the
corresponding vices that tempt us, we tend to classify jealousy among
the latter. Wasn't jealousy the second-ever recorded sin in the Bible, the
motivation that led Cain to murder his brother Abel? Isn't "You shall not
covet" (Exodus 20:17 ESV) one of the Ten Commandments?

But jealousy can have two senses—a negative and fleshly one and a
positive and spiritual one. In these verses from 2 Corinthians, Paul expresses
a divine jealousy for this flock of Christians he has shepherded, yearning that
they would continue walking earnestly in the faith and not be "led astray
from a sincere and pure devotion to Christ" (2 Corinthians 11:3 ESV).

Like the men and women of the Corinthian church, we are all made
in the image of God and designed for a relationship with him. While
Satan has tried to claim us as his own through the power of sin, the work
of Christ on the cross has restored us to the Father. "He has delivered
us from the domain of darkness and transferred us to the kingdom of
his beloved Son" (Colossians 1:13 ESV). It is good and right to feel a
divine jealousy toward fellow believers, a possessive zeal to remind our
brothers and sisters of who they are and whose they are.

The same God who commands us not to covet in the tenth
commandment also says in the second commandment, "You shall not
bow down to [any other gods] or serve them, for I the Lord your God am

a jealous God" (Exodus 20:5 ESV). Elsewhere in Exodus, God reveals that the divine name is even synonymous with jealousy: "You shall worship no other God, for the Lord, whose name is Jealous, is a jealous God" (Exodus 34:14 ESV).

While jealousy of our neighbor's belongings is sinful, jealousy for our neighbor's continuation in the faith is godly. As you pray, ask the Lord to give you a proper divine jealousy for your fellow brothers and sisters in Christ.

Recommended Closing Prayer

Almighty God, you created us out of love, and we belong to you. Your zeal for us to know and love you is great, and your desire for us not to be led astray by the deceit of sin is absolute. Cleanse us from our petty worldly jealousies and replace them with a proper divine jealousy for our fellow man and fellow woman to know you. All this we ask by the powerful name of Jesus, the supreme demonstration of your perfect jealous love for us. Amen.

Epiphany Day 47

MATT HOEHN

Reflect on 2 Corinthians 12:7–10

Call to Prayer

While the Bible is clear on the fundamentals, or "all things necessary for salvation," such as the character of God, the plight of sinful humankind, and the saving work of Christ, it also leaves many questions unanswered relating to tertiary issues.

Second Corinthians 12:7–10 raises one such question: what was Paul's thorn in the flesh? We simply don't know. Paul doesn't reveal the specifics to us here or elsewhere. While we can't know what Paul's thorn was, we can all relate to it. Following Adam's fall, all of us are afflicted in various ways. All of us have things in our lives—thought patterns, sinful inclinations, marred relationships—that we long for God to destroy or redeem. Adam chose sin and tainted the human condition for all, and now we all have hurts, habits, and hang-ups that beset our lives.

While Paul had previously repeatedly implored the Lord to remove this thorn, he later came to see that God had a purpose in it. Our thorns remind us of our true condition, sinful and frail, and rid us of our proclivities toward conceit and pride. Our thorns remind us that we are not in control of our own lives and are not our own saviors. We desperately need the power of Christ in our lives. Our thorns provide an opportunity for us to taste and see that God's grace is our portion. It is sufficient for us, regardless of our circumstances or struggles.

As you pray, bring to mind a thorn from your life and present it to the Lord. Rather than asking exclusively that he would remove it, pray that the Lord would use whatever the affliction, ailment, or circumstance may be to demonstrate his power in the midst of your weakness.

Recommended Closing Prayer

> Almighty God, whose most dear Son went not up to joy but first he suffered pain, and entered not into glory before he was crucified: Mercifully grant that we, walking in the way of the Cross, may find it none other than the way of life and peace; through Jesus Christ our Lord. Amen.
> *(Anglican Church in North America Book of Common Prayer)*

Epiphany Day 48
MATT HOEHN

Reflect on 2 Corinthians 13:11–14

Call to Prayer

When reading one of Paul's letters, one may find it tempting to gloss over the valediction, the parting farewell, and the final instructions to the letter's recipients.

But the conclusion of the epistle is crucially important and often captures the essence of Paul's heart, as is the case with 2 Corinthians. Throughout this letter, Paul has laid out a vision for how the church at Corinth should follow Christ communally as one body. Here at the close, Paul hammers home this theme with three "one another" exhortations: comfort one another, agree with one another, and greet one another with affection. Christians are not to be those who obstinately insist on their way to the point of division and disunity; they are to be those who "aim for restoration" and "live in peace" (2 Corinthians 13:11 ESV).

In our day and age where individuality is valorized and submission to a community is thought ludicrous, we would do well to heed Paul's instructions. We Christians should be known as a people whose corporate life together is characterized by restoration, mutual comfort, agreement, and peace.

As you pray, ask the Lord for unity in the body of Christ—in your immediate relationships, at your home congregation, and throughout the wider global church.

Recommended Closing Prayer

Almighty God, you sent your Son Jesus to purchase his bride, the church, with his own shed blood. In spite of its defects, you see the church as radiant and clothed in the righteousness of your Son. Grant your church to have the mind of Christ among its many members so that we may be knit together in love, concord, and peace, and so the watching world may know you through your church. Amen.

Epiphany Day 49
KARI WEST

Reflect on Romans 1:1–7

Call to Prayer

What comes to mind when you think about the gospel? Is it primarily an intellectual concept, a list of theological ideas, a rubric for moral living, a half-remembered story from your churched childhood?

Hear how Paul describes the good news in this passage: what God has done *for us*.

This long-promised reality of the Son of God clothing himself in humanity, living perfectly, dying sacrificially, and resurrecting in power—it was all done by God so we could belong to him. We who hated him, we who ran from him, we who had nothing to offer to our Creator God, we who would die in our miserable rebellion—now we are the friends of God.

Why did Christ live, die, and return again to life? Paul knew; it was so that God could give you grace and peace.

God did everything for us so that we could be his own.

As you pray, meditate on this passage and ask the Spirit to reveal the deep, personal, intimate love of your Father for you in these words. You are his, and he has moved heaven and earth to make it so.

Recommended Closing Prayer

Father, may you give us the strength to comprehend with all the saints what is the breadth and length and height and depth, and to know the love of Christ that surpasses knowledge, that we may be filled with all the fullness of you. Amen.
(Adapted from Ephesians 3:18–19 NIV)

Epiphany Day 50
MATT HOEHN

Reflect on Romans 1:16–17

Call to Prayer

We are regularly faced with circumstances where it would be easier to downplay our commitment to Christ. Whether a business situation where colleagues of ours are cutting corners, a social setting that has devolved into gossip, or a classroom context where the teaching of the instructor is confrontational toward a biblically shaped outlook, sometimes our faith can call us to live in ways that are inconvenient, socially awkward, and personally costly.

Paul's declaration in Romans 1:16 serves as a booming cannon of encouragement to us when facing such circumstances. "For I am not ashamed of the gospel, for it is the power of God for salvation to everyone who believes, to the Jew first and also to the Greek" (ESV). While it can be tempting in certain scenarios to shrink from our discipleship, our call is to be boldly unashamed of our identity in Christ.

The gospel reveals the righteousness of God—his covenant faithfulness to his promises and his perfect and holy character, which covers our sin and shame. While we are not righteous by our own natural inclination, we receive the very righteousness of God as a gift through faith in Christ, the "Righteous One" (Acts 3:14 ESV).

Jesus says in Luke 9:26, "For whoever is ashamed of me and of my words, of him will the Son of Man be ashamed when he comes in his glory and the glory of the Father and of the holy angels" (ESV).

These verses from Romans remind us that whatever the circumstance may be, our allegiance to Christ is ultimate. As you pray, ask for grace to live not for the approval of humankind, but with your eyes on the prize of salvation and the gift of Christ's righteousness, granted to you by faith.

Recommended Closing Prayer

> O God our King, by the resurrection of your Son Jesus Christ on the first day of the week, you conquered sin, put death to flight, and gave us the hope of everlasting life: Redeem all our days by this victory; forgive our sins, banish our fears, make us bold to praise you and to do your will; and steel us to wait for the consummation of

your kingdom on the last great Day; through Jesus Christ
our Lord. Amen.

(Anglican Church in North America Book of Common Prayer)

Epiphany Day 51

MATT HOEHN

Reflect on Romans 2:1–4

Call to Prayer

One of the most moving, powerful, and dramatic scenes of the entire
Old Testament takes place when the prophet Nathan confronts King
David about his sin with Bathsheba and his murder of her husband
Uriah. David is so blinded by his own sin that Nathan intuits that the
only way to get through to him is to set a rhetorical trap.

Desiring to evoke a visceral reaction from David, Nathan tells a
parable of a wealthy owner of many sheep who steals the lone beloved
sheep of a poor man. David "burned with anger" and rashly declared,
"As surely as the Lord lives, the man who did this must die!" Without
missing a beat, Nathan stares David straight in the eye and issues a
shocking rebuke: "You are the man!" (2 Samuel 12:5–7 NIV).

According to Romans 2:1, Nathan's rebuke is aimed at all of us. All
of us "have no excuse" for our sinfulness because we pass judgment on
others and then fail to live up to the standards of our own judging. All of
us are beset by hypocrisy. We are condemned by the very standards we
establish for others. If you can't escape your own judgment, then Paul
rightly reasons, "Do you suppose … that you will escape the judgment
of God?" (Romans 2:3 ESV).

Graciously, God does provide a means of escape from both our
hypocrisy and his judgment in the riches of his kindness, forbearance,
and patience, all of which lead us to repentance. Rather than our
hypocrisy caging us in shame, it is meant to serve as a reminder that
there is a just Judge with a perfect standard of justice. Though we fail

to meet his standard, the Judge has also become the judged and has absorbed the blow of his own justice in our place. Through repentance of our sin and placing our faith in him, our souls find forgiveness and our consciences find peace.

As you pray, consider that Nathan's rebuke of David is true of you as well. Reflect on God's kindness, forbearance, and patience in not judging you according to your own fickle standards, but rather sending his Son to be judged according to God's perfect standard in your place.

Recommended Closing Prayer

> O God, the strength of all who put their trust in you: Mercifully accept our prayers, and because, through the weakness of our mortal nature, we can do no good thing without you, grant us the help of your grace to keep your commandments, that we may please you in will and deed; through Jesus Christ our Lord, who lives and reigns with you and the Holy Spirit, one God, for ever and ever. Amen.
> *(Anglican Church in North America Book of Common Prayer)*

Epiphany Day 52
MADISON PERRY

Reflect on Romans 5:1–5

Call to Prayer

Paul's assertions startle us! Suffering leads to good things? Endurance improves our character? A person of character knows real, solid hope?

If we are honest, we know suffering can be good for us, but we prefer to find a way around it or to fight against it. How much easier it is to want life to be carefree and to hope in vanishing temporary things!

But in times of distress, we have the opportunity to be made strong by God, to learn to hope in the things that last, and best of all, to find the love of God being poured into our hearts in new ways.

As you pray, ask God to help you embrace your life as it is right now. Ask him to help you know the solid ground of his peace and grace. Think of someone else and pray for that person, asking that he or she would know courage and hope because of the grace and peace of the Lord Jesus Christ.

Recommended Closing Prayer

> O Lord, support us all the day long through this trouble-filled life, until the shadows lengthen, and the evening comes, and the busy world is hushed, and the fever of life is over, and our work is done. Then in your mercy grant us a safe lodging, and a holy rest, and peace at the last. Amen.
> *(Anglican Church in North America Book of Common Prayer)*

Epiphany Day 53

MARYRACHEL BOYD

Reflect on Romans 5:17–19

Call to Prayer

Paul is speaking in this passage to an audience who understood the law as a check on sinful human impulse. Indeed, it's easy for most of us to think that keeping the right rules will earn us good standing with God. But Paul points us away from our own efforts. He longs for us to see what the perfect obedience of Jesus has accomplished.

Because of Christ's obedience all the way to the cross, we are offered the free gift of righteousness. That gift doesn't just make us good; it frees us to be fully alive, to "reign in life" (Romans 5:17 NIV), as Paul puts it. No matter how large our intentions for good have been and no matter how deep our sin, God's grace in Jesus is abundantly larger and deeper. Christ himself is our redemption, not our adherence to the law.

This pushes against our tendency to be individualistic and self-sustaining. Through Adam's disobedience, *all* were made sinners. There are no exceptions. However, through the coming and crucifixion of Jesus Christ (the second Adam), the tables are turned. Our perfect, obedient, righteous King bestows the gift of grace on us, the unworthy. In this mercy through Christ, we are *made* righteous and, as heirs of the kingdom, given the grace that reigns through righteousness, leading to eternal life.

Truly *receiving* this gift is an active thing. It demands from us a full-hearted response, an engagement on a physical, spiritual, and emotional level. As you pray, listen for God's invitation to respond to his love. He longs for you to know the abundance of his grace; he longs for you to reign in life; he longs for you to be free of the burden of trying to make it on your own.

Recommended Closing Prayer

O Father God, give me a heart to say yes to all that you want to give me in Jesus Christ. Amen.

Epiphany Day 54
MARYRACHEL BOYD

Reflect on Romans 8:37–39

Call to Prayer

God has declared it to be true: nothing in all creation can separate us from the love of God in Christ Jesus our Lord! We are secure no matter what happens to us and no matter how we fail. But that is not all. Because Christ has offered us his perfect, rightly ordered loyal love, we can offer that genuine and steadfast love to each other.

To be able to turn outward in joy and treat others with a similar quality of faithful love, we have to draw from the deep well of Christ's love for us. His Spirit longs to fill us with a love that will not run dry.

With an open mind and open heart, ponder what the power of the Holy Spirit is able to do in you and for you. Trust God; he who began a good work in you will bring it to completion. Don't be afraid: He has known you from the beginning of time. He knows where you have been and what lies ahead of you. He is mighty, is just, and is an ever-faithful friend.

As you pray, thank your Father for how secure you really are in Jesus. Then ask him to show you how you can love others well out of that security.

Recommended Closing Prayer

O Father, I am kept by your love. Work that love so deeply into my whole being that I am able to love others with a steadfast and loyal love. For Christ's sake. Amen.

Epiphany Day 55

WILLA KANE

Reflect on Romans 9:1–8

Call to Prayer

In Romans 9, Paul's grief that his kinsmen are lost follows the great and glorious promises of Romans 8. Why this unexpected juxtaposition of high to low, great joy to great sorrow?

He does this to highlight a critical question for believers: how can we trust that God's promises will hold for us if we question his faithfulness to his chosen people? If they are cut off from the Savior, how can we trust the anthem of promises just sung across the verses of Romans 8?

Paul gives an emphatic answer: "It is not as though the word of God had failed" (Romans 9:6 NIV). But this response leads to another question: what kind of children belong in God's family as his true offspring—children of flesh or children of promise?

Finding this answer sends us back to Genesis. God had promised old Abraham that barren Sarah would bear a son with descendants as numerous as the stars. In impatience or disbelief that God could do what he promised, Sarah and Abraham turn from faith to flesh, to the handmaid Hagar. The result was not a child conceived supernaturally, but a child conceived in human flesh. Even so, God was good to his promise and Isaac was born "not of blood nor of the will of the flesh nor of the will of man, but of God" (John 1:13 ESV). Isaac is child of the promise.

As you pray, examine your heart. Is there an area where you are trusting human devices for an answer to God's promises? Is impatience for his timing or unbelief in his ability to meet your need an excuse to operate in your flesh? Have you trusted in the work of Christ as your personal Savior, or are you trying to work your way to salvation? Are you a child of the flesh or a child of the promise?

Jesus is both promise and promise keeper. If you belong to Christ, then you are "Abraham's offspring, heirs according to promise" (Galatians 3:28–29 ESV). As you pray, put your whole trust in him.

Recommended Closing Prayer

> Lord God,
> Take me to the cross to seek glory from its infamy;
> Strip me of every pleasing pretense of righteousness
> by my own doings.
> O gracious Redeemer,
> I have neglected thee too long,
> often crucified thee,
> crucified thee afresh by my impenitence,
> put thee to open shame.
> I thank thee for the patience that has borne with me
> so long
> and for the grace that now makes me willing to be thine.
> O unite me to thyself with inseparable bonds,
> that nothing may ever draw me back from thee,
> my Lord, my Saviour.
> (From *The Valley of Vision*)

Epiphany Day 56

WILLA KANE

Reflect on Romans 10

Call to Prayer

Salvation—nothing less!

Is this your desire for those apart from Christ? Do you want this with all your heart and pray for it all the time? If you're honest, you will see that you fall short of this standard set by Paul, whose heart beat constantly for the lost.

We live in a world where self-concocted "salvation shops" and "noisy knockoffs" are everywhere we turn. "You do you" is the acceptable mantra for finding purpose and peace. Rather than taking God at his word and believing he alone can set things right in lives that are perpetually intrinsically wrong, people create lives on their own terms. They incur insurmountable debt to manufactured saviors who cannot save. Even those "impressively energetic toward God" (Romans 10:1–3 MSG) get it wrong without Jesus.

Paul makes it clear in this passage that God's Word saves. God's saving grace—the incarnate Word—is Jesus. Christ, the Word that saves, is right here, near as your next breath.

All you must do is speak a word of welcome to the God who saves. Everything that is necessary has already been done. Jesus died, was raised, was exalted, and now reigns as Lord.

Who do you know who needs to hear, receive, and accept this gospel truth? Who needs to say the word of welcome to Jesus? Pray the Lord will give you a heart that aches for those who are lost and opportunities to share this simple, life-altering truth: If you confess with your mouth that Jesus is Lord and believe in your heart that God raised him from the dead, you will be saved. For with the heart one believes and is justified, and with the mouth one confesses and is saved.

Recommended Closing Prayer

Merciful God, creator of all the peoples of the earth and lover of souls: Have compassion on all who do not know you as you are revealed in your Son Jesus Christ; let your Gospel be preached with grace and power to those who have not heard it; turn the hearts of those who resist it; and bring home to your fold those who have gone astray; that there may be one flock under one Shepherd, Jesus Christ our Lord. Amen.

(Anglican Church in North America Book of Common Prayer)

Epiphany Day 57
WILLA KANE

Reflect on Romans 11:1–6

Call to Prayer

Facing a struggle bigger than we are can make us feel small and alone. Elijah experienced this nine hundred years before Christ. We feel this today as we are increasingly confronted by those who reject or ignore Jesus in a culture that may oppose our influence. As Paul looks back to Elijah and into his own life, he shines an encouraging light into our present darkness.

Here in Romans, Paul asks if God will reject his people, Israel. His emphatic "No!" rests on personal experience—he is a Jew from the tribe of Benjamin, yet he has not been rejected. He belongs to Christ. His response rests on God's exchange with Elijah, alone and hiding in fear, when God said, "I have reserved for myself seven thousand who have not bowed the knee to Baal" (Romans 11:4 NIV). Paul's answer rests on God's promise: "So too, at the present time there is a remnant chosen by grace" (Romans 11:5 NIV). If you are a follower of Jesus, this promise is also for you.

These words from our God are intensely personal. As you pray, is this the way you see yourself? kept by God the Father for himself?

God has always preserved a remnant. In the world's economy, remnants end up on a scrap heap. But in God's economy, his remnant is chosen, treasured, beloved, and kept.

This passage tells us clearly the way God chooses his remnant. He chooses not by works or by merit or at random, but by grace. God's grace weaves a remnant thread from the Old Testament to the New, through the lives of patriarchs, an ark builder and a wall builder, to fishermen, prostitutes, and lepers, all the way to a Jesus-persecutor on the road to Damascus. If you are a follower of Jesus, then this remnant thread weaves through your life as well.

As you pray, thank our God that you are not alone. Thank him that your place in the glorious tapestry he is weaving with his remnant is not dependent on works but is an extravagant gift of grace.

Recommended Closing Prayer

> Almighty God our Savior, you desire that none should perish, and you have taught us through your Son that there is great joy in heaven over every sinner who repents: Grant that our hearts may ache for a lost and broken world. May your Holy Spirit work through our words, deeds, and prayers, that the lost may be found and the dead made alive, and that all your redeemed may rejoice around your throne; through Jesus Christ our Lord. Amen.
> *(Anglican Church in North America Book of Common Prayer)*

Epiphany Day 58
WILLA KANE

Reflect on Romans 12:1–2

Call to Prayer

A living sacrifice. This is what the Lord desires of us. It is what he deserves from us. In light of all the mercies God has poured out on us and for us, we take the life he has given us—body, mind, and soul—and offer it back to him for his glory and his purposes. This is only possible as our life philosophy stops conforming to the world as the Lord transforms our minds.

Paul's call to be a living sacrifice followed fifteen hundred years of a sacrificial system that led to death, not life. Those sacrifices couldn't save, but they pointed to one who could. One afternoon on a hill outside the city, Jesus, the perfect Lamb of God, changed everything.

Jesus's death defeated sin and opened the way to new life flooded with an incomprehensible list of mercies—God-given things we don't deserve. As you pray, stop to consider the mercies God has poured out for you: divine love, faith to believe, peace, patience, forgiveness, hope, the Holy Spirit, eternal life, adoption, security, comfort, and power.

A mind focused on these gifts can't focus on the world and its counterfeit treasures. Jesus died to make you his treasure. Have you died to yourself to make him yours?

We worship what we treasure. If Jesus is your treasure, then your reasonable response is to live a life of worship toward him. Living in mercy toward others, giving life away sacrificially because Jesus gave himself for you, is a life of worship. This kind of merciful living grows out of God's mercies.

All around us people are in need of mercy. Ask the Lord where and to whom you might extend mercy. Ask for his eyes, ears, and heart to see, hear, and love the least, the lost, and the broken, mothers, fathers, sisters and brothers, children, neighbors, and strangers. See them in their need, and respond with mercy. Follow Jesus in this sacrificial way of living. Place yourself as a living sacrifice on the altar of God's love.

Recommended Closing Prayer

> O God,
> Fill the garden of my soul with the wind of love,
> that the scents of Christian life may be wafted to others;
> then come and gather fruits to thy glory.
> So shall I fulfill the great end of my being—
> To glorify Thee and be a blessing to men.
> Amen.

(From *The Valley of Vision*)

Epiphany Day 59
WILLA KANE

Reflect on Romans 13:11–12

Call to Prayer

The apostle Paul issues a wake-up call to believers in these verses from Romans 13. He says, "You know the time, that the hour has come for you to wake up from sleep" (Romans 13:11 ESV).

The dawning of a new day calls us to wake up. The sun's rays creep over the edge of the morning horizon, first casting a glow, then banishing darkness as night becomes day. The Son who brought salvation banishes darkness for those who believe as he ushers them from the dominion of darkness into his kingdom, the kingdom of light.

If you've been ushered from darkness to light, if a new day has dawned in your heart, why do some days still feel so dark? If Jesus's death and resurrection saved once for all, then how can salvation be nearer now than when you first believed?

Salvation is a process with past, present, and future realities. Past salvation deals with sin's penalty. Present salvation deals with sin's power. Future salvation deals with sin's presence. It is this future salvation that is "nearer to us now than when we first believed" (Romans 13:11 ESV), when Christ will return to make all things new and to gather his people to himself. Until then, we will experience darkness in a world infected by sin, even though its power over us has been broken.

Past salvation, the death of Jesus on the cross to pay the penalty of sin we could never pay, and present salvation works in hearts, minds, and bodies by the Holy Spirit to defeat the power of sin and prepare us for that day when we will see Jesus face-to-face. Because we've been forgiven in Christ and are being refined by the Spirit, we can cast off the works of darkness and live for the gospel, protected by the armor of light. Paul describes this armor in 1 Thessalonians 5:8 as "the breastplate of faith and love, and … a helmet the hope of salvation" (ESV). The armor of light is faith, hope, and love.

As you pray, cast off darkness and put on the armor of light. Put on faith in the Lord Jesus Christ. Put on hope in the Lord Jesus Christ. Put on love for the Lord Jesus Christ. Clothed in him, you should answer his wake-up call. The night is far gone; the day is at hand.

Recommended Closing Prayer

> Hasten, O Father, the coming of your kingdom; and grant that we your servants, who now live by faith, may with joy behold your Son at his coming in glorious majesty; even Jesus Christ, our only Mediator and Advocate. Amen.
> *(Anglican Church in North America Book of Common Prayer)*

Epiphany Day 60
WILLA KANE

Reflect on Romans 14:9–12

Call to Prayer

Paul's words of caution to first-century Christians are still as relevant and real now to a twenty-first-century church. Perhaps now more than ever, the body of Christ is divided in myriad ways, pulled apart by petty tyrannies.

In Paul's day, the church in Rome was divided about what to eat and what day of the week to meet. He spends thirty-five verses in Romans discussing how believers should not judge, but accept each other's stance on nonessential matters where they differ. It mattered to Paul because it mattered to Christ, and so it should matter to us.

Paul tells us clearly, using words from the prophet Isaiah, that every knee shall bow and every tongue confess that God, only God, is Lord. Lording your opinion over your brother is impossible if you remember that God is God and there is no other. We all will give an account to him. Do you harbor a spirit of criticism or condescension toward a brother or sister who holds a differing view? Confess it.

We must speak out if a matter threatens the truth of the gospel or the spiritual health of a church or person, but there are issues on which the Bible is silent or not clear about what to do. On some issues, godly believers differ. Ask the Spirit to confirm to you the non-negotiables of the Christian faith and to give you boldness to defend sound doctrine. Now ask the Spirit to show you any secondary issues you have elevated above primary status, and ask for the humility and grace to love others who hold differing views.

As you pray, search your heart for any ways you might stand in judgment of someone else in the body of Christ. Jesus died as Savior, rose as Lord, and ascended as Judge. You can't take his role as Savior or Lord. Neither should you usurp his role as Judge.

Jesus died and rose again to free us from petty tyrannies. Rejoice and live in the freedom Christ offers.

Recommended Closing Prayer

> Almighty God, you show those in error the light of your truth so that they may turn to the path of righteousness: Grant that all who have been reborn into the fellowship of Christ's Body may show forth in their lives what they profess by their faith; through Jesus Christ our Lord, who lives and reigns with you and the Holy Spirit, one God, now and forever. Amen.
>
> (*Anglican Church in North America Book of Common Prayer*)

Epiphany Day 61
WILLA KANE

Reflect on Romans 15:4–7

Call to Prayer

All throughout his letters, Paul quotes Old Testament scripture to support his teaching about Christ. Romans 15 is no different; Paul insists old scriptures were written to teach modern Christians. They are intended to bring encouragement and hope to God's people.

We need God's help and encouragement to endure. God's very nature demonstrates endurance: "'I am the Alpha and the Omega,' says the Lord God, 'who is and who was and who is to come, the Almighty'" (Revelation 1:8 NIV).

Endurance is the measure of a person's stamina or persistence. By sheer will, one can hold on for a season, but without a reason to persist, even the most determined will give up or give in. The scriptures give us a reason to hold on. They give us hope.

This kind of hope differs from a worldly hope that expresses uncertainty. Biblical hope, the kind that comes with encouragement from the scriptures, is faith that is directed to the future. It is trust in God's character and God's promises; it is deep belief that the death and resurrection of Christ brings new life that endures into eternity for those who believe. This kind of hope transforms relationships broken by hearts focused inward and transforms a world that shouts in competing screaming voices into one harmonious voice that glorifies the God and Father of our Lord Jesus Christ.

Pause to focus on the hope that is yours in Jesus. Because he died, your sins are forgiven. Because he lives, you live also. Nothing can separate you from his love. Add your voice to those of worshippers before the throne who proclaim, "Praise and glory and wisdom and thanks and honor and power and strength be to our God forever and ever. Amen!" (Revelation 7:12 NIV).

In all challenging circumstances, be encouraged to endure because your hope is in Christ. Now turn and welcome one another because he has welcomed you.

Recommended Closing Prayer

Heavenly Father, grant us to live in such harmony with one another, in accord with Christ Jesus, that lost people in a dying world will hear many voices made one in glorious praise to the one who made us and has made us one in Christ. Give us endurance that grows out of confident and settled hope in you, the Alpha and Omega. In Jesus's name and for your glory. Amen.

Introduction to Lent

STEVEN E. BREEDLOVE

Just as Advent without Christmas makes no sense, so Lent without Easter is meaningless. In the Christian year, celebration must follow fasting and preparation, as the seed that is sown must come to fruition. Fasting without an ultimate celebration is not Christian, but instead a pagan form of self-denial.

The forty-day fast of Lent follows the biblical pattern, and in every instance—Noah, Moses, Elijah, Jesus—a revelation from God, a blessing, or a new ministry follows the fast. The fast is preparation and not an end in itself. If we seek to deny our flesh and mortify ourselves as if this is the end, then we have missed the point. *Lent is for the sake of Easter.*

But we must also recognize that celebration in the Bible follows preparation, ministry follows testing, and blessing follows patience. To desire Canaan without the wilderness, the Noahic covenant without forty days of rain, or the Davidic throne without exile under the hand of Saul is to miss that God prepares his children for what he has for them. If Jesus had to prepare for his ministry—the temptation, and then Gethsemane—then we also must prepare.

Lent, through its deep fast of contrition, repentance, and self-denial, prepares the people of God to meet the risen Lord yet again. This is needed every year because the fallen world is always discipling us in the wrong direction. We need a season every year where we realize anew our need for the cross and empty ourselves of all false hopes so that we can receive the resurrection.

Prayer during Lent is uncomplicated, even though it is difficult. The constant call is to confess. The Spirit of God calls us to confess those places where we still rebel against the Lord, seek to make ourselves a god, and depend upon our own strength. The Spirit calls us, then guides us through scripture, to examine and judge ourselves. We are called to contrition and repentance, not with fear or despair, but in humble honesty. The full weight of our sinfulness, the darkness of our hearts, is drawn out into the open so that we are prepared to receive the life of the risen Lord yet again.

Lent Day 1 (Ash Wednesday)

FRANCIS CAPITANIO

Reflect on Isaiah 58:1–12

Call to Prayer

In the practice of the ancient church, fasting and almsgiving were partnered together, along with works of justice. Our selfishness often keeps us from practicing the love of God, both toward God and toward our neighbor. In our flesh, we want to keep for ourselves and to make sure we find ourselves safe in a shelter of our own construct, one often made of money and comfort. But our self-constructed shelter is often our prison. It protects us only in this life and is built on the sand of this present world. It keeps us safe within walls, but the walls often keep the love and presence of God out.

In Isaiah, we are reminded that fasting, though important, is pointless without the greater works of justice. We know fasting is important from the gospels; Christ testified to the fact that his people would fast, and we know that apostles and saints have fasted up until this day. But there is also a recognition that fasting from food is a small act that trains our flesh; it is only a reflection of the greater works we are called to do that not only train our flesh but also train our hearts. These greater works teach us to see the needs of others. Almsgiving teaches our wills to say yes to others, even as fasting says no to our stomachs. If we go through seasons of fasting, like Lent, but have no concern for the needs of the poor or to exercise our will for their sakes, then we fast in vain. We may increase in self-control regarding food, but we don't increase in self-control regarding our neighbor.

Fasting, almsgiving, and other acts of justice teach us not only what God wants in the way of self-denial but also the value of our priorities as Christians—and this is how we must pray, because we can't do it alone. We must ask to know even more deeply what God is like and what we are like when brought up against the shelters we built that we don't want to give up. As we seek to grow in him, prayer becomes the foundation upon which we build our life of self-denial and contend with our flesh. This is what the season of Lent is all about.

As you pray, consider the ways you might fast in Lent, and ask the Lord for what you need accordingly.

Recommended Closing Prayer

Are you fasting from food? *Lord, help me know that I don't need this food to live.*

Are you fasting from greed, struggling to give away money you think you may need? *Lord, help me to know that I can be generous and that I don't need this extra money to live. Help me to let go so that I can hold on to more of you.*

Lent Day 2

SALLY BREEDLOVE

Reflect on Psalm 120

Call to Prayer

Faithful Jews made the ascent to Jerusalem for at least one of three major festivals celebrated each year. Jesus was raised by parents who yearly made that pilgrimage, so as a boy he walked there alongside his kinfolk and neighbors.

With them, as they traveled, he prayed and sang. Like every Jewish child, he was learning to pray by praying the psalms. What was it like for the Prince of Peace to speak the words "I am for peace, but when I speak, [my words] are for war"?

His words as an adult stirred up controversy and hatred. While his message brought peace and life to many, in others his words ignited a plan to silence him by murder. When he drew near and saw Jerusalem, he wept over it, saying, "Would that you, even you, had known on this day the things that make for peace! But now they are hidden from your eyes …. You did not know the time of your visitation" (Luke 19:41, 19: 44 ESV).

We often live in times of turmoil, and we can't rearrange the building blocks of our world to secure peace of mind, peace in our relationships, or peace among political parties, among countries, or even within the scientific or religious community.

And we live in a world where God invites us to call out to him for help as we live our days.

As you pray, will you lament with Jesus? Will you pray for deliverance from lies, hostility, and divisive spirits both within you and around you? Will you tell the truth and admit that you need deliverance from the deception and posturing you yourself do? Will you ask Jesus to show you the things you can do in your own world that make for peace?

Recommended Closing Prayer

> Eternal God, in whose perfect kingdom no sword is drawn but the sword of righteousness, no strength known but the strength of love: So mightily spread abroad your Spirit that all peoples may be gathered under the banner of the Prince of Peace; to whom be dominion and glory now and forever. Amen.
>
> *(Anglican Church in North America Book of Common Prayer)*

Lent Day 3

SALLY BREEDLOVE

Reflect on Psalm 121

Call to Prayer

Sometimes the choice to believe is simply that: a choice made against despair, doubt, and fear. Can Jesus possibly understand what that tug-of-war feels like?

Imagine him as a boy. He knew the view north of Galilee with its panorama of Mount Hermon's majesty. In those trips to Jerusalem, he anticipated the hills rising to the towering temple against the southern sky. He likely sang with other pilgrims: "Does my help come from these mountains?" And he sang the response: "No, it comes from God, who created these mountains."

Christ knew the pull of doubt and the pressure to despair. Hebrews 4:15 speaks plainly about Christ's earthly experience. "For we do not have a high priest who is unable to sympathize with our weaknesses, but one who in every respect has been tempted as we are, yet without sin" (ESV).

The pull to disbelieve in the goodness and power of God, to want to find someone or something else to trust, is not a sin—it is a temptation. Jesus sympathizes and wants to help us.

We crave solutions to our problems, but Psalm 121—sung and prayed by pilgrims like Jesus on the road to Jerusalem—reminds us that God invites us to trust in him. In the midst of hardship, we need to be reminded again and again that we can indeed put our trust in God.

As you pray, tell your Father about your doubts, about the places in your life where it is hard to believe. Then, as Psalm 121 reminds you, say no to the doubting places in your heart. Reaffirm with Jesus and with all God's pilgrim people, "My help comes from the Lord, the maker of heaven and earth" (Psalm 121:1 NIV).

Recommended Closing Prayer

Lord, I believe. Help my unbelief. In Jesus's name. Amen.

Lent Day 4

SALLY BREEDLOVE

Reflect on Psalm 122

Call to Prayer

This psalm leans toward Jerusalem; it imagines the goodness of being within the city's gates. For the Jews, Jerusalem was God's city, and the temple was God's dwelling place. Its walls brought safety; its unity arose from worship of the one true God. It was meant to be a place of peace—an active peace that nurtured the well-being of all.

To travel toward Jerusalem for one of the yearly festivals was to acknowledge that the blessings we need—safety, belongingness, at-oneness with others, peace, fullness of life—cannot be achieved apart from worshipping God with other believing people.

As you pray, listen for the Spirit's voice. Repent of your past indifference toward gathering with other Christians. Repent of your pride that says you need to find "just the right church." Repent of your sense that you need to be a better person before you show up for worship. The psalmist says, "Our feet are standing within your gates" (Psalm 122:2 NASB). My dirty, travel-worn, misshapen feet—cleansed by the blood of Jesus—are welcome in God's presence.

Pray for unity. Pray for peace. Pray for leaders and pastors by name. Pray we become a people who bow in awe and love before the Triune God. Pray we become a people who seek the good of all.

Recommended Closing Prayer

Lord Jesus, you told the Samaritan woman that God seeks true worshippers. Help me to respond to your call. Shape my heart, my mind, my will, and my strength so I can live a worshipping life. Amen.

First Sunday of Lent, Day 5
SALLY BREEDLOVE

Reflect on Psalm 123

Call to Prayer

The Psalms of Ascent help us as we interact with fellow travelers and with the bystanders on the side of the road. These psalms teach us how to walk out our life together.

Are you in the midst of a hard season? What words come to your mind when you finish the sentence "I have had enough of ..."?

Perhaps what comes to you is best spoken only to God; it is too caustic to be said to another person. Perhaps what comes to you shames you. You ought to be a bigger person; other people have endured far worse. Tell the truth about your own heart. Our life with God, our opportunity for maturity, calls us to tell the truth about our lives as they are.

This psalmist had had enough of the contempt and pride of the people around him. Perhaps he'd had enough of those who seemed to skate through life, those who didn't see themselves as pilgrims, those who had no desire or need to turn to God for help.

Listen to what he prays as he faces a world filled with pride and contempt. He doesn't pray for power to set all things right, and he doesn't pray for an easier life. Instead, he reminds himself that he is God's servant. He seeks God's face. He cries out to God for mercy.

We can learn from him. When the road is hard, and when people and systems around us make it harder, what can we do? Remember we are God's servants. Seek God's face. Cry out to him for mercy.

As you pray, name the people and situations in your life that need the mercy of God. After you name each one, simply pray, "Lord have mercy, Christ have mercy." Then pause for a moment before you mention something else. Continue to pray like this until you have held up to God the things and people that trouble you.

Recommended Closing Prayer

To you, O Lord, we lift up our eyes. We are your servants; you are our Good Master. Have mercy, O Lord, on us and on all whom you have made. For Jesus Christ's sake. Amen.

Lent Day 6

SALLY BREEDLOVE

Reflect on Psalm 124

Call to Prayer

Far too often, this world brings us great anguish. In the midst of suffering, we find it hard to hold to deeper truths such as the ones presented to us in Psalm 124. And yet, one way our healing comes is through joining our voices with the testimony of scripture and declaring, despite our circumstances, "*God is for us.*"

Consider the other places in scripture that speak this, as follows:

Romans 8:31 asks, without apology, "If God is for us, who can be against us?" (ESV).

Psalm 118:6 proclaims, "The Lord is on my side" (ESV).

When they awake in a city surrounded by a hostile army, Elisha sees a host of angels ready to defend him, and he reassures his fearful servant, "Do not be afraid, for those who are with us are more than those who are with them" (2 Kings 6:16 ESV).

God is for us—but that does not mean he gives us a full explanation of why everything happens or why life can't be easier.

God is for us—but that does not mean he is for our greed, our schemes, or our prejudices.

It does not mean he is for us and, therefore, opposed to the ones we oppose.

This psalm compares the power of our enemies to the power of water: flash floods, tsunamis, dam breaks, and rising tides in hurricanes. Water—so necessary for life—in seconds is transformed into raging death. It's foolish to think we can take care of ourselves with such enemies. Still, the warrior king David rejoiced that God was for him.

The Psalms of Ascent are prayers that strengthen us to follow after Jesus. They move us out of the world of our feelings and into a world defined by God's will. They're not primarily about how we feel; they're about what's true. These psalms are perfectly formed hiking boots to keep us solidly on the road for another day of walking.

As you pray, hold the truth before your own heart—"God is for me." Then hold up to God the names of those you love and those you struggle to like or forgive, and declare, "God is for _____."

Recommended Closing Prayer

O Father God, Isaiah 43 tells us we don't have to be afraid, that we are precious in your sight and honored and loved by you. Reassure us of your love, and help us to lay aside our doubts and our cynicism. Give us the humility that submits to being loved by you. Amen.

Lent Day 7

SALLY BREEDLOVE

Reflect on Psalm 125

Call to Prayer

We live in a world where the evils of racial injustice and violence often assault us. Surely God cares for the poor and marginalized who cannot protect themselves. In the times in our lives when wickedness is on full display, how can we pray a psalm that assures us that God surrounds and protects his people as he surrounds and protects Jerusalem?

Perhaps it will help to consider what Jerusalem was like. It's not a city set in an exalted location. It's a city on a hill, in the midst of a cluster of hills; no impregnable plateau keeps it safe. Jerusalem has no natural resources, no important river, and no harbor. It's not a city in a stunningly spectacular setting. Hills; arid wilderness; small streams; dirt, sand, and rock; and a lake full of salt are its immediate environs. But for centuries, it has been fought over, captured, destroyed, and rebuilt. It is a city that God has never let fully die as other ancient cities have.

Might the very setting of Jerusalem remind us that God loves the lowly? Might Jerusalem's history assure us that though enemy after enemy may assault the lowly, the lowly will never be utterly destroyed?

As Jesus walked to Jerusalem singing this pilgrim song, he walked toward an occupied city. What burdened his heart as he sang, "For the scepter of wickedness shall not rest on the land allotted to the righteous" (Psalm 125:3 ESV)? His earthly experience contradicted that promise, but he did not turn away in despair or turn to violence. He turned to lament. He set his face toward laying down his life for sinners.

As you pray, lament for all that should be but is not. Lament for all that is and should not be. Ask God where you are to lay down your life for the good of others. Ask for steely-eyed endurance and a heart broken by compassion so that you will live like Jesus until God fully establishes his rule, his Jerusalem, on this earth.

Recommended Closing Prayer

Lord, make me like your dear Son. Make me gentle and lowly of heart, courageous, quick to protect the vulnerable, patient, and faithful to endure until your kingdom comes. In the name of Jesus Christ. Amen.

Lent Day 8

MADISON PERRY

Reflect on Psalm 126

Call to Prayer

Place brackets around your circumstances and enter the world of this psalm. God's people are on a journey. They have left their homes. Rich and poor are all walking together for days, slowly ascending to the temple of the Lord.

And then, midway through, others approach the group, stragglers who look to be from a foreign land. They regard one another, and then there are looks of recognition. Cries break out: "Look! Our friends are returning to us!"

No one thought this was possible. Israel had been fractured, and a large portion had been carried away and forced into exile. They were never to be seen again. But here they are! They have a future now, thanks to our great God.

Return to the psalm and read it once more. Let yourself be there. Like streams in the desert, so runs the grace of our God. His salvation is known and experienced as we taste his grace together. We are exiles being welcomed home.

You may pray this psalm through tears. You have real pain—intractable injustice, the loss of work, hopeless toil against an invisible enemy, dashed hopes, private griefs, or the thwarting of all your best intentions and faithful stewardship. But God will have the final victory. For now, that moment of victory may feel like a far-off dream. But one day, your present pain will recede beyond the horizon and will linger only as a scar, a travail that the Lord carried you through.

Whom are you separated from? Who has been swept away by the awful work of sin, struck by oppression and misfortune? Pray that the Lord's grace will find these souls and bring them to a home where his justice reigns. Who has been carried away by the enemy and has forgotten their way home—the deluded and hopeless? Pray for their forgiveness, repentance, and salvation. And in the midst of all this, pray that you will have a heart big enough to receive all exiles in love and joy. Pray that you will have the heart of Christ.

Recommended Closing Prayer

O Lord, may your justice, grace, and peace prevail in our hearts and reign in our world. Shield us from the attacks of the evil one, and grant us courage and hope. Thank you that the victory of your cross never fades and always guarantees our future. Give us real friends to help us endure until your glory comes in full. Amen.

Lent Day 9

Reflect on Psalm 127

Call to Prayer

In vain. This phrase is repeated three times in these first two verses. Is there anything that can prevent our lives from being lived in vain?

Our physical effort, strategic planning, careful hiring, best intentions, and emotional investment—none of that is a guarantee of fruitfulness. Even works done for God suffer the same fate when they aren't done by God. David and Solomon, writers of our psalms, were great builders, but the works of their hands were dashed and broken.

But notice: this psalm turns from vanity to progeny, the blessed fruit of the love of husband and wife. The fruit of our lives will be our children, including the people we have nurtured and cared for in love, prayer, and service. And the fruit of David and Solomon will not bring shame to their houses, for through their line came Jesus, son of David (Matthew 1:1).

Jesus, son of David, was a master builder, though he built no citadels, temples, or palaces. He left no children behind, yet his descendants outnumber the stars in the sky. He took in strangers and made them children of God by his victory on the cross, bestowing life without end.

Jesus will labor through us now, bringing life to our friends, neighbors, and enemies, reconciling all things unto himself. Even though time seems to mock us and our best intentions may never add up to much, we can join in the eternally significant and sure work of building up the children of God in the name of Jesus Christ. And yes, these children will need homes, schools, churches, and statehouses. But the people with bodies and immortal souls who fill these places and grow in them will be our legacy, not the monuments we leave behind.

Pray now and draw near to God's eternal temple. You are standing on a foundation that will never fade, built on the cornerstone of Christ. Jesus is expecting you, offering his blood so that you may enter this holy place. Will you allow him to welcome you and anoint you with his favor, blessing you as a child of God? Ask him for the courage to keep working even when you can't see fruit, trusting him and his will. Intercede for your parents, relatives, and friends and for this world. Ask him what you should do next.

Recommended Closing Prayer

Father God, only you can build what lasts forever. Help me show up as your servant, day by day, in the life you have given me. Use my life to build what you desire. Grant me peace when my hard work fails; grant me faith to pour into your people; and grant me the true hope of eternal life with you and your blood-bought church. For Jesus's sake. Amen.

Lent Day 10
MADISON PERRY

Reflect on Psalm 128

Call to Prayer

This psalm is a proclamation of blessing: the one who fears the Lord enjoys satisfying labor, family dinners, and a prosperous city. It feels so simple—uninterrupted by tragedy, unbroken by idolatry, and uncluttered by random commitments.

Maybe you feel that this prayer is a fantasy or a distraction. Read the psalm again. Doesn't it make you long to live in the land where God is King?

Here, then, is the best news you will hear today: our King has come, and you can dwell in his kingdom. Jesus offered a way to eat at God's table, to have children, and to lay up treasure in a place where moth and rust do not destroy, where thieves cannot break in and steal.

Jesus had many ways of describing the kingdom, a reality that you may begin to know here and now, something that is growing in strength and power with the movement of the Holy Spirit.

Reading this psalm's blessing should lead us to mourn the sin that has ravaged this world. At the same time, it calls us to begin dwelling with God in this very moment. Even now, we can receive our daily bread from the Lord. Even now, we can enjoy the slow growth of the Holy Spirit's presence. Even now, we can seek to see God's kingdom rule take hold as we respond to the circumstances of today with the heart of Christ.

As you pray, speak aloud your allegiance to the King of heaven and earth. Commit your own life to his rule and reign. Ask that his kingdom would come in fullness. Be specific about what will need to change in this world and, above all, in your heart as this happens. Praise the Lord, and rest in the confidence that he who raised Jesus from the dead is at work in you.

Recommended Closing Prayer

> Almighty and everlasting God, whose will it is to restore all things in thy well-beloved Son, the King of kings and Lord of lords: Mercifully grant that the peoples of the earth, divided and enslaved by sin, may be freed and brought together under his most gracious rule; who liveth and reigneth with thee and the Holy Spirit, one God, now and for ever. Amen.
>
> *(Anglican Church in North America Book of Common Prayer)*

Lent Day 11

MADISON PERRY

Reflect on Psalm 129

Call to Prayer

As this psalm begins, the pot is boiling over. For too long the unjust have afflicted Israel. So "let Israel now say …" (Psalm 129:1 ESV).

And then the psalm speaks through us with little for us to add, using images that make us recoil. "The plowers plowed upon my back; they made long their furrows" (Psalm 129:3 ESV).

For some of us, it is hard to know whom we are to pray this psalm about. We don't really have enemies so much as people we wish didn't exist. But for the marginalized and discarded, the images of being furrowed strike close to home; their oppressors have faces. This psalm encourages us to identify with the least of these and to have their enemies become ours.

It is possible to have complicated feelings toward someone—to desire both the person's shame and his or her salvation. "May all who hate Zion be put to shame and turned backward!" (Psalm 129:5 ESV). The curses contained in this psalm rain down upon evil, seeking to wash it away. These are prayers that God's mighty Spirit would excise injustice, burn away the dross, and unflinchingly restore the glorious image that sin has almost completely obscured. In asking for justice against evildoers, the psalmist is in fact seeking their good.

The center of this psalm is the key: "The Lord is righteous" (Psalm 129:4 ESV). The pilgrims who pray this psalm don't seek vigilante justice. They turn to the Lord, trusting his hand to hold the surgical knife and his timing to do so only when it is necessary. It is the Lord who will act against the unrighteous.

We must receive this psalm within the full context of scripture if we are to understand how to pray it. "God desires that all should be saved and come to knowledge of the truth" (1 Timothy 2:4). How does this salvation break in? Christ does not come with half-hearted blessings for the unjust and unrepentant. It is a great gift to be turned around when your every step carries you farther from God. And so, we pray for the salvation of all with the words, "Repent and believe in the gospel!" (Mark 1:15 ESV).

If you don't trust yourself to pray against enemies, then simply pray the words of this psalm. If you have enemies in mind, seek their strong repentance, knowing that for them to repent, God will intervene with his inbreaking justice. Be aware that as you do this, you are also praying for God to operate on your own heart. Offer yourself to him and trust that he will bring his good work to completion. Ask him to bring to mind people to whom you need to apologize or steps you need to take to bring your life more completely into his kingdom reality.

Recommended Closing Prayer

O God, we pray that your justice would reign. We pray that your will would be accomplished. We pray that saving knowledge of you would fill the earth as waters cover the sea. Come, Lord Jesus. Amen.

Second Sunday of Lent, Day 12

MADISON PERRY

Reflect on Psalm 130

Call to Prayer

The ascent is long, and the road has taken turns we had not have anticipated. Now we enter the last difficult upward portion of these Psalms of Ascent at the moment before God's temple comes into view. But having walked the dusty roads and prayed the soul-searching prayers, we are plunged into the depths again.

Where do we turn when our strength is failing? We remember our Lord, and we cry out to him. We turn to him in our exhaustion. We come to him in our hunger. We flee to him for shelter from evil. We ask him for mercy. The forgiveness we know in God is the first of his blessings toward us, a first fruit of the redemption of the whole cosmos.

In the second half of this psalm, the psalmist longs for God's redemption to be fully known. The last two stanzas are anthems to patience, the songs of someone hewn in the image of Christ who longs for daily bread and for God's kingdom.

The psalmist is aware of hunger and longing, but instead of reaching for a quick fix or instant gratification, he directs his attention to the Lord. "I wait for the Lord … my soul waits for the Lord more than watchmen for the morning" (Psalm 130:5, 130:6 ESV). A night watchman is on guard at all times in case of attack, but the watchman's longing is that daylight will come without any evil occurring. You can pray with eager expectation, tilting toward the east and waiting for the dawn that will be visible any second now.

What depths do you call out from today? Acknowledge them and ask God for mercy. God has redeemed Israel. Ask that God's just reign would extend over the whole cosmos. God's dawn is coming, and he will not disappoint. Ask that your life will reflect the resurrection of Jesus and give cause for others to hope in him. Encourage your own soul to hope in the Lord.

Recommended Closing Prayer

> Lord, you now have set your servant free
> to go in peace as you have promised;
> For these eyes of mine have seen the Savior,
> whom you have prepared for all the world to see:
> A Light to enlighten the nations,
> and the glory of your people Israel.
> *(The Song of Simeon)*

Lent Day 13

MADISON PERRY

Reflect on Psalm 131

Call to Prayer

After a long journey upward, at last we have passed through the gates of Jerusalem. The reality outside the walls of the city fades to secondary importance. Drawn inward toward the temple, we find ourselves approaching the Holy One of Israel.

To approach the Lord in his temple, worshippers brought sacrifices that they offered to the priest. The pinnacle of all such sacrifices was humility, as Psalm 51:17 teaches: "The sacrifices of God are a broken spirit; a broken and a contrite heart, O God, You will not despise" (ESV).

This short psalm captures the essence of the sacrifice God will not despise—the humility of a worshipper of the Lord. "My heart is not lifted up" (Psalm 131:1 ESV). The person praying it is not asking (as several of Jesus's disciples did) whether they may be the greatest in the kingdom. "My eyes are not raised too high" (Psalm 131:1 ESV). The psalmist does not demand to first know the mysteries of the universe or God's exact plan for righting the wrongs of the world. This encounter with God is rooted in humble dependence and leads to quiet intimacy and praise.

A unique and beautiful image captures the moment. "I have calmed and quieted my soul, like a weaned child with its mother" (Psalm 131:2 ESV). The child reclining against her mother no longer requires milk, yet she clings to her mother in joy, basking in her continued protection and nurturing.

As you pray, ask for this posture of humble joy in the presence of your Lord. Quiet your heart, refrain from clamoring for material blessings or high positions of authority, and rest securely in him. Thank God that his presence is all that we need, and ask him for the gift of hoping only in him.

Recommended Closing Prayer

Father, give me a calmed and quietened soul before you. Let my heart not be lifted up or my eyes raised too high. Grant me contentment and hope in your presence, from this time forth and forevermore. Amen.

Lent Day 14

MADISON PERRY

Reflect on Psalm 132

Call to Prayer

This psalm captures the moment of our ascent when we enter the temple, the dwelling place of God. The Lord has accepted the sacrifice of righteousness that is the accomplished work of Jesus Christ on the cross. We have taken on his humility. Now we dare venture in.

Praying this psalm aligns us with David as he dwells on the significance of the temple.

And what is the centerpiece of this psalm?

More than expressing David's heart for God and for God's temple, Psalm 132 captures the Lord's heart for Zion and for the people of Zion. It reveals God's intentions for his kingdom rule on this earth. The throne of Zion is the temple, God's dwelling place among humankind.

The temple was much more than an edifice of blocks or the best place to experience song, incense, or mystical symbols. It was the focal point of God's promises and the physical manifestation of God's unshakable intention to draw our story to an end where heaven meets earth. Standing at the temple as we make our ascent, we are overwhelmed by God's abiding love and goodwill toward us. We are unworthy, yet we are truly blessed.

Have you forgotten God's promises for you? Pray these verses aloud. God spoke them prophetically over his Son, and as you participate in Christ, they are promises for you as well. Praise him and thank him.

Recommended Closing Prayer

O Father, thank you that you have made your dwelling with us. Fill us with faith, and let us ever sing for joy. Amen.

Lent Day 15
WILLA KANE

Reflect on Psalm 133

Call to Prayer

Tragically, we cannot often use words such as *good*, *pleasant*, and *unified* to describe how people are getting along in our world. Our society, our churches, our workplaces, and our families are fractured by disagreements. We are perhaps more divided today than ever before in human history.

In Psalm 133, the psalmist tells us to pay attention. It is both good and pleasant when people in the family get along. This psalm is a word for the people of God. Only in God is real unity possible; it is where it must begin.

But we know this isn't simple or easy. The battle between evil and good, in us and all around us, started in the Garden. Broken connection with God makes unity in the human family arduous and elusive.

Can the difficulty in our lives truly work for our good and reveal God's glorious goodness? Can we find a way to truthfully say "I know the goodness of real unity with other Christians"?

Yes—but only as we draw near to God. Intimate fellowship with him is our greatest need, and his friendship makes intimate relationships with others possible. Draw near to the Father through the Son. Reflect on the deep love within the Triune God, who is Father, Son, and Spirit. Ask God for unity of spirit with others. Ask God to teach you to love.

Unity, centered on God, is like fragrant oil anointing Aaron the high priest and running down his head, onto his beard, and onto his collar in excessive abundance. Oil is a picture of the Holy Spirit. Let God's gracious Spirit flow over your life. Receive God's abundant provision of forgiveness, acceptance, and love.

Unity is like the dew from Mount Hermon, the highest peak, refreshing the arid climate of Mount Zion many miles away. Pause to be refreshed by the one who is living water. Psalm 133 promises us that goodness flows from lives lived in unity with others.

As you pray, ask the Father to plant you deeply in his goodness and his love.

Recommended Closing Prayer

Father, grant us true unity with our brothers and sisters, rooted in our restored relationship with you. Please give us the love that you have for all people. Forgive us our hatred and apathy. Let us linger at the cross and be freshly amazed at the lengths you went to, to bring us back to you. Grant us fresh faith to pursue friendship and love, for it is love that will mark us as your people. Amen.

Lent Day 16
WILLA KANE

Reflect on Psalm 134

Call to Prayer

Psalm 134 is the last of the Psalms of Ascent—those songs sung by pilgrims who journeyed from their homes in Israel to Jerusalem three times a year for festival celebrations. The Psalms of Ascent move from expressions of lament, to expressions of confidence, to cries for help, and finally, to shouts of praise. This last psalm, a benediction of sorts, dwells on temple worship. But notice that the setting for this psalm is nighttime. As we walk through Lent, anticipating Easter, it is like living in the darkness, waiting for dawn, and seeking to praise God even as we wait.

This psalm and this season both ask a question of us: how are we, as Spirit-filled servants of the Lord, to bless him when days like ours look as dark as night?

In this fallen world, we experience what the apostle John described: "People loved the darkness rather than the light" (John 3:19 ESV). Evil abounds on the earth—evidence that the world loves darkness.

This psalm exhorts us, even and especially in the night watches, to bless the God who "is light; in him there is no darkness at all" (1 John 1:5 NIV). We are called to lift our hands to the Lord as we praise him, not only for who he is, but also for what he has done for us.

We, too, once "were darkness, but now [we] are light in the Lord" (Ephesians 5:8 ESV). Through a miracle of grace and mercy, we have joined the company of priests serving in the night watches.

Now, even though it's hard, lift your hands in praise to the Lord.

Praise him that he is light and because in him there is no darkness at all.

Pray for those who are still trapped in the kingdom of darkness.

Pray for real revival in Jesus.

Pray the words of Isaiah from centuries ago: "The people who walked in darkness have seen a great light. Those who dwelt in a land of deep darkness, on them has light shone" (Isaiah 9:2 ESV).

Recommended Closing Prayer

> Lord, in the daytime stars can be seen from deepest wells,
> And the deeper the wells the brighter Thy stars shine.
> Let me find Thy light in my darkness,
> Thy life in my death,
> Thy joys in my sorrow,
> Thy grace in my sin,
> Thy riches in my poverty,
> Thy glory in my valley.
> Amen.
> (From *The Valley of Vision*)

Lent Day 17

SALLY BREEDLOVE

Reflect on Colossians 1:11–12

Call to Prayer

Every day, we are faced with the same fundamental decision: whether or not to walk with our Savior in simple obedience and there taste a deep and unshakable joy and peace.

God wants far more for us than to hunker down and make it through. So enter now into your Savior's joy, which shatters the fantasy of wishful thinking. Jesus calls you to strength. When you labor with this strength, you will know a serene peace. The Spirit prays that God the Father will give you glory strength, not just the endurance to survive. He wants to bind his church together in this strength.

Will you join the Spirit in praying for yourself in this way? How do you long to be strengthened? How has God shown you goodness even in difficulty? Thank him for the goodness in your life, just as it is right now. Ask him to give you joy-strength.

Finally, turn your attention to those you love. What strength do you long for them to have? Pray what you notice back to your Father.

Recommended Closing Prayer

Lord of heaven and earth, we your people turn our hearts to you now. We ask you to strengthen us, to allow us to be glorified in our acts of service, and to fill us with your peace. Amen.

Lent Day 18
SALLY BREEDLOVE

Reflect on Matthew 11:28–30 and Hebrews 4:9–11

Call to Prayer

God has always invited all of us to find rest in him. From the Genesis beginning, he has held it out as a gift: Sabbath rest for the people of God.

For centuries, Saturday for the Jewish people and Sunday, the Christian Sabbath, were seen as set-apart days. Yes, the Sabbath has been abused and turned into a legalistic club. But now, might the Lord be inviting you to reexamine Sabbath rest?

The Hebrew word for Sabbath means many things, but three meanings stand out. Sabbath means to take a break, celebrate, and let the present be imperfect.

Will you take a break and stop checking things off your to-do list for one day? Stopping is one way to trust God and to grow more discerning. Tomorrow is a Sunday. How can you make tomorrow a day of stopping?

Will you choose to celebrate? Goodness, beauty, and truth have not left this world. The insight to see and to say thank you is an offering to God that reshapes your life.

And finally, will you let the present be imperfect? Will you accept life as it is? God guarantees a future of joy, but for now, we walk a pilgrim path in a dimly lit valley. Will you submit to its being enough?

You are invited to rest. From the beginning, God has offered rest. In Jesus, he reaffirms that offer. Come to Jesus, run to Jesus, and rest in Jesus.

Are you willing to choose a life of regular Sabbath? Will you say yes to God's invitation?

Recommended Closing Prayer

> Almighty God, after the creation of the world you rested from all your works and declared a day of rest for all your creatures: Help us to put away our anxieties and prepare us to worship you without distraction and with our whole hearts. We come to you for protection and security, looking forward to the eternal rest promised in heaven; through Jesus Christ our Lord. Amen.
>
> *(Anglican Church in North America Book of Common Prayer)*

Third Sunday of Lent, Day 19

KARI WEST

Reflect on Matthew 22:15–22

Call to Prayer

What a foolhardy mission of the Pharisees, setting out to entangle the Word made flesh in his own words. The Word of power, the Word that formed the universe and mysteriously holds it together, the Word that would show all hypocrites the way of repentance and truthfulness—this Word will not be stopped by the design and tricks of sinful, deceitful human beings and their empty words.

If only these Pharisees had listened to what they were saying about Jesus, if only they had taken their own descriptions seriously, then they could have come to Christ and gained all he had to give them.

He is Truth. He can show you the real way to the Father. He is not swayed by appearances. He knows what is in the heart of humankind.

Stop coming to him with your agendas, and your flattery, and your maneuverings for power or prestige. Take him on his own terms. Render to God what is God's—most importantly, your own soul.

As you pray, let this short gospel scene examine you: What will you do with the witness and words of Christ? Will you believe he is the Word of Life and surrender your own life to him?

Recommended Closing Prayer

Christ, help us to render ourselves to you, the Maker, lover, and sustainer of our souls. Amen.

Lent Day 20

KARI WEST

Reflect on Mark 1:35–39

Call to Prayer

Do you pray in the desolate places?

Other translations of these verses use the word *lonely, solitary,* or *deserted* to describe the place Christ sought early in the morning so he could speak to his Father. The word has connotations of a desert—arid, dry, and isolated.

Why does Jesus pray in such a place? Surely he does so in part for the solitude it offers him. As Simon points out, everyone is looking for Christ. The crowds search for him as Jesus searches for silence to deeply connect with his Father.

But still, why didn't Jesus seek out a beautiful and quiet setting in which to pray? Isn't there something in the loveliness and majesty of creation that draws our hearts to God? Aren't the psalms full of effusive delight in God's handiwork that turns to rich praise of God? Jesus knows this, and yet he chooses to pray in a lonely, dry, desert-like space.

Perhaps he knew, and wants us to know, that God will meet us in all the solitary, arid moments of our lives. It is easy to pray in an oasis; it is hard to offer petition and praise to God in a wasteland. And yet Christ rises early and seeks the face of his Father in a desolate place, knowing God will meet him there. Lent is a time when we seek those desert places to be with our Father and to pour out our hearts to him.

As you pray, remember you are in Jesus. God will always meet you in your turning toward him. Be at peace in the desolate places.

Recommended Closing Prayer

Christ, enable me to cast all my cares upon you. Let me remember how very much you care for me. Fill me with your peace. Amen.

Lent Day 21

SALLY BREEDLOVE

Reflect on Mark 5:21–24, 5:35–43

Call to Prayer

People who have it made in life often have a hard time accepting help. Jairus has arrived. He is the ruler of the synagogue in his region. He is known; he is important. Jesus is the controversial young itinerant rabbi who is welcomed by some and run out of town by others.

But Jairus is desperate. His beloved twelve-year-old daughter is dying. He'll risk his reputation and do anything to save her, even if it means asking Jesus for help. Humbling himself, he doesn't send a messenger but, instead, comes and falls at Jesus's feet.

Wonderfully, Jesus begins to follow Jairus to his house, but then Jairus faces another opportunity for humility. Jesus stops in his tracks to help a nobody woman. She is not the adolescent daughter of a well-to-do man. She is middle-aged, unclean, hopeless, and without family. But she, too, is determined to seek Jesus's help.

Despite the protests of his disciples, Christ stops to care for this woman. Likely, desperate fear and anger rise up in Jairus. They mustn't delay! His daughter is dying.

The worst happens. Although the woman is healed, people arrive from Jairus's household with a soul-killing message: his daughter is dead.

Pause. Let Jairus's despair touch you. Was he simply overcome with his loss? Was he angry at the woman and at Jesus's delay? Were his thoughts flashing ahead to his wife's anguish and the emptiness in their home from now on? Did he have a stab of fear that he'd likely lost status by turning to Jesus?

Before Jairus can respond, Jesus speaks. The verbs Mark uses in this passage are best translated "Don't *go on fearing* the worst. *Keep on believing* the best."

Pause now as you prepare to pray. Lent is a time to learn humility. Are you willing to humble yourself and ask Jesus to help you? Are you willing to humble yourself and accept the hope he offers? Don't go on fearing the worst; keep on believing the best. Pray for the grace to run to Jesus, to wait for Jesus, and to know that Jesus is stronger than death itself.

Recommended Closing Prayer

Lord, all of us grieve someone who has died. O help us in the depth of our loss and pain. Help us to trust that you will make all things new. Lord, all of us find stubborn places in our hearts where we don't want to ask you for help. Forgive our anger, our impatience, our sense of entitlement, and our despair. Teach us to keep on believing. For Jesus's sake. Amen.

Lent Day 22

WILLA KANE

Reflect on Psalm 147

Call to Prayer

"It is good to sing praises to our God; for it is pleasant and a song of praise is fitting" (Psalm 147:1 ESV), says the psalmist.

Amid the uncertainty of our world, is this the way you feel? The last psalms of the psalter build together into a crescendo of praise. Psalm 147 calls us four times to praise or sing thanks to the Lord.

Can we honestly offer praise in these days if challenges press in on every side? We can if we will let ourselves see all the ways God cares for us.

He builds up, he gathers outcasts, he heals the brokenhearted, and he binds up their wounds. Our God is tender and personal, even though he is all-powerful—creating, numbering, and naming the stars, covering the heavens with clouds, and preparing rain for the earth. He bends low to gently lift the humble. He takes pleasure in those who fear him and trust him, who hope in his steadfast love.

Are you overwhelmed? Are you living as an outcast? Come to Jesus. Are you brokenhearted, wounded, and broken in spirit? Come to Jesus. He knows brokenness because he entered into it. He is not a stranger to any challenge you face.

He is the Word the Father sent, the Word that runs swiftly to meet your every need. Let the wind of his Spirit blow fresh life and infuse living water into your burdened heart. Experience his strength, his pleasure, and his peace.

The beauty of the gospel is simple, but it is not small: put your hope in the love of God.

Now rise to praise him, for he inhabits his people and takes delight in their praise. It is good to sing praises to our God.

Recommended Closing Prayer

O Father, it is unbelievable to me that I, a sinner, though forgiven, am the object of your pleasure and delight. Thank you that I am among those you've gathered to you. I praise you with all my heart. Amen.

Lent Day 23

S A L L Y   B R E E D L O V E

Reflect on Philippians 2:5–8

Call to Prayer

In the ancient world, foot washing was a necessity. Roads were dusty and muddy, and animals walked the same paths and roads as people. Not everyone wore shoes, and most shoes were only sandals. It was a matter of hygiene and comfort to provide a way for people to wash their feet when they entered a home. If you had any means, you provided a servant to do the job for your guests or family.

But at the Last Supper, the Eternal Son of God strips down like a servant to wash his disciples' feet even as they are jousting among themselves over who deserves first place with Jesus.

Peter protests that Jesus will not wash his feet. Jesus insists. Then, as he finishes and sits down among his stunned and chastised disciples, he explains what he has done. "You call me Teacher and Lord, and you are right, for so I am. If I then, your Lord and Teacher, have washed your feet, you also ought to wash one another's feet. For I have given you an example, that you also should do just as I have done to you" (John 13:13–15 ESV).

The command for us is to follow Jesus and take a servant's place.

Look around you. You will see the presence of Christ being lived out in choices other people are making.

Will you pray in thanksgiving for those who serve as Christ serves?

When you chafe against life as it is, will you pray and ask God for specific ways you can serve our world?

Will you hold Christ's words and pray that he make your heart like his? "For even the Son of Man came not to be served but to serve, and to give his life as a ransom for many" (Mark 10:45 ESV).

Recommended Closing Prayer

> Lord God, whose blessed Son our Savior gave his body to
> be whipped and his face to be spit upon: Give us grace to

accept joyfully the sufferings of the present time, confident of the glory that shall be revealed; through Jesus Christ your Son our Lord, who lives and reigns with you and the Holy Spirit, one God, for ever and ever. Amen.
(Anglican Church in North America Book of Common Prayer)

Lent Day 24

SALLY BREEDLOVE

Reflect on Isaiah 50:4–11

Call to Prayer

These words from Isaiah 50, written centuries before Jesus's birth, paint a picture of a person responsive to the Father's voice. Morning by morning, the prophet tells us that he lets God wake him up so he can listen and be taught.

Jesus is the fulfillment of Isaiah 50. He is the eternal God-man. As a man, he lived this listening-to-God life. He submitted to the process of being taught and of learning obedience. He determined he would not turn away or rebel. He chose to submit to injustice, disgrace, and pain.

Jesus knows what it means to suffer, to be worn out, to be mocked and mistreated, to have the light of God's presence with him snuffed out, and to die. That listening obedience shapes his earthly life all the way to the cross.

As you walk with Jesus, be assured that he will help you. His listening obedience and his endurance haven't turned him into a tough drill sergeant impatient with your stumbling and your doubts. He overflows with compassion. He is able to help you when you are weary. He will sit in the darkness with you until God brings light.

Perhaps Jesus is inviting you to follow him in new ways. Pray for the state of your own soul. Will you let yourself be awakened to God's Word morning by morning? Will you accept the hardships and injustices life is bringing your way? Will you choose to trust? Will you lay down your life in the particular ways Christ calls you to do?

Christ sits with you in this darkness. Are you willing to wait with him for the light that only he can bring?

Pray that God will give you the heart of a disciple, and pray that he will make you eager to listen and to obey. Ask him to calm your heart so you can wait in the darkness with Jesus. Ask him to calm the hearts of those you know who are fearful and weary. Ask him to make you a person of peace for others.

Recommended Closing Prayer

Lord, we come to you because you are True Life. Though we may see only death around us, when we look upon your Son, we can finally rest. Give us the energy and strength that comes from your life, leaving our fear and sadness behind. Jesus bore the unimaginable weight of the sin of the world. Please give us, your feeble children, the strength to bear whatever burdens we face. Your eternal life stretches out before us uninterrupted by our present dangers, and we hope in you. Amen.

Lent Day 25

SALLY BREEDLOVE

Reflect on Mark 6:45–52

Call to Prayer

After feeding the five thousand, Christ makes his disciples get in a boat and begin the journey across the Sea of Galilee. Perhaps, as John hints in his version, Jesus knows his disciples could be caught up in the movement by the crowd to make him king. Maybe he is protecting them from shortsighted foolishness. Jesus dismisses the crowd (and his disciples) and climbs a mountain to pray. Finally, he has time to be with his Father. He lingers long there.

But as the night unfolds, Jesus looks toward the water. It is whipped into a fever pitch by a windstorm. Perhaps the moon is full; perhaps dawn is emerging. Jesus sees his friends straining to cross the lake. He walks down to the shoreline and begins to walk on the rough sea. We assume he will join his friends in the boat and help them. We assume he will quiet the sea.

But Mark surprises us: "He meant to pass them by" (Mark 6:48 ESV). "Why?" we ask. For their part, the disciples are frightened. Thinking that Jesus is a ghost, they cry out in fear. Where is their faith? Can they not reason that the one who fed five thousand would also be able to walk on water or calm a storm?

This simple story raises questions we can't answer. We'll never understand everything Jesus does. We become afraid in overwhelming circumstances. Often, we don't even hold onto the faith we were given the last time we went through a similar crisis. What do we do?

Perhaps the best thing is simply to return to the words of Christ. "Take heart: it is I. Do not be afraid" (Mark 6:50 ESV). We can hold these words when we are deeply confused and scared. Christ is near, and he is with us. His reality is greater than any confusion and every storm. We will never be abandoned.

As you pray, thank Jesus that he is always present and always able to help you. Submit by faith to what you do not understand. Ask him to strengthen your believing.

Recommended Closing Prayer

Lord, I believe. Help my unbelief. For Jesus's sake. Amen.

Fourth Sunday of Lent, Day 26

SALLY BREEDLOVE

Reflect on Jeremiah 8:20–9:1

Call to Prayer

Are you in a season of waiting for answers or solutions that haven't come? Do you lament with Jeremiah, "We are not yet saved" (Jeremiah 8:8 ESV)?

Lent is often about waiting and sitting in darkness. With Psalm 74:10, you may find yourself crying out, "How long, O God?" (ESV).

You may be forced into the corner called waiting, called hope, called faith in the Lord God, the one who is good, and wise, and all-powerful, the one who loves you even when life has gone pitch-black.

As you pray, confess your own longings and fears with a ruthless honesty. Pray you will become a person who is willing to wait, to watch, and to hope.

End your prayers with the waiting words of Psalm 130.

Recommended Closing Prayer

> Out of the depths I cry to you, O Lord!
> O Lord, hear my voice!
> Let your ears be attentive
> to the voice of my pleas for mercy!
> If you, O Lord, should mark iniquities,
> O Lord, who could stand?
> But with you there is forgiveness,
> that you may be feared.
> I wait for the Lord, my soul waits,
> and in his word I hope;
> my soul waits for the Lord
> more than watchmen for the morning,
> more than watchmen for the morning.
> O Israel, hope in the Lord!
> For with the Lord there is steadfast love,
> and with him is plentiful redemption.
> And he will redeem Israel
> from all his iniquities. Amen.
> *(Psalm 130 ESV)*

Lent Day 27

KARI WEST

Reflect on John 6:27–40

Call to Prayer

Do you hear the invitation in these words of Jesus? He tells us that he is the bread of heaven that gives life to the world. To believe in Jesus isn't an intellectual exercise where we give a mental nod to certain facts about our Savior. It's an acknowledgment of that gnawing, constant hunger inside us and that deep desperation of knowing that we can't find true bread. And it's an embracing of Jesus as the one and only person who holds out the true feast—him.

Are you starving? Has your life revealed how little you can truly provide for yourself?

Go to Jesus. Embrace him as the only source of true life, and rest in his promise that he will never drive you away. He will keep you. He will hold you. He will love you. At the last day, he will raise you up to eternal life with him. His kingdom is inaugurated with a feast, the marriage supper of the Lamb. One day, that gnawing hunger you know now will be fully satisfied.

As you pray, ask for fresh faith to know—in your head and your heart and your bones and your stomach—that Jesus *is* the bread of life. He is all we need, and we are his forever.

Recommended Closing Prayer

Jesus, you are the bread, broken so that we may be whole. Let us feast, and let us trust you, bread from heaven, our Immanuel. Amen.

Lent Day 28

KARI WEST

Reflect on Psalm 109:21–31

Call to Prayer

In Psalm 109, the goodness and steadfastness of our ruling God is in stark contrast to the evil, lying leaders oppressing David. These men are so aligned with a life of wickedness that David says they wear cursing like a garment and display their shame as their outer garment. Because of their malice, David feels he is fading away like a shadow in the evening. He feels as insignificant as an insect.

But in the midst of these deep difficulties, David seeks the face of God. He calls on the Lord to act according to his character, according to his faithful love. Although these leaders curse, David calls on God to bless. Although these leaders oppress the poor and tread over the lowly, David names God as the one who stands at the right hand of the needy.

Rather than give in to despair because of these men's brutality and power, David recalls the supremacy of God. He pleads with the Lord of heaven and earth to bring justice against those who malign and abuse his people. He rests in the surety that he will praise God in a throng of worshippers. God will sit enthroned forever, long after all evil rulers are put to shame. His justice will shine like the noonday sun.

As you pray, take heart in God's reigning power. Yes, Lent is a time of sorrow and of repentance, but it is never a time of despair. Ask God to bring justice and deliverance to this world. Hope in his eternal throne.

Recommended Closing Prayer

With my mouth I will greatly extol you, Lord; in the great throng of worshippers I will praise you. For you stand at the right hand of the needy, to save their lives from those who would condemn them. Amen. *(Adapted from Psalm 109:30–31 NIV)*

Lent Day 29

SALLY BREEDLOVE

Reflect on Isaiah 43:1-4a

Call to Prayer

"Perfect love casts out fear," 1 John 4:18 (ESV) promises us. What a profound mystery that love can displace fear. Most of us have known someone whose love made us feel safe. But even if we have never had that experience, our hearts long to be loved, held, and protected.

There is indeed good news that banishes fear. The Triune God loves each one of us wholly. He is perfect strength and power, perfect wisdom, perfect kindness and compassion, perfect holiness. He is the God who fully sees us—in our fears, our sin, our brokenness, and our doubt. And he is the mighty and merciful God who nonetheless fully cherishes us and protects us.

Where is your soul today? Does it feel as if the waters are rising around you? Turn to God as you pray. Be honest about where you are. Then thank him. He declares, "You are precious in my eyes, and honored, and I love you" (Isaiah 43:4 ESV). Even before any feelings of being loved arise in you, thank him that he does indeed hold you in his love.

Recommended Closing Prayer

> Most loving Father, you will us to give thanks for all things, to dread nothing but the loss of you, and to cast all our care on the One who cares for us. Preserve us from faithless fears and worldly anxieties, and grant that no clouds of this mortal life may hide from us the light of that love which is immortal, and which you have manifested unto us in your Son, Jesus Christ our Lord. Amen.
> (*Anglican Church in North America Book of Common Prayer*)

Lent Day 30

WILLA KANE

Reflect on Luke 18:35–43

Call to Prayer

Jesus is making his way through Jericho to Jerusalem and to the cross. He has just described in detail what lies ahead, but his closest friends are blind to his teaching.

Yet even though he is headed to the cross, Christ's heart is still full of compassion. For three years, Jesus has blessed people with countless miracles, beginning in northern Israel at a wedding in Galilee. Now this last miracle before his resurrection takes place on his journey to Jerusalem.

As he travels, Jesus is surrounded by loud throngs of pilgrims who are also on their way to celebrate Passover in Jerusalem. From the crowd, a beggar cries out, "Jesus, Son of David" (Luke 18:38 NIV). The crowd tries to hush him, but he persists. The very fact that he calls Jesus "Son of David" would have startled the crowd. What makes this man think that Jesus is the promised Messiah?

We wonder as well how this blind man knows that the Messiah is on the Jericho road?

"Have mercy on me!" (Luke 18:39 NIV), he cries out again. Jesus calls out for the blind man to come to him. A blind beggar believes, and his dead eyes are transformed by the power of Christ. Unlike the rich young ruler who chose possessions over Jesus, this man throws away the only thing he has, a worn-out cloak, and runs to Christ.

Christ asks him a simple question: "What do you want me to do for you?" (Luke 18:41 ESV).

His answer: "Lord, I want to see!" (Luke 18:41 ESV).

As the crowd looks on, faith becomes sight. Seeing, the man follows his Savior.

Take a moment to consider Jesus. The one he blesses in this story is a blind beggar. In first-century Israel, he was an outcast at the bottom of society, rejected by family and dependent on charity from strangers.

But in his blindness, he can see more than the disciples who've been with Jesus for three years. He sees with the eyes of his heart.

As you pray, ask Jesus to open the eyes of your heart. Thank him for the miracle of new life in him, and ask for renewed purpose to follow him well, not just during Lent, but for all the days of your life.

Recommended Closing Prayer

> Lord, high and holy, meek and lowly, You have brought me to the valley of vision, where I live in the depths but see You in the heights; hemmed in by mountains of sin I behold Your glory. Let me learn by paradox that the way down is the way up, that to be low is to be high, that the broken heart is the healed heart, that the contrite spirit is the rejoicing spirit, that the repenting soul is the victorious soul, that to have nothing is to possess all, that to bear the cross is to wear the crown, that to give is to receive, that the valley is the place of vision. Lord, in the daytime stars can be seen from deepest wells, and the deeper the wells the brighter Your stars shine; let me find Your light in my darkness, Your life in my death, Your joy in my sorrow, Your grace in my sin, Your riches in my poverty, Your glory in my valley. Amen.
> (From *The Valley of Vision*)

Lent Day 31
FRANCIS CAPITANIO

Reflect on Habakkuk 3:17–19

Call to Prayer

Add whatever it is that's not going well in your life to this scripture, and you will have a prayer that's always deep, always timely, and always important to have in your heart. There's a game kids like to play called Mad Libs, where they find a paragraph full of blank spaces and are asked to put in a noun, verb, adverb, or adjective of their choice. What they get in the end is a comical and nonsensical paragraph that will usually make them laugh.

This scripture, when filled with all our struggles, is not so funny. But what it expresses is vital to finding the secret of contentment when we come to pray. If you add in your own worries and hardships here, what you get in the end is a very real picture of your own need for God, not just a Savior for your sins but also a Savior for your whole life, able and willing to help you with whatever you may need. This scripture provides a prayer of true faith, a faith not based on whatever is seen around us but based on the faithfulness of God *despite* what we see around us.

As you pray, take these words on your lips and rest in the steadfastness of God.

Recommended Closing Prayer

Though the car won't start, though there is no food on our table, though we can't pay our utility bills this month, though I just lost my job, and though it seems in the news the world is falling apart, I will rejoice in you, Lord. I will be joyful in God my Savior. Amen.

Lent Day 32

SALLY BREEDLOVE

Reflect on Mark 8:31, 8:34–37

Call to Prayer

How did we ever get it into our heads that the way to the life we really want would be an easy journey?

The universe reminds us that life is born out of death. There is a rhythmic dying hidden in each season: the loss of the safety of the womb through the risk of birth, the laying down of one's independence and autonomy for the good union of marriage, the seeds that die for vegetables and flowers to grow, and the peach blossoms that wither and fall to the ground so bubbly hot peach crisp can crown a summer supper. Death is the door to life.

It's almost Easter, the yearly celebration of the Lord Jesus Christ's death and resurrection. The resurrection is God's lived-out-in-history proclamation that life is stronger than death, and it is the reminder that in God's mystery, life must pass through death if it is to offer life to others. A Jesus who never died would be only a paragon of virtue, not the Son of God, whose death gives life. The death of Jesus destroyed death and opened the door to life.

What has been dying in you lately? God promises to bring real life out of what dies.

As you pray, can you hold up what you love, what you count on, and what gives you joy as offerings to God? Pray that the deaths you die may bring life to others. Pray that God will give you a heart and vision for the kind of dying that can bring life to others.

Ask God to show you something life-giving you can do for someone who is hurting or alone.

As you pray, call to mind someone whose losses and griefs are far greater than your own. Pray that over time, the Holy Spirit will help this person see life emerge from the death he or she is experiencing.

Recommended Closing Prayer

Father, there is death at work in us, pulling us toward despair. Our attempts to comfort ourselves and to ignore our condition have not worked. And so we lay down our lives before you now, acknowledging you as Master and Lord. Purge sin and death from us, both in the depths of our souls and in our daily decisions. Keep us from living to make ourselves happy. We embrace the true life that comes to us through the death and resurrection of Jesus Christ. In ways large and small, may we die to ourselves and know your immovable peace and energizing joy. May you be glorified in our lives, Father, Son, and Holy Spirit. Amen.

Fifth Sunday of Lent, Day 33

FRANCIS CAPITANIO

Reflect on Hosea 6:1–3

Call to Prayer

"Come, let us return to the Lord" (Hosea 6:1 NIV). This is the way to fulfill the first and greatest commandment: to love the Lord your God with all your heart, with all your soul, and with all your mind. To love God, we must return. To return, we must pray.

On the third day, the Lord rose up from death. It was *he*, rather than Israel, who was torn to pieces this time. For the sake of his people, it was *he* who was injured, even to the point of death. But on the third day he was restored, along with all of Israel, back to the fullness of the divine life promised to humankind by God the Father. Through that resurrection, Jesus the Messiah made the way for Israel and the nations to live in the presence of their God forever and find eternal peace.

That's what we tap into every time we pray. The third day opened the way for us into God's presence each and every day, so that we know it is there when we return to the Lord in prayer. We are third-day people. We return to the Lord from our lives of worry, injury, heartache, sin. We forget the Lord, we get buried by the world, and then we remember that we must return—we must push through and turn back to face the one who can and will revive us. Every time we turn to behold his presence through prayer, it is a reminder of what the Lord made possible on the third day a little more than two thousand years ago and of his promise to always be there when our hearts turn back to him.

As you pray, remember this reality, recall this promise, and be at peace.

Recommended Closing Prayer

Lord, I return to you today. You healed me. You bound up my wounds. You revived me. You restored me. You made me alive with you on the third day. So I come to you with confidence, knowing that I can live in your presence and receive your love. Amen.

Lent Day 34

BRANDON WALSH

Reflect on Mark 11:1–26

Call to Prayer

When Jesus arrives at the gates of Jerusalem in Mark 11, the pressure has been building. Jesus's ministry has spread across Israel, with miracles and signs stirring up wonder and hope among all God's people. In chapter 8, Peter declares Jesus the Son of God, but Jesus insists that his disciples keep this a secret until they understand what his kingship will look like—crucifixion and resurrection. They do not yet see rightly.

In chapter 11, Jesus arrives to great anticipation. The crowds throng around him, declaring as Peter did that Jesus is the Messiah. Hosanna! Blessed is he who comes in the name of the Lord. Blessed is the coming kingdom of our father David! Hosanna in the highest!

Every word the people proclaimed was true, but they didn't understand what they were saying. They wanted Jesus to be King on their terms. They were not rejoicing in the kingdom of God, but in a kingdom they imagined—one where they were on top again.

But when the Lord enters, he does not give them what they want. Instead, he gives all of us what we desperately need and do not yet understand.

In hindsight, we can see the irony and tragedy of this triumphal entry, but we are so often guilty of making the same mistake. We want the Lord to enter into our lives and circumstances and give us victory and relief. But the Lord so often gives us what we need, not what we want. He invites us to walk the narrow path of suffering love, to venture into the darkness with only his rod and his staff as our guide and comfort.

As you pray, ask the Lord to come and be your Lord—not as you wish, but as he wills.

Recommended Closing Prayer

> O Holy Spirit, beloved of my soul, I adore you. Enlighten me, guide me, strengthen me, console me. Tell me what I should do; give me your orders. I promise to submit myself to all that you desire of me and to accept all that you permit to happen to me. Let me only know your will. Amen.
>
> *(Anglican Church in North America Book of Common Prayer)*

Lent Day 35

BRANDON WALSH

Reflect on Mark 12:13–34

Call to Prayer

Religious leaders, trying to trap Jesus, ask him a hot political question: "Is it lawful to pay taxes to Caesar?" (Mark 12:14 ESV). Jesus's answer offers us a framework for thinking about our own politics.

Jesus asks them to bring a coin to him. Then he looks at it, and asks, "Whose image and inscription is here?" They all reply, "Caesar's." Jesus says, "Render to Caesar the things that are Caesar's, and to God the things that are God's" (Mark 12:16b–17 ESV).

To modern readers, this statement can be perplexing. We are supposed to pay taxes because of the picture on a coin? What is Jesus driving at? What does it have to do with us now?

In Exodus 20:4, Moses presents the Ten Commandments to the Israelites, the second of them being, "You shall not make for yourself a carved image or any likeness of anything that is in heaven above, or that is in the earth beneath, or that is in the water under the earth" (ESV).

This commandment instructs God's people to refrain from worshipping anything other than the Lord and to refrain from creating images on objects for worshipping.

The deep logic being, in the temple of creation, human beings are the ones who bear the image of God. So when Jesus takes a coin graven with the image of Caesar, he is making the point that if Caesar wants some of his silver, then you should give it to him, but that you are made in the image of God and you belong to him.

The same is true today. As Christians, we live in a society and should "give unto Caesar," meaning we should be faithful to fulfill our civil obligations, pay taxes, and work toward the common good. But we must never confuse the image on the coin for the image written onto us. Our deepest, fullest, and most primary identity must be found in the living image of the invisible God, Jesus Christ (Colossians 1:15). Some trust in chariots and horses, but our ultimate hope always rests not on any temporal political reality, but rather on the kingdom of God (Psalm 20:7).

We have something greater to love than images on coins or those people whom they represent. We have a true and living God. We should take heart. As you pray, remember that he whom you worship is greater than he who is in the world. Thank God for his supremacy, and ask for greater faith to trust in him.

Recommended Closing Prayer

> Almighty God, our heavenly Father, send down on those who hold public office, especially those just elected, the spirit of wisdom, charity, and justice; that with steadfast purpose they may faithfully serve in their offices to promote the well-being of all people; through Jesus Christ our Lord. Amen.
>
> (Anglican Church in North America Book of Common Prayer)

Lent Day 36

BRANDON WALSH

Reflect on Mark 12:35–44

Call to Prayer

Jesus's words in today's gospel reading offer insight into the nature of worship and giving. Jesus compares wealthy persons making big donations, their coins loudly clanging into the temple coffers, with a humble widow quietly offering her two coins. The first group offers a huge amount of money but do not offer themselves to God; instead they offer themselves up for the praise of others. The widow, on the other hand, gives out of her poverty. She gives herself.

The resources we offer to the Lord are symbols of our whole lives, offered up to the Lord as an ongoing act of worship.

The Lord wants your pocketbook, but not because he needs the money! The Lord owns the cattle on a thousand hills. The Lord desires our offerings, sacrificial offerings, because they represent all that we are and all that we have. The actual amount of money, time, and talents we offer the Lord may change depending on our circumstances—but we are all called to offer ourselves wholeheartedly.

As you pray, ask the Lord for an increased heart of generosity. Ask to grow in true worship in offering your whole life to him. Thank him for his provision and his love.

Recommended Closing Prayer

> Give me, O Lord, a steadfast heart, which no unworthy thought can drag down; an unconquered heart, which no tribulation can wear out; an upright heart, which no unworthy purpose can tempt aside. Bestow upon me understanding to know you, diligence to seek you, wisdom to find you, and faithfulness that finally may embrace you. Amen.
> *(Anglican Church in North America Book of Common Prayer)*

Lent Day 37

BRANDON WALSH

Reflect on Mark 13:14–37

Call to Prayer

The time grows short for Jesus's earthly ministry in Mark 13. This section on the end of things is Jesus's last teaching before the Lord's Supper and Passion.

Jesus also says, "But concerning that day or that hour, no one knows, not even the angels in heaven, nor the Son, but only the Father. Be on guard, keep awake. For you do not know when the time will come" (Mark 13:32–33 ESV). We do not know when the Lord will come to make all things new.

Spending our energy on trying to predict the future isn't productive or helpful. Instead, we should "keep awake"—making ourselves, our families, and our communities ready for the kingdom of God. This does not mean hoarding food in our basements; on the contrary, it means sharing it with our food bank or neighbors in need. In the words of Saint Paul, now we see through a glass darkly, but then we shall see face-to-face. Until that day, when all things become clear and we are standing in the fullness of the kingdom, three things remain—faith, hope, and love.

What does it mean to "keep awake"?

It means to faithfully live according to the faithfulness of God in Jesus Christ.

It means to allow the hope of the gospel to completely transform one's imagination, longings, and vocation.

It means to let the love of God illumine one's heart and animate one's life even when the earth quakes and the seas roar.

As you pray, ask the Lord for steadfast love, trust in his providence, and the ability to keep awake until his return.

Recommended Closing Prayer

> O gladsome light,
> pure brightness of the everliving Father in heaven,

O Jesus Christ, holy and blessed!
Now as we come to the setting of the sun, and our eyes behold the vesper light,
we sing your praises, O God: Father, Son, and Holy Spirit.
You are worthy at all times to be praised by happy voices,
O Son of God, O Giver of Life,
and to be glorified through all the worlds.
(Anglican Church in North America Book of Common Prayer)

Lent Day 38

BRANDON WALSH

Reflect on Mark 14:12–25

Call to Prayer

The word *companion* comes from two Latin words and literally means "with bread." A companion is one with whom you share bread. When Jesus and his disciples celebrated this final meal, this Last Supper, they had been through so much. Jesus, the miracle worker, had calmed the sea, raised the dead, humbled the proud, and exalted the humble. Hopes and ambitions alike kindled in the disciples' hearts. A Messiah, a King, a Lord. All the lights of prophetic hope focused as if through a magnifying glass on Jesus.

Jesus takes bread, blesses it, and breaks it. He lifts a cup, gives thanks, and offers it. He will be broken like the bread. He will be poured out like the wine.

Jesus takes these twelve men and makes them companions, but more than that, he breaks his body to make all of us companions with God. We who walked in darkness have seen a great light—not primarily in heavenly splendor, but in ordinary bread and wine. God has come near to us and continues to invite us to his table to be his companions.

Remember Christ as you break bread at your dinner table. Give thanks for his goodness when you drink from your cup. Call to mind his sacrifice when you next take Communion. As you pray, rejoice that Jesus is our companion now and always.

Recommended Closing Prayer

> Dear Jesus, I believe that you are truly present in the Holy Sacrament. I love you above all things, and I desire to possess you within my soul. And since I cannot now receive you sacramentally, I beseech you to come spiritually into my heart. I unite myself to you, together with all your faithful people gathered around every altar of your Church, and I embrace you with all the affections of my soul. Never permit me to be separated from you. Amen.
> *(Anglican Church in North America Book of Common Prayer)*

Lent Day 39
BRANDON WALSH

Ecclesiastes 6

Reflect on Psalm 49

Call to Prayer

Sometimes it's hard to trust what we know. We know a second dessert is rarely a good idea, but we go back for seconds anyway. We know we need more sleep to feel better in the morning, but still we stay up longer than we should.

In the same way, most of us know that wealth, honor, and security are terrible ends in and of themselves, but we long for them anyway. Yet it is all vanity, vapor—here today, gone tomorrow.

Psalm 49 and Ecclesiastes 6 warn us of the dangers of placing our hope in wealth. Jesus too has harrowing things to say about wealth and its dangers. He admonishes us that pride, self-righteousness, and the desire for wealth are destructive to our souls.

What is it about a longing for material wealth that it so dangerous? God created the world good. Food for feasting, clothes for wearing, and gold for artistry are part of his creation. Jesus himself turns water to wine for a wedding, and is accused of gluttony (Luke 7:34f). (But he also fasts for forty days in the wilderness and has no place to lay his head.)

Wealth is not dangerous because physical things are bad. Wealth proves dangerous because it falsely promises us that it can satisfy our deep longing for security, affection, glory, and power. But only God can fill up our hearts. Material things must be seen for what they are: blessings, yes, but never blessings that can fill up our longings.

As you pray, ask God to show you where you are too eager for material blessings. Ask him where you can be a generous person instead. The best cure for your overfocus on what you want or need is often generosity. It's hard to be possessed by something, to obsess about it, if you give some of it away. Nothing puts wealth in its proper place more than sharing it with others. So pray for the grace of generosity. Then ask God to satisfy your deep longings and heal your fears and insecurities.

Recommended Closing Prayer

> Eternal Word, only begotten Son of God,
> Teach me true generosity.
> Teach me to serve you as you deserve.
> To give without counting the cost,
> To fight heedless of wounds,
> To labor without seeking rest,
> To sacrifice myself without thought of any reward
> Save the knowledge that I have done your will.
> Amen.
> (Saint Ignatius of Loyola)

Introduction to Holy Week

STEVEN E. BREEDLOVE

Holy Week offers us the chance to enter directly into the life of Christ. We wave palm branches; we celebrate the Last Supper and wash each other's feet; we place crosses in our churches, sometimes kneeling before them or nailing our sins to them; we fast on Saturday, perhaps waiting in vigil that evening; and then we break forth in joy and celebration on Easter morning. Over the course of this week, the life of Christ—the specific things he did and said, and the things done to him—dominates our devotions and worship.

This is as it should be, for our hope is grounded in the life, death, and resurrection of Christ. *Our growth in the faith must also revolve around this.* We need a yearly moment when we rehearse and reenter the foundation of our faith. During this week, we are given the chance to center our life on Christ in an explicit way and let our prayers respond to what he did that week.

On Palm Sunday, as we cheer with the throngs, our prayers should be, "Hosanna! Save us, Son of David!" From Monday to Wednesday, as we read the final words Jesus spoke in the temple, our prayers should be, "Lord, examine me! May I be built upon you, my cornerstone!" On Thursday, we should meditate on the washing of feet, marvel at the Last Supper, and pray that we too would love one another and be preserved when our faith is tested. We should grieve in prayer with the Lord as we enter Gethsemane, asking that we might stay awake in prayer during temptation. And on Friday, a day that can only be called "good" because our redemption was purchased, the cost of our life should drive us to prayers of both sorrow and joy. Yet when Sunday comes, our prayers should become victory songs—not merely joyous, but fully triumphant—as we remember the resurrection of the Lord.

Holy Week Day 1 (Palm Sunday)

SALLY BREEDLOVE

Reflect on Matthew 21:1–5

Call to Prayer

In the Western church, today has historically been observed as Palm Sunday—the celebration and remembrance of Christ's triumphal entry into Jerusalem. In truth, it's only a pause on the road to the cross, but it resounds with meaning. Jesus is the humble King. As John 12:15 tells us, we no longer have to be afraid. As Mark 11:10 reminds us, the coming kingdom of our father David is blessed.

But pause with Jesus one more time on that high place of the Mount of Olives, look down into the Kidron Valley, and then lift your eyes with him to see the city of Jerusalem. Jesus must descend and then climb before he enters the Holy City. Is this panorama a picture of the real descent he will make? the walk through the valley of death that leads to the cross?

On that morning, how did he endure the thought of all that lay ahead? Hebrews 12:2 declares that the joy set before him strengthened him. That passage concludes with this encouragement to us: our ultimate destination is the city of joy, which cannot be shaken, the city where all who belong to God are gathered together. Angels in party clothes will celebrate alongside us in that place.

Listen:

You've come to Mount Zion, the city where the living God resides. The invisible Jerusalem is populated by throngs of festive angels and Christian citizens. It is the city where God is Judge, with judgments that make us just. You've come to Jesus, who presents us with a new covenant, a fresh charter from God. He is the Mediator of this covenant. The murder of Jesus, unlike Abel's—a homicide that cried out for vengeance—became a proclamation of grace.

So don't turn a deaf ear to these gracious words. … Do you see what we've got? An unshakable kingdom! And do you see how thankful we must be? Not only thankful, but brimming with worship, deeply reverent before God. (Hebrews 12:22–25, 12:28 MSG)

What lies ahead of us on this Lenten evening? Perhaps a deeper descent into the valley of suffering, but even if this is so, we are never abandoned there. As Psalm 23:4 reminds us, in the darkest valley, the truth is still the truth. Christ is Immanuel, God with us, no matter where the road leads.

He is indeed leading us to the city that endures forever, the New Jerusalem, which will come down from heaven. His alone is the unshakable kingdom, the dwelling place of joy, where God wipes away every tear, heals every disease, dispels every fear, and makes all things new. We can endure.

Recommended Closing Prayer

Almighty and everlasting God, in your tender love toward us you sent your Son, our Savior Jesus Christ, to take on our flesh and to suffer death upon the cross for our sins. Mercifully grant us to join in his resurrection from the dead by the power of the Holy Spirit and to follow him all our days. Give patience and strength to those who are serving others during these days of hardship. Bring comfort to those who are suffering, and let all turn unto you for everlasting life. Amen.
(Adapted from the *Anglican Church in North America Book of Common Prayer*)

Holy Week Day 2

BRANDON WALSH

Reflect on Mark 14:26–52

Call to Prayer

Each year cinemas fill up bigger screens with bigger special effects to show to bigger audiences. Blockbusters depict heroes in cosmic battles for the fate of the world. Stories like these fill our imaginations and hearts with wonder. We love heroes.

In our gospel reading today, a different kind or hero and a different kind of battle come into focus. The Son of God enters into a cosmic struggle with sin and death, and the final action sequence is set up. But this struggle occurs in a dark and quiet garden. Jesus, the Son of God, tells his disciples, "My soul is very sorrowful, even to death. Remain here and watch" (Mark 14:34 ESV).

Jesus feels the weight of what will soon happen. It tears him up. The text says he falls to the ground, affirms that the Father can do all things, and asks for him to remove this cup. Here the Lord experiences the fullness of his humanity. But in this moment of sorrow unto death, he delivers the death blow to sin and Satan, the final knife thrust through the heart of creation's rebellion.

Jesus prays, "Yet not what I will, but what you will" (Mark 14:36 ESV). The Crucifixion fulfills these words and succeeds where all before failed.

When Jesus asks his disciples to carry their crosses, he means that they must also submit to the will of the Father, to make his words their words. "Yet not what I will, but what you will." For all of us who follow Jesus, these words offer freedom. In accepting the Father's will, we are free to flourish into the image of God in Christ, for which we were created.

In our own lives, the greatest battles we fight are not like those in epic movies. They look like Jesus in the garden, wrestling with his own soul. As you pray, consider this question: will you say "Thy will be done" even when you ask the Lord to let the cup pass? Come before your Savior and King and ask for submission to his will, even as he submitted to the Father.

Recommended Closing Prayer

> Lord Jesus, Master Carpenter of Nazareth, on the Cross through wood and nails you wrought our full salvation: Wield well your tools in this, your workshop, that we who come to you rough-hewn may be fashioned into a truer beauty by your hand; who with the Father and the Holy Spirit live and reign, one God, world without end. Amen.
> *(Anglican Church in North America Book of Common Prayer)*

Holy Week Day 3

SALLY BREEDLOVE

Reflect on John 12:20–28

Call to Prayer

It's Passover Week. Jesus has entered Jerusalem in triumph, but the acclamation he received just days before is deteriorating. The Jewish leaders who serve as enforcers for Roman rule have decided that Jesus has to die.

In that context, the story of Greeks wanting to meet Jesus seems like a sidebar event, not one to make the front page. But in truth, it is the real story. Jesus's mission is so large, and God's compassion for all the world is so great, that the container of the Jewish nation cannot hold it any longer. It spills over to the Gentiles.

This is good news and sobering news. Christ knows this outpouring of God's mercy requires his own death. He says, "Now is my soul troubled. And what shall I say? 'Father, save me from this hour'? But for this purpose I have come to this hour" (John 12:27 ESV).

Rather than explaining his coming crucifixion in this passage, Christ illustrates it. A seed has to be put in the ground and die, or else it will never be more than a seed. But if it dies, it reproduces itself. In the world of farming, one wheat kernel planted in the ground gives birth to between three hundred and five hundred new seeds. Jesus knows his death opens the door to life for countless others.

As Christ continues in John 12, he turns the focus to us: "In the same way, anyone who holds on to life just as it is destroys that life. But if you let it go, reckless in your love, you'll have it forever, real and eternal. If any of you wants to serve me, then follow me" (John 12:25–26 MSG).

Do we insist on holding onto our life as it has been? None of us has the power to keep our lives from changing. What would it be like to live a life of reckless love, following Jesus wherever he leads you?

Will you pray this night for your own willingness to follow Jesus into this chaotic and deteriorating world? Will you let die what he asks you to let die? Will you ask him to help you love like he loves? Will you give your fears and sadness to him?

Pray. We are up against more than we can solve on our own, but the mighty eternal God is with us.

Recommended Closing Prayer

Lord Jesus Christ, thank you for this time to praise your name and call upon you for help. There are so many hurting right now, not only where we live, but also around the world. Please bring your swift rescue to the sick, the sorrowful, and the wounded. Your salvation goes beyond temporary security and health. We know that there are places you want to reign in our lives, but we are reluctant to let you step in. We look to you for complete help and salvation. Deliver us from our desire to control our world. We look to you for complete and total rescue, and we declare you to be Lord of our lives. Please save us. Amen.

Holy Week Day 4
PHIL ASHEY

Reflect on Luke 22:39–53

Call to Prayer

Jesus faced a dark night and a dark hour in the garden of Gethsemane. He faced it as he so often did, in prayer, only this time he was laboring hard until he was sweating drops of blood. This detail alone speaks volumes about the spiritual, physical, and emotional burden that Jesus was carrying as he faced crucifixion. It is a vivid picture of the humanity of Jesus in the midst of his divine obedience, almost coming apart at the seams. Here, darkness fell. Jesus faced anxiety and fear, dread of his impending crucifixion, grief, weariness, friends letting him down in his hour of need, betrayal, loss, and the temptation to take a swing and fight back.

How do we pray when the darkness descends and we cannot see the light or the life on the other side? Gethsemane may come to us as an unwelcome diagnosis of a life-threatening disease, the loss of a job, betrayal by a friend, or some other grievous loss. What can we learn from Jesus about to how to face such deep difficulty?

Jesus entered this hour of utter darkness in a place that was familiar to him—a place of prayer. When the darkness falls for us, we pray as Jesus did, not allowing the crisis to consume us, as it did the disciples, but rather allowing it to drive us to our knees. Like Jesus, we face both the facts before us ("Father, if you are willing, take this cup from me" [Luke 22:42 NIV]) and our feelings ("And being in anguish he prayed more earnestly" [Luke 22:44 NIV]). The facts and our feelings may be desperate, but we give voice to both *in prayer* just as Jesus did.

Only God could show Jesus the way forward through the onslaught of hell itself. Jesus did not surrender or submit to the reign of darkness. Rather, he surrendered and submitted to his Father: "Father, if you are willing, take this cup from me; yet not my will, but yours be done" (Luke 22:42 NIV).

Are you ready to pray as simply and as intimately as Jesus prayed: "Father, what do you want?" Are you ready and willing to surrender yourself to the path the Father has set down before you? Are you ready to continue to entrust yourself to the Father just as Jesus did and to receive the same strength he received from heaven itself?

Recommended Closing Prayer

> Dear Lord and Savior Jesus Christ: I hold up all my weakness to your strength, my failure to your faithfulness, my sinfulness to your perfection, my loneliness to your compassion, my little pains to your great agony on the Cross. I pray that you will cleanse me. Strengthen me, guide me so that in all ways my life may be lived as you would have it lived, without cowardice and for you alone. Show me how to live in true humility, true contrition and true love. Amen.
>
> *(Anglican Church in North America Book of Common Prayer)*

Holy Week Day 5
(Maundy Thursday)

PHIL ASHEY

Reflect on Luke 22:54–62

Call to Prayer

Peter failed. After following Jesus very closely for three years, he now began following Jesus at a distance. Under peer pressure, physical distance gave way to emotional distance, emotional distance gave way to emphatic denial, and that denial finally gave way to cursing and swearing (Matthew 26:74). When Jesus turned at that final denial and looked straight at Peter, all Peter could remember were Jesus's words, "You will disown me" (Matthew 26:34 NIV). In that moment, Peter realized he was a total disappointment.

How do we pray when we embrace our failures, our following Jesus at a distance, and the conviction that we, too, have denied him in word and deed?

We remember that "weeping may stay for the night, but rejoicing comes in the morning" (Psalm 30:5 NIV). There is another side to failure: it's called grace and forgiveness, redemption and restoration, hope and a future in Christ alone. We remember that Jesus had many more words for Peter than "You will disown me." Jesus prepared Peter for the sifting he was about to experience by Satan, the loss of his faith, and the restoration of his leadership (Luke 22:31–32). Knowing Peter's heart, Jesus then did restore him (John 21:1–14) in a threefold consecration, redeeming each one of Peter's denials. In Acts 2, we see a Peter not only restored and redeemed but also filled with the Holy Spirit and proclaiming Christ faithfully to all the nations.

The resurrection of Jesus Christ vindicated every promise Jesus ever made to Peter and every promise he makes to you and me, so that we too can live with hope on the other side of our failures. Let the story of Peter's denial and restoration open your eyes to the redemption and restoration Christ has for all of us through his resurrection power. Let us pray with thanksgiving as Peter did (1 Peter 1:3–5).

Recommended Closing Prayer

Almighty God and Father, we praise you for sending your Son Jesus Christ to die on the cross for all our sins. By your great mercy, we have been born anew to a living hope through the resurrection of Jesus Christ from the dead. By your Holy Spirit, strengthen our faith so that in this life we may possess the fullness of that living hope and that in the life to come we may possess our imperishable, undefiled, and unfading inheritance in Christ. Through him who reigns with you and the Holy Spirit, one God, now and forever! Amen.
(Adapted from 1 Peter 1:3–5 NIV)

Holy Week Day 6
(Good Friday)

PHIL ASHEY

Reflect on Luke 23:1–25

Call to Prayer

We possess a natural human need to have the last word. Have you noticed how often online comments degenerate into arguments that are never-ending (until a moderator shuts them down) because every person feels the need to get in the last word on the matter at hand?

In this passage, Jesus surrenders his right to have the last word. Politics, personalities, and unjust legal proceedings swirled about him. Herod plied him with many questions, "but Jesus gave him no answer" (Luke 23:9 NIV). Pilate questioned him again and again, and when asked, "Are you the King of the Jews?" Jesus barely replied, "You have said so" (Luke 23:3 NIV). Jesus was assaulted by false and vehement accusations, personal ridicule and mocking, and eventually, shouts of "Crucify him!" (Luke 23:21 NIV) that overpowered the evidence of his innocence. Jesus did not defend himself. "When they hurled their insults at him, he did not retaliate; when he suffered he made no threats. Instead, he entrusted himself to him who judges justly" (1 Peter 2:23 NIV).

Through Christ, God's supreme act of love for you and me was to suffer a gross miscarriage of justice *silently,* surrendering his right to have the last word. Yes, we know the end of the story—that in Christ and his resurrection, God still has the last word. But in *this* moment Jesus manifests God's love for the world in silence, surrendering his right to have the last word this side of the cross and suffering the greatest injustice of all.

Following Jesus means that we will also "share his sufferings" (Philippians 3:10 ESV). Is God calling you in Christ to exercise that discipline of silence, just as Jesus did, in the face of criticism, a false accusation, or even gross injustice? How will you pray as you share in the fellowship of Jesus's silence?

Recommended Closing Prayer

> Almighty God, whose most dear Son went not up to joy but first he suffered pain, and entered not into glory before he was crucified: Mercifully grant that we, walking in the way of the Cross, may find it none other than the way of life and peace; through Jesus Christ your Son our Lord. Amen.
> *(Anglican Church in North America Book of Common Prayer)*

Holy Week Day 7
(Holy Saturday)

PHIL ASHEY

Reflect on Luke 23:26–49

Call to Prayer

Imagine your last dying declaration. What would you choose to say? A goodbye to loved ones? a blessing upon them? an expression of awe at the horizon of heaven that you are now approaching?

Jesus's final word from the cross was simply the summation of the way he lived his whole life. The breakers of death are about to roll over him. He is so near death that he is no longer attentive to anything but his own Spirit. He is not preaching. He is not trying to convince anyone. These words utter his heart: they are between Jesus and the Father alone.

These words are a prayer from Psalm 31:5, which every Jewish mother taught her little boy to pray before drifting off to sleep. But Jesus added something to it, one little word: *Abba*, meaning father. "Father, into your hands I commit my spirit" (Luke 23:46 NIV). In the midst of his abandonment, Jesus speaks this personal, intimate prayer from his heart to the Father. *Hell itself could not invade that place!*

Jesus had a conviction that Father God was waiting for him with open arms. He trusted in the Father's goodness, in his plans, and in his wisdom, which dwarfed all fears of the unknown. He was able to let go, with a calm, voluntary, purposeful release of his life into the Father's hands. Finally, there was passion—not a feeble, whimpering surrender, but a great, loud, victorious embrace of the Father.

In his dying, Jesus's prayer, conviction, trust, letting go, and passion gives us a model for hoping in God for the breakthrough, wherever we may see it and need it. In reality we cannot fix, cure, or heal anyone or anything. Only God can do that. Is there someone in your life, perhaps even you yourself, who needs such healing? Is there something in your life that needs such a fix? Can you pray as Jesus did with a passionate trust in and abandonment to God for the breakthrough?

Recommended Closing Prayer

I am no longer my own, but thine. Put me to what thou wilt, rank me with whom thou wilt. Put me to doing, put me to suffering. Let me be employed by thee or laid aside for thee, exalted for thee or brought low for thee. Let me be full, let me be empty. Let me have all things, let me have nothing. I freely and heartily yield all things to thy pleasure and disposal. And now O glorious and blessed God, Father, Son and Holy Spirit, thou art mine and I am thine. So be it. And the covenant which I have made on earth, let it be ratified in Heaven. Amen. *(Anglican Church in North America Book of Common Prayer)*

Introduction to Easter

STEVEN E. BREEDLOVE

For the disciples who encountered Jesus between his resurrection and ascension, forty days likely felt far too quick. After his crucifixion and resurrection, there were so many questions to ask, and every moment with the risen Lord was precious! Yet fast-forward two thousand years, and Easter season seems incredibly long. How can we sustain resurrection joy for the seven weeks between Resurrection Sunday and Pentecost? If it is difficult to celebrate for twelve days at Christmas, how much more difficult is it to celebrate through the whole Easter season?

Perhaps this difficulty is partially the fault of our inability to prepare. When we skip Advent and Lent, we don't build the spiritual muscles necessary for a whole season of Christmas or Easter. In order for celebration to fit in to our souls, we need preparation. The celebration will always be in proportion to the depth of the preparation. This is why those Christian traditions that practice Lent most deeply also seem to celebrate Easter most richly.

But there is more going on. Keeping our eyes fixed on the resurrection—the first fruits of all things being made new, the testimony of our own future in Christ, the shattering of all that is evil and grievous in the world—is just hard to do! We run out of steam because what we are celebrating is at odds with what we experience in the world. Celebration will come easy in the new heavens and earth because our experience will be in accord with reality.

Yet we can still learn to pray in accord with Easter. From Easter to Pentecost, the resurrection can undergird our prayers. This is as straightforward as actually acknowledging the brokenness and death in the world, and stating to the Lord, "Yet this, too, is not your final word, for the resurrection is coming!" It is as simple as asking our risen King, "Would you raise me up in this struggle, this relationship, even as I wait for the day when death is swallowed up in victory?" For a season, we can devote ourselves to prayers that *assume that the corruptible will be made incorruptible, and the perishable made imperishable*, even if in our doubt we struggle to understand what this will finally mean.

Resurrection Sunday

PHIL ASHEY

Reflect on Luke 23:50–24:12

Call to Prayer

The last thing the women expected to find that morning was the stone rolled away from the tomb. They had seen his body laid in the tomb; now they were coming to anoint Jesus's body with the spices they had prepared. Their entire frame of reference was a collapse of faith in the face of his death. The huge heavy stone rolled across the tomb was a physical sign of the impossible situation they faced—Jesus was dead and decaying in that stone-cold tomb, and with him their hopes and dreams.

What impossible and uncontrollable reality are you facing in your life today—what burden too heavy to bear, what situation too impossible to move, what mistake or hurt so costly that it has entombed your hopes? What is out of control in your life—with your children, your health, your job, your finances? What habits are you trying to break but failing to do so, no matter how hard you try? What is it in your life that you'd like to change but you find yourself unable? Even with your best efforts, it's not working.

Listen to the good news Luke brings from resurrection morning! When everything seemed out of control, when a hope and a future seemed impossible, after hours and hours of living with powerlessness, these women were jolted out of the impossible by the rolled-away stone and the words of the angels:

"Why do you look for the living among the dead? He is not here: he has risen!" (Luke 24:5 NIV).

The resurrection of Jesus means that God has the power to roll away the impossibilities in our lives! As you pray, remember that the same resurrection power that raised Jesus from the dead is the power God offers us in Christ. It is the power Jesus promised his followers long before he died, when he said to them, "With man this is impossible, but not with God; all things are possible with God" (Mark 10:27 NIV).

Recommended Closing Prayer

Almighty God, I ask you to give me the spirit of wisdom and revelation so that I might know you better. I ask also that the eyes of my heart may be enlightened in order that I may know the hope to which you have called me, the riches of your glorious inheritance in the saints, and your incomparably great power for us who believe. May the same power that you exerted in raising Jesus from the dead be at work in my life, my family, my workplace, and my community, to roll away the impossibles so that Christ himself will be exalted as head over all. Through Jesus Christ our Lord, to whom, with you and the Holy Spirit, be all honor and glory now and forever. Amen. *(Adapted from Ephesians 1:15–22 NIV)*

Easter Week Day 2, Monday
SALLY BREEDLOVE

Reflect on Revelation 21:1–8

Call to Prayer

The resurrection of Jesus has broken apart the old inevitable cycle of death. That very first Easter evening, the resurrected Christ made himself visible and recognizable to Mary, to his friends walking the Emmaus road, and to his locked-in-a-room-in-fear disciples.

And now it is Easter Monday, a day to breathe a sigh of relief. Christians sometimes call this Monday "the eighth day," a reminder that we no longer live in the old creation with its seven days repeating themselves again and again. We live instead in the new order.

In times like ours, this new order of reality may often seem dim. The world is still broken by sin. We still suffer. Life is not as it should be. But while these things are true, they are not all that is or will be.

The real and ultimate truth is the future that Revelation 21 paints. The earth is remade and restored, and the barrier between heaven and earth is removed.

Will you choose to live as an eighth-day person in a world staggering with troubles? The promises God has given us are real. Will you learn them by heart and not just with your head?

No matter how deeply death and grief has touched you, the eighth day has arrived. Will you accept both—the reality of the world you live in and the goodness of Christ's coming reign on earth?

As you pray, take time to speak aloud what you most look forward to in that eighth-day world. Pray in thanksgiving for what is already true and what will one day arrive in fullness.

Pray for those who grieve. Pray that alongside their grief, they may experience a sure sense of the hope that lies ahead. Pray they are comforted and strengthened by the risen Christ.

Recommended Closing Prayer

This is the day that the Lord has made. We will rejoice and be glad in it! O Lord, we thank you that we are alive now in a new world. We see the passing of sin and death, and we taste the fruit of Christ's resurrection. We are hurting and we lament as we behold the toll of this world's falling away from you. Yet we rejoice as we rest, seeing how you have pursued us and will never let us go. Please comfort the afflicted. Give them tender relief and hope in your salvation. Preserve us and help us never to forget what you have already done. Amen.

Easter Week Day 3, Tuesday

SALLY BREEDLOVE

Reflect on Luke 24:15–32

Call to Prayer

It's Eastertide, seven weeks of joy spilling out until Pentecost. Good news has come, Christ died to atone for all sin, and God has raised him from the dead. Life has the final word.

We know the risen Jesus is more real than our current circumstances. Still, we long for glimpses of his presence as we walk through life, particularly through hardship. We need assurance that we are not alone and that he is with us.

What can we learn from those followers of Jesus who walked that road to Emmaus? What habits of the heart and what choices shaped their ability to recognize him?

The two on that road were honest. They let their confusion and grief speak. They wondered about the things Jesus had said and what the women who went to the tomb meant. They didn't run from what they were experiencing.

Are you willing to tell the truth about your own confusion, frustration, and fears? Will you turn away from the temptation to fill hard times with endless distractions? A plasticized Christianity of perfect belief will not stand the test of trial. A distracted life will reap no harvest from what you endure.

Second, these two listened to the scripture and to the stranger with new ears. They didn't assume they already knew the answers. God wants us to turn to him and turn to his Word. He wants our humility and our willingness to be taught. Will you admit you don't know everything? Will you ponder? Are you willing to listen and obey?

Finally, these two welcomed the stranger. Like Mary, who was willing to ask the gardener for help, the Emmaus couple turned to a stranger on the road with them. Are you willing to be open to those around you and to see the presence of Christ in unexpected people?

Pray for yourself. Pray you will let go of your presumptions. Pray for the humility to be honest, to listen to the Word with new ears, and to receive the stranger. Pray you have eyes to see Christ. He is here.

Recommended Closing Prayer

O Lord, soften our hearts and open our ears to hear afresh the good news that you have truly conquered the grave. May your name be glorified above all names as you are our worthy God and King. Please be at work in us. Show us how to love our neighbors in acts of service and steady prayer. You have provided us with true life through your son Jesus, and we trust in your leading and continued provision, now and forever. Amen.

Easter Week Day 4, Wednesday

SALLY BREEDLOVE

Reflect on Revelation 1:12–18

Call to Prayer

Does it seem to you as if good news hasn't made the headlines in a very long time? Perhaps on a personal level you've experienced blessings, but corporate good news? It can feel as though it doesn't exist.

But at the birth of Christ, we discover extravagant promise after extravagant promise declared by people and angels: a brilliant future was in store where longings would be met, mercy poured out, the strong shamed, the downtrodden exalted, and those sitting in fear and the shadow of death visited by the sunrise from on high. Those promises jumbled together, they were so plentiful. Perhaps they are best summed up in the words the angles gave the shepherds the night Christ was born: Good news of great joy for all people.

And yet, for the thirty-something years of Jesus's life, corporate good news was still scarce. Yes, Jesus healed, raised some from the dead, released others from demonic bondage, extended forgiveness, calmed storms, and fed thousands. But none of that touched everyone, and none of it lasted. And then he was crucified. It was over.

Except it wasn't. The promises had taken root. We are in Eastertide, celebrating Jesus's resurrection. The good news of great joy for all people has been accomplished. Death no longer rules; the indestructible life of Jesus saves us to the uttermost.

The Lamb who was slain and who now lives forever as the eternal Son at the Father's right hand has met our deepest longing with extravagant abundance. He is the First and the Last. He is the Living

One; he was dead, and now look, he is alive forever and ever! He invites you to trust him. Will you do that? Let your prayers this night be of praise, adoration, and thanksgiving.

Recommended Closing Prayer

Our heavenly Father, we praise your name! You have caused us to be born again to a living hope by the resurrection of Jesus Christ from the dead. For surely we were once dead—our hearts were barren, our sin was great, our betrayal of you was undeniable. Yet you took upon yourself our weakness and treason, and in your tender mercy from on high you gave us your only begotten Son. And so now we pray as did your servant Simeon. Sovereign Lord, you may now dismiss your servant in peace. For my eyes have seen your salvation, which you have prepared in the sight of all nations: a light for revelation to the Gentiles and the glory of your people Israel. Amen. Hallelujah.

Easter Week Day 5, Thursday

SALLY BREEDLOVE

Reflect on 1 Thessalonians 2:17 and 2 Corinthians 4:6

Call to Prayer

Paul missed his friends in Thessalonica. Hearing they were doing well wasn't enough for him.

We have always longed for embodied life with others and for tangible companionship. Someone dear to us dies, and as the person's face grows dim in our minds, we grieve. Once again. It is not just the particulars of the person's appearance we long for; we could go look at a picture for that. What we long for is the person's presence.

In some mysterious way, we know that faces communicate the very presence of someone. Face and presence are inextricably linked.

In the Old Testament, God is sometimes called "the Presence," and the Hebrew words for presence and face are the same. Moses met with God in person, face-to-face, as a friend meets with a friend (Exodus 33:11).

It is Eastertide. Christ has risen indeed. He was once again present with his friends. He ate, walked, and talked with them. He prepared breakfast for them. They saw his face, and he saw theirs. They experienced each other's presence.

Who do you wish you could see face-to-face? Do you have family who live far away? a friend who has died? Or perhaps there is someone whom you are estranged from and you long to see this individual in person and make things right.

We long for in-person connection. Receive that longing as a gift. You were made for it. Pour out your heart to God this night. Tell him the ones you long to see. Pray for those people.

Then pause again. One day you will see Jesus face-to-face, as Paul declares in 1 Corinthians 13:12. Death does not have the final word. Sit in awe with the truth that Christ was indeed raised from the dead and that one day we too will have new bodies. Pray that your longing for the full presence of Jesus and your longing for that day will grow within you.

Recommended Closing Prayer

O Lord Jesus Christ, we rejoice in your victory over death! You live and reign, and by the power of the Holy Spirit you are with each of us. By your Spirit, we are together with those who are united in you. Please be with those who are living alone or are cut off from loved ones. For those who carry great burdens, join them in carrying those yokes and bring them peace. We live in your resurrection world. As the old fades away, may we see your new creation. Father, may we catch glimpses of the face of your Son Jesus and know his presence in our hearts. Amen.

Easter Week Day 6, Friday

ELIZABETH GATEWOOD

Reflect on Hosea 2:16–23

Call to Prayer

God is a relentless lover. He is a lover without what we would call "good boundaries."

In the book of Hosea, God commands Hosea to bind himself in faithfulness to an unfaithful woman as a living embodiment of God's covenantal relationship with Israel. Despite Israel's repeated unfaithfulness, God relentlessly pursues her in covenantal love.

As it turns out, each of us is the unfaithful lover. As Gentiles, we are grafted into Israel's story. God has extended Israel's covenantal promises to us who are in Christ. And, as it turns out, we show just the sort of scattered unfaithfulness that this woman did to Hosea and that Israel did to God. We Christians need just as much of God's unyielding, relentless love and mercy.

The unfaithful woman seeks to secure her basic provisions (bread, water, clothing, fuel) from immoral work (Hosea 2:5). She is offered marriage to a faithful man who would provide for her. Yet she fills her life with idolatry, sin, and anxious striving for her basic provisions, securing them by dubious means.

The woman seeks to impress others, pursuing attention and fame. She "adorned herself with her ring and jewelry, and went after her lovers and forgot me" (Hosea 2:13 ESV). She mocks her husband's fidelity by seductively parading herself.

We find in her life an uncomfortable resonance with our own lives. We often forget that our basic provisions come not from our striving or work, but from God's faithfulness. Further, we are anxious to refine our reputations, craft our brands, and become respected in our fields of work. Fame and attention are our idols, and we dress ourselves up for social media. But to put it bluntly, we forget God.

Yet despite the woman's unfaithfulness, Hosea is faithful. Despite Israel's unfaithfulness, God binds himself in covenantal love.

And despite our unfaithfulness, forgetfulness, and idolatry, God is relentlessly faithful.

As you pray, thank God for his faithful pursuit of you. Ask God for illumination to see your own waywardness of body, mind, and heart. The poem-prayer of John Donne is an apt one, filled with evocative imagery and a prayer for God to overcome our wayward loves.

Recommended Closing Prayer

> Batter my heart, three-person'd God, for you
> As yet but knock, breathe, shine, and seek to mend;
> That I may rise and stand, o'erthrow me, and bend
> Your force to break, blow, burn, and make me new.
> I, like an usurp'd town to another due,
> Labor to admit you, but oh, to no end;
> Reason, your viceroy in me, me should defend,
> But is captiv'd, and proves weak or untrue.
> Yet dearly I love you, and would be lov'd fain,
> But am betroth'd unto your enemy;
> Divorce me, untie or break that knot again,
> Take me to you, imprison me, for I,
> Except you enthrall me, never shall be free,
> Nor ever chaste, except you ravish me. Amen.
> ("Batter My Heart, Three-Person'd God" by John Donne)

Eastertide Day 7, Saturday
ELIZABETH GATEWOOD

Reflect on Hosea 11

Call to Prayer

We might say that parenting is a thankless job, but perhaps a more apt description is that it is a hidden job. What we parents do each day is to provide tender and proactive care in a thousand small and unnoticed ways.

We make sure there is milk in the fridge for morning cereal. We put the towels in the right spot so they're ready after a bath. We pick up the discarded toys so they're not broken or lost. We schedule the well-child visits and the dentist appointments. We remember to order the spring clothes and the sun hats and the sunscreen.

These small things add up to the tender care that allows a child to flourish.

In Hosea 11, God is the parent and Israel the child. God has tenderly cared for Israel. He's called Israel out of Egypt—a rescuing from bondage that prefigures the infant Christ's sojourn to seek protection in Egypt. He has taught Israel to walk. He has given Israel laws for their flourishing and protection—cords of kindness and bands of love.

And Israel is the child who neither notices God nor thanks him for his provision and nurture. This is a child who is bent on turning away from God.

Yet the mercy and love of God swell and crest like waves, overcoming his anger. He simply cannot punish or abandon Israel as they deserve. His love pours forth in a roar full of emotion, righteousness, love, anger, and invitation all at once, a roar that will be familiar to any "mama bear" who fiercely loves her children.

God will not allow the destructive bent of his children to be the final word. He will bring them home and redeem them. He will be faithful even when his children are not.

As you pray, consider the places where you are tempted to keep score and give up loving. Ask for God's mighty power to wash over you so that you might participate in his relentless love. His love is not overwhelmed or canceled by our actions. Consider also the places where you feel beyond the reach of the greatness of God's love. Imagine his love overpowering you and surrounding you.

Recommended Closing Prayer

God, thank you for your hidden love. You have sustained us in a thousand ways that we neither see nor acknowledge. We thank you for life and breath, for the blessings of family and friends, and for the sustenance and shelter that you have provided. Thank you also for your relentless pursuit of us. We can't grasp the wonder that you have been loving and pursuing us since the day we were born. We confess that we are wayward children, bent on idolatry, which leads to destruction. We are forgetful and capricious. And we have trouble believing that we are worth your time and attention. Help us to rest in our belovedness. Amen.

Second Sunday of Easter, Day 8

ELIZABETH GATEWOOD

Reflect on Hosea 14

Call to Prayer

God's love and mercy have the last word. Hosea does not mince words about the depth or severity of Israel's sin. And he doesn't blunt the force or power of God's anger. Yet the book of Hosea ends on a hopeful note with God's promise to heal and bless.

In chapter 14, we have a prayer and a vision. Both are instructive for us.

First, God gives his people a prayer to pray. "Take words with you" in your return to the Lord (Hosea 14:2 NIV). Hosea seems to know that sometimes we grasp for language, not even sure what we should say to or ask of God. In this prayer, the people are to ask for his forgiveness. Then they are to name their idols. For Israel, these idols are trust in foreign might and the gods they've made by their own creativity and skill. And finally, they are to proclaim to themselves and one another that in God the fatherless will find compassion.

Second, God gives his people a vision. Depending on your climate, the imagery may not grab your imagination or stir your senses. Hosea mentions six different plants: the lily, the cedar of Lebanon, the olive tree, grain, a grapevine, and a juniper. Israel will again flourish as do these plants in full health and bloom, offering beauty, shade, nourishment, and fragrance. The grace of God, like dew, will saturate them.

Call to your mind what spring is like as it renews our sense of the goodness of God. Purple coneflowers are lush in the midst of their green bunches of leaves. Fragile columbine flowers bloom. The naked limbs of trees morph into the shelter and shade of new oak and maple and dogwood leaves. The shy, potent smell of nicotiana flowers fills the evening air. Zinnias and sunflowers offer summer color. And gardens flourish—tomatoes, beans, and fragrant herbs abound.

What if we were to see the lush abundance of this blooming as an image of God's present and future work in us? God's dew will rest upon us, and we will flourish as these plants do in the glorious early summer months.

As you pray, follow the structure of Hosea's prayer: confession and plea for forgiveness, naming of idols, proclamation of God's faithfulness. And imagine God's dew of grace resting upon you and bringing fruitfulness and healing to your life.

Recommended Closing Prayer

God, it's unimaginable that we who are so wayward and forgetful, so idolatrous and doubtful, should flourish like those plants. We feel dried up and fruitless. So we ask:

Forgive all our sins, specifically, _____.

Our idols and the creations of our skilled hands and minds cannot save us or fulfill us, specifically, _____.

In you the fatherless find compassion.

Lord, we long to be fruitful, healthy, and whole. We marvel at your faithfulness and your commitment to us. Soak us with the dew of your grace and renew your life in us. Amen.

Eastertide Day 9

MADISON PERRY

Reflect on Luke 24:36–43, 24:50–53

Call to Prayer

This is the end of Luke's Gospel. The most important event in history has occurred: Jesus has been resurrected from the dead.

If this were a story written by one of us, Jesus would immediately assume power. Justice would roll down. History would accelerate to its end. Peace and prosperity would ensue.

Yet, the revolution we would expect to follow doesn't explode into motion. After conquering the grave, Jesus encounters his disciples in very gentle ways. He doesn't demand apologies or cow them by a revelation of his glory and splendor. He approaches them and waits for them to understand. When they are troubled, he shows them his scars, wrought for them. He notes that he is hungry and asks for food. And then without warning, Jesus "parted from them and was carried up into heaven …. And they worshiped him and returned to Jerusalem with great joy, and were continually in the temple blessing God" (Luke 24:51, 24:52 ESV).

Instead of full resolution, we are given relational reconciliation, the sharing of food, and the worship of God. These are the crucial things we need to prioritize.

God does not need us for his revolution—and his revolution has not paused. Jesus reigns, even now in the midst of our unresolved pain and questions, and will reign forever. What a privilege that by the Holy Spirit we can be drawn into heavenly worship.

So now, wherever you are, turn to God in praise. "Holy, holy, holy is the Lord of hosts; the whole earth is full of his glory!" (Isaiah 6:3 ESV). Proclaim this to God several times. As you do so, you edge into eternity. Ask him that his kingdom would come and his will would be done on earth as it is in heaven. Trust that there will be earthly resolution. We have known Christ's resurrection life, and one day it will fill our bodies and brokenness to the brim. If you do not feel joy, consider praising God until you sense a measure of peace.

Praise the Lord, my soul.
Lord my God, you are very great;
you are clothed with splendor and majesty.
The Lord wraps himself in light as with a garment;
he stretches out the heavens like a tent
and lays the beams of his upper chambers on their waters.
He makes the clouds his chariot
and rides on the wings of the wind.
He makes winds his messengers,
flames of fire his servants …
May the glory of the Lord endure forever;
may the Lord rejoice in his works—
Amen.
(Psalm 104:1–4, 104:31 NIV)

Eastertide Day 10

BRANDON WALSH

Reflect on Psalm 46:4–11

Call to Prayer

"Be still." These are words that every parent knows all too well! Little kids fidget, squirm, and make noises all the time. Knees bounce under the table, fingers tap on car windows, and chairs rock back and forth at just the moment when the noise is most noticeable.

We are not so different from children. Sure, at some point we learn a bit of impulse control. We stop fidgeting quite so much, or we develop quieter and less distracting ways to do it. All the while, beneath a more presentable exterior, we are squirming on the inside. Our brains flit from thing to thing, looking for distraction. Our smartphones throw gasoline on this fire. The distraction of technology may make our restlessness worse, but in truth, our nervous anxiety comes from a deeper root.

In Psalm 46:10, the Lord invites us, "Be still and know that I am God" (NIV).

Be. Still.

This psalm paints a picture of the world in tumult. It is a world giving way to chaos, to uncreation, where the mountains are thrown into the very heart of the sea. Mountains are firm and reliable; the sea, capricious and strange. So when mountains are hurled into the sea, things have gone awry. But even in moments when the world seems least peaceful and reliable, we can find our full refuge in God.

The psalm reassures us that a river runs through the city of God, the city where the Most High dwells. But in truth, there is presently no river in Jerusalem! The psalm refers to a future hope, seen in Ezekiel 47 and Revelation 22, when a river will pour out from the temple of God and restore all of creation.

When the waves crash and the earth shakes, when pandemic isolates and politics divide, we need to be still, to turn away from the taunting voices of distraction and hysteria, and to return to the living waters of God. Only in such a place will the fidgeting of our souls find its rest.

That peace is offered today as well, the psalmist reassures us. As you pray, practice living into the invitation of this psalm. Be still. Be still and know that the Lord is God. In him all things hold together and find their completion. If you belong to Jesus, the Spirit will make rivers of living water flow through your heart.

Recommended Closing Prayer

Almighty Father, make us still—still enough to feel your breath on our faces and in our lungs. Make us still enough for you to tame the raging waters within us and around us. Make us still enough to know you even as we are fully known by you. From the throne of your Son, true waters flow into your people by your Holy Spirit. May we be still enough to drink, still enough to bear fruit in every season. In the name of Jesus. Amen.

Eastertide Day 11

BRANDON WALSH

Reflect on Psalm 63

Call to Prayer

Our hunger or our satisfaction shapes how we see the things around us.

Psalm 63:1, 63:3 reads, "O God, you are my God; earnestly I seek you; my soul thirsts for you; my flesh faints for you, as in a dry and weary land where there is no water .... Because your steadfast love is better than life, my lips will praise you" (ESV).

Sometimes we read a text like this and think, *Wow, I wish I felt that way about God.* But what if there is another way to read these words? What if these words give us a clue about what we are really hungry for? What if these words in Psalm 63 express the state of our souls more clearly than we often feel or can articulate? What if it's just a fact that "our soul thirsts for God" and that our flesh "faints for [him]" (Psalm 63:1, 63:3 ESV)?

We might be living our whole lives hungry for something that we can't quite name or get to, which results in our going through life as if it is a hungry trip to the grocery store. We are forever seeing things with hungry and thirsty eyes.

We enter the world doing hungry math. Our hearts are restless, hungry, thirsty, and faint until we find our rest and satisfaction in the Lord.

As you pray, wonder about your own deep hunger. Confess to God your longing for him.

Recommended Closing Prayer

> O God, of your goodness, give me yourself, for you are enough for me. I can ask for nothing less that is completely to your honor, and if I do ask anything less, I shall always be in want. Only in you I have all. Amen.
> *(Julian of Norwich)*

Eastertide Day 12

Reflect on Psalm 67

Call to Prayer

A tension exists throughout the Old Testament between the elect people of God and God's divine purpose for all the nations. In Abraham all the nations will be blessed. But Abraham has to carry that promise and be the avenue through which the particular blessings of God flow.

In Psalm 67, the psalmist desires election, the blessings and graciousness of the Lord, not simply for Israel, but for the ultimate purposes of God: that Yahweh might be known throughout the whole world and that the nations might sing and be glad. The blessings of God for the people of Israel have a purpose beyond the well-being of his people. It is a blessing for the sake of the world.

In the same way, the Lord shares his Spirit abundantly with us. We pray that the Lord might turn his face toward us and bless us. However, all the blessings we receive are not for us alone, but for the sake of the world. The vocation, the calling, of Israel was to be a light to the nations, a place where peoples look and see something different. Jesus continues that image in the Sermon on the Mount, calling us to be a city on a hill, salt and light in the world.

Beyond anything else, Christ's greatest gift to the church is himself, his own life, which is the light of humankind. In Christ the Lord does turn his face toward us as he invites us to go forth into all the world both to proclaim and to *be* that good news. The gift of Christ and the Holy Spirit is not simply a balm to make us feel better, but oil in our lamps to light the way for others.

As you pray, pray that your life might be a conduit of blessing to others.

Recommended Closing Prayer

O God, our heavenly Father, you manifested your love by sending your only-begotten Son into the world, that all might live through him: Pour out your Spirit on your Church, that we may fulfill his command to preach the Gospel to all people. Send forth laborers into your harvest; defend them in all dangers and temptations; and hasten the time when the fullness of the Gentiles shall be gathered in, and faithful Israel shall be saved; through your Son Jesus Christ our Lord. Amen.

(Anglican Church in North America Book of Common Prayer)

Eastertide Day 13

ELIZABETH GATEWOOD

Reflect on Ephesians 1:1–14

Call to Prayer

The beginning of Paul's letter to the Ephesians reads like a child excitedly recounting the gifts she received on Christmas morning. It feels like one run-on sentence, like what would spill out of a child's mouth on this most hallowed day of gift giving and materialism. "And then I got this, and then I got this! And then my parents even gave me this! And then I got this and this and—oh wait, I forgot to tell you about *this*!"

Paul can hardly get past his greeting to the church at Ephesus before he pours forth with a story of who God is, what God has given us, and who we are in Christ.

What would it look like to be so rooted in God's story and so saturated in thankfulness that we simply could not help joyfully recounting a list of all the rich blessings that God has given us?

Too often we forget. We are distracted by our current ailments, however legitimate, or by the confining boundaries of a particular situation, the pain of a failing relationship, or the longing for a child, or a new job, or a path out of depression, or a friend. We come to God not with joyful remembrance but with tired, and sometimes faithless and cynical, prayers.

But Paul brings us back to God's big story. And here is what is gloriously true for those of us who are in Christ. We are:

- blessed with every spiritual blessing in Christ;
- chosen before the creation of the world;
- predestined for adoption to sonship as God's children;
- freely lavished with grace;
- forgiven of our sins;
- redeemed by God's blood;
- marked with the seal of the Holy Spirit.

Perhaps this seems real to you today. Perhaps it doesn't. Or perhaps, even if it is real, it seems irrelevant to your actual problems.

As you pray tonight, consider this list. Which gift stirs you? Which leaves you with questions? Which do you struggle to believe God has given you? Which do you simply forget?

Recommended Closing Prayer

Pray aloud the words from Ephesians 1:3–14, substituting *I* or *me* for *we* and *us*, respectively.

Eastertide Day 14

ELIZABETH GATEWOOD

Reflect on Ephesians 1:15–23

Call to Prayer

There are certain pockets of Christianity across space and time that have tended toward envisioning God as muscular, victorious, conquering. Some have wielded the name of Jesus as a weapon to accomplish their own ends and perhaps had an overrealized expectation of what God would choose to accomplish in certain present circumstances, be they political, financial, or otherwise.

But there are also certain pockets of Christianity across space and time that have so domesticated God that they hardly expect anything of him anymore. God is reduced to a flat figure in our "moralistic therapeutic deism," a vague and only vaguely comforting or significant figure in our spiritual imaginations.

What we see in Ephesians is something quite different, if we will slow down enough to parse what is going on in this tremendously long sentence of Paul's.

God has worked his power to raise Jesus from the dead and seat him at the right hand of the Father in the heavenly realms. Jesus is established as ruler of all times and places.

And catch the wild part: this same power of "immeasurable greatness" (Ephesians 1:19 ESV) is at work in us who believe in Jesus. This is not a power that we can wield for our own ends. It's also not a power that we can domesticate or deny. God's power is *power itself.* And this power is at work in you. This power is at work in me.

This power isn't only or primarily at work when we *feel* holy: at church, or when doing something explicitly Christian such as tithing, feeding the poor, sharing the gospel, or disciplining our children. This power is at work in our *ordinary* lives—at the kitchen sink, on the webcam, and on the T-ball field. God's Spirit indwells us and his power is in us—made perfect, in fact, in our very weakness.

As you pray, consider whether you tend toward claiming God's power for your own ends or denying and forgetting that God is powerful. Ask God to reveal his power and presence in the midst of your ordinary life.

Recommended Closing Prayer

God, what a surprise it is that you would show up in the midst of our ordinary lives. How incredible it is that your power is at work in us, the same power that raised Jesus from the dead! It feels too great, Lord, like a wind that is too strong. We aren't quite sure we believe that, and if it's true, we aren't quite sure what to do with it. Remind us that your power is never absent from your love. Remind us that your Holy Spirit enfolds us, empowers us, and indwells us. Give us a strong assurance of your power and presence. Let us submit to this power and to your loving embrace of us. Amen.

Third Sunday of Easter, Day 15

WILLA KANE

Reflect on Ephesians 2:1–8

Call to Prayer

At the doctor's, we dread a dire medical diagnosis. Here in his letter to the Ephesians, Paul delivers a different sort of diagnosis, one even direr: "dead in trespasses and sins."

We were spiritually dead and separated from the God who made us, unable to escape the many consequences of our sins.

In the face of such hopelessness, what could possibly happen?

"But God" (Ephesians 2:4 ESV; emphasis added).

They've been called the two most beautiful words in the Bible—our gospel prescription in two little words.

But God. But God stepped in. But God intervened. But God came after us. But God drew near to spiritually dead people and, because he loved us, made us alive together with Christ.

These two words were the pivot point at which everything changed. We were flatlined on the operating table, our hearts choked in spiritual death. But God, in his mercy and kindness, performed a complete heart transplant. We were hopeless, helpless, and alone. But God, rich in mercy, made us alive together with Christ!

As you pray, settle into these two words: "But God." Let them fill your mind, heart, and soul. Challenge the challenges you face with these words. Thank God for his great love for us, for his extravagant mercy, for the gift of kindness that promises us immeasurable riches in Christ. If our God has done all these things, how much more can we count on him to be with us in the night, during days that are hard, and on into eternity?

Recommended Closing Prayer

> Dear Lord and Savior Jesus Christ: I hold all my weakness to your strength, my failure to your faithfulness, my sinfulness to your perfection, my loneliness to your compassion, my little pains to your great agony on the Cross. I pray that you will cleanse me, strengthen me, guide me, so that is all ways my life may be lived as you would have it lived, without cowardice and for you alone. Show me how to live in true humility, true contrition, and true love. Amen.
>
> *(Anglican Church in North America Book of Common Prayer)*

Eastertide Day 16

WILLA KANE

Reflect on Ephesians 2:12–17

Call to Prayer

Paul loves to highlight the difference that Christ makes in our lives. Just a few verses earlier, he recalled how things used to be and rejoiced in how they are. Yes, we were dead in sin. But God is rich in mercy, and out of his great love, he has made us alive in Christ.

Paul begins with another impossible situation: the messy, insurmountable interpersonal divisions in our lives. "The dividing wall of hostility" (Ephesians 2:14 ESV) is such a good image illustrating how it feels to be separated from another person. When you are in conflict with other people or are divided by a vast array of differences, you may feel that the problem is impossible to overcome.

But the good news is that God has overcome for us. God himself has *demolished* the dividing wall of hostility. Jesus himself is our peace, even when all hope for reconciliation seems lost. Loving other people well is not just up to us. It's not even possible on our own. If we are in Christ, the walls that divide us have been torn down, and love pours out.

As you pray, pause and take some moments to look at your life with ruthless honesty. What relationships in your life need to be restored? Where is love in short supply? Where do walls still exist? Blessedly, there is a remedy. Open up your heart to God in confession, and come to the cross where love and mercy meet, where the love of Jesus pours down and out. Ask the one who has paid the price and made the way for your own reconciliation to pour out love and forgiveness through you.

Recommended Closing Prayer

O Lord, you have met me in mercy and love. You have not dealt with me as my sins deserve. As Jesus hung on the cross, he offered forgiveness to those who had not even asked for it. Help me this night to forgive the one I hold a grudge against. Teach me to love freely and generously. Thank you for the love of Jesus, which you long to pour into me and through me. Amen.

Eastertide Day 17

ELIZABETH GATEWOOD

Reflect on Ephesians 3:1–13

Call to Prayer

Paul has a clarity about his story and his vocation.

Paul has been given a particular grace and revelation from God. His particular vocation is to preach the gospel to the Gentiles, telling them that they've been included in God's kingdom and also telling them about the boundless riches of Christ. Paul sees himself as a messenger and participant in God's big story. He's spilling over with excitement as he describes God's big story in chapter 1, and now he simply gives the footnotes in Ephesians 3:9–12.

It might seem easy for us to grasp that someone like Paul has a clear calling and a place within God's big story. Paul, after all, is a colossal figure in the early church. Perhaps it's a harder leap for us to believe that God has given each of *us* a particular vocation and a particular place within

God's big story. Our lives feel ordinary, full of struggle, insignificant, pragmatically driven, speckled with failure, and plagued by suffering.

Yet Paul is very much like us. He persists in doing his work even though he feels unworthy to do it. He persists in doing his work even though his work is causing him to suffer.

What might we learn from looking to Paul as an ordinary person? He is a sinner and he struggles and suffers his way through ministry. Yet he persists in courageously and energetically doing the task that God has called him to do.

As you pray, consider what call God has placed on your life. Pray that God might clarify his will and encourage you in your vocation, regardless of what occupation happens to be yours at the moment. Meditate on Paul's story, on his sufferings, and on his courage.

Recommended Closing Prayer

God, it is difficult for us to believe that you have called us and equipped us. We feel so ordinary, and our days are filled with ordinary things: diapers and emails, car pool lines and meetings, paperwork and chores. Have you truly called each of us with a specific vocation and given us a particular role in your big story? We ask that you might encourage us by Paul's story. Equip us in the midst of our ordinary days to bring glory to you. Clarify that to which you have called each of us. And give us courage to persist in the midst of self-doubt, suffering, and failure. Amen.

Eastertide Day 18
ELIZABETH GATEWOOD

Reflect on Ephesians 3:14–21

Call to Prayer

As Paul prays for the Ephesians in chapter 3, he makes three references to God's power.

First, he prays that God's power would strengthen them so that Christ may dwell in their hearts through faith. Though this isn't a theological treatise on faith and free will, this passage seems to suggest that faith in Christ is a joint effort between the animating power of the Holy Spirit and an individual's will.

Second, Paul prays that the Ephesians would have the *power* to grasp the love of Christ. This is a love that is higher, wider, and deeper than they can imagine. And this is a love that surpasses knowledge. Paul spills over with joy and excitement about the *love* of God. He deeply desires for this budding church at Ephesus to grasp this love as fundamental to the gospel.

Third, Paul references God's power that is at work within us. He has made this point already in chapter 1: the same power that raised Jesus from the dead is at work in those who are in Christ. The astonishing reality is that we are animated by the same power that conquered death.

God is power! But God's power is worked out in *love*. It is not a power marked by greed, selfish gain, self-centeredness. God's power is marked by love. It takes the shape of the cross. It moves in the illuminating and empowering wind of the Holy Spirit.

As you pray, consider that the most powerful thing in the entire world is a power that is love-shaped. It is a power that moves toward you and me in self-sacrificial love and embrace. It is a power that brings life.

Recommended Closing Prayer

Let your ending prayer simply be Paul's words in Ephesians 3:14–21, substituting personal pronouns so that you are praying Paul's words for yourself.

Eastertide Day 19

GAYLE HEASLIP

Reflect on Ephesians 4:1–16

Call to Prayer

Looking at the world around us, and often the one within us, we see division, fragmentation. Our holy longing for wholeness is challenged by so very much brokenness. As we sit among the fragments of shattered dreams, do we dare to envision the healing presence of God's kingdom as a growing reality?

Our God has promised to bring what is broken into a singular wholeness and unity through Christ. We are mended through the one faith and one baptism into a oneness with the one God and Father of all. His is the unifying power; his is the mending love.

In his wisdom, the Lord has generously gifted his body on earth to those who serve to equip us for ministry in our wounded world. And in that preparation we are built up and grown in love so that we might reflect, right in the midst brokenness, the wholeness of the one who joins us and holds all things together.

Growth into maturity comes slowly within a Spirit-led transformation into Christlikeness. As we grow in the knowledge of the person of Christ, and as each of us inhabits our roles for the sake of others, the church grows into a fullness none of us can achieve alone.

As you go to prayer, pause and consider what is going on in your own heart. What do you imagine wholeness to look like in Christ's body on earth? Will you dare to trust the Lord to mend brokenness, heal wounds, and bring unity? Will you give yourself to his process to do so and live into your own maturity under the Spirit's tender and powerful leading? Will you do this in community?

Recommended Closing Prayer

Lord, may I be content with my place in your body on earth. May I be willing to lean on others for the support given by my brothers and sisters in the grace, love, and wisdom supplied by your overseeing love. May I boldly embrace the unifying, maturing work of the Spirit to bring us all into the whole measure of the fullness of Christ. Amen.

Eastertide Day 20

GAYLE HEASLIP

Reflect on Ephesians 4:17–32

Call to Prayer

"God is light, and in him is no darkness at all," John proclaims in 1 John 1:5 (ESV). Paul urges us in this passage from Ephesians to live as children of light, to be a mirror reflecting and a window revealing God our Father.

Living as children of the light means that we choose our way forward each day, always opening our hearts to the Lord. If we harden our hearts to him, we lose sensitivity to his presence and leading; our understanding becomes increasingly darkened until we become separated from the life of God.

Instead, we put off the old self of our darkened minds and put on the new self in Christ. For in Christ there is abundant light, light that makes clear to us what true righteousness and holiness looks like as we gaze on him whose life is the light of humankind shining in the darkness. We want to live continually in this bright new life that is his gift to us.

How difficult such daily choices can be, however. How easy to tear down others with our words, to hold bitterness, anger, and hatred in our hearts, to grieve the Holy Spirit. How easy to be self-centered instead of speaking to build others up and working with the intent to share with those in need.

Where do you find yourself in darkness today, separated from the light? What relationship cries out for the light of Christ's upbuilding love through your words, your other-oriented generosity, and your kindness and compassion that flow from a light-drenched heart? What prayer rises up from within you, beloved of God, for his light in place of darkness?

Pray that you will respond to God's invitation to you to live as a child of the light.

Recommended Closing Prayer

Lord, you know the places within me that lean toward darkness. How I long for your light to fill me! As I bring myself before you now, I freely choose to put off the old self and live in the light of your holy presence. At each intersection of choice tomorrow, strengthen me to choose again and again from a heart and mind surrendered to the light of your love. In so doing, may I discover flowing from me the loving words and actions that reveal you, Father of lights. Amen.

Eastertide Day 21

GAYLE HEASLIP

Reflect on Ephesians 5

Call to Prayer

Imagine a landscape drenched in an early spring sunshine that illuminates every meadow flower, every dew-kissed blade of grass. As you step into this sunny field, your fingertips graze the soft tips of new growth reaching for the light. Lifting your face to the sky, you stop and close your eyes, receiving a deep sense of warmth and well-being.

Such is the inheritance of God's beloved. Once we lived in darkness, bereft of light. Our hands groped before us, seeking a way forward. Our feet stumbled, seeking stability. Our minds were darkened and fearful.

Now we are light and walk as children of the light in Christ, full of glory. Our hearts are illuminated; our minds, cleared by this truth: he is, and we are his. We drink this truth in and taste its bright goodness and slaking satisfaction.

Where else but in this bright landscape would we long to dwell? What other path but this path of goodness and truth would so satisfy? As we embrace these desires from the inmost places of our hearts, we will discover, in the Lord's responsive affection for us, what pleases him, and we will come to understand what his will is for us so that we might follow this light always.

As you pray, ask the Lord to fill you with longing for his goodness and truth.

Recommended Closing Prayer

O God, enable us to walk in the light of your love. Amen.

Fourth Sunday of Easter, Day 22

GAYLE HEASLIP

Reflect on Ephesians 6:1–12

Call to Prayer

All is held in God's gaze, and every desire of the Lord is rooted in his nature to love. Though there is surely a great power differential between the Lord and his people, he relates to us only in love and exercises his authority for the sake of love. When we realize that all relationships— whether they are between children and parents, husbands and wives, or servants and masters—are also held within his loving desires for us, we may see them in a fresh way.

The knotted tensions of power within relationships can be loosened when we choose to serve the Lord's will to love others within each relationship. Yoked to him, we are invited to live in freedom from thinking in terms of one over and against another. What is more, the Lord promises that he will reward us for whatever good is done, no matter our position.

Such choosing does not come easily, and daily living in this choice requires strength beyond us, a power born of the Spirit. Be strong *in* the Lord and in *his* mighty power. To do this, we put on spiritual armor given to us through dependence on him. Then we can stand against the schemes of unseen spiritual evil and the machinations of a world that values utilization above honor. In his strength we can resist the external forces that work to frame relationships by power alone so that we are free to love in giving, not grabbing. In this will we bear witness to the Lord's overcoming love.

Pray that you will learn to love as God loves.

Recommended Closing Prayer

Father, teach me how to love. Amen.

Eastertide Day 23

SALLY BREEDLOVE

Reflect on Ephesians 6:13–18

Call to Prayer

Paul writes these words from prison. His circumstances urge us to ask: Can good come out of being so severely restricted? Can imprisonment be turned to blessing? The Bible tells stories that assure us it can be so. Joseph did excellent work for each person who kept him in bondage: the rich Potiphar, the head jailer, and even Pharaoh himself. The exiled Moses learned how to live in the desert and gained shepherding skills as he served his father-in-law for forty years as a herdsman. Daniel never got to go home; he spent his life at the beck and call of foreign kings. Jesus said no man ever born was greater than John the Baptist, but John's exit from prison was his beheading. Paul wrote much of the New Testament while in shackles.

How is the Spirit calling you to receive the restrictions that shape your own life right now? How is he inviting you to see your minutes and hours as a gift?

Any distress or restriction we face does not have to undo us. It can make us more deeply human if we let it. Paul urges us to let truth, righteousness, peace, faith, and salvation shape our lives. He reminds us that the scriptures and prayer give us the strength we need.

Ponder Paul's words here in Ephesians. How does God want to grow you so that you become stronger and wiser? How is he inviting you into new rhythms of loving and living?

Pray for yourself. Pray you will steward your time well. Pray you will embrace new disciplines for your life with God. Pray you will enter into new ways of being at rest. Pray you will see the opportunities right before you to love and to serve.

Recommended Closing Prayer

O Lord, I pray to you, alongside brothers and sisters around the globe. All good things come from you. Please pour into us truth, righteousness, peace, and salvation. Open our lips so that we may praise you and pray for others. Please let the world know of your salvation. Wake us all up to our sin and inadequacies. Fill the hungry; comfort the brokenhearted; and give rest to the weary. May you be praised in all things and at all times now and everywhere, our Rock and our Redeemer. Amen.

Eastertide Day 24

MADISON PERRY

Reflect on Psalm 20

Call to Prayer

This is the prayer of a people at war who are united behind their king. It would have been sung on the day of battle, starting with the people of Israel united behind King David. Today, we pray this with our eyes fixed on the Lord's Anointed One, Jesus Christ. Jesus is the focal point of the action in heaven and on earth. His battle against evil is the most important conflict. When we pray, "Now I know that the Lord saves his anointed" (Psalm 20:6 ESV), we understand that the resurrection is the best evidence that the Lord saves Christ.

Consider this: "May [God] grant you your heart's desire and fulfill all your plans!" (Psalm 20:4 ESV). If you were to read this out of context, no doubt you would take it differently. But in context, this verse doesn't refer to our desires, but to those of our King. Jesus similarly teaches his disciples to pray, "Your kingdom come, your will be done, on earth as it is in heaven" (Matthew 6:10 ESV).

How would it feel to pray this way? Our responses can vary, ranging from fear at our loss of control to sweet relief at no longer having to pretend to be a ruler. Do you resist praying this psalm, or is it like a song drifting to you from a land you would love to visit and remain in forever, the land where Christ rules?

Begin your time of prayer by worshipping God—Father, Son, and Holy Spirit. Call on the Lord for victory in your own battles, and ask that our Lord's kingdom would come. Plead for God's will to be done, not only in the world outside, but also in your own life.

Recommended Closing Prayer

Father, we are tempted to trust in everything but you. Give us the grace and strength to trust in your name alone, O Lord our God. Amen.

Eastertide Day 25
GAYLE HEASLIP

Reflect on 3 John

Call to Prayer

How wonderfully encouraging it must have been for Gaius, in the midst of deceiving philosophies and opposition, to receive a letter from John. The apostle has great joy in hearing about Gaius's faithfulness to the truth of the gospel and about his commitment to walking in the truth and doing what is good in the Lord's sight. Gaius is commended for the hospitality he offers to traveling evangelists who, though they are strangers to him, are received as those unified in the truth of Christ. They are each working toward the same goal of bringing eternal life to those who would receive it.

John also affirms Gaius by contrasting him with a prideful church leader who refuses to offer this hospitality. He cuts off those under his authority who do so and spreads malicious rumors about the elders set over area churches. He is divisive, impeding the gospel's freeing access to the kingdom of God.

What really matters is fidelity to the truth of the gospel, walking in this truth, and offering oneself to it in word and deed. Gaius can rest in the security that what he has done confirms that he belongs to the Lord, for the Lord is the Author of his good actions.

Have you experienced a time when your actions of faithfully walking in the truth of the gospel brought conflict into your life? God sees your faithfulness and commitment to do what is good, and he commends you for it. He affirms that your life of faith comes from him. You bring him great joy as you unite, offering whatever you can, with those who also bring the truth of Christ to others.

Today, will you receive his affirmation and offer yourself anew to serve this truth? If there is one who comes to mind who also follows faithfully, you might send a note of encouraging affirmation just as John did for Gaius.

Recommended Closing Prayer

Lord, I can wither under oppression, feel overwhelmed by competing worldviews, and draw back from engagement. Ah, but how generous you are, how unending your resources! You invite me to commit to the truth of the gospel, fully living in it with confident expectation of your great joy in me as I continue to do what is good. May I not draw back from opportunities to do good but freely give what has been given to me by your generous hand in service to the truth. Amen.

Eastertide Day 26

KARI WEST

Reflect on Philippians 1:3–11

Call to Prayer

Paul's consistent, joyful prayers over the Philippians stem from his confidence that God will finish what he has started. God is the one who planted the gospel deep within the Philippians. He is the one bringing forth fruit in them now, and he will grow them into perfected, matured believers at the day of Christ.

Is this your confidence when you pray for yourself and other believers?

God will be faithful to grow the seeds he has planted in us. We can pray with this same kind of joyful confidence in God's commitment to our wholeness, our flourishing, and our maturity as his people.

Paul goes on to say that he loves this church with the affection of Jesus Christ. Pause and consider: how often can you say that about other people in your life? Rather than feeling condemned over a perceived lack of Christlike love, see Paul's statement as an invitation. God can form us into people who love other people with the very love of Jesus! What was true for Paul can be true for you and me. We can know the deep, powerful love of Christ for fellow believers.

What does this deep love of Christ compel Paul to do? It compels him to pray the kind of rich, piercing, poignant prayer that we find in verses 9–11.

As you come before the Lord, read through these final verses again and ask that God will do this for you and others.

Recommended Closing Prayer

Father, please enable our love to abound more and more in knowledge and depth of insight, so that we may be able to discern what is best and may be pure and blameless for the day of Christ, filled with the fruit of righteousness that comes through Jesus Christ—to your glory and praise. Amen.

Eastertide Day 27

KARI WEST

Reflect on Philippians 1:12–18

Call to Prayer

Paul is in chains as he pens this letter to the church at Philippi. And yet he calls to mind reason after reason to rejoice. In the preceding verses, he is full of joy over the Philippians' partnership in the gospel and over God's commitment to continue his good work in them.

Here in these verses, we find that Paul rejoices that Christ is being honored through his imprisonment. Paul sees how his suffering is furthering the kingdom of God. He peers past his present difficulties to find a deeper purpose to what is happening to him.

All the prison guards know that Paul is in chains because of his commitment to Jesus. More and more believers are compelled to preach the gospel boldly because of Paul's faithful witness. And even though some are proclaiming the gospel from wrong motives, Paul still rejoices that the message of Christ is reaching farther and farther into the world.

What trials lie before you today? What difficulties are strewn across this season of your life? Will you come before the Lord and ask him to fill your mind and heart with reasons for rejoicing? Will you ask for the faith to peer past what you are experiencing and to hope in the deeper things that God promises to work in your life?

We aren't promised an easy road, but we are promised an ever-present helper. Call out to him and ask for the eyes of faith, for joy, and for a heart that treasures the gospel. Trust that he hears you. Trust that he cares. Trust that he will always do you good in the end.

Recommended Closing Prayer

As you end your time of prayer, speak the words of this beloved hymn aloud, and receive these promises from your heavenly Father:

> When through fiery trials your pathway shall lie
> My grace, all-sufficient, shall be your supply
> The flame shall not hurt you, I only design
> Your dross to consume and the gold to refine
> The soul that on Jesus has leaned for repose
> I will not, I will not desert to His foes
> That soul, though all hell should endeavor to shake
> I'll never, no never, no never forsake.
> ("How Firm a Foundation" by John Rippon)

Eastertide Day 28

KARI WEST

Reflect on Philippians 1:18b–26

Call to Prayer

What comes to mind when you think about death?

Can you even consider it, or does your mind quickly grasp hold of any fleeting distraction? Paul is imprisoned as he writes these words to the Philippians. It seems as though he's taken quite some time to contemplate the possibility of his imminent death. What is his conclusion?

It's a far better thing to die and be with Jesus in fullness.

How can he come to say something so remarkable, so counterintuitive? Death is the enemy, 1 Corinthians 15:26 reminds us. Death is the wage paid for sin. It is a fearful thing, a terrible thing. Anyone who has lost a loved one can feel the wrongness of death. No matter how many times it brushes our lives, it will always feel like a monstrous aberration.

The only thing that makes death bearable is our Savior standing on the other side of it, holding the keys to the grave.

And because he stands there, waiting to embrace us and draw us into the utter magnificence of his full presence, it is a far, far better thing to die.

Are you fearful of death? We worship the one who trampled that old enemy. It need not hold sway over you, beloved of Jesus. As you pray, ask our resurrected Lord for such a trust in his goodness, grace, and glory that you can say with Paul: to live is Christ, and to die is gain.

Recommended Closing Prayer

Lord Jesus, you are the Living One. You died, and now you are alive forever and ever! You hold the keys of death and Hades. We praise you, our resurrected King. Amen.

Fifth Sunday of Easter Day 29
KARI WEST

Reflect on Philippians 1:27–30

Call to Prayer

"Whatever happens" (Philippians 1:27 NIV) is quite the all-encompassing phrase. Paul seems to believe that through all our circumstances, our trials, our emotional upheavals, and our successes or failures, we can conduct ourselves in a manner worthy of the gospel.

How does that sit with you? Does that idea draw up disbelief, cynicism, or guilt in you? Does it feel like an impossible standard to reach? Take those feelings before the Lord.

The truth is, we can embrace these words of Paul as a promise. It is God who saves us, and it is God's power that works within us. If we offer up our lives to him—daily, hourly—asking him to transform us, he will take our offering and do as we request. No cyclical trial, no emotional turmoil, and no days of drudgery have the ultimate ability to keep us from living lives worthy of the gospel.

And what is the result of this kind of life? Paul tells us earlier in his prayer over the Philippians: "being filled with the fruit of righteousness that comes through Jesus Christ, to the glory and praise of God" (Philippians 1:11 ESV).

Fruit is a sign of rich soil, of deep roots, of true life, of a wise and worthy gardener. The fruit of righteousness in our lives comes *through* the power of the Lord Jesus as we continually bow our knee to him and his kingdom rule, to the glory and the praise of God.

As you pray, ask for a renewed love of God's Word and trust in his power. Confess the ways you live that do not adorn the gospel. Submit again to Christ's lordship, and praise him for his faithfulness to you.

Recommended Closing Prayer

> Go, then, earthly fame and treasure
> Come disaster, scorn and pain
> In Thy service, pain is pleasure
> With Thy favor, loss is gain
> I have called Thee Abba Father
> I have stayed my heart on Thee
> Storms may howl, and clouds may gather
> All must work for good to me. Amen.
> ("Jesus, I My Cross Have Taken" by Henry Francis Lyte)

Eastertide Day 30

KARI WEST

Reflect on Philippians 2:12–18

Call to Prayer

There is a connection between joyful, contented living and firmly holding to the Word of Life, namely, Christ. That connection can't be

230

severed by personal hardships or the crookedness of the world around us. That connection keeps us from devolving into the natural responses of complaining and grumbling when life is difficult.

If we are wholly alone in suffering and hardship, if all we can see is the darkness in our world, then complaining and grumbling would be an understandable response to the times we live in. But Paul calls us to put away complaining and arguing when we face hardship and a bleak world. How can we?

Paul says he is able to rejoice because holding on to Christ brings joy. He is rejoicing because a life of holding on to Christ is never in vain. He is honest about this life being one of service; it feels like being poured out as a drink offering. It is full of intense sacrificial work. But this kind of life is possible because Paul hopes in the day of Christ and in the coming of the King.

It can be the same for us today. Are you facing a season of deep trial, of sleeplessness, of anxiety, of pain? Hold to Jesus, and more importantly, know that he holds you. He will work in you his good will. Christ is King, and he will come again.

As you pray, confess your grumbling. Ask for a fresh awareness of the abiding presence of Christ, and ask for the strength to rest in his sovereign love for you.

Recommended Closing Prayer

O God, in your mercy and grace, supply my every need according to your riches of glory in Jesus. Amen.

Eastertide Day 31
SALLY BREEDLOVE

Reflect on Philippians 3

Call to Prayer

What do we have to look forward to in this life? Perhaps you are in a season where the horizon of your future seems to be shrinking. But in

Philippians 3, Paul gives you plenty of reasons to stay grounded in hope and confidence no matter what does or doesn't happen in your life.

Paul offers us all a different way to live when life is hard.

Find your joy in the Lord. As Christ faced his own death, he promised he had joy to give us. Do you believe that? Will you accept the kind of joy he offers? Will you believe Jesus is the only source of unfading happiness?

Stop trusting the things that make you feel as if you have a secure and important place in this world. Paul sweeps the things we often long for into a trash pile: a flawless life, an important job, the right connections or education. He says to let them go or let them be taken from you. They don't add up to half a thimbleful of joy compared to knowing Jesus.

In these verses, Paul calls us to know Jesus more fully. We need humility since none of us will ever fully arrive, but we can be hopeful as well. Jesus has laid hold of us, and he'll never let us go.

And finally, Paul encourages us to follow and imitate godly leaders. Whom do you want to be like? It is a serious question.

We are called to live in a new way, but the heart of joy is about something beyond this present brief life. Our real joy is that we are citizens (already!) of heaven and are waiting for our Savior King to arrive.

As you pray, listen to this counsel from the apostle Paul. What do you need to pick up or put down for you to know joy even in a world like ours? Then take a minute to thank God that one day when Jesus comes, we will know joy in full.

Recommended Closing Prayer

> Give me, O Lord, a steadfast heart, which no unworthy thought can drag down; an unconquered heart, which no tribulation can wear out; an upright heart, which no unworthy purpose can tempt aside. Bestow upon me understanding to know you, diligence to seek you, wisdom to find you, and faithfulness that finally may embrace you. Amen.
> *(Thomas Aquinas)*

Eastertide Day 32

SALLY BREEDLOVE

Reflect on Philippians 4

Call to Prayer

The way Paul describes prayer in this passage might be summed up like this: *Ask God for whatever you want, and thank him for whatever he gives.* It doesn't say, "Tell God the things a good Christian would tell him" or "Ask in the right way and you will get it." No, it is far simpler. Be like a child—turn your desires (as confused or misshapen or small as they may be) into prayers to our holy God. Then receive with gratitude what he gives you.

Ponder the call to think about good things and imitate the actions and words of godly people. Our minds so quickly slip out of alignment, and we fall back into our favorite rut of fear, envy, or resentment. A desire to corral our thoughts is like the desire to herd cats: largely impossible. It is far better, Paul says, to choose something else to think about, something good and true. Notice what you are thinking about, and then shift your focus to things that are lovely and honorable. Then choose to act like people you admire, whether you feel like it or not.

Consider your circumstances: your life may be too large or too small, too challenging or too boring, too full or too empty. But ask yourself, is the life you've been given enough? Even if it is small, or damaged, or limited, God is so very present with you. Contentment is saying to God, "Thank you. I have enough. You are with me, which is more than plenty." Even when everything in you rages that you deserve more, saying thank you for everything you possibly can takes you back to contentment and back to God.

Our life with God is shaped by prayer, thinking, acceptance, and thanksgiving. Not everything in our story is good, but it is all held in the hands of the good and beautiful God.

In the middle of whatever hardships we find ourselves in, Christ invites us to open up our hearts to joy. As you pray, do just that—pour out your heart to God, being as honest and grateful as you can possibly be. It will be enough.

Recommended Closing Prayer

O Lord God, we can no other answer make than thanks and thanks and ever thanks. Because of Jesus Christ. Amen.

Eastertide Day 33

SALLY BREEDLOVE

Reflect on Colossians 1:1–20

Call to Prayer

What about this world would you love to see changed? What have you had enough of? Be honest as you listen to your own heart. We live in a stressful world that keeps hearing more of "the same bad" at every turn of the news cycle.

Perhaps you need to take ten steps away from the latest crisis or dire prediction and remind yourself of the big picture. Colossians says Jesus was supreme in the beginning and will be supreme in the end. We, on the other hand, may be in the middle of deep difficulty and struggle. Our strength will come from seeing the whole story and living into it. It won't come, as *THE MESSAGE* says in Colossians 1:11, "from the grim strength of gritting our teeth."

What is the real story? The Triune God has always been and will always be. As Jesus himself declares in Revelation 1:8, he is "the Alpha and the Omega." In his great goodness, he created a beautiful cosmos where his kingship would bless everything he made. But rather than responding with gratitude, we chose mutiny and rebellion. Our rejection of his kingship still spreads out like shock waves from an earthquake. The result? We live in a broken and dislocated universe where little knows its meaning or place.

But Paul is not in despair. In Jesus, God is rescuing people who will join him in this work of reestablishing the rightful rule of King Jesus.

It sounds very cosmic (and it is), but it is also personal and ordinary. It is you listening to someone you disagree with. It is you acting with compassion rather than ignoring the need of another. It is you responding with kindness when insulted. It is you choosing humility rather than standing on your rights. It is you delighting that the King is near and will one day come in fullness.

Today—this, another day in the middle—matters. Live this day for *that* day when the King will come in fullness.

As you pray, ask God for one specific way you can live out the prayer "Your kingdom come, your will be done."

Recommended Closing Prayer

> O God, grant that we may desire you, and desiring you seek you, and seeking you find you, and finding you be satisfied in you for ever. Amen.
> *(Francis of Xavier)*

Eastertide Day 34

SALLY BREEDLOVE

Reflect on Colossians 1:21–2:7

Call to Prayer

Paul doesn't pull any punches, does he?

We live in a world that is intrigued by spiritual things but that gets squeamish if we say, "Jesus Christ, God come in the flesh, is the center of all." Paul, however, is blunt: "The mystery in a nutshell is just this: Christ is in you, so therefore you can look forward to sharing in God's glory. It's that simple. That is the substance of our Message" (Colossians 1:27 MSG).

Maturity is the profound simplicity found in clinging to Jesus.

Paul was a citizen in the most sophisticated empire of his time. He was a highly educated Jew in a culture that valued reading, thought, and dialogue. By the end of his life, he was widely traveled, debating and presenting the work of Jesus from the Areopagus in Athens to the courts of kings, from slave girls and wealthy women to the Praetorian Guard who worked for Caesar in Rome. But he never changed his tune. It was always, always Jesus.

His life's passion was to help develop Christ followers whose lives were deeply centered and well-built on Jesus.

The truth, Paul says, is in Jesus alone. The truth is Jesus. But Paul says even more in this letter that is very controversial in terms of our culture's sensibilities. He says he gladly participates in the suffering of Jesus—in Jesus's rejection, in his sorrow over the broken lostness of the world, in his laying down of his own life for the world.

We can wake up tomorrow morning trusting that Jesus is the center of the universe and that he holds all things together. We can be confident of Jesus and live our day seeking to be poured out for the sake of others. As you come to him in prayer, rest in these certainties.

Recommended Closing Prayer

O Lord Jesus, help me to remember that the sufferings of this present world are not worthy to be compared to the glory that awaits us when your kingdom comes in fullness. Help us to live today for that day. For Jesus Christ's sake. Amen.

Eastertide Day 35
SALLY BREEDLOVE

Reflect on Colossians 2:8–19

Call to Prayer

Listen again to how *THE MESSAGE* puts Paul's words in Colossians 2:10: "You don't need a telescope, a microscope, or a horoscope to realize the fullness of Christ, and the emptiness of the universe without him. When you come to him, that fullness comes together for you, too."

We are people of longings. It starts at the beginning. We are thrust into this world, and we long for air, for milk, for warmth, for closeness, and for touch. Without longings, are we really human?

Paul tells the Colossians that because of Jesus, they belong in God's family. But it's not just belonging we desire—we want to know we are wanted and that we are good enough to be in the group. Paul assures us that we do measure up because of Jesus's death on the cross and our baptism into his life.

We are insiders because of Christ, but it doesn't stop there. We don't need to concoct a self-improvement course in order to maintain our place in God's family. Special diets, rituals, and secret knowledge all add up to nothing in God's eyes. Grace and mercy are so very large that Christ is always enough.

In our world, it's easy to feel isolated and to slide into loneliness and self-doubt about our worthiness.

As you come to pray, turn away from those thoughts. Listen to the real truth about yourself and about the overflowing love of Jesus Christ. Thank your Father God that you belong to Jesus, to his family, and to his grand purposes in this world. No matter what else you have or don't have, know that you have Christ and that it is an empty universe without him.

Recommended Closing Prayer

> O God, of your goodness, give me yourself, for you are enough for me. I can ask for nothing less that is completely to your honor, and if I do ask anything less, I shall always be in want. Only in you I have all. Amen.
> (*Julian of Norwich*)

Sixth Sunday of Easter, Day 36

SALLY BREEDLOVE

Reflect on Colossians 2:20–3:11

Call to Prayer

In the preceding chapters of Colossians, Paul urges us to realize that a life full of rituals and insider religious talk is not at all what life in Jesus is like. Here he continues that theme as he focuses on our character and everyday choices. The bottom line? We need to clean up our act, as the saying goes. What is wrong with us after we come to Jesus arises from a heart that focuses on things and feelings instead of on God. That wrong focus stirs up everything from sexual promiscuity to a bad temper in us.

The solution, Paul makes clear, is not doubling down on a self-congratulating self-discipline about outward things that perish and don't matter in the long run. Fastidious choices about what we do or don't do, or what we eat or don't eat, may make us look pious, humble, or ascetic, but they don't deal with our self-serving and self-deceived hearts. As Jesus tells us in Luke 6:45, "Out of the abundance of the heart his mouth speaks" (ESV).

As you begin your time of prayer, pause and consider: What filled your heart and your mind as you went about your day? Where do you wish you had made a different choice from the one you made? What thoughts or emotions plagued you that you couldn't shake off? How do you long to change?

Paul's counsel makes such good sense. Christ has given you his resurrection life, so look up, be alert, and see life from Christ's perspective.

Praise God as you pray. It is his life in you that will remake you. Join him in the work he is doing.

Recommended Closing Prayer

O Lord God, remake so I look like your Son the Lord Jesus Christ. Amen.

Eastertide Day 37

SALLY BREEDLOVE

Reflect on Colossians 3:12–25

Call to Prayer

The end goal of the Christian life it to be remade so we are like our Master, our Friend, our Savior, our big brother Jesus Christ. What does it mean to be like Jesus? Paul says in this passage that it is to live a life of love.

Isn't it easy to want something else even as we follow Jesus? Even if we never speak it out loud, we find it easy to believe that we have to have something in addition to Jesus. If only we had success, a church we really liked, a spouse or a better spouse, children, grown children out of the house, a job or a job that really mattered, the right political party in power, or freedom from fear of disease, then we could better follow the command to walk in love.

But Paul makes it clear that love is fundamental; it is the one thing we need. "It's your basic, all-purpose garment. Never be without it" (Colossians 3:14 MSG).

The real truth about love is that it starts with small choices, such as determining you will live by the peace of Christ so that you can respond properly to those who offend you; choosing to be thankful; living deeply in the scriptures day by day so they guide your understanding of life; singing joyfully, even when your heart is heavy; and determining to serve others in the everyday relationships of your life.

Paul puts it in stark terms in 1 Corinthians 13—"Without love we are nothing."

As you pray, ask God to teach you to love as he loves.

Recommended Closing Prayer

> Lord, make me an instrument of your peace.
> Where there is hatred, let me bring love.
> Where there is offence, let me bring pardon.
> Where there is discord, let me bring union.

Where there is error, let me bring truth.
Where there is doubt, let me bring faith.
Where there is despair, let me bring hope.
Where there is darkness, let me bring your light.
Where there is sadness, let me bring joy.
O Master, let me not seek as much
to be consoled as to console,
to be understood as to understand,
to be loved as to love,
for it is in giving that one receives,
it is in self-forgetting that one finds,
it is in pardoning that one is pardoned,
it is in dying that one is raised to eternal life. Amen.
(Saint Francis)

Eastertide Day 38

MADISON PERRY

Reflect on Psalm 29:9–10

Call to Prayer

At every moment of your life, you can live firmly ensconced in God's kingdom. Here you are in exile. But at the same time, you play and pray in the throne room of the heavenly King. Your place has been secured by the death and resurrection of our Savior.

The Lord will surely watch over you and keep you. Now you only see the start of an eternal adventure. Perhaps in this season, it feels as if you are treading backward. Maybe your work feels fruitless, or perhaps you are in an extended season of sickness. Maybe you cannot help but sense the deep pain of the world.

Regardless of your circumstances, on a much deeper lever, there is forward movement. God is renewing you, redeeming you, and saving you to the uttermost.

Let this moment do its work in you. Receive your season as a gift. Turn your eyes upward to your Father and King. In his kingdom, the limits of the present age are shattered. You may feel hemmed in here, but in God's kingdom all things are possible. He will hold you fast.

Recommended Closing Prayer

Father, we ascribe to you the glory due your name. We worship you in the splendor of your holiness. Please give strength to your people, and bless us with peace.
(Adapted from Psalm 29:1–2, 29:11 ESV)

Eastertide Day 39
WILLA KANE

Reflect on Psalm 34

Call to Prayer

David teaches us in psalm after psalm that our hearts were made for worship; our voices, designed for praise. This is especially poignant for us to remember during Eastertide as we celebrate the resurrection and power of God. Here in this psalm, David calls us to join him in living, breathing, and—every chance we get—praising the God who saves.

This call is countercultural in a world dominated by negative headlines and nanosecond messaging, in a world focused on me and mine. As king of Israel, David might have expected, even demanded, adulation from his subjects. But he has found another way, a better way.

His lungs expand with praise for the God who met him halfway, who freed him from his fears, and who rescued him from enemies and desperation. He calls us to join him and gives a lesson in how to worship God.

As you pray, open your mouth and taste, and open your eyes and see, the goodness of God. Run to him and be blessed. Seek beauty. Don't lie or use profanity. Turn your back on sin. Do good. Seek peace.

When you need him, cry out to God—he listens and rescues.

Are you kicked in the gut, heartbroken, in trouble? God is there every time.

The Lord himself has paid the ransom. He has bought your freedom. He will never leave you or forsake you. Praise him and thank him.

Recommended Closing Prayer

O God, we praise you and thank you because you will rescue your servants; no one who takes refuge in you will be condemned. Amen.

Eastertide Day 40
(Ascension Day)

BRANDON WALSH

Reflect on Acts 1:1–14

Call to Prayer

For forty days the resurrected Jesus appeared to the disciples and taught them about the kingdom of God. They had the chance to see Jesus in his glory and, by him, see the world in a whole new light. This period after the resurrection is a crash course in resurrection life.

Luke, the writer of Acts and the Gospel of Luke, addresses the patron of this work, Theophilus (which literally means "lover of God"). As Acts begins, Luke tells Theophilus that in his Gospel he has recorded what Jesus *began to do and teach* (Acts 1:1) before his ascension. But Luke knows for certain that the work of Christ is not finished. Christ will send his Spirit to continue his work. The Spirit will empower the disciples to witness to him in Jerusalem, Judea, and Samaria and to the ends of the earth. The book of Acts follows that road map as the resurrection of Jesus sends shock waves that are felt across the world.

It would have been a gift to join the disciples in that forty-day crash course that Jesus offered. But in truth, the class is not over. Jesus didn't stop empowering his disciples and teaching them; he continues to empower and teach his disciples through the Holy Spirit and through each other.

When we open scripture together, when we share the Lord's Supper, when we rejoice and weep with each other, we are sharing in Christ's presence among us. The Lord is teaching us what it means to live in light of the resurrection, in light of the kingdom he has already inaugurated and will one day fulfill.

As you pray, thank the Lord for the gift of the Spirit, for the gift of the scriptures, for the gift of other Christians. Pray for freedom to gather as the body of Christ.

Recommended Closing Prayer

> Soul of Christ, sanctify me. Body of Christ, save me. Blood of Christ, inebriate me. Water from the side of Christ, wash me. Passion of Christ, strengthen me. O good Jesus, hear me. Within thy wounds hide me. Permit me not to be separated from thee. From the wicked foe defend me. In the hour of my death call me, and bid me come to thee, that with thy saints I may praise thee for ever and ever. Amen. *(Anglican Church in North America Book of Common Prayer)*

Eastertide Day 41
BRANDON WALSH

Reflect on Acts 1:15–26

Call to Prayer

What is the first order of business for the disciples after Jesus ascends? They need to replace Judas. Peter exhorts his fellow disciples that it must be someone who has been with Jesus from the baptism of John until he was taken up to heaven. But notice the exact phrase he uses: someone who can "become with us a witness to his resurrection" (Acts 1:22 ESV).

This new twelfth disciple must be a *witness*. The Greek word translated "witness" is from the same root as the word *martyr*. The whole book of Acts depicts how the followers of Jesus, starting in Jerusalem and rippling outward to the ends of the earth, become witnesses to what the God of Israel has done through Christ for the sake of the world.

Crucially, this witness includes preaching and proclamation, but by no means does it end there. Each of the main characters in Acts starts to look like Jesus in their own flesh; they too become martyrs/ witnesses. Their lives become little Christs (which is why they are first called Christians). Stephen, the first martyr recorded in the book of Acts, as he is being stoned to death, asks the Lord not to hold the sin of his murderers against them. He then asks God to receive his spirit. These mirror the final words of Jesus in Luke.

So what does this mean for us?

All of us are called to become *witnesses to* Jesus's resurrection. Not only telling people about the good news of God in Christ, but also *becoming* an announcement of that good news in our own bodies. For some of our brothers and sisters around the world, that might look much like the witness of Stephen. For all Christians, it leads to a life of laying down our rights and our privileges so that we draw from Christ our fundamental identity, an identity that directs and orders all the other aspects of our lives around his lordship.

As you pray, ask your Father to make you a witness to Jesus. Offer him your sexuality, your finances, your career, your politics. Submit to being crucified and resurrected so that your life will give testimony to his goodness, truth, and beauty.

Recommended Closing Prayer

O God, you have made of one blood all the peoples of the earth, and sent your blessed Son to preach peace to those who are far off and to those who are near: Grant that people everywhere may seek after you and find you; bring the nations into your fold; pour out your Spirit upon all flesh; and hasten the coming of your kingdom; through Jesus Christ our Lord. Amen.

(Anglican Church in North America Book of Common Prayer)

Eastertide Day 42

KARI WEST

Reflect on Psalm 145:9–16

Call to Prayer

Reading, believing, and praying the psalms is often an act of faith. When life is arduous, we need hearts that trust God. That trust can then lead us to take verses such as these on our lips, even when the truths may feel distant from us.

We can speak them, hoping in God's promise to remove our hearts of stone and give us ones of flesh. We can say them, trusting in his Spirit to renew our faith.

The truth is that in all circumstances, we have a gracious and compassionate God who is slow to anger and rich in love.

The truth is that the Lord is good to his whole creation and that his compassion extends to all.

The truth is that God's kingdom is marvelous and enduring— stretching throughout all time.

The truth is that our God is trustworthy, our God is faithful, our God will provide, and our God will uphold us, from this time forth and forevermore.

Our God remains all of these things in all our hardest moments. He remains through our doubts, through our struggles, and through our fears. He will remain to the end, until we no longer need eyes of faith, for we will behold his kingdom in its fullness.

As you pray, take one of these traits of our Father God and meditate on it. Ask him for faith to believe even when it is hard. Rest in the fact that he will always say yes to that prayer.

Recommended Closing Prayer

Father, enable me to praise you for all your goodness, your faithfulness, and your love. For Jesus's sake and by his blood. Amen.

Seventh Sunday of Easter
(Sunday after the Ascension)

KARI WEST

Reflect on Psalm 147:1–11

Call to Prayer

Do you look at the physical world and see the close, active love of God? These verses tell us that he is the one who pushes clouds into the sky, pours rain onto the earth, and pulls grass up from seeds to sprout on green hills. Ravens call to him for food, and he gives it to them. He numbers and names the stars in the heavens. All of creation is cultivated and cared for by his hand.

Take a moment to consider God's nearness and active love as shown in a world that continues to turn, in plants that break through the soil each spring, in newborn animals, in cloud-spread skies, and in life that is preserved and flourishing.

But the care of God doesn't stop at the physical world. It crescendos, like a symphony, to the abiding, sustaining, specific love for his chosen people. He gathers his exiles; he binds their wounds and heals their broken hearts. He takes deep joy in those who honor him, and he sustains all those who are humble before him. On this side of the cross, we see that love culminating in the death and resurrection of Christ.

This psalm shows us how to respond to these beautiful realities. In humility, we can rely on our good God to provide what we need. We can come before him with awe at his transcendence and his power. We can put our hope in his unfailing love.

Does the sustaining love of God feel far from you? Speak this psalm out loud to the Lord in prayer. Ask for his Spirit to give you fresh insight into his perfect power, his tender care, and his abiding love for you.

Recommended Closing Prayer

Father, you clothe the lilies, you feed the sparrows, and you sustain all life in the world, including mine. Thank you for your nearness and your care. Give me a spirit of humility and a heart that depends on you. For Jesus's sake. Amen.

Eastertide Day 44

KARI WEST

Reflect on Psalm 150

Call to Prayer

"Praise the Lord." We hear that phrase so often in Christian circles that we can forget what it means. Perhaps we only associate it with a certain portion of a church service or a specific kind of music. But praising God encompasses far more. It means to see something true about God and then to communicate gratefulness and gladness in response.

The genesis of praise is God's character and his actions. In this psalm, we are charged to praise God because of both his surpassing greatness and his acts of power—in other words, for both his character and how his character is manifested in the world.

But we aren't just passive observers of God's goodness. The psalmist commands us here to take up our part in the dance of creation and the music of the spheres. Do we know anything of God's graciousness, his steadfast love, or his mighty acts? Then we can strum a harp, clash some cymbals, pick up our feet, and use our breath to praise God for who he is and what he has done, is doing, and will do.

No matter where you find yourself, you can praise God. Will you read through this psalm again and ask Christ to take your eyes off your circumstances and fix them on him, the Author and perfecter of your life and faith? Come to Jesus and ask for the ability to praise him, to trust him, and to rest in him.

> Father, help us to praise you.
> in your sanctuary,
> in your mighty heavens,
> for your acts of power,
> for your surpassing greatness.
> Let us,
> with your breath,
> with your Spirit,
> praise you.
> Amen.
> *(Adapted from Psalm 150:1–2 NIV)*

Eastertide Day 45

MADISON PERRY

Reflect on Psalm 14

Call to Prayer

The psalmist has diagnosed his day's woes, and they are summed up in the heart of the fool. The fool has turned aside to corruption, disregarding God and preying on others.

This reflects scripture's deep position that creation has gone awry because God's people have failed to worship their King. We see Adam and Eve set up to govern the garden, but they disregard God's law and seek to overthrow him, sending the cosmos into a tailspin. And we see humanity's revolt at its worst when the masses come together to demand the crucifixion of the one who could tame nature and put all wrongs to right.

This prayer of the psalmist is not a quiet spiritual moment or a time to ignore the world's obvious disarray. No, hear the psalmist bring up the ruin of this world epitomized by evil people. And amazingly he sees himself implicated in it all. For under heaven, "there is none who does good, not even one" (Psalm 14:3 NIV).

When you see the darkness tearing this world apart, do you link it with the heart. Do you link it with your heart?

But the psalmist is not absolutely crushed. Hundreds of years before Christ, he writes this: "Oh, that salvation for Israel would come out of Zion! When the Lord restores his people, let Jacob rejoice and Israel be glad!" (Psalm 14:7 NIV).

Indeed, salvation has come out of Zion. God found one who was righteous, Jesus of Nazareth, and our Savior has borne the weight of our betrayal. Our fortunes have been restored and we have peace with God. We hail a resurrected King.

But we are still in the midst of brokenness. As you pray, join the psalmist in raging against the evil at work in this world. Do not neglect your place in it. Have an eye to those who have suffered. Now turn to the cross of Jesus Christ. Jesus died and rose so that we might all have life. This darkness is already passing, for we have seen the salvation of our Lord. Be joyful in this season. We know how the story ends.

Recommended Closing Prayer

> Blessed are you, O Lord, the God of our fathers, creator of the changes of day and night, giving rest to the weary, renewing the strength of those who are spent, bestowing upon us occasions of song in the evening. As you have protected us in the day that is past, so be with us in the coming night; keep us from every sin, every evil, and every fear; for you are our light and salvation, and the strength of our life. To you be glory for endless ages. Amen.
> *(Anglican Church in North America Book of Common Prayer)*

Eastertide Day 46

MADISON PERRY

Reflect on Psalm 15

Call to Prayer

The author of this psalm begins with a longing for God's home. God's tabernacle and mountain are filled with God's holiness, his consistent and resplendent glory. Home is where God's holiness dwells, and the psalmist desires to live there in unending and unsentimental fellowship with his Father.

The person who dwells with God does not find fault with those nearest him. That is, he does not judge others despite their flaws and mistakes. He does not label a person according to her faults, always allowing for God's mercy and grace to prevail.

This seems to be an impossible standard—only the best and most merciful person could ever join God in his dwelling. God's home seems peaceful but inaccessible and always out of our reach. However, you have been invited to dwell in God's mountain house.

How? The righteous person's actions begin with truth spoken in the heart (Psalm 15:2). God wants to truly dwell with you, but unlike the legalistic person who lives on the surface, God will begin with your heart. If you will allow the Word of God to dwell within you, he will fill all of you. From the inside out, your thoughts and acts will begin to resemble those of Jesus Christ, the only truly righteous and merciful person. Once you let God through the door of your heart, he won't stop until he dwells in every square inch, preparing you for your eternal dwelling on his holy mountain.

Come to the Lord with a longing for home on his peaceful and unshakable mountain. Dwell with him now, inviting him into your thoughts, words, and deeds. Name places where you have left off God's way and barred his entry. Thank your Father for his welcoming embrace, and thank Christ for his sacrificial love. Finally, ask that God's kingdom might prevail in the world and within your own heart.

Recommended Closing Prayer

> Lord God, whose Son our Savior Jesus Christ triumphed over the powers of death and prepared for us our place in the new Jerusalem: Grant that we may praise thee in that City of which he is the light; and where he lives and reigns, for ever and ever.
> Amen.
> *(Anglican Church in North America Book of Common Prayer)*

Eastertide Day 47

SALLY BREEDLOVE

Proverbs 14:8

Reflect on Galatians 6:1–5

Call to Prayer

Pause and ask the question "How have I been changed recently?"

As you begin your time of prayer, would you be willing to ask yourself a few questions about your current season of life? Don't try to dress up your answers; don't resist what comes to you; and do not move into self-condemnation as you respond to these questions, as follows:

- If Jesus Christ were to ask you what has been the hardest thing about this season, what would you tell him?
- What are you afraid Jesus might ask you about this season?
- What do you wish Jesus would ask you or tell you about this time?
- Is there something this season has given you that you are deeply grateful for? If so, what is it?
- Is there some new way of living or small habit you have learned that you want to take into future seasons?

As you move into prayer, simply read Psalm 103 aloud and thank the Lord for his presence and provision.

Recommended Closing Prayer

> Bless the LORD, O my soul,
> and all that is within me,
> bless his holy name!
> Bless the LORD, O my soul,
> and forget not all his benefits,
> who forgives all your iniquity,
> who heals all your diseases,
> who redeems your life from the pit,
> who crowns you with steadfast love and mercy,
> who satisfies you with good
> so that your youth is renewed like the eagle's.
> The LORD works righteousness
> and justice for all who are oppressed.
> He made known his ways to Moses,
> his acts to the people of Israel.
> The LORD is merciful and gracious,
> slow to anger and abounding in steadfast love.
> He will not always chide,
> nor will he keep his anger forever.
> He does not deal with us according to our sins,
> nor repay us according to our iniquities.
> For as high as the heavens are above the earth,
> so great is his steadfast love toward those who fear him;
> as far as the east is from the west,
> so far does he remove our transgressions from us.
> As a father shows compassion to his children,
> so the LORD shows compassion to those who fear him.
> For he knows our frame;
> he remembers that we are dust.
> As for man, his days are like grass;
> he flourishes like a flower of the field;
> for the wind passes over it, and it is gone,
> and its place knows it no more.

But the steadfast love of the LORD
is from everlasting to everlasting
on those who fear him,
and his righteousness to children's children,
to those who keep his covenant
and remember to do his commandments.
The LORD has established his throne in the heavens,
and his kingdom rules over all.
Bless the LORD, O you his angels,
you mighty ones who do his word,
obeying the voice of his word!
Bless the LORD, all his hosts,
his ministers, who do his will!
Bless the LORD, all his works,
in all places of his dominion.
Bless the LORD, O my soul!
Amen.
(Psalm 103 ESV)

Eastertide Day 48

MADISON PERRY

Reflect on John 14: 1–7

Call to Prayer

For centuries, Christians buried their dead in the churchyard surrounding the church. One could not enter the church without seeing grave markers of generations clustered together—little children, young mothers, the aged. The markers comforted the grieving as reminders that their loved ones were now gathered with the saints of all ages. Those markers spoke the truth we often avoid: death comes for all.

Our world leaves dying to the experts. But what have we lost by not considering our own death? Would we live more fully, more humbly, and more wisely if we were to actively accept the reality that our time on this earth is brief? If we admit we too will die, will we care more deeply about those who will follow us?

God invites us to remember that we will die. Have we entered into the forgiveness he offers us in Jesus Christ? Are we seeing the fragility of all life, and are we respecting and esteeming those around us? Do we need to remind ourselves that Jesus alone offers us eternal life? Do we need to ask if our lives will leave a blessing to those who follow us?

As you pray, consider whether you know that Jesus is your Good Shepherd who has laid down his life for you. Do you know he keeps you as you live and will keep you when you die? Thank your Shepherd Jesus that he is always with you. Pray for courage to live well and to die in faith, so that your living, and even your dying, might bring blessing to others. Remember that Christ has been resurrected and that we too will live in fullness beyond the grave.

Recommended Closing Prayer

> Lord Jesus, be mindful of your promise. Think of us, your servants, and when we shall depart, speak to our spirits these loving words: "Today you shall be with me in joy." O Lord Jesus Christ, remember us, your servants who trust in you, when our tongues cannot speak, when the sight of our eyes fails, and when our ears are stopped. Let our spirits always rejoice in you and be joyful about our salvation, which you through your death have purchased for us. Amen.
> *(Anglican Church in North America Book of Common Prayer)*

Eastertide Day 49

STEVEN E. BREEDLOVE

Reflect on Acts 1:4–8

Call to Prayer

Since Thursday, we have been *between Ascension and Pentecost.* During Holy Week we seek to walk in the footsteps of Jesus, but as we move from Ascension to Pentecost, we walk in the footsteps of the disciples. Indeed, much of life can feel like learning to walk between Ascension and Pentecost.

At the Ascension, Jesus told the disciples to go to Jerusalem and wait for the power of the Holy Spirit, who would be given by the Father, so that they could accomplish the task Christ had called them to. The image of the disciples receiving a call and yet having to wait in patience for God's powerful presence fits with much of our experience. The disciples didn't know how long the wait would be and didn't know what it would be like to receive the presence of the Holy Spirit. They just had to wait in patience and faith.

We, too, often know that there is something for us to do. Perhaps it's a particular task, job, or goal that we know is ours. Perhaps it's a new spiritual discipline or a deeper level of pursuing God. We know we are called, yet we can't seem to succeed.

Perhaps it is a level of contentment and peace that we desire but cannot achieve on our own strength. Perhaps it is reconciliation of a particular relationship. We all have moments where there is something before us, something from God, that we cannot yet reach. In these moments, we are called, like the disciples, to wait in faith. We are waiting for God to show up, waiting for the strength of the Holy Spirit to do what we are called to do, waiting for the promise to be given.

We don't get to dictate the length of the wait. We don't know what it will be like for God to arrive. We don't know how the calling will be fulfilled. Like the disciples, we are simply called to remain in our particular Jerusalem until God arrives.

As you wait for Pentecost on Sunday, let the fact that we are between Ascension and Pentecost encourage you to keep waiting for the presence of God, who will lead you into the calling he has for you in his timing! Pray that you will wait with patience and hope, eager for his help.

Recommended Closing Prayer

> Oh God, the king of glory, you have exalted your only son Jesus Christ with great triumph to your kingdom in heaven: Do not leave us comfortless, but send us your Holy Spirit to strengthen us and exalt us to that place where your savior Christ has gone before, who lives and reigns with you and the Holy Spirit, one God, in glory everlasting. Amen.
>
> *(Anglican Church in North America Book of Common Prayer)*

Pentecost Sunday
BRANDON WALSH

Reflect on Acts 2:1–21

Call to Prayer

Jesus told them to wait. So the disciples retreated from public view, praying for something they really couldn't predict or understand. At this point they are in Jerusalem, along with so many others from around the ancient world, for the Feast of Pentecost. For Jews, Pentecost celebrates the giving of the law of Moses and the beginning of the wheat harvest.

One day, God had promised to write his law in the hearts of his people. And at this first Pentecost after the resurrection, the Spirit comes to rest on each one gathered. The same divine wind that the Lord breathed into Adam fills their lungs. As they speak to the diverse crowds about what has happened, each listener hears Christ proclaimed in his or her own language.

This story might feel as foreign to you as that of Moses parting the Red Sea or of the burning bush. Likewise, the call of Christ can feel daunting, impossible even. How can we become like Christ? How can we be his *witness* in our lives? But the Holy Spirit who fell on Pentecost, who animated the life and proclamation of the first apostles, is offered to us as well. The Holy Spirit lives in all who proclaim Christ as Lord and continues to work miracles in this world.

Pray that the Father will make you aware of the Holy Spirit in your life. Pray that the Spirit will be present in your hard conversations at work, around your family dinner table, and in your most important relationships. Invite the Holy Spirit to do in you what you cannot do on your own strength. Ask him to make you like Jesus. Ask the Spirit to blow through the church and bring in the harvest.

Recommended Closing Prayer

> Breathe in me, O Holy Spirit,
> That my thoughts may all be holy.
> Act in me, O Holy Spirit,
> That my work, too, may be holy.
> Draw my heart, O Holy Spirit,
> That I love but what is holy.
> Strengthen me, O Holy Spirit,
> To defend all that is holy.
> Guard me, then, O Holy Spirit,
> That I always may be holy. Amen.
> *(Saint Augustine)*

Introduction to Ordinary Time

STEVEN E. BREEDLOVE

The season after Pentecost, commonly called "Ordinary Time," is the longest season of the Christian year. It completes the three-season cycle that began in Lent, and it offers the chance to live as Christians in the *here and now*. In spite of the term *Ordinary Time*, the *here and now* is anything but ordinary (the term itself simply refers to the way the Sundays were ordered) because of what Jesus did.

In the season after Pentecost, the church is called to live the life of Christ by the power of the Holy Spirit. This is what the disciples did in the days that followed Pentecost. They were living Jesus's life, as his body, in the strength and presence of the Holy Spirit. Week after week, this is also what we are called to do. We are called to be faithful disciples in this season, through the Spirit given at Pentecost.

The prayers and readings of this season are thus focused on growing in the faith and being witnesses to the world. We read the scriptures and pray in response to the readings so that we will grow in understanding together, so that we will devote ourselves to prayer together, so that we will come to the Lord's table together, and so that we will take care of each other in love. The life of the church, in all its aspects, is our focus during this season. As we read, our prayer ought to be, "Lord, strengthen and sanctify your body, filling it with your Spirit, so that we might be your witnesses in the world!"

Ordinary Time Day 1

KARI WEST

Reflect on Psalm 90:12–17

Call to Prayer

See how the psalmist looks to the Lord for everything. God must give wisdom. God must satisfy with his love. God must show his work and glorious power. God must establish the work of our hands.

As you step into a new season in the liturgical year, pause and consider: Do you come to the Father with the same kind of neediness, the same kind of expectancy? Do you plead for his return, for a deeper experience of his presence? There is no life apart from him. There is no lasting gladness apart from his steadfast love. We are like flowers that will wither and die without the sun.

As you pray, step into the same vein of desperation as the psalmist. Abandon all pretense of self-sufficiency. Pray this psalm to the Lord, asking him to mold you more and more in humility and give you a true understanding of the impossibility of life without his abiding presence.

Recommended Closing Prayer

You are our life and our length of days, O Lord our God. Let us know that life is a misery apart from you. Manifest your presence in us, and let us grow in our need of and our hope in your great sustaining love. Amen.

Ordinary Time Day 2

KARI WEST

Reflect on Galatians 1:1–9

Call to Prayer

In this opening passage of Galatians, notice how Paul doesn't see the gospel as a disembodied idea. It is not an interesting theological concept to bat around in our minds or debate in seminary classes.

The Lord Jesus Christ gave *himself* for our sins to rescue us from the present evil age. Christ presents himself in the gospel. It is the story of his life, death, and resurrection. Through it, we encounter a person, very alive and very real.

This is why Paul is so incensed in these beginning verses. If the Galatians desert the gospel, if they turn from the atoning sacrifice of Jesus and begin to believe there are other avenues to friendship with God, they will lose everything. In turning from the gospel, Paul says, they are deserting the one who called them to live in the grace of Christ.

They aren't simply swapping out one philosophy of life for another. They are turning from the one living, reigning Lord who bridges the chasm between their souls and their souls' Maker.

We run the risk of making the same mistake today. Jesus offers himself to us through the gospel. Do not turn from him to any other savior. Embrace him as your Lord and live in the grace he gives. As you pray, confess any wanderings from Christ. Ask for fresh faith to see the gospel as the one beautiful true way to eternal life with God.

Recommended Closing Prayer

Christ, let us hold fast to you, our Savior and Sustainer. For your sake and in your name. Amen.

Ordinary Time Day 3

SALLY BREEDLOVE

Reflect on Galatians 1:10–24

Call to Prayer

We have just finished remembering and celebrating Christ's death and resurrection, and now we turn to consider a man wholly changed by the power of that death and resurrection.

Paul experienced an about-face in his life—turning from hating Jesus Christ and the good news that was made real in Christ's death and resurrection to worshipping Jesus, loving his message, and knowing it was from God. Having abandoned a life of intense religious observance that had morphed into a murderous hatred of the new Christian believers, he became a man determined to proclaim Jesus as the only one who could give "himself for our sins to deliver us from the present evil age" (Galatians 1:4 NIV).

Do you ever wish that you yourself could be so radically changed? Are you ever sick and hopeless because you keep on being the same person and doing the same thing year after year?

Look at what changed Paul—a powerful encounter with Jesus on the road to Damascus, where he saw the depth of his own sin and the deeper reality of Christ and his mercy. Are you willing to turn from your sin and say yes to God's mercy?

Something else reshaped Paul's life as well. He took time after that Damascus Road encounter to listen long to Jesus. Paul tells us he went to the Arabian Desert for three years to be with Jesus in solitude and be taught by him.

As you start this new season, are there any about-face decisions you need to make concerning how you treat your family, your own body, or the community around you? Will you encounter Jesus and let him be Lord? Are you willing to make time regularly to be with Jesus in quiet and let the Spirit teach you?

As you pray, ask God to help you repent where you need to repent. Thank him for his great mercy. Ask him for the will to make time to simply be with him day by day.

Recommended Closing Prayer

> Thanks be to thee, My Lord Jesus Christ, for all the pains and insults thou hast borne for me, and for all the benefits thou hast given me. O most merciful Redeemer, Friend, and Brother: Grant that I may see thee more clearly, love thee more dearly, and follow thee more nearly, day by day. Amen.
> *(Anglican Church in North America Book of Common Prayer)*

Ordinary Time Day 4

SALLY BREEDLOVE

Reflect on Galatians 2:17–21

Call to Prayer

We have a new phrase in our culture: virtue signaling. It's a rampant game, easy to play. Pick an issue that's important to you—whether it is morality, or politics, or how to raise your children, or how you treat your dog—then find those who see things differently and deride them for their opposing view.

Perhaps you've been a victim of this game, or perhaps you've been the culprit.

What can we do about our fractured society, the judging that is done against us as believers in Jesus and the judging we do of others?

Our friend the apostle Paul invites us to join him in a new freedom, the freedom of not having to be the person who's always at the top of the virtue pecking order. What do we need to do to join him in this new spacious life?

We need the humility to know we are broken people who hurt others. We need to confess of our egos and our desire to be seen as the right one, the best one, or the one who is trying the hardest.

But if we let go of our pride of place, our desire to be praised and vindicated, how can we know we matter? How can we be safe? Once again Paul helps us. He says that Christ lives in him. Christ has loved him and given his life for Paul. If you belong to Christ, the truest thing about you is not how virtuous you are, but how much you are loved.

As you go to prayer, will you join the tax collector in Luke 18:13 and pray his prayer: "God, have mercy on me, a sinner" (NIV)? Then will you thank your Father that his mercy toward you overflows? When he sees you, he sees the beautiful life of his Son alive in you; he does not see your battle-weary, battle-stained soul. He does not see your protests that you are trying as hard as you can. He simply sees his beloved Son's love for you.

Lay down your ego and come to him.

Recommended Closing Prayer

> Lord Jesus, Master Carpenter of Nazareth, on the Cross through wood and nails you wrought our full salvation: Wield well your tools in this your workshop, that we who come to you rough-hewn may be fashioned into truer beauty by your hand; who with the Father and the Holy Spirit live and reign, one God world without end.
> Amen.
> *(Anglican Church in North America Book of Common Prayer)*

Ordinary Time Day 5

SALLY BREEDLOVE

Reflect on Galatians 3:1–6

Call to Prayer

Have you ever daydreamed about what it would be like to receive an enormously large, unexpected inheritance? Perhaps a far-flung childless great-aunt leaves you her fortune.

Stay with that imagining. What if you barely made enough for rent month by month and knew you would never have the money for a down payment on a home of your own? What if you depended on the government for food programs and health care? What if you worked every job you could find, but they were always temporary, paid minimum wage, and offered no hope of advancement?

What if you went by your post office box (you never had mail delivered to your home address because your address changed too often) and found a notice for a certified letter in your box? When you retrieved the letter from the postal clerk, you learned an estate lawyer wanted you to call him because you had an inheritance in store.

What would you do? Would you leave the post office, pray your car would start, and drive to your next odd job? Or would you find a way to call the lawyer? Would you start dreaming about a whole new life—an education, a car with less than two hundred thousand miles, a home of your own, and new clothes that didn't come from the thrift store?

Paul is at pains in Galatians 3 to explain how this gift of new life in Christ is utterly comprehensive and transformative. It began with the death of Christ on the cross, and it is sustained daily by the Spirit. It is an abundant inheritance we did not earn; it is treasure beyond all imagining.

It's as if Paul is saying, *Live like a person who's just received that certified letter. Start making plans to become the well-resourced person you actually are. And look around you—everyone who has received this same inheritance is your sibling, your equal. Be encouraged, and encourage each other!*

As you pray, ask God to help you lay down all your striving to save yourself or remake your life. Thank him that you have so much more than an earthly inheritance. Thank him for the lavish gift of the Father, Son, and Holy Spirit in your life.

Recommended Closing Prayer

What shall I render to the Lord
for all his benefits to me?
I will lift up the cup of salvation
and call on the name of the Lord,

I will pay my vows to the Lord
in the presence of all his people. Amen.
(Psalm 116:12–14 ESV)

Ordinary Time Day 6
SALLY BREEDLOVE

Reflect on Galatians 4:1–7, 4:19

Call to Prayer

Adoption has always been part of this world. In Galatians 4, as Paul explains how fully our adoption into God's family has changed us, he turns to the Genesis account of Abraham's two sons, Ishmael and Isaac. Their story is full of all the relational brokenness we encounter so often in our world. At the heart of this story is the reality that although Abraham had two sons, he only had one *real* son, Isaac. All Abraham's promises, blessing, and wealth would be passed to that *real* son.

If you have an adopted child, or if you yourself are adopted, then you know the deep longing an adopted child has to know that he or she is indeed a *real* son or *real* daughter. No matter how much the adoptive parents love their child, their love and the legal paperwork are not enough. Something in the heart of an adopted child has to shift. The child has to submit to how deeply he or she has been longed for, chosen, loved.

Paul's longing for the Galatians to accept the truth that they are real sons and daughters of their heavenly Father is so intense that it is painful—as painful as childbirth, he says. Likely he has watched or heard of the intensity of a woman in labor and had experienced some of the agony that precedes the gift of a new life.

Paul's longing is just a shadow of God's longing for you and for me. He is in heart agony waiting for us to submit to being loved, being wanted, being made family with him.

The Spirit wants to help you receive and trust the reality that God loves you as his beloved child. As you pray, ask the Spirit to help you cry out to God, "Abba, Father."

Recommended Closing Prayer

As you pray, hold up before God someone you know who needs to know the Father love of God. Put the person's name in the appropriate places in this prayer adapted from the American Church in North America Book of Common Prayer:

Watch over your child _____, O Lord, as his [or her] days increase; bless _____ and guide _____ and keep _____ unspotted from the world. Strengthen _____ when he [or she] stands; comfort him [or her] when discouraged or sorrowful; and raise _____ up if he [or she] falls. And in his [or her] heart, may your peace that passes understanding abide all the days of his [or her] life, through Jesus Christ our Lord. Amen.

Ordinary Time Day 7

SALLY BREEDLOVE

Reflect on Galatians 5:13–26

Call to Prayer

In Galatians, Christ offers us freedom from having to prove our own goodness, and promises a new kind of freedom beyond our imagining. It is a freedom to learn to love well. It is the only freedom that can't be taken from us, and it is ours as we let God love us. We can't churn out love on our own. But if the Spirit is alive in us, this love will begin to reveal itself in our lives, just as truly as new life erupts in a spring garden.

Here is what God longs to grow in our hearts, things he tends in us by his Spirit:

- Affection for others
  Do you really like the people in your life?
- Exuberance about life
  Is your life characterized by hope and gratitude?
- Serenity
  Does peace keep you even when things are unsettled?
- A willingness to stick with things
  Are you easily frustrated? Do you give up easily?
- A sense of compassion in the heart
  Are you tenderhearted?
- A conviction that a basic holiness permeates things and people
  Do you respect the people in your life, or are you plagued by contempt for them?
- Involvement in loyal commitments
  Do you easily give up on people? or family? or your church?
- Not needing to force your way in life
  What do you do when things don't go your way?
- The ability to marshal and direct your energies wisely
  Do you live wisely and sanely? Do you take Sabbath times?

It's the beginning of Ordinary Time. All around us, we see meadows, farmlands, and gardens teeming with new growth. Let the life around you teach you. You too are to be a garden of life and love that God is tending.

Walk with him around your heart and your life right now. Ask God to show you what is growing in your life that you haven't made happen on your own. Ask God to help you see the tenacious weeds and briars that need rooting out. Confess the barren places in your heart. Ask your Father to change you.

Thank God for the ways he is teaching you to love; confess the ways your love needs to grow; and ask him to increase your love.

Recommended Closing Prayer

> O Lord you have taught us that without love, all our deeds are worth nothing: Send your Holy Spirit and pour into our heart that most excellent gift of charity,

the true bond of peace and of all virtues, without which whoever lives is counted dead before you; grant this for the sake of your Son Jesus, Christ, who lives and reigns with you and the Holy Spirit, one God for ever and ever. Amen.

(Anglican Church in North America Book of Common Prayer)

Ordinary Time Day 8

SALLY BREEDLOVE

Reflect on Galatians 6:1–8

Call to Prayer

Paul has used every means at his disposal to teach us about grace: his own story, arguments from law courts and inheritance rights, the story of Abraham and his sons, and metaphors from the agricultural world. Everywhere Paul looks, he sees the freedom grace brings, the freedom a beloved son has to learn to love like his father loves.

Ordinary Time calls us into a life of daily discipleship so that we become more like Jesus—and Jesus lived a life of love.

Paul's aim in this final chapter of Galatians is to teach us how to get about the business of everyday loving. If you make your days about yourself, Paul says, you'll watch everything collapse into corruption in the end.

Or you can face the things that keep you from love and learn how to love in the complexity and brokenness of your own world. A life of love is a mosaic shaped by everyday repeated decisions. It is a life of humility, a life of taking risks to help people who are living in destructive ways. It is a life of bearing the burdens of others and carrying your own daily burden. It is a life where you quit ranking yourself and instead ask God to show you the truth about yourself. It is a life where you don't give up and where you keep doing good.

Jesus is the glorious interjection of love into our futility. He has loved us and loved this world in far greater ways than we will ever be called on to love, so don't be afraid to be the first one to love in your own broken and pain-filled relationships. Be like Jesus, and peace and mercy will flood into your life.

As you pray, ask God to give you new and specific ways to love the people in your world.

Recommended Closing Prayer

> Lord, make me an instrument of your peace,
> Where there is hatred, let me sow love;
> Where there is injury, pardon;
> Where there is doubt, faith;
> Where there is despair, hope;
> Where there is darkness, light;
> Where there is sadness, joy;
> O Divine Master,
> Grant that I may not so much seek
> To be consoled as to console;
> To be understood as to understand;
> To be loved as to love.
> For it is in giving that we receive;
> It is in pardoning that we are pardoned;
> And it is in dying that we are born to eternal life.
> Amen.
> *(Saint Francis of Assisi)*

Ordinary Time Day 9

Reflect on Galatians 6:1–2, 6:9–10 and Matthew 11:28–30

Call to Prayer

The call to bear each other's burdens comes to us this night as it did to believers in Galatia almost two thousand years ago. Theirs was a time when religious zealots tried to add requirements to the freedom promised by grace alone in Christ alone. Ours is often a season of division and unrest when the needs within and around us far exceed our resources.

Many of us are weary. How are we to bear our own burdens, much less help shoulder the burdens of those around us?

In the sacrificial simplicity of his love, Jesus says, "Come to me, all you who are weary and burdened, and I will give you rest. Take my yoke upon you and learn from me, for I am gentle and humble in heart, and you will find rest for your souls" (Matthew 11:28–29 NIV).

Rest for the weary is more than a physical need. It's a deep desire of our souls only satisfied in Christ. As we come to him with empty hands and on bended knee, his love pours rest into our weary souls.

Jesus's love is selfless, sacrificial, sympathetic, and sure.

- Selfless
  We come, and Jesus gives.
- Sacrificial
  Jesus bore in his body the crushing burden of sin for all humanity.
- Sympathetic
  He was tempted in every way as we are, so he knows our pain and struggle.
- Sure
  Our hope in him is an anchor for the soul.

This Jesus, our burden-bearer, admonishes us to bear each other's burdens and in so doing fulfill the law of Christ. Galatians 5:14 reads, "For the entire law is fulfilled in keeping this one command: 'Love your neighbor as yourself'" (NIV).

To obey the law of Christ is to love one's neighbors with his love: selfless, sacrificial, sympathetic, and sure. This is only possible as Jesus pours his love through us. Though expressed in a myriad of practical ways, this love always draws us and points others to a relationship with Christ—to know Jesus and grow in him.

Where is God calling you to extend this kind of love? What opportunities to fulfill the law of Christ are right in front of you? Pray and listen. The Spirit will lead you.

Recommended Closing Prayer

Heavenly Father, we are weary. These times are hard, and we are broken. Would you give us humility to lay our burdens down at the foot of the cross, to receive help and rest in Jesus, and to receive strength and compassion to stoop low to bear the burdens of those around us, especially our brothers and sisters in Christ? Amen.

Ordinary Time Day 10

WILLA KANE

Reflect on 1 Thessalonians 1

Call to Prayer

Perhaps for you, this early summertime doesn't seem to promise much joy. Perhaps it feels more like bleak midwinter, living in the minor key of a plaintive hymn. Are you experiencing another month of discord, peril, pain, or uncertainty? Do you wonder when, O Lord, it will end?

Some of us are isolated physically and emotionally. The news around us invites us to outrage, not joy; to doubt, not trust.

Paul's message to a young church in Thessalonica is a message of hope for all of us this night, despite where we find ourselves. He reminds them, and us, of who they (and we) are to God the Father, demonstrated in the life of Jesus the Son, poured into us by the presence of the Holy Spirit.

You are beloved and chosen to be his own by God the Father.

Beloved and *chosen*. Let these words saturate your very being.

Now turn to consider the gospel message that comes not just with words, but with Holy Spirit power, to change us from the inside out. Jesus has saved us. Even now he lives in us and intercedes for us. He will come again to make all things new.

Desert the God substitutes of your old life and make room for true God worship. Let joy invade your suffering. Christ, our rescuer, will come again in glory. Allow that hope to form strength like steel in your soul.

Living like this pours God's message through us to others, not just in words but also as a living display of Christ our Light, our Redeemer.

Pause to ponder these divine truths. Hear God your Father call you his beloved. Thank him that he has chosen you to be his own. Receive his strength to endure dark days. Let the joy of who you are in Christ settle in your inmost being. Delight in the expectant hope of Christ's return. Let these realities transform the landscape of your heart.

Recommended Closing Prayer

Grant us, Lord, not to be anxious about earthly things, but to love things heavenly; and even now, as we live among things that are passing away, to hold fast to those that shall endure; through Jesus Christ our Lord, who lives and reigns with you and the Holy Spirit, one God, for ever and ever. Amen.

(Anglican Church in North America Book of Common Prayer)

Ordinary Time Day 11

WILLA KANE

Reflect on 1 Thessalonians 2:4–13

Call to Prayer

Paul uses the imagery of family relationships to describe his love and care for this newly planted Thessalonian church. His message is personal. Paul the evangelist has been faithful to reach these converts. Paul the edifier is faithful to teach them. Eight times in these verses, Paul points them to God.

Paul himself is under God's authority. The result? He exudes humility like a little child. No demands, no impure motives, just unselfish love.

A mother's love shares and cares intimately, exemplified in a mother feeding and caring for her own children. In some Bible translations, the image is one of a nursing mother on whom a child relies completely for nourishment. Love like this means opening your own life as you share the gospel.

A father's love leads, pleads, encourages, and urges children toward worthy living and a share in God's kingdom and glory. A father's love points to the Father through the Son, in the Spirit. Love like this is leadership in action.

Love holds nothing back. Pause. What is your own heart toward those around you who desperately need the good news of Christ? Does unselfish love describe the orientation of your heart toward those who believe but are fatigued or falling away during a difficult season?

Pause and pray. Who needs your time, your tender affection, and your intimate care? Who needs encouragement toward godly living? Who needs you to share your life with them?

The gospel is the only thing of value you can give away, over and over again, and still possess in its entirety.

It is the opposite of hoarding; it's a life of joyful generosity.

How is this possible? Jesus, our source, never runs out and never runs dry. He is not a cistern but a fountain. He fed five thousand people

273

with five loaves and with much to spare. He is the living water and the bread of life.

Come to the family table, feed on the Word of God, and then share its nourishment with others. Let the gospel change you—then give it away.

Recommended Closing Prayer

Heavenly Father, replace hunger and thirst for things that pass away with a holy and insatiable desire for you and your Word. Fill us with a gospel that satisfies deep in our souls and overflows to a desperate waiting world. Give us your tenderness and love, and hearts of joyful generosity. Amen.

Ordinary Time Day 12

WILLA KANE

Reflect on 1 Thessalonians 3:1–8

Call to Prayer

In our passage, Paul speaks to a young church about suffering. Unable to return to them himself, he sends Timothy to them so that he could be "cheering [them] on so [they] wouldn't be discouraged by these hard times" (1 Thessalonians 3:2 MSG).

Our times are hard, and many of us are discouraged. What can we learn from Paul's message? How are we to suffer well in this season?

Suffering shouldn't come as a surprise. We need to remember that it is a promised part of our calling. In Paul's words, "we are destined for such troubles" (1 Thessalonians 3:3 NLT), so we must be on guard. Satan, the tempter, loves nothing more than to use hard times to weaken our faith and draw our eyes away from Jesus onto our circumstances.

If suffering is our destiny, how do we receive it? We must stand firm in the Lord, in faith, and in his promises. We can stand firm in Christ because he is our Rock.

> I waited patiently for the Lord;
> he turned to me and heard my cry.
> He lifted me out of the slimy pit,
> out of the mud and mire;
> he set my feet on a rock and
> gave me a firm place to stand.
> (Psalm 40:1–2 NIV)

> You keep him in perfect peace
> whose mind is stayed on you
> because he trusts in you.
> Trust in the Lord forever,
> for the Lord God is an everlasting rock.
> (Isaiah 26:3–4 ESV)

> From the end of the earth I call to you
> when my heart is faint;
> lead me to the rock
> that is higher than I,
> for you have been a refuge for me,
> a tower of strength against the enemy.
> (Psalm 61:2–3 ESV)

With a quiet heart, ponder these verses. Wait patiently, stay your mind on Jesus, and let him be a rock and refuge—a tower of strength against the enemy.

This kind of waiting is active, steady, and expectant.

As you turn to him in prayer, stand firm in the Lord. He is your strength.

Recommended Closing Prayer

> Most loving Father, you will us to give thanks for all things,
> to dread nothing but the loss of you, and to cast all our care

on the One who cares for us. Preserve us from faithless fears and worldly anxieties, and grant that no clouds of this mortal life may hide from us the light of that love which is immortal, and which you have manifested unto us in your Son, Jesus Christ our Lord. Amen.
(Anglican Church in North America Book of Common Prayer)

Ordinary Time Day 13
WILLA KANE

Reflect on 1 Thessalonians 4:1–12

Call to Prayer

The Christian life is intended to be lived from the inside out. God himself designed our bodies as a temple for the Holy Spirit—Christ in us as we walk this earth and learn his ways.

Paul's letter to the Thessalonians urges us to live a life from the inside out: a life of purity, holiness, and dignity. Sit with his words for a moment. Do they describe the way you're living—beautiful and holy from the inside out? Or do you struggle with disorder in your thought life, your sex life, your work life, or your family life? Where is your life unkempt?

When hearts are disordered, relationships are too. Life feels like a mess, not a beautiful dance.

Running roughshod over others is easy to excuse when times are hard. Wearing emotions on one's sleeve, using words lit by short fuses, selfishly dismissing the concerns of others—this is not the way to live a life of love.

Pause to examine your heart by looking at your excuses. What do they reveal? "I'd be more patient if only …"; "My thought life would be purer if only …"; "I wouldn't say this or do that if only …"; "I'd be more generous or loving if only …"; "My life would be more beautiful if only …"

Pray. Confess to the Lord the things in your heart that are disordered and unkempt. Lay these things at the cross, at the feet of Christ.

God's gift to you is the Holy Spirit. As he indwells you, his job is to transform—to bring purity, holiness, and beauty to your inmost being.

Receive this gift. Don't reject it. Invite the Spirit in and be transformed.

Recommended Closing Prayer

> Holy Spirit, breath of God and fire of love, I cannot pray without your aid: Kindle in me the fire of your love, and illumine me with your light; that with a steadfast will and holy thoughts I may approach the Father in spirit and in truth; through Jesus Christ my Lord, who reigns with you and the Father in eternal union. Amen.
>
> *(Anglican Church in North America Book of Common Prayer)*

Ordinary Time Day 14
WILLA KANE

Reflect on 1 Thessalonians 4:13–5:11

Call to Prayer

We live tethered in tension. We're told that Jesus reigns, but we know that the world is broken and that our lives are messy. A virulent enemy stalks and steals. Most days, one negative headline bleeds into another. The question lurks: what if death has the final say?

Against a backdrop of confusion and despair, Paul tells the Thessalonians and us that there is hope. We are children of the day, not people of the dark, so we can have confidence that all those who believe the gospel will be caught up together to meet Christ when he returns. We can hope in this ultimate encouragement: we will be with the Lord forever.

We can't seem to move past living in turmoil and isolation in our world. Nothing seems to draw us together. So much seems off, conflictive, uncertain. Against a backdrop of loneliness and with little to look forward to, we have this amazing encouragement from God: a time will come when there will be one huge family reunion with the Master. It's not a date on the calendar but a deep assurance in our hearts. Jesus will return, he will gather us to himself, and we will be together with him forever.

Pause to consider this, to be encouraged and even delighted, as you receive this promise. Imagine eternity with Christ and the family of God.

This is such good news that we cannot, must not, keep it to ourselves. We are told to build each other up and reassure one another with these words. Whom do you know who is still in darkness? Who is discouraged? Who is in despair?

As you pray, ask the Lord to send you as an encourager with this great good news—the best news of all.

"He died for us so that, whether we are awake or asleep, we may live together with him" (1 Thessalonians 5:10 NIV).

Recommended Closing Prayer

O God, thank you that new birth in Christ gives way to life eternal. Send me with your message of hope and peace as an encourager into a world that is lost and dying. In Jesus's name and for your glory. Amen.

Ordinary Time Day 15
WILLA KANE

Reflect on 1 Thessalonians 5:12–24

Call to Prayer

Paul ends this first letter to the Thessalonians with a litany of to-dos—like a parent to a child who is leaving home. *Remember this! Don't forget that! Do this!* He gives seventeen practical instructions about living as believers.

Even halfway through, the list feels onerous and impossible. Honor your leaders and overwhelm them with love. Get along among yourselves, warn freeloaders, and encourage stragglers. Be patient and attentive. Don't snap, but look for the best in others and do your best to bring it out. Be cheerful and thank God no matter what. Pray all the time. Don't suppress the Spirit or discount prophecies. Don't be gullible. Keep the good and throw out the evil.

These instructions *are* onerous and impossible—until Paul delivers the most encouraging words that believers in Christ can hear: the one who calls you is faithful, and he will do it.

He will do it. He will make you holy and whole. He will put you together—spirit, soul, and body. He will fit you for the return of Christ.

As you pray, thank him for his faithfulness, for his perfect plan to forgive, redeem, and restore you, for the assurance that he himself will do the work to sanctify you completely.

Recommended Closing Prayer

> Blessed Lord Jesus,
> No human mind could conceive or invent
> the gospel.
> Acting in eternal grace, thou art both
> its messenger and its message,
> lived out on earth through infinite compassion,
> applying thy life to insult, injury, death,
> that I might be redeemed, ransomed, freed.

Blessed be thou, O Father, for contriving this way,
Eternal thanks to thee, O Lamb of God,
for opening this way,
Praise everlasting to thee, O Holy Spirit,
for applying this way to my heart.
Glorious Trinity, impress the gospel on my soul.
Amen.
(From *The Valley of Vision*)

Ordinary Time Day 16

KARI WEST

Reflect on 2 Thessalonians 1

Call to Prayer

It's summer in the midst of Ordinary Time, when we choose day by day to walk out our lives with God. But we are not simply plodding along with no hope of a final destination; we are headed toward a magnificent culmination. There will be a future moment when Christ will be revealed as the mighty, just, and splendid King of the cosmos. This is the hope that Paul holds out to the Thessalonians and to us—remember that you are in the middle of the grand narrative of redemption. Remember that your King reigns now but that his majesty, justice, perfection, and rule will be revealed and enacted in fullness on that final dawn.

It will be a glorious day—but not for everyone. For some, it will be a reckoning. Paul doesn't mince words: Christ will come in judgment against those who persist in evil and who refuse the path of obedience and trust. He will fulfill all justice on the earth.

How does that sit with you? Does it make you angry, or confused, or hopeful? Allow yourself time to process the emotions that arise from this picture of the coming judgment. And then ask the Holy Spirit for fresh awareness of those who need to hear about this just and grand God. Thank him that he will reveal himself in fullness and that he will bring perfect rule to the earth. Praise him that we will one day have our deepest heart's desire met—to see and marvel at our King of glory.

Recommended Closing Prayer

> O God and Father of all, whom the whole heavens adore: Let the whole earth also worship you, all nations obey you, all tongues confess and bless you, and men and women everywhere love you and serve you in peace; through Jesus Christ our Lord. Amen.
>
> *(Anglican Church in North America Book of Common Prayer)*

Ordinary Time Day 17

K A R I   W E S T

Reflect on 2 Thessalonians 2:13–17

Call to Prayer

How often do you slow down and let the words of scripture seep into your soul? Do you believe that the Word of the Lord is sweeter than honey? We are quick to read marvelous truths such as the ones found in this passage and then move on to something else. We don't often sit and savor.

Hear the Word of the Lord now:

- "Brothers and sisters loved by the Lord" (2 Thessalonians 2:13 NIV).
  You are his beloved, joined to his family.

- "God chose you" (2 Thessalonians 2:13 NIV).
  You have been seen, singled out, and cared for by the Almighty.

- "Saved through the sanctifying work of the Spirit" (2 Thessalonians 2:13 NIV).
  Your salvation is not your own doing; it is the gift of God.

- "That you might share in the glory of our Lord Jesus Christ" (2 Thessalonians 2:14 NIV).
  Your story will be fulfilled in a marvelous way.

- "By his grace gave us eternal encouragement and good hope" (2 Thessalonians 2:16 NIV).
  God has lavished unending encouragement and good hope upon you.

Sit and savor. Meditate in a quiet place. Ask the Holy Spirit which truth you most need to receive today. Ask him to plant it deep within your soul.

May God encourage your heart and strengthen you in every good deed and word.

Recommended Closing Prayer

> The Lord bless you and keep you; the Lord make his face shine on you and be gracious to you; the Lord turn his face toward you and give you peace. Amen.
> *(Numbers 6:24–26 NIV)*

Ordinary Time Day 18

KARI WEST

Reflect on 2 Thessalonians 3:1–5, 3:16

Call to Prayer

Our own prayer life will deepen when we learn to echo the prayers of God's Word. Over time, by praying for the things God asks us to pray for in scripture, the contours of our words, our vision of the world, and our desires will come more and more into line with our heavenly Father's. That is the need and the hope of every believer.

Paul asks the Thessalonians to pray for the same things we need to pray for today. First and foremost, we need to pray that the message of the Lord will spread rapidly and be honored. Our world desperately needs the truth of God. Paul encourages us to ask not only for the gospel to spread, but also for people to see it for what it truly is— the life-giving, humanity-forming, powerful message of grace for all people.

Pause and consider: how often do you petition the Lord to do this great work?

Next, Paul asks the Thessalonians to pray for deliverance from those opposed to Christ. His request reveals his understanding of God as both Judge and refuge. Rather than acting on a desire for personal vengeance to get even with those who have wronged him or made his life arduous, Paul asks for God to deliver, to save.

Pause and consider: when the sin of another person wreaks havoc on you, how quick are you to turn to the Lord and plead for deliverance and justice?

Pray for these things. Ask the Holy Spirit to conform you more to the image of Christ as you make these requests your own.

"May the Lord direct your hearts into God's love and Christ's perseverance...May the Lord of peace himself give you peace at all times and in every way" (2 Thessalonians 3:5, 3:16 NIV).

Recommended Closing Prayer

> O God, the source of all holy desires, all good counsels, and all just works: Give to your servants that peace which the world cannot give, that our hearts may be set to obey your commandments, and that we, being defended from the fear of our enemies, may pass our time in rest and quietness; through the merits of Jesus Christ our Savior. Amen. *(Anglican Church in North America Book of Common Prayer)*

Ordinary Time Day 19

KARI WEST

Reflect on 1 Corinthians 1:1–9

Call to Prayer

After this introduction, Paul will go on to address the issue of divisions within the church at Corinth. What a timely topic for our day and age. We live in a world rife with contempt and fracture along every conceivable fault line, both in our culture at large and in our churches.

But first, Paul takes the time to remind the Corinthian believers who they are in Jesus, what Jesus has done and will continue to do in them, and what they can expect at the end of days.

Before urging unity, Paul draws the church's gaze back to the Savior who has sanctified them, who has given them the blessed name of his holy people, and who has enriched them in every way. Sustained love for one another can only come out of a deep-rooted hope in the person and work of Jesus. Christ has given us all we need for life and godliness. Christ has made us holy, and he will keep pulling us into holiness. Christ will pour faith into our souls, enabling us to stand firm to the end.

We can wait eagerly for Christ to be revealed in fullness; we can hope in our future blameless state before the judgment seat of God; and we can know friendship with God today.

Are you weary of the divisions all around you? Are you exhausted from relational fractures? True unity between brothers and sisters in the Lord will flow from hearts of faith and trust in God. Remember your deepest identity—loved and called by God, joined to and made for his family.

As you read these verses, pray that the Holy Spirit will give you a deeper understanding of God's love for you, Christ's work for you, and your own calling to build up others in love. Ask the Spirit to bring you to repentance and change where you have despised a brother or sister. Plead for the strength to live peaceably and humbly.

Recommended Closing Prayer

> O God the Father of our Lord Jesus Christ, our only Savior, the Prince of Peace: Give us grace to take to heart the grave dangers

we are in through our many divisions. Deliver your Church from all enmity and prejudice, and everything that hinders us from godly union. As there is one Body and one Spirit, one hope of our calling, one Lord, one Faith, one Baptism, one God and Father of us all, so make us all to be of one heart and of one mind, united in one holy bond of truth and peace, of faith and love, that with one voice we may give you praise; through Jesus Christ our Lord, who lives and reigns with you and the Holy Spirit, one God in everlasting glory. Amen.
(Anglican Church in North America Book of Common Prayer)

Ordinary Time Day 20

K A R I   W E S T

Reflect on 1 Corinthians 1:26–31

Call to Prayer

Pride is a poison; self-reliance, an abyss. As we come before God's throne, all the things we put so much credence in—our own intellects, our social posturing, our physical, political, or economic strength—are shown to be inconsequential at best and a hindrance at worst. God looks to the humble.

We idolize ourselves, our success, our status, and our socioeconomic positions of power and prestige. But God in his mercy warns us away from this trap of lauding trivial realities.

He tells us: *See those whom the world forgets, those the world considers foolish, weak, lowly, and beyond notice or care? I will choose to accomplish my glorious purposes through such people.*

God's power will flow through those who acknowledge their desperate need for him. If we are wrapped up in arrogance and fixated on our human achievements, then we will miss a great many chances to be caught up in the greater story God is telling on the earth.

Do you hunger for humility? Do you seek out those in your community who could teach you about dependence? Do you honor and follow leaders—in the church, in your workplace, in the political sphere—who model graciousness and lack hubris?

As you pray, confess pride. Plead for a right understanding of yourself that will lead to humility and dependence. Trust that God will answer and God will bless. Ask the Holy Spirit to reveal how you might gather people around you who will encourage dependence on the Lord. Ask for the courage to honor leaders in every sphere of life who display humility. Refuse to throw your lot in with those steeped in arrogance.

Be at peace. As we live into holy habits of confession and repentance, God will grant us what we most deeply need—reliance on and conformity to his Son, the one who is our righteousness, holiness, and redemption.

Recommended Closing Prayer

> Father, please give us this mind among ourselves
> which is ours in Christ Jesus,
> who, though he was in the form of God,
> did not count equality with God a thing to be grasped,
> but emptied himself, by taking the form of a servant,
> being born in the likeness of men.
> And being found in human form,
> he humbled himself
> by becoming obedient to the point of death,
> even death on a cross.
> Therefore God has highly exalted him
> and bestowed on him the name that is above every name,
> so that at the name of Jesus every knee should bow,
> in heaven and on earth and under the earth,
> and every tongue confess that Jesus Christ is Lord
> to the glory of God the Father.
> Amen.
> *(Adapted from Philippians 2:6–11 ESV)*

Ordinary Time Day 21

KARI WEST

Reflect on 1 Corinthians 3:1–4, 3:16–23

Call to Prayer

"Are you not acting like mere humans?" (1 Corinthians 3:3 NIV).

At first glance, Paul's accusation against the Corinthians seems to be strange and puzzling. Aren't we all human beings? What's the problem with acting like one?

We find a clue to what Paul means in the word *mere*. Paul is jealous for the Corinthians to catch the grand vision of how God is working in his people. They are not merely individual human beings any longer, trapped in the pettiness and anguish of self-worship and self-aggrandizement. The bogs of pride no longer smother their hearts, corrupt their desires, or thwart their ability to worship the right things in the right order. They have been freed!

But freed for what? The answer is the same for the Corinthians then as it is for us today: to be God's temple, together with our new family of other believers. We are freed to become the place where God *dwells*.

Do you treasure God's presence in the midst of his church? Is it your deep desire? Do you see it as the best, the most precious reality? It's better than receiving honor from other people, better than one's political party staying in or stepping into power, better than any crisis ending, better than our economy thriving, and better than stability in our country and our homes.

God is forming us *together* into his holy temple, a place for the Spirit of God to dwell. There is something deeply sacred about the church and the relationships between the blood-bought brothers and sisters of Christ. How we need eyes of faith to see what God is working in his people by his Spirit. We are his temple.

And those who persist in jealousy, rivalry, and arrogance damage that holy dwelling place of God. We can build up the temple in humility, or we can tear it apart with pride.

As you pray, ask the Spirit to reveal the depth of the beauty of his work in and through his church. Confess pride, and plead for greater humility. Meditate on the glory of our identity and our end: we will one day be fully knit together as the dwelling place of God.

Recommended Closing Prayer

Father, make us into a humble people. Enable us to hold the right things sacred. Deepen our imaginations to grasp the glory of your work in our midst. Give us your peace and your love. Amen.

Ordinary Time Day 22

KARI WEST

Reflect on Psalm 51

Call to Prayer

When sin is revealed in your life, is your first reaction to hide it, justify it, or minimize it? Or do you take it to God in prayer? How often do you confess your failures to the Lord?

The arrogant are blind to their own iniquity, but a person who seeks to walk in humility and live with a right understanding of his or her own soul before a mighty God will discover how much sin still lurks within. It takes a humble heart to acknowledge and confess that sin.

But the beautiful reality is that the more you make a habit of confession and repentance, the more you will grasp God's deep capacity to cleanse you from sin, to pull you farther into sanctification, and to purify your heart and your mind. God is the one who gives clean hearts, who renews right spirits, who restores and upholds. All we must do is continue to ask for humility and for grace, to continue to confess and repent. God promises to blot out our transgressions, to wash us thoroughly, and to save us to the uttermost.

Take time to sit in silence before the Lord, asking him to reveal any sins that you need to confess. Allow the Holy Spirit to do his convicting work in your soul. Confess and repent, and receive God's mercy and grace to walk in a way that honors him. Be at peace.

Recommended Closing Prayer

> Create in me a clean heart, O God,
> and renew a right spirit within me.
> Cast me not away from your presence,
> and take not your Holy Spirit from me.
> Restore to me the joy of your salvation,
> and uphold me with a willing spirit. Amen.
> *(Psalm 51:10–12 ESV)*

Ordinary Time Day 23
SALLY BREEDLOVE

Reflect on 1 Corinthians 4:20–5:13

Call to Prayer

It's easy to focus on the parts of scripture that fit our views and values. We want a God who is soft on our comfortable sins but ruthlessly opposed to the sins we despise. But when we read the Bible without editing out the parts we don't like, we are all confronted by God. His holiness is a blazing fire of purity. His generosity and compassion make our virtue-signaling embarrassingly self-congratulatory, and his directness in calling what is evil, evil, silences our secret hope that other people's sins are worse than ours.

In our age, Christians are deeply divided over the issue of practical godliness. Is godliness about protecting life? Is it a traditional view of gender and sexuality? Is it about prioritizing economic and racial justice? embracing all forms of inclusiveness?

We divide into camps. We take our view of God's agenda in to our politics, and the spirit of our political world becomes the spirit of our local church. We judge each other's faith; we turn friends and family into enemies.

But look at this passage in Corinthians. Paul ends chapter 4 with this: "The kingdom of God does not consist in talk but in power" (1 Corinthians 4:20 ESV). What does he mean by power? Perhaps he means the power of a thoroughly godly life. Godliness makes visible the kingdom of God.

Then Paul underscores the grace Christians have received: "You really are [already] unleavened" (1 Corinthians 5:7 ESV)! Paul defines the far reach of an unleavened life of godliness: keeping sex within the bond of covenant marriage, turning from malice and evil, rejecting greed and not taking advantage of others, stopping derogatory talk about others, renouncing addictions, laying down idols that imprison us, loving those outside the faith, even when they live lives antithetical to God, and calling other Christians to join us in pursing wholehearted holiness.

As you pray, ask God to reveal where you need to repent. Commit yourself to a greater godliness. Ask him to give you compassion for this world. Ask him to make you like his Son Jesus. A life of power is a life of ongoing godliness, and godliness makes visible the kingdom of God.

Recommended Closing Prayer

> Lord, Jesus, Master Carpenter of Nazareth, through hard wood and sharp nails of the Cross, you wrought our full salvation. Wield well your carpenter's tools in us, your workshop, that we who come to you rough-hewn may be fashioned into truer beauty by your hand; who with the Father and the Holy Spirit live and reign, one God, world without end. Amen.
>
> (Adapted from *The Anglican Church in North America Book of Common Prayer*)

Ordinary Time Day 24

SALLY BREEDLOVE

Reflect on 1 Corinthians 6

Call to Prayer

Paul's stance toward the Corinthian church is fierce. Imagine having a preacher, Bible teacher, or writer you admire confront you about the lawsuit you are planning to file, your sex life, how much you think about winning at all costs, how much you drink, and how often you get angry. You, like many of us, would flinch and put up your defenses. You will likely flinch now if you let Paul's words sink in deeply.

What's his point? Is Paul the behavior inspector-corrector? In truth, he does hold all God's people to the highest imaginable standard, namely, the standard of becoming like Christ, of being a "little Christ" in this dark world.

But Paul's heart is for our well-being, our freedom, and our joy, not set out to shame us or simply improve our ethics. We will one day inherit God's kingdom in all its fullness. In this life we are being prepared for that future. Our daily choices—who we are becoming by way of our desires and habits—really matter.

But here is the key: Paul tells us that God has already made us holy. God wants us to live into the person God has made us to be in Christ and into the gift of a clean heart made right with God. We don't have to manufacture our own goodness. God invites us to live in line with who we already are!

God desires an intimate friendship with us. We belong to him. He wants us to be free, not enslaved to lesser choices.

As you pray, consider the dignity and privilege that God has heaped upon you. Lift your heart, your choices, and your thoughts up to him. Let God's Word give you hope so that you can choose a life of holiness, freedom, and joy.

> O Holy Spirit, beloved of my soul, I adore you. Enlighten me, guide me, strengthen me, console me. Tell me what I should do, give me your orders. I promise to submit myself to all that you desire of me and to accept all that you permit to happen to me. Let me only know your will. Amen.
> *(Anglican Church in North America Book of Common Prayer)*

Ordinary Time Day 25

SALLY BREEDLOVE

Reflect on 1 Corinthians 7:32b, 7:35–37

Call to Prayer

First Corinthians 7 is an interesting and confusing chapter. When we sit with the whole chapter, we may wonder what Paul means. Does Paul see marriage as a less worthy choice and lifelong singleness and devotion to Christ as a better choice, for all time and for all people?

Despite our confusion, parts of chapter 7 are straightforward, and perhaps troubling in their implications. Notice if you find yourself resisting one of the places where his meaning is clear. Marriage is a relationship of mutuality, not one of submission and domination. Singleness with self-control is a gift some are given. The covenant that binds two people together is sacred and should not be lightly disregarded. Contentment with one's place in life is a good thing. This world won't last forever.

Our world wants to control the discussion about marriage. Perhaps you feel your own pushback to Paul's words. But how you see marriage and how you live as a married person or an unmarried person is either a road to well-being and peace or a road to disharmony, confusion, and pain. Paul says that living into God's truth about marriage and singleness leads to a less anxious and less complicated life. He says that this kind of life frees one up to pay attention to God and his kingdom.

As you pray, sit with your own story of married life or your own story of singleness. How do you long for God to free you from anxiety and confusion? How is God inviting you to a life of following after him?

Recommended Closing Prayer

> Merciful Savior, you loved Martha and Mary and Lazarus, hallowing their home with your sacred presence: Bless our home, we pray, that your love may rest upon us, and that your presence may dwell with us. May we all grow in grace and in knowledge of you, our Lord and Savior. Teach us to love one another as you have commanded. Help us to bear one another's burdens in fulfillment of your law, O blessed Jesus, who with the Father and the Holy Spirit live and reign, one God, for ever and ever.
> Amen.
> *(Anglican Church in North America Book of Common Prayer)*

Ordinary Time Day 26

SALLY BREEDLOVE

Reflect on 1 Corinthians 8

Call to Prayer

One hears a passage like this one and wants answers to what one thinks are the obvious questions: "How much freedom do I have to follow my own conscience? Does another person have the right to shape my choices? What if I disagree with that person? Do I have to make *my* life work for *that individual*?"

We all have places where we disagree with another Christian's choices or freedoms. So what do we do? Put our energy into convincing the person that our perspective is right? Why do we keep on arguing when we know from all our past experience that arguments about who is "more right" rarely solve anything?

All the facts and knowledge we amass only move us farther apart. We live in a world that is fracturing into a million pieces because of all we argue about and all the ways we are convinced we are right.

We need to listen to the first three verses in this chapter. Paul tells us that when an issue matters deeply to people, knowledge rarely solves a disagreement. Love is the builder of people and relationships. Humility, not perfect knowledge, keeps us connected to God. Admitting that God knows us all the way to the core of our beings keeps us honest. We matter because of God's love for us, not because of our rightness.

Is there an ongoing broken relationship in your life right now? Ask God how he is inviting you into love, into humility, and into being known. Lay down your need to be right. See those around you as full recipients, just like you are, of the mercy of God. Be at peace. God loves you miraculously and mercifully, but not because you are right about everything. Submit to being loved, and therefore embrace God's call to love.

Recommended Closing Prayer

> O God the Father of our Lord Jesus Christ, our only Savior, the Prince of Peace: Give us grace to take to heart the grave dangers we are in through our many divisions. Deliver your Church from all enmity and prejudice, and everything that hinders us from godly union. As there is one Body and one Spirit, one hope of our calling, one Lord, one Faith, one Baptism, one God and Father of us all, so make us all to be of one heart and of one mind, united in one holy bond of truth and peace, of faith and love, that with one voice we may give you praise; through Jesus Christ our Lord, who lives and reigns with you and the Holy Spirit, one God in everlasting glory. Amen.
> *(Anglican Church in North America Book of Common Prayer)*

Ordinary Time Day 27

SALLY BREEDLOVE

Reflect on 1 Corinthians 9:19–27

Call to Prayer

Ordinary Time in the church year lasts quite a long time. Each day before us offers us an opportunity to throw our lots in with Jesus's. It is so easy to think, *Nothing ever changes. I have the same problems, disappointments and heartaches I have always carried.*

But when we read Paul's words, we see a man who isn't bound by the drudgery of day after day. He's free, and he's using his freedom to fully participate in living for Jesus and loving this world—today! He's committed to living well and to making it to the finish line of his life without flagging. He wants the "Well done" of Jesus at the end of his days.

What do you want? An easy life, a safe life, a successful life, and a life where you are seen and appreciated? Paul says he wants to *live* the gospel, not just know about it. He wants to enter the world to serve as Jesus did. He wants to understand people's lives and perspectives so he can speak the truth of Jesus in ways that make sense to them.

The atmosphere of Paul's soul is electric with anticipation. He is excited about the life he has chosen, as excited as an athlete before a championship game.

Our world can be so dreary, broken, complicated, and empty. What if you were to choose to enter the world right around you and live into the fullness of your life in Christ? What if you were to decide to build a deep friendship with someone who doesn't yet know Jesus? What if you were to spend real time seeking to understand and enjoy this person? What if you were to pray that your words and your life might become a bridge to bring the person to Jesus?

As you pray, ask for the desire to join in God's gospel work. Ask him to bring someone to mind whom you could befriend. Be the gospel to that person. Pray.

> Almighty God our Savior, you desire that none should perish, and you have taught us through your Son that there is great joy in heaven over every sinner who repents: Grant that our hearts may ache for a lost and broken world. May your Holy Spirit work through our words, deeds, and prayers, that the lost may be found and the dead made alive, and that all your redeemed may rejoice around your throne; through Jesus Christ our Lord. Amen.
>
> *(Anglican Church in North America Book of Common Prayer)*

Ordinary Time Day 28

S A L L Y   B R E E D L O V E

Reflect on 1 Corinthians 10:11–14

Call to Prayer

Paul loved the Corinthian church. He spent more time with these believers (and with the church in Ephesus) than with those at any other place. Paul knew this church, warts and all, but he never walked away from them in disgust. He wrote four letters we know of (two of which are in the Bible) to help teach them and disciple them.

Paul longed for the people of Corinth to follow Jesus wholeheartedly. He longed for them to become true disciples, not casual yes-people to the gospel.

Chapter by chapter in 1 Corinthians, Paul calls out the sin of the Corinthian church and brings up the controversies and arguments that plague them. First Corinthians 10 makes his motive clear: he does he wants them to be discouraged. Their situation is not hopeless. The trials they face, like the trials we face, are the same issues all people everywhere have faced. We, and they, have not been uniquely singled out for pain or difficulty.

Life is hard. Perhaps it would help to place our distress in perspective if we were to just accept that reality. As Acts 14:22 tells us, "Through many tribulations we must enter the kingdom of God" (ESV).

But far bigger than the difficulty of life is the faithfulness of God. Paul tells us that in every temptation, God is offering us grace to escape the pressure to give in and grace to endure until the temptation passes.

Is there a place in your life right now where you feel pushed beyond your ability to endure? Confess that to God; and as you pray, thank him for the truth that he is so much larger than your weariness and temptation. God is faithful; he will help you. He will give you endurance. As you end your prayer time, reenter your life as one who knows that God will be faithful.

Recommended Closing Prayer

> Dear Lord and Savior Jesus Christ: I hold up all my weakness to your strength, my failure to your faithfulness, my sinfulness to your perfection, my loneliness to your compassion, my little pains to your great agony on the Cross. I pray that you will cleanse me, strengthen me, guide me, so that in all ways my life may be lived as you would have it lived, without cowardice and for you alone. Show me how to live in true humility, true contrition, and true love. Amen.
> *(Anglican Church in North America Book of Common Prayer)*

Ordinary Time Day 29

SALLY BREEDLOVE

Reflect on 1 Corinthians 11:1

Call to Prayer

- To imitate Jesus is to follow Jesus.

- To imitate Jesus is to know the gospels in such a way that the stories about him shape your mind and your imagination. Only then will you know what imitation looks like in the everyday situations of your own life.
- To imitate Jesus is to find wise and godly Christians and then pattern your life after theirs.
- To imitate Jesus is to choose to love across all the lines that divide you from others.
- To imitate Jesus is to be an unrecognized servant.
- To imitate Jesus is to be willing to lay down your life for the sake of others.
- To imitate Jesus is to care more for the Father's approval than for the approval of anyone else.
- To imitate Jesus is to live a holy life.
- To imitate Jesus is to be willing to oppose the greed and hypocrisy of religiosity.
- To imitate Jesus is to spend time with the Father.
- To imitate Jesus is to know the scriptures.

What statements of your own can you add to this list? As you pray, ask God where he is particularly inviting you to imitate Jesus. Then take up that invitation, day by day.

Recommended Closing Prayer

> Thanks be to thee, my Lord Jesus Christ, for all the pains and insults thou hast borne for me, and all the benefits thou hast given me. O most merciful Redeemer, Friend, and Brother: Grant that I may see thee more clearly, love thee more dearly, and follow thee more nearly, day by day. Amen.
>
> *(Anglican Church in North America Book of Common Prayer)*

Ordinary Time Day 30

KARI WEST

Reflect on Psalm 73:1–7, 73:21–28

Call to Prayer

Asaph, the writer of this psalm, immediately pulls us into the narrative. In the opening verses, Asaph recounts his observations of the wicked. He sees an old, jagged, vicious pattern that has cut through the centuries—we easily recognize it today. Arrogant, ruthless individuals amass wealth and power and then wield these instruments to oppress the poor and the downtrodden. They are opposed to God and openly mock him; they cloak themselves in pride and violence. Despite their evil, they seem to live privileged, comfortable, carefree lives.

Asaph envies such people. He wants the ease of their lives for himself. He wants the wealth, the prestige, and perhaps the lack of conscience. He has spent his life trying to honor God, but what does he have to show for it? Punishment by the wicked and daily affliction. If we are honest, we will admit that we often feel like Asaph.

But Asaph could only perceive one small part of the story. And his envy had so corroded his heart that he forgot who it was who held his right hand—the God of all heaven and earth, the God of justice, mercy, grace, and glory. He forgot that God has not finished his great work of justice on the earth. And he forgot that even now—in the midst of all the anguish and confusion of a world undone by evil—God is always present, always guiding, and always strengthening his people. He will be our portion forever, and he will bring us to glory.

Ask God to search your heart and reveal any unclean way within you. Confess if you, like Asaph, are envying the wicked and questioning whether God will do what he has promised to do. Ask for fresh conviction of God's all-sufficiency to bring about his purposes, restore his world, and be a strong refuge for his people. Ask for patience and for peace.

Ordinary Time Day 31

KARI WEST

Reflect on 1 Corinthians 13

Call to Prayer

In Psalm 1, the godly person is likened to a tree next to a stream of water—rooted, lasting, and significant as it bears forth good fruit in season. The wicked, in contrast, are described as chaff, weightless and worthless, blown about by the wind. Here in 1 Corinthians, Paul tells us that it is possible for a person to look very impressive and godly and yet not truly resemble that tree. Without love, all our efforts are smoke and ash. They will amount to nothing. More than that, without love, we ourselves become nothing—like chaff driven before the wind.

Love. Not accomplishments, not to-do lists, not résumés, not feats of "godliness," but *love* is the measure of our humanity.

But that, by itself, is a terrifying reality to consider. As we read Paul's many descriptions of love, we see how short we fall of this all-important eternal virtue. We'd rather measure ourselves by our smaller accomplishments or by check marks of godliness. How can anyone love as Paul describes it?

Thank God that love is both the measure and the means of our humanity. We are pulled into this utterly impossible and deeply good calling of love by the powerful love of Jesus, the one who knows each of us fully.

Read Paul's description of love again, but this time, substitute the name of Jesus—the full and final manifestation of love.

Jesus is patient, *Jesus* is kind. *Jesus* does not envy, he does not boast, he is not proud. *Jesus* does not dishonor others, *Jesus* is not self-seeking,

Jesus is not easily angered, *Jesus* keeps no record of wrongs. *Jesus* does not delight in evil but rejoices with the truth. *Jesus* always protects, always trusts, always hopes, always perseveres.

Jesus never fails.

As you pray, rest in the perfect and perfecting love of your Savior. Ask him for greater obedience to heed this great call of love.

Recommended Closing Prayer

Eternal Love, maintain thy life in me. Amen.
(From "Leave Me, O Love, which Reachest but to Dust" by Sir Philip Sidney)

Ordinary Time Day 32

KARI WEST

Reflect on Jeremiah 29:4–14

Call to Prayer

The Lord Almighty carried his people into exile and promised to carry them back to their homeland. In the meantime, while they waited in a land not their own, he commanded them to seek the welfare of their captors. He told them to pray for the peace and prosperity of those who had inflicted massive suffering on them.

On the heels of this seemingly impossible charge, God gives them a promise that we often hear quoted today: He knows the plans he has for his people. He plans to care for them, to give them hope, and to give them a glorious future. He promises to bow low and hear each prayer offered to him. He promises to be found.

His deep and powerful words of promise were not given to populate a floral-decorated Instagram post to make us feel good about ourselves. They were meant to propel the Israelites toward love for their enemies and toward seeking the peace and prosperity of a group of people who had wreaked havoc on them.

By the great work of Christ, we have been grafted in as part of God's people, so we can take these words of promise to the Israelites and embrace them as a promise for us. But we must also let these beautiful words lead us where they were always designed to lead God's people—to seek the peace and goodness of those who despise, mistreat, malign, or disregard us.

Meditate on God's great and powerful words and ask him to propel you toward love for your enemies. Hope in this great promise—God will be found by his people.

Recommended Closing Prayer

> Proceeding Spirit, our defense...
> Refine and purge our earthly parts;
> But, oh, inflame and fire our hearts!
> ...And, lest our feet should step astray,
> Protect and guide us in the way.
> Make us eternal truths receive,
> And practice all that we believe:
> Give us thyself, that we may see
> The Father and the Son, by thee.
> Amen.
> ("Come, Creator Spirit" by John Dryden)

Ordinary Time Day 33

KARI WEST

Reflect on Psalm 78:19–40

Call to Prayer

> True, he struck the rock,
> and water gushed out,
> streams flowed abundantly,
> but can he also give us bread?
> (Psalm 78:20 NIV)

How quickly the Israelites come to distrust the God who had rescued them from slavery by signs and wonders and who had provided for their needs through miracles. And though he continued to care for them by giving them bread from heaven and causing meat to rain down like dust, he also struck down some of the people because they distrusted his faithfulness and disregarded his power.

We may be quick to flinch because of the way God judges his people in this passage. We may wonder if God has overreacted. We may think he was too harsh. But what if our gut response reveals our numbness to the severity of sin? But what if a story like this one is meant to reawaken us to the reality that God is holy and just, as well as merciful and loving? Distrust of the Father matters; disregard for his laws matters; our flattering tongues and deceitful hearts matter.

For such things, the bread of heaven was broken.

Ask the Lord to reveal where your heart is more controlled by our culture's attitudes than by his character as revealed in scripture. Thank him that this passage is not the end of the story, but that in the fullness of time, God sends better bread from heaven, broken for the healing of the world. Praise the Father that his justice is perfectly satisfied in Jesus. Ask for a soft heart that confesses sin as heinous, Christ as beautiful, the Spirit as powerful, and the Father as trustworthy.

Recommended Closing Prayer

> O God, whose thunder shakes the sky,
> Whose eye this atom globe surveys,
> To thee, my only rock, I fly,
> Thy mercy in thy justice praise.
> Amen.
> ("The Resignation," Thomas Chatterton)

Ordinary Time Day 34

KARI WEST

Reflect on 1 Corinthians 15:1–11

Call to Prayer

Christ died for our sins; Christ was buried; and Christ rose from death to reign in life. If we lose this central story, we lose everything.

By this gospel, we are saved. Christ's death has bought us peace with God and ushered us back into his family. His resurrection has inaugurated the coming kingdom and secured his final, full victory over the cosmos.

This resurrected Christ appeared to multitudes—many of whom were still alive at the time when Paul was writing. This resurrected Christ appeared to Paul himself and wrought an incredible transformation in his life—from hating and persecuting the church to pouring himself out for its good. For all their proximity to the resurrection, the Corinthian believers were in danger of losing their focus. We need to take care that we also do not lose sight of the death and resurrection of Jesus.

Paul wants the truth to sink into the Christians at Corinth and into us today: embrace the resurrection.

In this gospel, we find fresh power for life and godliness, as Paul did. Through this gospel, we learn that Christ will make all things new.

As you pray, remember the one in whose name you come before the Father. Praise him for his sacrificial death, praise him for his victory over all lesser powers, praise him for breaking the curse of death, praise him for his current reign, and praise him for his promised restoration of all things.

Hail our risen and reigning Lord and Savior Jesus Christ, God over all.

Recommended Closing Prayer

As you end your time of prayer, rejoice in the truth of these words in the presence of your heavenly Father:

> Death and darkness, get you packing.
> Nothing now to man is lacking.

All your triumphs now are ended,
And what Adam marred is mended.
Graves are beds now for the weary,
Death a nap to wake more merry.
Amen.
(From "Easter Hymn" by Henry Vaughan)

Ordinary Time Day 35

KARI WEST

Reflect on Psalm 84

Call to Prayer

The aim of our hearts will determine the beauty and depth of our lives.

Here the psalmist catches a vision of the glorious dwelling place of God—unparalleled in its beauty, its solace, or its strengthening power. Where God dwells is so lovely and the psalmist yearns for it so deeply that he says it would be better to spend just one day there than a thousand days in any other place in the world.

Those who have hearts set on pilgrimage find power from on high to live faithfully. The psalmist declares that those who have set their affections on God go from strength to strength. More than that, they can pass through the Valley of Baca, or Valley of Weeping, and even their tears will be turned into a spring. Even their sorrows will bear fruit in season, and nothing will be wasted, nothing ultimately lost.

God makes all this possible. God is our sun and shield.

Do you long for your life to reflect his power, his light, his strength, and his comfort? The truth is that God's dwelling place is now within you and within the gathered and scattered church. As you pray, ask him to give you this all-consuming vision of his presence. Ask for greater faith to trust that one day in the Lord's presence is truly better than a thousand elsewhere. Contemplate the glorious dwelling of God.

Recommended Closing Prayer

> How lovely is your dwelling place,
> Lord Almighty!
> My soul yearns, even faints,
> for the courts of the Lord;
> my heart and my flesh cry out
> for the living God.
> Lord Almighty,
> bless us, who trust in you.
> Amen.
> *(Adapted from Psalm 84:1–2, 84:12 NIV)*

Ordinary Time Day 36

KARI WEST

Reflect on Psalm 85

Call to Prayer

Let this psalm be a rubric for your prayer.

Rehearse the past goodness of God. Remember how far he has flung your sin and rebellion from you. Speak out loud to him about his deep forgiveness. Thank him that at such a great cost to him, he set aside his wrath and turned from his anger. List the many ways you've seen God work in your life and in the lives of those in your community.

Plead the perfect sacrifice of Christ on your behalf. Ask him for restoration. Ask him for fresh, renewing power in your life and within your family and your church so that you may seek him more faithfully and rest in his goodness.

Listen to what God has said to you, and revel in his promises of peace, the nearness of his salvation, and the current and future dwelling of his glory here with us. Pray fervently that we would not fall into folly and sin but would walk in a way that honors the Holy Spirit within us.

Hope in the beautiful picture laid before us—love and faithfulness greet each other like old friends; righteousness and peace kiss; faithfulness springs forth like water from the depths of the earth; and righteousness peers down from the heavens. The land will yield a great and plentiful harvest. God walks the earth, and righteousness prepares the way.

God will always give what is good. Let your heart be at peace.

Recommended Closing Prayer

> Teach me, my God and King,
> In all things Thee to see,
> And what I do in anything
> To do it as for Thee.
> Amen.
> (From "The Elixir" by George Herbert)

Ordinary Time Day 37

MADISON PERRY

Reflect on Psalm 88

Call to Prayer

Psalm 88 is known as one of the hardest psalms to pray. It is very dark; it seems entirely hopeless.

Consider the strangeness of this psalm and how surprising it is that it is incorporated into God's book of prayers. No other god today would offer it to us as a prayer. Many faiths on offer preach a law of attraction, where we must think positive thoughts if we are to attract positive outcomes. Other faiths say, yes, there is darkness, but it can be avoided if we will just mutter the right formula, or jump through the right hoops, or do enough right things. Why pray such depressing thoughts as those expressed in this psalm? It is bad enough just to have them. Amazingly, the historical church has prayed Psalm 88 daily, at the start of the day in fact, as a reminder of death—each of our own deaths and the death of our Savior.

Note that the psalm begins "O Lord, O God of my salvation" (Psalm 88:1 ESV). There is no better encapsulation of who God is to us than this line of text. God has saved us, saves us, and will save us. We remain rooted in God even as our lives spiral downward through darkness and into alienation. As the psalm leads us, we come to see that the weight of death we feel is the judgment of God. As we pray, we feel death wrap itself around us, ending our prayer in *darkness*.

Yet for all this, God's goodness is not spent, for Christ is still with us. As surely as we begin with this psalm turning toward the God of our salvation, Jesus joins us there and sustains us through these immensely heavy lines. These lines eventually end, yet we do not. For just when death thinks it has pinned us down, it finds that it no longer has hold of Jesus. Jesus, the firstborn from the dead, inverts this movement of sin and death. He thrusts us up into the light, infinitely exceeding the power of death all the way through to complete and total life.

Because of the God of our salvation, we can look unflinchingly on death that feels like death. Because of our victorious Savior, we can speak honestly about the fullness of sin, knowing that if we will not look away from the worst of deaths, we will never have to take our eyes off the fullness of life.

Praise be the God of heaven and earth, the God of our salvation.

Recommended Closing Prayer

> O God, who by the glorious resurrection of your Son Jesus Christ destroyed death and brought life and immortality to light: Grant that your servants, being raised with Christ, may know the strength of his presence and rejoice in his eternal glory; who with you and the Holy Spirit lives and reigns, one God, for ever and ever. Amen.
> *(Anglican Church in North America Book of Common Prayer)*

Ordinary Time Day 38

MADISON PERRY

Reflect on 2 Corinthians 3:7–18

Call to Prayer

Thank the Lord for the gift of his Word! It is challenging, foreign, and so unlike the thoughts our world teaches us to think. It is very likely that you did not wake up this morning thinking about Moses and Israel or about Jesus and the outpouring of the Holy Spirit.

But for Paul, the Christian life is not a matter of a onetime spiritual event, a single mountaintop experience that you can leave behind and keep going on as before. Paul talks here about being among those who "with unveiled face" are "beholding the glory of the Lord" (2 Corinthians 3:18 ESV).

What would it look like for you to contemplate the Lord's glory? Can you squeeze it onto your list of priorities?

Second Corinthians 3:16 gives us a hint about the first step—we must turn to the Lord. We must take our eyes off other things and look to the Lord. This can only happen if we are willing to look on something that may shatter us, reconfigure our priorities, threaten our identities, and gift us with an exalted hope. Are you willing to abandon yourself and find yourself?

Let us contemplate the Lord. Praise the Lord, the Creator of heaven and earth. Praise the Lord, in whose hands are the caverns of the earth. The heights of the hills are his also. The stars run their courses according to his paths and do his bidding. Praise the Lord, who chose Israel to be his people. Praise the Lord, who offers discipline to those he loves, and who will never leave us or forsake us. Praise the Lord, born in a manger of the young girl Mary, born to die and conquer death. Praise the Lord, whose Spirit guides today us today and into eternity. He will transform us in his glory.

Recommended Closing Prayer

Lord, forgive us for our dull minds and dull hearts. Thank you for refreshing us in your Word and restoring to us the joy of our salvation. In every way that we do not honor you, correct us as a gentle and loving Father. In every way that we can serve you, equip us, call us, and accompany us by the power and presence of your Holy Spirit. Amen.

Ordinary Time Day 39

MADISON PERRY

Reflect on 2 Corinthians 4:6–12

Call to Prayer

The gospel promises us extravagant things. God puts within his people the light of the knowledge of the glory of God in the face of Jesus Christ. We bear great treasure and are filled to overflowing with the life of Jesus.

But in truth, the gospel is manifested in us—not in our creaturely strength and passing fleshly glory, but in our very weakness. This is the great contradiction of our everyday lives as we embrace the way of Christ, where we at once take up our crosses and also know life and rest.

Glorious ruins are we, afflicted and perplexed vessels of the living God. Saint Paul says here without despair, "We always carry around in our body the death of Jesus" (2 Corinthians 4:10 NIV), revealing his resurrection life.

Have you given up yet? Is there any part of your life that you have surrendered to death, to the realm of utter pointlessness, to suffering and despair?

Come to Jesus now for rest. Name your burdens and ask him to share in them. Ask for the strength to continue to struggle. Finally, ask for the privilege of beholding the light of the knowledge of the glory of God, a glimpse of God's beauty far beyond anything this world could ever offer.

Recommended Closing Prayer

O Lord Jesus, we believe; help our unbelief. We cannot fathom your purposes, and we have ceded ground to hopelessness. May your fullness of life well up in our hearts, and may your Spirit bring life to us and glory to your name. Amen.

Ordinary Time Day 40
MADISON PERRY

Reflect on 2 Corinthians 5:16–21

Call to Prayer

In our age of self-improvement, we have been urged to take up the task of self-creation, of fashioning ourselves according to our own (inevitably shallow) vision of what is good and beautiful. In an age like ours, Paul's celebration of a "new creation" (1 Corinthians 5:17 NIV) might sound like an invitation to finally become the people we want to be.

However, Paul's words do not fit well into a universe built to exalt people. He has in mind not the passing glory of the flesh, but the eternal and resplendent glory of the living God.

To be a new creation is to be born anew, not only as true sons and daughters of the King, but also as ambassadors for Christ and ministers of reconciliation. Ever since the beginning of evil's war against our Lord, creation has become polluted by sin and alienated from God. God's holiness will not abide sin.

The task that falls to us is to enter into Christ's reconciliation of heaven and earth by offering this world to God so that he might make it righteous. Our hope is that every square inch of creation will be filled with the presence of God, becoming a new and transfigured creation. And the first offering that we make is ourselves. As God cleanses us and renews our hearts, we become the first fruits of his new creation.

God's restoration is cosmic, and his renewal will be all-encompassing.

Offer your heart and your life to God. Give him permission to renew you, to lift you out of hopelessness and rebellion and into new life. Ask him to give you a truer picture of his heart for the reconciling of all things to himself. Ask him how your life can reflect his heart. Glorify him. It won't be long before this reconciliation is fully accomplished.

Recommended Closing Prayer

Almighty God, you called your church to bear witness that you were in Christ reconciling the world to yourself. Give us boldness to proclaim the good news of your love, so that all who hear it may be drawn to you. Through him who was lifted high up on the cross, Jesus Christ our Lord. Amen.

Ordinary Time Day 41

MADISON PERRY

Reflect on 2 Corinthians 6:1–13

Call to Prayer

Open wide your heart to God and his people. Do not let yourself be restrained in your affection. If you harbor in yourself love of riches, a vain desire for glory, the nagging impulse toward sloth, or the bitter, consuming darkness of despair, then listen to the heart of Christ in the words of Paul. Unbind your affections and receive Christ, as today is the day of salvation.

Reread the middle portion, 2 Corinthians 6:3–10, again. Let it sink in. If your heart rejoices, read it again. Praise the Lord for his salvation!

Recommended Closing Prayer

Father, we are hungry for you and for your path. Lead us on, come what may, and never depart from us. We hunger and thirst to know your salvation more fully. Please give us the joy of sharing your salvation with others in the days and weeks ahead. Amen.

Ordinary Time Day 42

MADISON PERRY

Reflect on 2 Corinthians 6:16b–7:1

Call to Prayer

Hear God's promises: "I will make my dwelling among them and walk among them. I will be their God …. I will welcome you, and I will be a father to you" (2 Corinthians 6:16b, 6:17b–18 ESV).

Paul exhorts those reading his letter to live into the full completion of these promises. As Jesus often urged his disciples, Paul asks his friends to be ready for the time when God's holiness is revealed in full.

We who know Christ have been given his Holy Spirit to dwell in us. Yet, restrained by sin as we have been for so long, we often abandon the call to holiness.

Do you desire the completion of holiness in your own life? God's desire is not to use you but to complete you. And he will never abandon you to anything less than what is best for you.

God's holiness is not austere and lifeless. It is the fullness of his life brought to bear on creation, the intense and complete indwelling of his mercy, joy, and justice. To know God's life is to know both his all-embracing love and his swift and lifesaving intolerance of evil.

First meditate on God's promises. Thank him for his infinite mercy and unstoppable love. Ask him for the grace and strength to walk in a manner worthy of your call in Christ.

Recommended Closing Prayer

> Almighty and ever-living God, let your fatherly hand ever
> be upon us; let your Holy Spirit ever be with us, and so lead

us in the knowledge of and obedience to your Holy Word, that we may faithfully serve you in this life and joyfully dwell with you in the life to come. Through Jesus Christ our Lord. Amen.

(Adapted from the *Anglican Church in North America Book of Common Prayer*)

Ordinary Time Day 43

MADISON PERRY

Reflect on 2 Corinthians 8:1–9

Call to Prayer

"But as you excel in everything—in faith, in speech, in knowledge, in all earnestness, and in our love for you—see that you excel in this act of grace also" (2 Corinthians 8:7 ESV).

Paul here asks the Corinthians to examine whether or not they are generous. It can be easy for a Christian to say, "What I do with my resources isn't spiritual enough to think deeply about."

To counter that idea, let's notice how Paul understands giving. He talks about it as an *act of grace*. Every area and segment of our lives—from words, to deeds, to wallets—is a place where God's grace can enter and his salvation can be known. Pity the person who is only partially baptized, who has held himself or herself back from a complete and full-body immersion in God's grace.

When we give to someone else, in that very act God is present in his grace, freeing us on the one hand and blessing someone else with his bounty on the other. We give in love for God and to someone made in the image of God. Here we declare our freedom from greed, insecurity, and pride. Thanks be to the Lord for giving us people to give to, for giving us an amazing opportunity to know and be filled by his love and his grace.

Are there places in your life where you do not yet know the fullness of salvation? Could one of these be your wallet? What else comes to mind?

Come and lay it all at the foot of the cross. Ask that God will make his grace known to you in every moment and in every act and that as you live, your own thoughts, words, and deeds will glorify him. Thank him for his salvation, and rest in the peace that you are eternally provided for beyond measure.

Recommended Closing Prayer

> Lord Jesus Christ, you stretched out your arms of love on the hard wood of the cross that everyone might come within the reach of your saving embrace: So clothe us in your Spirit that we, reaching forth our hands in love, may bring those who do not know you to the knowledge and love of you; for the honor of your Name. Amen.
> *(Anglican Church in North America Book of Common Prayer)*

Ordinary Time Day 44
KARI WEST

Reflect on 2 Corinthians 9:10–15

Call to Prayer

We often live with a mindset of scarcity and conservation. With only a limited amount of time, money, and abilities, we have to act accordingly, doling out those resources carefully within clearly defined parameters.

But in this passage, we come face-to-face with an abundant, overflowing, limitless God—the great farmer who desires to produce massive stores of righteousness within his people. Paul is not trying to nickel-and-dime the Corinthians; he is not trying to guilt or coerce them into giving up a bit of their hard-earned limited incomes so the church can stay out of the red each month.

He invites them into a deeper, more powerful, more abundant way of living. He says, *Give cheerfully, knowing that our plentiful God is more than able to provide for you out of his infinite hidden storehouses.*

More than that, as we respond to God with free and openhanded generosity, he will produce a lavish harvest of godliness and increased generosity within our hearts. And if that isn't enough, God will use our generosity to yield yet another harvest as it meets the needs of other believers, producing thankfulness in their hearts toward God and deep affection for his body, the church.

As you pray, pause and meditate on this vision of our boundless, generous God overflowing with grace and mercy, and ready to produce great harvests of righteousness in his people. Ask him to reveal one way you could grow in cheerful generosity. See that way as an invitation to this great dance of giving and receiving life in his name.

Recommended Closing Prayer

Give us a vision of your abundant grace, O God, and fashion in us trusting and generous hearts. Amen.

Ordinary Time Day 45

KARI WEST

Reflect on Psalm 106:34–48

Call to Prayer

God called the Israelites to be set apart and to show the world a wholly different way to live. His laws for his people were meant to demonstrate his holiness and to portray a better way to be human as God's chosen possession.

Instead, God's people chose to conform to the cultures around them, ultimately turning to the most vicious sort of idol worship—sacrificing their own infant boys and girls on the altars of the Canaanite gods.

Perhaps we are tempted to sit in judgment of the Israelites. How could they have done such a thing? How could they have descended to the point of performing such horrific deeds? How had they failed so devastatingly?

But the truth is, all of our hearts are terribly powerful things, able to bear much good fruit when cleansed by Christ's blood and empowered by his Spirit, but also capable of the deepest depravity when twisted and corrupted by idolatry.

What we give ourselves to in worship matters so very much.

But what matters even more is what the psalmist has to say about God. God didn't forget his covenant; he returned and rescued his people again, pouring out his mercy on his stubborn people. His immense love led him to Golgotha, where he finally freed our idolatrous hearts once and for all.

As you pray, ask the Spirit for fresh conviction to know where idolatry has taken hold in your soul. Confess and receive his perfect mercy. Rejoice in his name.

Recommended Closing Prayer

> Blessed be the Lord, the God of Israel, from everlasting to everlasting! And let all the people say, "Amen!" Praise the Lord! Amen. *(Psalm 106:48 ESV)*

Ordinary Time Day 46

KARI WEST

Reflect on Psalm 107:23–32

Call to Prayer

God is at the helm of the world. His voice stirs the wind, and his whisper commands the oceans. No part of creation is outside the reach of his lordship; no corner of the world is beyond the bounds of his realm.

This isn't just an interesting theological fact; it is a permeating reality that has the power to shift your understanding of the world and the way you experience your circumstances. God is the one who rules the world, and God is the one who draws near each time you lift your voice to him.

God is compassionate and powerful, merciful and mysterious, loving and mighty.

The storm-tossed helpless sailors, staggering like drunkards under the weight of the wind and waves, cried to God, and God answered them.

Let the reality of God's reign and God's nearness pull you to your knees in prayer. Exalt him for his great love and the wonderful things he has done. Ask him for rescue, for succor, for strength. Be at peace, living under the rule of our great King.

Recommended Closing Prayer

> O God, the protector of all who trust in you, without whom nothing is strong, nothing is holy: increase and multiply upon us your mercy; that with you as our ruler and guide we may so pass through things temporal that we lose not our hold on things eternal; grant this, heavenly Father, for our Lord Jesus Christ's sake, who is alive and reigns with you, in the unity of the Holy Spirit, one God, now and for ever. Amen.
>
> (*Anglican Church in North America Book of Common Prayer*)

Ordinary Time Day 47

KARI WEST

Reflect on Psalm 109:1–5, 109:26–31

Call to Prayer

Do David's opening words bring any specific situation to your mind?

It's a hard thing to bear the hatred and accusations of other people, and it's even harder when that vitriol is undeserved and comes from those we love, those we pray for. How do we handle the anguish of unmerited animosity from those we considered—at least at one point in time—to be friends?

David spends most of this psalm telling God in detail about the vicious lies and the verbal attacks thrown at him by his false accusers. Perhaps this is our first clue. Before we rush to contemplating God's character or asking for his help, as David will by the end of this psalm, we must be honest with the Lord. We must lay before him the details of our deep struggles. We must offer up the intricacies of our hardship to the one who cares for us. We must spit out the poison of our anger and bitterness to God before it takes its toll on our own hearts.

After this honesty with God, David then asks him to intervene. He asks for rescue and deliverance. He pleads with God to work according to his steadfast love and his good character. He says that as long as God rescues him by his love, then others can curse him if they like. With the blessing of God, it no longer matters. David remembers that God stands beside the needy, giving strength and salvation.

David begs for salvation, for the unfailing love of God. We know even more about God's love than David did. We now know Jesus, our Savior, the perfect image of the Father's love. In our hardships, in our struggles, in those barbed circumstances that David's words call to mind, there is rest to be found in Christ. He bled out on a cross under false accusations and in front of a crowd that spewed mockery and hatred. Our Jesus, who patiently bore each lie and all vitriol, died unjustly to bind himself to us and give us peace with God.

Remember that our God still stands beside the needy. He is with the mistreated and abused.

Pray for honesty toward God, endurance, peace, and justice from God. Pray for a deeper full-being knowledge of Jesus, our sinless sin-bearer, whose blessing is all that you need.

Recommended Closing Prayer

O Lord, let us know your love deeply. Amen.

Ordinary Time Day 48

KARI WEST

Reflect on Mark 1:16–20

Call to Prayer

Jesus's ministry is just beginning at this point in Mark. His fame has yet to spread, as it will just a few verses later on in this chapter. What can possibly have convinced these blue-collar workers to abandon their livelihoods and follow an uneducated carpenter from the backwater town of Galilee? What do their fellow fishermen think as Simon and Andrew abandon their still torn nets in the boat? Does Zebedee call after his sons in anger or confusion as they walk away?

"Follow me" (Mark 1:16 NIV). With a sentence, Jesus alters the course of these four men's lives. Why do they listen? Why do they trust him?

By the mysterious grace of God, they see something true, something compelling, in Christ.

"Follow me" (Mark 1:16 NIV). Christ's words, recorded for us in scripture, have that same mysterious, drawing power as much today as they did two thousand years ago when they fell from his lips.

As you pray, allow these words to work in your soul. Dwell on Christ's command given to all his disciples. Dwell on the beauty and trueness of Jesus that compels you to obedience, even when all around you misunderstand or scorn your steps toward the Savior.

> Lord, to whom shall we go? You have the words of eternal life, and we believe, and have come to know, that you are the Holy One of God. Amen. *(John 6:68–69 NIV)*

Ordinary Time Day 49

KARI WEST

Reflect on Mark 3:20–34

Call to Prayer

The strong man is bound. Someone greater has entered the house, set on holy plundering.

This is the great truth that Christ's own family and the religious rulers miss in this passage. Christ's actions gesture toward who he is and what he will do, but those around him don't allow themselves to see it. Instead, both his detractors and those who love him turn to easier-to-swallow ideas: his family calls him crazy, and the teachers of the law say he's possessed by the devil.

Just a few verses earlier in this chapter, unclean spirits fall before Christ and declare him to be the Son of God. And yet here, foolish leaders accuse Jesus of being in league with Satan. These men are willfully blind to the great works of Jesus and what those acts reveal about his kingship and his aim. Christ rebukes them for their unbelief and arrogance.

Similarly, he tells his blood family that only those who live in accordance with God's will are truly his kin. Allegiance to Jesus and belief in his lordship must supersede all earthly claims of family.

All—no matter their family status, no matter their religious knowledge or prestigious place in society—must acknowledge the lordship of Christ. He reigns over Satan, over death, over every throne and ruler and authority. He has tied up the strong man. He rules, and he will set all to rights.

As you pray, don't miss this reality as many in the passage did. Ask the Lord for fresh awareness of his dominion over all the earth and every lesser power. Pray to be an ambassador of his peace. Take refuge in him.

Recommended Closing Prayer

> Jesus, you are the image of the invisible God,
> the firstborn over all creation.
> For everything was created by you,
> in heaven and on earth,
> the visible and the invisible,
> whether thrones or dominions
> or rulers or authorities—
> all things have been created through you and for you.
> You are before all things,
> and by you all things hold together.
> Let us worship you in spirit and in truth.
> In your great name. Amen.
> *(Adapted from Colossians 1:15–17 NIV)*

Ordinary Time Day 50

KARI WEST

Reflect on Mark 4:35–41

Call to Prayer

"Do you not care that we are perishing?" (Mark 4:38 ESV).

Christ responds to this question with a display of his absolute power over the creation he has made. Then he turns and asks his disciples,

"Why are you afraid? After all this time, do you still not know who I am? Is your faith still so weak?"

Christ replaces their fear with a better one. Instead of towering waves, swift winds, or the threat of death, he puts himself on display as the one to hold in awe as the Supreme Ruler of the earth. But Christ is very different from earthly rulers: he uses his power to protect, to care, and to bring peace. He directs his might to harness chaos and to still the storm.

The disciples feared death and distrusted Jesus. But Christ knew, with the long path of discipleship stretching ahead of them—ending for most in their martyrdoms—that they needed a radical reorientation of their fears. He displayed his power so that when the time did come for the disciples to face death, they would trust their resurrected, risen Savior, creation's Lord, and death's trampler.

As you pray, remember that Ordinary Time is all about following after Christ in this long walk of obedience and faith. Thank Christ for his power, his care, and his love. Hope in him as death's foe, as the earth's ruler, and as your ever-near friend. Ask him again for the steadfastness to follow where he leads.

Recommended Closing Prayer

Jesus, please be our peace. Amen.

Ordinary Time Day 51

SALLY BREEDLOVE

Reflect on Daniel 11:33–35, 12:1–3

Call to Prayer

We are unaccustomed to biting prophetic words. It's good to wonder why. Are we afraid of talking about a righteous God who is working a grand-scale plan of redemption in the midst of terrible evil? Do we resist being a part of a story that is cosmic and eternal, a story that is about much more than ourselves? Or perhaps we resist a Jesus who has more in mind than giving us abundant lives of prosperity and protection from all pain?

We can learn from Daniel. He was born into advantage in the kingdom of Israel, but as a young man he watched his nation fall. Jerusalem was razed. The elite, the educated, and the wealthy were killed or taken captive. From his late teens, Daniel lived in exile at the service of a foreign king. At times he was in favor; at times, discarded; at times, serving an insane ruler; and at times, in mortal danger from those in power. God also gave him the burden of terrifying and beautiful visions of what lay ahead for humanity.

Perhaps because of all he carried, the "watchers from heaven" came to him at least three times to tell him he was greatly loved. Was it knowing that he was seen and loved that gave him the power to endure? Can we endure like Daniel? We, too, are seen by the Triune God. We are greatly loved just as he was. Daniel had his opportunity to live faithfully in the midst of trouble. We have that same opportunity in our lives.

Will you pray for the grit and the courage to endure? Will you ask for the wisdom to live well when life is hard? Will you pray for someone you know who is deeply struggling? Will you pray for all of us who are God's people that we will stay courageously loyal to him?

Recommended Closing Prayer

Father, empower us to live in a way that honors you as we depend on you for all things. Amen.

Ordinary Time Day 52

Reflect on Psalm 27

Call to Prayer

Consider Psalm 27:5: "For in the day of trouble he will keep me safe in his dwelling; he will hide me in the shelter of his sacred tent and set me high upon a rock" (NIV).

Who is God to this psalmist?

God is a strong building, a fortress. The psalmist invites us to build our lives under the sheltering protection of God's presence. When we learn to inhabit spaces bounded by his grace, we find rest and shelter. We find protection from the enemy. God is our sheltering place, not because he replaces an earthly sheltering place and certainly not because he gives us permission to ignore those who need a sheltering roof over their heads. God is our sheltering place because his protection is so fundamental to our human needs, both spiritual and physical.

God is also the host, welcoming us to a grand house. We find our protection and refuge in him; he invites us to dwell close to him, in his house. Israel's story is one of exodus and exile and then return to the land. In it all, the desire for a home is central. For much of their existence, the Israelites are yearning and pressing toward home. Their tents, the tabernacle, and ultimately the temple do not neatly meet their spiritual hunger for finding a refuge in God.

Jesus, carpenter that he is, continues to invite people to take refuge in the sheltering God even as he renews their bodies. And in a magnificent though mystifying twist, when we are in relationship with this refuge God, our bodies become his house—the temple of the Holy Spirit.

As you come to pray, ask yourself these questions: "How do I experience the refuge that God provides? Do I identify it more with a personal sheltering in God or more with a corporate participation in worship at the church, his house?" Thank the Lord for his sheltering presence, and ask for deeper trust in him as your refuge.

Recommended Closing Prayer

Sheltering God, who invites us into his house and into his very presence, what does it look like to take refuge in you? We are so comfortable and so secure in our physical houses and with our bank accounts, our social networks, and our jobs that we hardly notice the need for shelter in you until we feel the world unraveling. Then we crawl toward you, asking the question why instead of simply taking refuge. Calm us with your presence. Welcome us into your house with a gloriously warm hearth and table set for all. And help us to surrender our own lives to become your dwelling, our bodies filled by your Holy Spirit. Amen.

Ordinary Time Day 53
SALLY BREEDLOVE

Reflect on Mark 6:1–6

Call to Prayer

Mark takes pains to show us that many people reject Jesus: the skeptical scribes as he offers forgiveness and healing to a paralyzed man; John's disciples and a group of Pharisees who question if Jesus is truly righteous; and both the Pharisees and the politically powerful Herodians in their murderous opposition. After Jesus's Sabbath miracles, unclean spirits try to expose him, his own extended family doubts his sanity, the scribes accuse him of being demon-possessed, his own disciples complain that he doesn't really care about them, and the Gerasenes banish him from their town.

This rejection continues in Mark 6. Jesus has gone home to Nazareth. He's no longer a carpenter. His band of disciples and his teaching both mark him as a rabbi, and the miracles he has done suggest he is far more than a rabbi. Surely in Nazareth he will be welcomed?

After all, the people in Nazareth are his kinfolk and neighbors. They have bargained and traded with Jesus for him to build them a table, a house, or a new yoke. Jesus has been a workingman like all of them.

They know his character. He has never been false, never used anyone, never pawned off shoddy workmanship, and never erupted in anger, or drunkenness, or greed. Even as a boy, he was truly a good person. How could they not believe? But Mark makes it clear. Their astonishment that their local boy is no longer simply a carpenter turns to contempt and resistance. They don't want to listen, to believe, or to receive Jesus's help.

As you pray, thank Jesus for enduring your own hostility toward him, for being patient with your doubt, and for forgiving your contempt. Ask Christ to give you a child's welcoming heart, one eager to believe him, trust him, and follow him.

Recommended Closing Prayer

> Almighty God, give us the increase of faith, hope, and love; and, that we may obtain what you have promised, make us love what you command; through Jesus Christ our Lord, who lives and reigns with you and the Holy Spirit, one God, for ever and ever. Amen.
>
> *(Anglican Church in North America Book of Common Prayer)*

Ordinary Time Day 54

MADISON PERRY

Reflect on Mark 7:14–23

Call to Prayer

This passage reveals to us Jesus's overwhelming concern for us and his desire to protect us from ourselves.

In Jesus's time, "religious people" struggled under the weight of a ubiquitous worry that they had to protect themselves from negative influences in the world around them. They believed that if they could isolate themselves from outside trouble and corrupting objects and people, they would finally be holy.

This same instinct is very much with us now. If only we could be left alone and spared the awful influence of any number of morally repugnant outsiders, then we could live lives pleasing to God.

But Jesus changes the conversation and puts the focus on our own hearts. "There is nothing outside a person that by going into him can defile him, but the things that come out of a person are what defile him …. For from within, out of the heart of man, come evil thoughts" (Mark 7:15, 7:21 ESV).

We have sold our very hearts for a mess of pottage—cheap thrills, easy pleasure, gratifying anger—and now we are in bondage. Our "religious instinct" is to lose track of our moral failings by fretting constantly over the evils being played out on the world stage or in our neighbor's living room. Jesus puts the focus back on us.

As we turn to the Lord in prayer, let us remember that God is real, unchanging, and ever present, regardless of whatever we fear is at work in the world. Jesus, our Creator and Author, knows more of the human heart than we ever will. Take another look at the evil things that Jesus says come from within. Pray that God will renew your heart. Return to the joy of the salvation wrought in Christ!

Recommended Closing Prayer

> O God, the King eternal, who dividest the day from the night and turnest the shadow of death into the morning: Drive far from us all wrong desires, incline our hearts to keep thy law, and guide our feet into the way of peace; that, having done thy will with cheerfulness while it was day, we may, when the night cometh, rejoice to give thee thanks; through Jesus Christ our Lord. Amen.
> *(Anglican Church in North America Book of Common Prayer)*

Ordinary Time Day 55

MADISON PERRY

Reflect on Mark 7:31–37

Call to Prayer

We read here an astonishingly intimate scene. Jesus works a miracle in private for someone who could never do anything for him.

"And taking him aside from the crowd privately, he put his fingers into his ears, and after spitting touched his tongue" (Mark 7:33 ESV).

Putting fingers in ears, spitting, and touching his tongue—these are the kinds of actions parents perform for their children. But here we see Jesus, the Author of life, perform an act of creation on behalf of a beloved child.

This scene overflows with weakness and tenderness. We feel embarrassed to look. But we mustn't turn away. Let this pitiful person who lacks ears to hear or even a tongue to speak show us what we need to understand. We too are children, unable to help ourselves, children who need to choose to be vulnerable to the tender care of our Father.

As you approach the Lord, consider his offer of salvation for you and for those you know. Call to mind your weakness. Allow Jesus to see you for who you are and to do what he must do, even if he must put his fingers in your ears and touch your tongue with his spit. Rejoice that the one who made you has recreated you.

Recommended Closing Prayer

O Christ, who meets us in our weakness, work in us once again your good and perfect will. Grant us humility, grant us sight, grant us hearing, grant us joy. For your sake and in your name. Amen.

Ordinary Time Day 56

MADISON PERRY

Reflect on Mark 8:27–30

Call to Prayer

What brings you back to the Lord today? routine and rhythm? the need to make someone else happy? the hope of receiving healing or blessing?

At this moment in Mark 8, Jesus is turning toward the cross. He has revealed his immense power and his all-encompassing heart for others. He has begun to fend off a host of expectations placed upon him by religious and political authorities. He has set his face to deal the decisive blow against sin and evil. The stakes couldn't be higher, but so few have even begun to grasp who he is.

This scene invites us to stand alongside Jesus's disciples. The one we sometimes make into a plaything or a dispenser of blessing stands before us. His love encompasses the whole world and descends into the deepest depths of your very soul. Jesus has come to set his creation free, to set you free. He wants to liberate you so you can see him for who he is and proclaim him in thought, word, and deed all the days of your life.

Jesus's question is meant to probe the depths of your hearts. Listen as he asks you, "Who do you say that I am?" (Mark 8:29 ESV).

Search yourself, and answer in prayer. Embrace Jesus as Savior. Disregard the competing voices in your world that would make little of Jesus. Ask Jesus himself for a strong faith and solid convictions. Lift your voice to the Lord in praise of who he is and the works of his hand.

Recommended Closing Prayer

Jesus, you are the Christ, the Son of the living God. Let us live joyful, steadfast lives rooted in who you are and what you have done. Amen.

Ordinary Time Day 57

BRANDON WALSH

Reflect on Psalm 7

Call to Prayer

Christians often speak about "intimacy" with God. Most of the time they mean a sense of the Lord's consoling nearness, a place where the Lord speaks, or a place where we know the Spirit's peace. But this is not the only kind of intimacy with the Lord the scriptures offer us.

Psalm 7 speaks of an intimacy with the Lord that has room for brutal honesty and frustration.

First, the psalmist names the atrocities the wicked commit. They oppress the poor and allow their pride to swell. When will God act? The writer doesn't bridle the anger, frustration, and confusion stirring inside his heart.

When a person speaks with a superior at work or with someone he or she knows in a strictly professional setting, his or her words become calculated and restrained.

But words flow more freely with the people we trust. A spouse will vent to a spouse, or a close friend to a close friend, if they trust each other deeply. The same can be said of this psalmist and the Lord; this is a relationship close enough for brutal honesty.

In truth, it sometimes feels as if the Lord is far off and oblivious to injustice. When we doubt, when our frustration and anger rise up, we have a choice: turn away from the Lord and be silent, or lean in and speak honestly with him. This second option is a path to deep faithfulness and intimacy.

The church calendar calls this time of year "Ordinary Time." Sadly, it seems our ordinary is often a long walk through frightening and unsettling days. We are anxious about finances, health, the stability of our world, and the future. Ask yourself: "How will I respond?" As you pray, move toward the Lord with your true heart, no matter how brutal and messy. Choose intimacy with your God.

> Dear Lord and Savior Jesus Christ: I hold up all my weakness to your strength, my failure to your faithfulness, my sinfulness to your perfection, my loneliness to your compassion, my little pains to your great agony on the Cross. I pray that you will cleanse me, strengthen me, guide me, so that in all ways my life may be lived as you would have it lived, without cowardice and for you alone. Show me how to live in true humility, true contrition, and true love. Amen.
> *(Anglican Church in North America Book of Common Prayer)*

Ordinary Time Day 58

SALLY BREEDLOVE

Reflect on 2 Corinthians 6:16 and Revelation 21:3

Call to Prayer

These days, does your life feel like a steep climb or as if you're on a long journey with no clear arrival date?

God's chosen people knew that reality. Three times each year, they journeyed to Jerusalem for religious festivals. The road of travel was long and the incline grew sharp as they neared the Holy City.

At its highest point, Jerusalem is twenty-five hundred feet above sea level. While just twenty-two miles to the east lies the Dead Sea, the lowest point on earth.

Getting to Jerusalem was quite a climb.

The people made this trek because they needed to worship their God in his temple. Built by Solomon, the temple was where the very Spirit of God dwelt in the holy of holies.

The Israelites sang songs along the way, and we know them as Psalms of Ascent. This was not just a physical journey; it was a spiritual one.

Perhaps you're exhausted by the hills you're forced to walk over during a challenging season. Maybe you feel as if you climb and climb yet make no progress. But even now, there is good news for you.

Although we face physical climbs in a fallen world, we do not face a spiritual one. In a miraculous change of address, God's Spirit has moved from a temple built by craftsmen on a hill in Jerusalem to hearts reclaimed through the blood of Christ.

We no longer face a journey of ascent. Instead, our Lord Jesus descended to the earth, lived among us, and died a criminal's death to pay for sins not his own. He came to us. He conquered death. Then as he ascended to the throne to sit at the right hand of the Father, he sent his Spirit to live in those who receive his free gift of salvation.

"Do you not know that you are God's temple and that God's Spirit dwells in you?" (1 Corinthians 3:16 ESV).

Pause to soak in the reality that the God of the universe has sent the Spirit of his Son Jesus Christ to reside in your heart. Celebrate the blessing that you, built together with other believers, are the temple of our living Lord. Thank him for this extraordinary gift, and choose to walk forward in this reality.

Recommended Closing Prayer

O Christ, thank you for descending to earth and redeeming your people so that we could forever know your nearness. Even in the midst of our exhaustion, give us grace to hold to the reality and to hope in the promise of full and unbroken friendship with you. Amen.

Ordinary Time Day 59

ART GOING

Reflect on 1 Peter 1:3–9, 1:13–16, 1:22–23

Call to Prayer

Peter wrote his first letter to people scattered among many different countries, uncertain about their future. They were marginalized in society, alienated in relationships, and threatened with loss of honor and socioeconomic standing. Paul calls them exiles, resident aliens in an alien culture. But he's also clear that they are God's Easter people. His encouragement and challenges still speak clearly to us, who are also aliens in an increasingly hostile world.

Peter's message is this: We are the following:

- People with a **past**
  Gospel transformation means we put the past behind us, not that we pretend we don't have one.

- People with a **love**
  What would it mean in practice for us to "love one another deeply from the heart"?

- People with an **appetite**
  Some of us will need to recover our spiritual hunger and open God's Word regularly again.

- People with a **purpose**
  God's mercy and hope is not for us to enjoy on our own or keep to ourselves. It is a treasure to give away. It was designed for passing on, so it gets better as we give it away! We are a people belonging to God "that you may declare the praises of him who called you out of darkness into his wonderful light," as 2 Peter 2:9 tells us.

- **People with a future!**

Jesus's resurrection gives us a radically better future than anything we could have dreamt of or imagined. It is a guaranteed new world and future together, a salvation to rejoice in, through all the griefs and trials of the here and now.

Living hope arises from being born anew through the resurrection of Jesus! Living hope comes not from surveying the world around us, but from believing in the resurrection.

And living hope leads to rejoicing! Rejoicing even if various trials come. Rejoicing even amid adversity, what Paul elsewhere calls "this light momentary affliction" (2 Corinthians 4:17 ESV).

You can't rejoice in trial unless your love has been transformed—you love Jesus and you trust him even though you have not seen him. You possess inexpressible joy in an invisible (but risen) Christ!

As you go to prayer, ask the Lord to kindle in you a living hope, and then beg the Spirit for joy, even in the midst of sorrow.

Recommended Closing Prayer

> May the Son of God, who is already formed in you, grow in you, so that for you he will become immeasurable, and that in you he will become laughter, exultation, the fullness of joy which no one will take from you.
> *(Isaac of Stella)*

Ordinary Time Day 60
ART GOING

Reflect on 1 Peter 2:11–17, 2:21–25

Call to Prayer

Peter doesn't address his friends in terms of their ancestry, social status, or wealth, but as strangers and resident aliens, as "God's chosen people who are living as foreigners" (1 Peter 1:1 NLT).

They are exiles with no power, no prestige, and no public impact. They exist on the sideline, beginning to experience persecution. This world into which God is sending them doesn't hear the gospel as good news, and it rejects its messengers. Very soon the persecution will intensify. If these Christians are going to be faithful witnesses, they need to understand who they are and what their world is like.

But they are chosen, by the mercy of God, to be made holy by the Spirit for a particular purpose.

Christians live a double life as dual citizens: inhabitants of a place and citizens of God's new world. They are pointers to a new reality, a new creation coming into being.

But this living as beloved exiles is not a ghetto strategy, and there is no universal blueprint. The particulars of what it means to be a Christian exile have to be worked out in a particular place. This exile life leaves us still embedded in the authority structures of the society we inhabit. We're called not to separation but to submission.

But remember the purpose laid out in 1 Peter 2:9: we are called to proclaim! We are a people with a story to tell.

We are called to be like Jesus—following the pattern he established, walking in his footsteps, bearing suffering patiently. This is what came with the terms of your call. So, as you pray this evening, pause to name your suffering, and then pray for a Spirit-endowed capacity to bear it with equanimity and patient endurance. Pray that God will use you as a signpost.

Recommended Closing Prayer

> Hasten, O Father, the coming of your kingdom; and grant that we your servants, who now live by faith, may with joy behold your Son at his coming in glorious majesty; even Jesus Christ, our only Mediator and Advocate. Amen.
> (*Anglican Church in North America Book of Common Prayer*)

Ordinary Time Day 61

ART GOING

Reflect on 1 Peter 3:8–9, 3:13–18

Call to Prayer

Peter knows how we yearn to be blessed. But he knows something we must pray to learn or rediscover, namely that blessing is not the presumption of privilege and the acquiring of stuff. "Do not repay evil with evil or insult with insult. On the contrary, repay evil with blessing, because to this you were called so that you may inherit a blessing" (1 Peter 3:9 NIV).

To be sure, we may expect blessing from God, but only when we offer blessing, when we live in blessing. And blessing is all about how we respond to mistreatment. Remember how frequently, in his first letter, Peter held up the example of Jesus's quiet and patient endurance of suffering on our behalf and called us to be willing to suffer likewise.

Peter encourages us, "Always be prepared to give an answer to everyone who asks you to give the reason for the hope that you have. But do this with gentleness and respect" (1 Peter 3:15 NIV).

We usually read that as a model of evangelism. But surely Peter had also in mind gentle and hopeful testimony of redemptive suffering.

Pray for the power to suffer this way, hoping in Christ.

Recommended Closing Prayer

O God our Father, whose Son forgave his enemies while he was suffering shame and death: Strengthen those who suffer for the sake of conscience; when they are accused, save them from speaking in hate; when they are rejected, save them from bitterness; when they are imprisoned, save them from despair; and to us your servants, give grace to respect their witness and to discern the truth, that our society may be cleansed and strengthened. This we ask for the sake of Jesus Christ, our merciful and righteous Judge. Amen.
(Anglican Church in North America Book of Common Prayer)

Ordinary Time Day 62

ART GOING

Reflect on 1 Peter 4:7–10

Call to Prayer

Called not to separation from the world but to *submission*. Everywhere we turn, we are embedded in relationships and called to follow the pattern of Jesus's own humble and patient submission. We are called to *suffer* in the same manner as Jesus.

And now we discover another essential S-word in our life as God's people in the world: *stewards*—stewards of the manifold grace of God. Pause at that job description! We are called to be stewards and caretakers of this glorious grace in all its hues and shapes. The Lord of resurrection, who has launched the new creation in and among us, is entrusting to us the task of tending his gifts to and for others. In all his manifold goodness, he has distributed his gifts to us in unimaginable diversity. Your gifts are not my gifts. But all of us are called to "use whatever gift you have received to serve others" (1 Peter 4:10 NIV).

Gifts are for serving, not merely for having or even enjoying. We're called to give our lives away, and God has given us the means—his own gifts of grace. Some of us do this with words; others, by way of acts of mercy; and still others … well, where to begin? It's manifold!

Hospitality is the open door of our lives, inviting others in, welcoming them with their gifts and receiving them as one more opportunity to serve.

And don't miss Peter's simple reminder to be disciplined in our praying. There will be countless situations in our exile life where we feel helpless or clueless as to how to serve, how to make inroads, and how to witness. Often we will be left with our prayers, sometimes even left so wholly in grief for a hurting world that we will have to trust the Spirit to pray in us, with sighs too deep for words. But disciplined praying for our families, our friends, our neighbors, and our enemies is itself a precious stewardship of grace.

Imagine the richness of a life given to discovering your gifts, nurturing them, and offering them in service to others. As you pray, ask for eyes to see how you have been gifted, and pray for opportunities to give your life away.

Recommended Closing Prayer

Almighty and eternal God, so draw our hearts to you, so guide our minds, so fill our imaginations, and so control our wills that we may be wholly yours, utterly dedicated to you. And then use us, we pray, as you will, and always to your glory and the welfare of your people. Through our Lord and Savior Jesus Christ. Amen.

Ordinary Time Day 63

ART GOING

Reflect on 1 Peter 5:1–11

Call to Prayer

A word to pastors: be humble shepherds!
A word to ordinary Christians: stay awake!

Humble shepherds. Shepherd is what the word *pastor* means. We all need leaders who watch over themselves, who live as examples of Jesus-centered compassion and tenderness, and who watch over us. Do you welcome oversight? Do you seek it out from your pastor, a spiritual director, or a friend?

In our celebrity culture, it's so easy for pastors to become absorbed in developing careers, acquiring followers, or as we hear so often today, "building a platform." Social media has magnified these efforts. In light of this, we all need the kind of pastor who recognizes that leadership is not acquiring a name, but tending the flock entrusted to one's care.

That's the calling all of us have received from God. It's what calling is: tending to those who have been entrusted to our care. Calling is not in the first place about my gifts, or my passions, or my fulfillment. It's about the people entrusted to my care—listening to their longings and fears, loving them, and serving them.

Pastors, be humble shepherds! Christians, stay awake!

Peter warns us to stay awake, to stand firm in God's power, resolute in faithfulness, mindful of other suffering brothers and sisters in the rest of the world. Stay alert to the prowling evil one, who wants nothing more than to devour us—to seduce us into self-serving and self-promoting.

As you pray, ask for protection. Pray for your pastor and for your being pastored. And pray for the people God has entrusted to your care.

Recommended Closing Prayer

> Visit this place, O Lord, and drive far from it all snares of the enemy; let your holy angels dwell with us to preserve us in peace; and let your blessing be upon us always; through Jesus Christ our Lord. Amen.
>
> *(Anglican Church in North America Book of Common Prayer)*

Ordinary Time Day 64

ART GOING

Reflect on 2 Peter 1:1–12

Call to Prayer

It's always helpful to keep the big picture in view: what God wants for, not from, his people. Peter reminds us that "his divine power has given us everything we need for a godly life" (2 Peter 1:3 NIV).

He provides all we need for an abundant and flourishing life and a deep commitment to what matters most. To that end, he has granted to us "his very great and precious promises" (2 Peter 1:4 NIV), as follows:

- Provision
  We need to be awakened to the realization that too often we function as though God were not the big thing in our lives.

- Power

  We can forgive, speak the gospel, and be God's healing presence.

- Promises

  Think of the capstone promise God gave at Pentecost—the Holy Spirit, Jesus's presence. You can be born anew into hope. Jesus will return, and you will live forever with him in a new heaven and new earth. In the meantime, know that no one can take away your joy.

What is the ultimate goal of this provision, this power, and these promises? That you may become partakers in the divine nature, so that you can become ever more like Jesus. That is God's purpose for God's people: Christlikeness.

Look at the virtues Peter calls for as confirmation of our calling. Do you hear echoes of the fruit of the Spirit from Galatians 5? It's all about the shape of the promised Christ life in us.

Pray now for a deeper awareness of the promises, the power, and the constant provision you have received from God.

Recommended Closing Prayer

Gracious God and most merciful Father, you have granted us the rich and precious jewel of your holy Word: Assist us with your Spirit, that the same Word may be written in our hearts to our everlasting comfort, to reform us, to renew us according to your own image, to build us up and edify us into the perfect dwelling place of your Christ, sanctifying and increasing in us all heavenly virtues; grant this, O heavenly Father, for Jesus Christ's sake. Amen.

(Anglican Church in North America Book of Common Prayer)

Ordinary Time Day 65

ART GOING

Reflect on 2 Peter 2:1–19, 3:1–13

Call to Prayer

Do we need reminding that there are false prophets and deceptive teachers motivated by greed who bring swift destruction down on themselves and poison their ministries? The stories abound. Leaders who have wielded global influence are brought down, leaving a wake of disheartened followers and, too often, damaged victims of their perversion, not to mention the flood of defectors from the faith.

"Waterless springs" (2 Peter 1:17 ESV), Peter calls them. "They promise … freedom, but they themselves are slaves of corruption" (2 Peter 1:19 ESV). We must pray fervently that we may not fall for the lies or be sucked in by the false promises, that we may have discerning minds and hearts.

But where does such discernment come from? Peter tells us: "I want you to recall the words spoken in the past by the holy prophets and the command given by our Lord and Savior through your apostles" (2 Peter 3:2 NIV).

It's the same reminder Jesus gave his disciples before the Ascension: "I will not leave you as orphans; I will come to you …. The Holy Spirit, whom the Father will send in my name, will teach you all things and will remind you of everything I have said to you" (John 14:18, 14:26 NIV).

Jesus knows we are perennial amnesiacs and need to be reminded of the precious and great promises, of the presence and power of Jesus's own Spirit, of the commandments, and of the grace to obey.

There is only one sure way to maintain a capacity to spot false teaching and to maintain faithfulness: read the scriptures!

How we live as we wait for the coming of the Lord in judgment matters. Peter calls us to live not casually or presumptuously, but in hopeful anticipation of the new heavens and the new earth. In the meantime, we must not be carried away by the empty promises of false teachers, but rather "grow in the grace and knowledge of our Lord and Savior Jesus Christ" (2 Peter 3:18 NIV).

Ordinary Time Day 66

BILL BOYD

Reflect on Matthew 26:17–29

Call to Prayer

In Matthew's account of the Last Supper, the disciples begin to second-guess even their own hearts. Each one seems to ask, "Is it I, Lord?" (Matthew 26:22 ESV).

Jesus's words cut his friends to the heart. But what about us? Would his words have troubled us? *What if I am the one Jesus is talking about?* Would we ask him that same question?

Or perhaps we are too glib? We assume that if we had been with Jesus, we never would have betrayed him. We never would have deserted him.

Do we perhaps need to examine our own hearts?

Do we assume that Christianity guarantees us freedom from doubt, pain, confusion, disappointment, or fear?

We need to slow down and spend time in prayer and contemplation before the Lord and his Word.

The true gospel always drives us humbly to the salve of Jesus's body and blood. It makes us hungry to be with God's people, to worship, to pray, to take Communion together, and to hear the words "Blessed are the poor in spirit, for theirs is the kingdom of heaven. Blessed are those who mourn, for they will be comforted" (Matthew 5:3–4 NIV). Only in accepting our brokenness will we have room to ask for his strength to follow and believe.

Recommended Closing Prayer

We do not presume to come to this your table, O merciful Lord, trusting in our own righteousness, but in your abundant and great mercies. We are not worthy so much as to gather up the crumbs under your table; but you are the same Lord whose character is always to have mercy. Grant us, therefore, gracious Lord, so to eat the flesh of your dear Son Jesus Christ, and to drink his blood, that our sinful bodies may be made clean by his body, and our souls washed through his most precious blood, and that we may evermore dwell in him, and he in us. Amen.

(Anglican Church in North America Book of Common Prayer)

Ordinary Time Day 67

SALLY BREEDLOVE

Reflect on Isaiah 30:15–18

Call to Prayer

For such a long time we have believed we could solve our own problems, haven't we? Israel faced the overwhelming Assyrians in the day of King Hezekiah, and many of them were convinced that the only safe course was to turn to Egypt for help. Egypt. The very place God had told them not to turn.

But in the midst of their stubborn fear and their belief that they could find their own solutions, God continued to offer himself.

Can we solve the issues of our hurting world and our lives on our own? Can we build a fortress strong enough to protect our health, our economy, or the life we have constructed?

Do we hear the invitation from God? He longs to show us mercy.

Draw near to him now. His mercy is exceedingly abundant, not just for you but for his whole created world.

Recommended Closing Prayer

Lord Jesus Christ, Son of God, have mercy on me, a sinner. Amen.

Ordinary Time Day 68

KARI WEST

Reflect on Psalm 119:33–40

Call to Prayer

What are the prayers that come up from the depths of your heart? Are they in tune with the requests found here in Psalm 119?

In these words, the psalmist displays a soul-deep conviction of the goodness, beauty, and worth of God's law. He delights in God's commands; he seeks understanding to better follow the Lord with all his heart; and he trusts that in the Words of God true life is found.

Pause and reflect. Do you possess the psalmist's love for the law of God?

One of the beautiful aspects of prayer is that when we offer verses like these up to the Lord, he will work within us to make them our true desires. If we ask for understanding so that we may grow in obedience, God delights not only to answer that prayer, but also to slowly transform us into the kind of people who want that more than anything else.

When we ask for our eyes to be turned away from worthless things and to instead hold to the supremacy of God's Words, we slowly become people who know, deep in our bones, that "everything else is worthless when compared with the infinite value of knowing Christ Jesus" (Philippians 3:8 NLT), the Word made flesh.

Offer up each of these requests to your Father and ask him to transform your heart to want the best things. Trust by the power of his Spirit that he is indeed forming you as his beloved disciple and child. Be at peace.

Recommended Closing Prayer

Father, give us the assurance that you who began your good work in us will bring it to completion at the day of Jesus Christ. In his name and for his sake. Amen.

Ordinary Time Day 69

MARYRACHEL BOYD

Reflect on Psalm 119:73–88

Call to Prayer

We live in an age of image. Our inner worlds—even our outer worlds, in some cases, these days—have the tendency to go unseen, and knowing and being known feels like a complicated pursuit. Where there is a lack of knowing, loneliness is close at hand.

With loneliness can come fear, grief, anxiety, and a host of other challenging feelings. But the psalmist unabashedly proclaims the achingly deep beauty of knowing God and of being known by him. This being known by God and letting God know us strengthens us and equips us to embrace the truth. And that truth, as Jesus says, will set us free—not just despite our circumstances, but in the mess of them.

In this light created by the darkness of the cross, we are reminded that we do not rest in our own ability or capacity to fashion peace or comfort. We can rejoice with the psalmist that there is a Creator who powerfully, delicately, and intentionally crafts each one of us into existence in our mothers' wombs.

This Creator's heart knows no bounds in its capacity for compassion. He possesses an unshakable, groundbreaking sense of justice that gives dignity to the weak and lowly, and he hears the cry of the lonely and needy.

As humans, we run dry and grow weary over time when confronted with even the most mundane of challenges. The psalmist understands this, but that is not the whole story. He also declares that it is God's unfailing love that preserves him.

As you pray, confess your weariness to your Creator. Think of others you know who are struggling as well. Then thank your Father for his unfailing love, made known in Jesus Christ.

Recommended Closing Prayer

Heavenly Father, you see us and you know us. You created us and our neighbors, and you reign gloriously over all creation with grace and compassion. Remind us of your decrees and of how deeply you love us, as well as this earth and all who dwell on it. Lead us farther into faithful hoping, rejoicing in life, and thriving in obedience. Feed us the food that is needful for us. Preserve our lives in you. Amen.

Ordinary Time Day 70

KARI WEST

Reflect on Psalm 119:129–136

Call to Prayer

O how we need hearts that stand in awe of God's words. Too often we find other things to admire and seek after—power, reputation, family, rest, sex, friendship, knowledge, food. We orchestrate our lives around our awe of the lesser. But here we find the psalmist delighting in scripture like one who has come upon unexpected treasure.

God speaks to his people. We are so familiar with this idea that it loses its incandescence and unfathomability. God speaks to us, his people. God wants to talk with us. We have his words as lights to our paths, as honey on our tongues, as diamonds in our hands, as the embrace of a father, as thunder.

Sit with this psalm and ask God to give you rightly attuned awe.

Ask him to mend again the broken compass of your soul that so often veers off course. Pray for ordered loves and a heart that seeks him foremost. Ponder the glory of this reality—God speaks to you. Thank him for the precious gift of scripture and the precious incarnation of Christ the Word.

Recommended Closing Prayer

Father, grant us a deep and abiding love for your Word and for you. For Jesus's sake. Amen.

Ordinary Time Day 71

M A R Y R A C H E L   B O Y D

Reflect on Psalm 119:161–168

Call to Prayer

Like all Jewish children, Jesus memorized, spoke, sung, and prayed the words of scripture. So, read back through this stanza from Psalm 119 in light of what you know about the life, death, and resurrection of Jesus Christ. What was it like for him to speak and pray these words? How might these words have given him hope, joy, and confidence?

We too often read scripture as a means of self-reflection or as a way to make sense of our own lives, but this psalmist has a far larger landscape in mind. He proclaims honor and awe for God's righteousness and its effect in his life; he knows God is his only hope for salvation; and he determines to pursue a life of obedience.

Pause. Doesn't this sound like the heart of Jesus? His soul was shaped by the scriptures.

In his final days before the Crucifixion, Jesus prayed as this psalmist prayed; he spoke of his love for God and his determination to obey. As you pray, say these words from Psalm 119. Let the Triune God bring comfort and strength to your anxious heart.

Recommended Closing Prayer

O Father, give me the heart of Jesus. Make me quick to trust, determined to obey. Help me to long for your glory and hope in your love. Amen.

Ordinary Time Day 72
KARI WEST

Reflect on Psalm 119:169–176

Call to Prayer

Listen to some of the psalmist's requests of God:

- "May my cry come before you" (Psalm 119:169 NIV).
- "Give me understanding" (Psalm 119:169 NIV).
- "Deliver me" (Psalm 119:170 NIV).
- "Help me" (Psalm 119:173 NIV).
- "Seek your servant" (Psalm 119:176 NIV).

One thing we never learn from this holy prayer book is independence. The psalms continually put us in the place of the supplicant, asking God for what we need.

There is a freedom in this knowledge that we are dependent creatures, needing the gracious care of our Father, which he promises to give us. There is freedom in not having to posture and pretend that we are fully capable in every way on our own.

Choose a verse from this stanza of Psalm 119 that captures your most pressing spiritual need. Do you need fresh assurance that God hears you? Do you need to confess your straying and ask him to seek you again? Do you need understanding or lips that can overflow in praise?

Come to your good heavenly Father and pray that verse; trust that he will give you all you require for life and godliness. Then praise him for his gracious and perfect provision for you and for all his people.

Recommended Closing Prayer

O God, may you be gracious to us, and bless us, and turn your face upon us, and give us peace. For Jesus's sake. Amen.

Ordinary Time Day 73

WILLA KANE

Reflect on Isaiah 64:8, Isaiah 45:9, and 2 Corinthians 4:7–9

Call to Prayer

Have you ever watched a potter at his wheel? He starts with a lump of clay moistened with water to make it pliable, pounds it onto the wheel with enough force to center it perfectly, and then spins the wheel slowly and carefully as he applies just the right amount of pressure. His fingers push deep inside the ball of clay while his palms hold firmly on the outside. He adds water as he spins and forms a vessel into the shape he desires.

Isaiah and Paul teach us that we are unformed clay in the hands of the Father. He is our Potter.

What can we learn as we watch the potter? Water makes clay pliable so it can be molded. Similarly, we need the water of God's Word so his hands can mold us. Clay must be centered on the wheel, and we must be centered in Christ, surrendered to Jesus as our Lord and Savior. Only then can God himself begin to mold, shape, and transform us, as he uses the wheel of time and the pressures of life inside and outside of us.

God knows just how and why he's using pressure in your life. Affliction, persecution, and being forsaken and struck down are all things our Lord Jesus experienced. These very things, in the hand of the Master Potter, can be used by God to form us into a perfect vessel for his Spirit.

Will we strive against the Lord and his design for us, or will we submit to the pressures he is using to fit us for the life he has planned? Pause to honestly consider your attitude toward the challenges you face. Confess your doubts, resentments, and opposition to his will. Then turn to him in submission. He can't mold you when you're resisting him. Drink in the living water of his Word. Pray for the desire to cooperate with him, even as the wheel of these hard days turns and even if the pressures increase. Trust the hand of the Master Potter to form you, to fill you, and to use you.

Recommended Closing Prayer

> Have thine own way, Lord! Have thine own way!
> Thou art the Potter, I am the clay.
> Mold me and make me after thy will,
> while I am waiting, yielded, and still. Amen.
> (From "Have Thine Own Way, Lord" by Adelaide Pollard)

Ordinary Time Day 74

WILLA KANE

Reflect on Psalm 4

Call to Prayer

In this prayer for help, David calls with passion to God, his defender. God is his protector: the Lord has helped him in times of trouble.

Trouble is promised as part of our earthly existence. Most of us know trouble all too well. Today may have been such a day, filled with trouble for you and those you love. Illness, broken relationships, job loss, food insecurity, and political instability wrap cords of grief all around us. Predictably but sadly, trouble is our companion.

In the day of trouble, whom do you trust and where do you turn? Do you first look for the sort of help and answers the world offers? Do you count on your own ingenuity? Or do you turn to God?

The psalmist's enemies love what is worthless and go after what is false.

Examine your heart. What do you love? What do you seek? The world is filled with worthless and false things we use as substitute saviors. But they cannot save, and they never satisfy.

David knows there is a better way. God is our righteousness. In Jesus Christ, he has chosen us and made us his own. He hears when we call. When the Lord himself claims us as his own, substitute saviors lose their allure.

Meditate on this great good news and offer a sacrifice of praise to God. Then offer your life itself as a sacrifice. Take your everyday, ordinary, "sleeping, eating, going to work, and walking around" life and place it before God as an offering.

As you pray, be like David; cry to God your Defender, your Helper. Thank him for the ways he has helped you in the past and for the joy of being kept by him, and trust him to do the same tomorrow. Because he never slumbers, you can lie down and sleep in peace.

Recommended Closing Prayer

I adore you, O Lord, my helper, my defender, and lover of my soul. I rest in the safety of your embrace and praise you as my King. Amen.

Ordinary Time Day 75
WILLA KANE

Reflect on Romans 4:19–25

Call to Prayer

Unlikely people all over the world and all throughout the ages have seen the whole course of their lives change just by trusting God's promises.

Abraham believed the unbelievable: a hundred-year-old man with an infertile wife would have a son, and his descendants would be as many as the stars in the night sky.

Noah built an ark when there was no sign of rain. Moses led the

Israelites out of bondage through the Red Sea with the Egyptian army in hot pursuit. The young girl Mary accepted her role as the mother of God's Son.

More than seven thousand promises from God to humanity are recorded in the Bible. How can we, like Abraham, be "fully convinced that God is able to do whatever he promises"? We only have to look back at the history of Israel and know, "None of the good promises the Lord had made to the house of Israel failed. Everything was fulfilled" (Joshua 21:45 CSB).

During each season, even in the long, hard, uncertain days, remember and believe. Today, embrace these assurances of God:

- "As far as the east is from the west, so far does he remove our transgressions from us" (Psalm 103:12 ESV).
- "And I will give you a new heart and a new spirit I will put within you. And I will remove the heart of stone form your flesh and give you a heart of flesh" (Ezekiel 36:26 ESV).
- "The Lord himself goes before you and will be with you; he will never leave you nor forsake you. Do not be afraid; do not be discouraged" (Deuteronomy 31:8 NIV).
- "I have said these things to you, that in me you may have peace. In the world you will have tribulation. But take heart; I have overcome the world" (John 16:33 ESV).

Our God is a promise maker and a promise keeper, unchanging, faithful, strong, true, and sovereign. As we hold to God's promises, he gives us strength to persevere, trust to overcome fear, and hope to claim a brighter future.

Will you build your life on his words, rather than the shifting foundations of this world? As you pray, remember these promises from the Lord. Tell God that you want to build your life on his Word. Pray for friends who need to be reminded that God is faithful. Then praise God for his faithfulness! God will make good on what he has said.

Recommended Closing Prayer

O merciful God, grant us the grace we need to trust in your promises and build our lives around your Word. Holy Spirit, increase our faith and help our unbelief. We ask this, trusting in the good and powerful name of Christ, in whose blood we are covered, in whose righteousness we are clothed, now and for eternity. Amen.

Ordinary Time Day 76

MARYRACHEL BOYD

Reflect on Romans 6:5–9

Call to Prayer

How very great a cost Christ paid when he willingly shed his blood for all of us.

Christ's death was not only pain and suffering on behalf of his own body. It was also taking physically upon himself the intensity and anguish of everyone else's death. The result? We are no longer enslaved to sin. We are free. God will not change his mind. The death of his Son instituted and finalized our freedom from the dominion of evil. We have been made alive, and the call now to us is to consider ourselves "dead to sin and alive to God in Christ Jesus" (Romans 6:11 ESV).

As you pray, thank your Father that because of Jesus's shed blood on the cross, he is offering you forgiveness, freedom, and life. Ask him to show you what it means for you personally to live into this new life.

Recommended Closing Prayer

Father God, you have made me alive in Jesus Christ. Help me to embrace my new life of freedom by loving and serving you and your world. For Jesus Christ's sake. Amen.

Ordinary Time Day 77

BILL BOYD

Reflect on John 2:1–11

Call to Prayer

The small Galilean village of Cana is revered and celebrated as the place of Jesus's first miracle, and that first miracle, of water turned to wine, is undoubtedly the prototype for the Son of God's life and ministry. Jesus proclaims and reveals at this wedding the real truth about kingdom life. Time and again Jesus will respond to invitations to dinners and festivals, small and large. He will talk, listen, eat, and drink just as we all do. And he will do many miracles. But like the water turned into wine, the *doing* of many of these miracles will be invisible. Only the outcome will be visible.

The message of Jesus's first miracle is profoundly simple: the wine of human hopes and designs always runs out, and usually at the worst possible moment. The help we need will never come through human effort, but through divine love. We are invited to ask for help, as Mary did, when we are dismayed by the circumstances of life.

John begins his Gospel with a wedding story. Why? Could it be that Christ wants to emphasize the great gift God has given us in marriage and family? And could it be that the blessing of this Galilean marriage points us toward the union of Christ and the church? We see the lavish love of Jesus: he is the Bridegroom who will provide for his bride on her wedding day.

"Do whatever he tells you" (John 2:5 ESV), Mary says to the servants at the wedding. Isn't she speaking to us as well?

Christ's desire is to bless us and help us when things are out of control, when our resources dry up, when the unexpected crashes down on us. As you pray, ask yourself, "What do I do when the wine runs out?"

Turn to Jesus. Listen for his voice. Obey. Seek blessing and restoration for yourself and for others.

Recommended Closing Prayer

O Father, keep me from the foolishness of trying to solve all my problems and the problems of those I love. Help me to be quick to ask for your help and to do what you call me to do. In Christ's most precious name. Amen.

Ordinary Time Day 78

WILLA KANE

Reflect on Psalm 145

Call to Prayer

In his last recorded psalm, David's extols the greatness and goodness of God and calls us to join him in praise. In contrast, we live in a world and a time where real goodness and true greatness seems in short supply. What is there to praise in our world? Incivility and violence abound. Fires, floods, myriad natural disasters, and crises in health, peace, and justice spread around the globe. Confidence in the stability of governments is at a low ebb.

Psalm 145 reorients us: it calls us to turn our eyes away from a world that is broken and to look at a God of unsearchable greatness, a God who does good because he is good.

We will see evidence of God's greatness when we meditate on his wondrous works in creation. Stop to consider the glorious things God has made. Speak them out loud. Now declare the greatness of the one who made them.

Turn your thoughts to God's goodness. He is righteous, kind, gracious, and merciful. Because of his great love for us, he gives us what we don't deserve and what we could never earn. And blessedly, unbelievably, mercifully, he doesn't give us what we do deserve. The cross of Christ showcases God's grace and mercy. Here we see in full the steadfast love of God: his Son pays sin's penalty. He laid down his life to be our undeserved ransom.

Loving us even when we were still sinners demonstrates God's goodness. Stop to consider this goodness poured out for you. Speak it out loud. Declare the goodness of the one whose perfect love, kindness, mercy, and generosity paid for your entrance into his everlasting kingdom. Thank the one who raises you up when you fall, upholds you when days are hard, and satisfies your deepest desires when everyone and everything else falls short. Thank him that he has heard your cry and has saved you.

When Moses asked to see God's glory, God said, "I will make all my goodness pass before you" (Exodus 33:19 ESV). God's goodness is his glory.

Our God is great, he is good, and he is glorious. He is worthy of our praise every day and into eternity.

Praise him.

Recommended Closing Prayer

Holy, gracious, merciful Father, I praise you that you are great, good, and glorious. Thank you for your love poured out to me on the cross. Amen.

Ordinary Time Day 79

WILLA KANE

Reflect on John 5:1–18

Call to Prayer

"Do you want to get well?" (John 5:6 NIV). On the surface, this seems like an unnecessary—even a cruel—question for Jesus to ask when he learns of this man's condition. He's been an invalid for thirty-eight years, lying right by water that reportedly has healing powers, and yet he's never able to get into the pool before someone else beats him to it. How frustrating and humbling this man's life must have been, so close to what he believes may bring him healing and yet unable to grasp it.

His answer is telling. Instead of a resounding, "Yes! I want to be healed!," the man says that it's impossible. There will be no healing for him because he doesn't have help and can't help himself. Can you feel his resigned despair in such an answer?

Perhaps Jesus's question is meant to rekindle this man's desire for restoration, for new life. I am not quite sure if it did remove his despair. But the focus of the story shifts, from a pool that offers healing and from the hopeless mindset of the man who can't make it to the pool to Jesus, the compassionate healer. The one who knitted this man together in his mother's womb stands before him, full of power, full of love. He commands, "Get up!" (John 5:8 NIV), and the man finds himself healed after thirty-eight years of misery.

Do you find yourself hemmed in by the impossibility of your circumstances? Are your friends and family far away? Are you facing your own helplessness? Look to Jesus, full of grace, for fresh hope. In his command to the invalid, hear his loving commitment to the good of his people. Though his ways are beyond us and he does not always act according to our timetable, he will right wrongs and restore what the locusts have eaten (Joel 2:25).

As you pray, meditate on this act of Jesus, one of taking what is broken and making it whole again. Consider our good God, our great healer, and rest in his love for you.

Recommended Closing Prayer

O Christ our Restorer, thank you that you will always do us good in the end. Amen.

Ordinary Time Day 80

KARI WEST

Reflect on John 5:19–29

Call to Prayer

Christ, the one through whom the cosmos was wrought, declares in this passage that he can do nothing by himself. The scriptures are filled with stories of Jesus's supernatural birth, his miraculous acts of provision and healing, his transfiguration, and his ultimate power over sin, death, and hell. Did he act alone? Not at all. Here in John 5, the Son of God states that he is not an "independent agent."

This challenges our own assumptions: we often link power with autonomy. But Christ gives us this incredible insight into the perfect, mysterious, foundational relationship in the Godhead—the Father, out of love, shows the Son his perfect work, and the Son enacts the will of the Father. No power grabbing, no usurping, no one-upmanship.

And what is the great, awe-inspiring work of the Father and the Son? They reach into the grave, knit bones back together, bestow a beating heart, and breathe life into the dead. They raise up a people to join in the vibrant, loving relationship of the Godhead.

As you pray, consider the great work of salvation. Ask yourself if you honor the Son as the bringer of new life to the world, enacting the will of the Father. Ask yourself if you've submitted to his lordship, knowing he will come back as Judge and King. Pray for the great power of the Spirit to walk in humility and love.

Recommended Closing Prayer

O Christ whose voice raises the dead to life, we praise you for the great gift of salvation bought with your blood. Let us walk as you walked, in the power your Spirit to the praise of the Father. Amen.

Ordinary Time Day 81

KARI WEST

Reflect on John 5:30–47

Call to Prayer

"How can you believe since you accept glory from one another but do not seek the glory that comes from the only God?" (John 5:44 NIV).

It is a terrifying possibility to contemplate: you can forfeit the glory of God, the riches of his presence, and the promise of the future inheritance of his saints because you prize a lesser thing, the praise of other people.

When this lesser thing is your highest goal and desire, you might study the scriptures diligently and live a moral life but still miss everything in those scriptures that point to the identity and supremacy of Jesus. And you will miss the great invitation that Christ holds out to follow him and thereby seek a higher glory.

It's an insidious thing—seeking and accepting glory from other people rather than seeking the glory of Christ. None of us who have been redeemed and who hold to Jesus as our Lord are immune to this temptation.

Sit with Christ's words and let the convicting power of the Spirit do its work. Do you truly believe that Jesus is Lord and worthy of glory, or have you been caught in the trappings of religion for your own elevation? Have you allowed your love of others' admiration to eclipse your desire for Christ's name to be lauded in all the earth?

As you pray, confess to your Savior and receive his full forgiveness. Thank him for these words and ask that his Spirit convict you and change you, molding your heart for the coming fullness of his presence, a splendor beyond imagining.

Recommended Closing Prayer

Jesus, yours is the kingdom, the power, and the glory forever and ever. Amen.

Ordinary Time Day 82
S A L L Y   B R E E D L O V E

Reflect on Exodus 35:30–36:2

Call to Prayer

We were made for work. Yes, Sabbath rest is a necessary and gracious rhythm that turns work from the shrill sounding of a fire alarm into music, but still we need real work.

The creation story is an invitation to engage in the satisfying work. The words "tend and watch over" in Genesis 2:15 (NLT) are the same Hebrew words used to describe the work of the priests as they led temple worship. Work matters; it can even be called a holy thing. Work is a way to care for all God has made and to unfold the possibilities contained in the gift of creation.

Moses picked two men to oversee the construction of the tabernacle and the creation of the elaborate artisan work that would adorn it. These two "project managers" were to be men filled with the Spirit of God, with skill, intelligence, and the ability to teach others. Their work depended on God's help and looked upward to God for meaning.

In Acts 6, the new deacons who were to care for widows had to be disciples of good reputation, filled with the Spirit and wisdom. Their work mattered, so their character and ability mattered.

We flourish when we engage in good work. So, what do we do when we can't work? What do we do with our restless boredom, with our sense of defeat? Rather than chafe or sink into fear and doom, might we serve those around us by doing the unpaid jobs that need doing?

If we are working, will we pause and consider how to accept the work we have with deep gratitude?

Pray in thanksgiving for the gift of work. If you have lost your job or are unsure if you will have a job, pray for courage and strength to face your life as it is. Pray by name for those who need a job. If you are responsible for other people's employment, pray for God's wisdom and grace as you lead. If you are working, pray for the grace to see your work as a way to love as God loves.

Recommended Closing Prayer

Heavenly Father, we remember before you those who suffer from want or anxiety or from lack of work. Guide the people of this land so to use our public and private wealth that all may find suitable and fulfilling employment and receive a just reward for their labor, through Jesus Christ our Lord. Amen.

Ordinary Time Day 83

KARI WEST

Reflect on Psalm 139:13–18

Call to Prayer

You were formed by the hand of God. Tonight, take a few moments to meditate on that reality. Know the nearness of the God who has carved every intricate way in you, who has searched out the depths of you, who has crafted the inmost parts of your soul and your being, and who knows you more fully than anyone has ever known you, including yourself.

And now let the truth of God as your near and intimate Creator give you a deeper trust in his thoughts and commands. They are for your good. They fit with what it means to be truly human. They will satisfy your soul. They will carry you farther into the life you actually long for, even if you don't have the words for it—a life of truly being human where you are free to become a deeply godly person.

Let the unfailing love of God be your consolation this evening. Seek a wholehearted life of love and obedience toward your Creator, who is your Father. Hope in the Lord's promises, ask for his comfort, and rest in his gracious compassion.

Recommended Closing Prayer

Our Christ, lover of our souls, Maker of ourselves, grant us trust in you, obedience to you, love for you, and grace because of you. In your most holy, most precious, and most powerful name. Amen.

Ordinary Time Day 84

SALLY BREEDLOVE

Reflect on 1 John 1

Call to Prayer

Jesus called the disciple John and his brother James "Sons of Thunder" (Mark 3:17 ESV). Perhaps that nickname only meant they were vocal and enthusiastic, but most of us aren't sure we want to be friends with a son of thunder. Such a person would likely be loud, authoritarian, dangerous, and quick-tempered.

How could an aggressive person fitting such a description write the words we read in 1 John 1? Here we find a John who longs for us to know Jesus. He assures us that the incarnation of the Son of God is so solidly true that if we had been in Jesus's presence as he was, we would have known Jesus in his humanity and yet known so much more. For in Jesus is friendship, life, and light.

We do not have to fear that we are unworthy to be near Jesus. John assures us that our sin, past, present, and future, can be taken care of by Jesus's blood and his prayers for us.

John wants to share his friend Jesus with us. Talk about transformation. This son of thunder has become the kind of friend we long for. He's humble, quietly confident, and generous.

Perhaps you feel that you've never had a real friend, never been chosen, or never been told you matter. Perhaps you believe you are hopeless; your failure and hypocrisy are too much for God. As you pray, listen for the voice of God's Spirit. How is he calling you to a life of greater honesty, obedience, and love? How is he reassuring you that Jesus's death on the cross is more than enough for all your sin and shame?

Thank God for the solid reality of Jesus, for the full forgiveness he offers, and for his ability to transform all of us who are willing to enter into friendship with him.

Recommended Closing Prayer

O Father God, transform my life so I am like your Son Jesus Christ. Make me a true friend as he has been to me. In the name of the Father, the Son, and the Holy Spirit. Amen.

Ordinary Time Day 85

KARI WEST

Reflect on 1 John 2:1-6

Call to Prayer

What does it mean for the love of God to be made complete in us? It's a strange turn of phrase. Isn't God's love perfect, lacking nothing? And yet here, John says that by keeping Christ's commands—most notably, his command to love others—the love of God is made complete in his people.

John isn't insinuating that God's love is less than perfect and that we, by our actions, make up for something morally lacking in the love of the Almighty. He means completion here in terms of finishing a race, of making it to the finish line. The love of God, which God has "poured into our hearts through the Holy Spirit" (Romans 5:5 NIV), now must pour from us into the lives of others in order for it to reach its intended end. God's love is not to halt with us.

We are to be joyful conduits of God's deep compassion for all people, so that more may know Jesus Christ the Righteous, our advocate with the Father, and the propitiation for the sins of the whole world.

These words are an invitation: Take your place in this great river of gladness. God is continually pouring out grace and mercy over you, treasuring you as his dearly bought child. Now turn and direct that powerful love to those around you, that they may drink the living water and never thirst again.

No person can do this on his or her own, but God longs to meet us in our need. As you pray, ask him for deep, still places in your soul where you may know the riches of his delight in you. Ask him to show you one person in your life who is thirsty for the living water of his presence.

Recommended Closing Prayer

Father, complete your love in us, we pray. Amen.

Ordinary Time Day 86
SALLY BREEDLOVE

Reflect on 1 John 2:7–10

Call to Prayer

"What's the goal of life?" All sorts of answers rise up in us when we ask that question: to be free of our struggles, to find someone who really understands us, to have kids, to have an interesting job, to make a bucket of money, to be a better person, to have our doubts about God finally come to an end, to be rid of the anxiety we carry, or to get even with the people who have hurt us or at least hear them apologize. We want a life that has meaning, a life where we belong.

But in this passage, John lays out a different goal: to grow up in keeping the greatest commandment. That commandment is a seamless call to love God with all your heart, mind, soul, and strength and to love your neighbor as yourself. John likely heard Jesus speak often about this greatest of all commandments and then in the upper room right before he was crucified. He heard Jesus say the same thing again and again—learn to love.

Our world runs on the notion that position, power, and privilege are all that matter. We are destroying our cities, our cultures, and our relationships with the insistence that we are right and the whole world needs to bow to our beliefs. Everyone is afraid to simply love.

Will you be willing to pray, "Lord, teach me to love like you love"? Will you receive the reality that you are greatly loved by God? Will you let his love touch you so deeply that you are set free to love others?

Recommended Closing Prayer

O Lord God, teach me to love like you love. In Jesus's name. Amen.

Ordinary Time Day 87

KARI WEST

Reflect on 1 John 2:12–14

Call to Prayer

Listen again to the reasons John is writing to these believers. He offers these words—like small benedictions—to Christians thousands of years ago and to you today:

- "Your sins have been forgiven on account of his name" (1 John 2:12 NIV).
- "You know him who is from the beginning" (1 John 2:13 NIV).
- "You have overcome the evil one" (1 John 2:13 NIV).

- "You know the Father" (1 John 2:14 NIV).
- "You are strong, and the Word of God lives in you" (1 John 2:14 NIV).

Take each of these declarations and turn them over in your mind. Speak them out loud. Ask the Holy Spirit to bring one in particular to bear. Which truth do you most need to hear and believe today? that your sins are forgiven? that you know the everlasting Father? that the Word of God *lives* in you, and that which lives will bring forth fruit?

Sit and meditate on these verses. Stay until your mind is quiet and your soul is stilled. Then thank the Lord for the gift of his living Word, doing its good work in your heart.

Recommended Closing Prayer

> O God, of your goodness, give me yourself, for you are enough for me. Amen.
> *(Julian of Norwich)*

Ordinary Time Day 88

K A R I   W E S T

Reflect on 1 John 2:15–17

Call to Prayer

Later on in this letter, John writes that the world is under the control of the evil one. When he speaks of the world in these verses, he doesn't mean our physical environment, or bodily existence, or the good creation that God has wrought and sustains by his presence. The world here means everything that is contrary to the abiding, eternal kingdom of God that he is building through the atoning work of Jesus and the witness of the church, washed in his blood and called to love as the church has been loved.

Here John specifies three things that are opposed to God's life-giving, rich, ruling presence: the lust of the flesh, the lust of the eyes, and the pride of life. In other words, evil desires—whether they be rooted in sexual immorality, greed, or covetousness—and the belief that we don't need our Father.

John doesn't attempt to shame or bully us into shallow morality. Instead, he tells us very simply that these things don't come from God and that we were made for the abundant forever life found at God's right hand, while the things set against this kind of life will pass away like the mist burned away by the rising sun.

As you begin your time of prayer, read through these verses again and ask the Holy Spirit to reorient your heart. Confess any love for the things set against the kingdom of God. Confess all pride and all evil desires. Receive his renewing mercy. Ask for deeper commitment to the way of Christ and deeper belief that in his steps, true, lasting life will always be found.

Recommended Closing Prayer

> O God, without whose beauty and goodness our souls are
> unfed, without whose truth our reason withers: Consecrate
> our lives to your will, giving us such purity of heart, such
> depth of faith, and such steadfastness of purpose, that in
> time we may come to think your own thoughts after you;
> through Jesus Christ our Savior. Amen.
> *(Anglican Church in North America Book of Common Prayer)*

Ordinary Time Day 89

KARI WEST

Reflect on 1 John 2:18–29

Call to Prayer

There were those among these believers who denied the deity of Christ and left the fellowship of the church. John writes this letter to be circulated among a series of house churches to encourage them as churches that belong to the household of God and to put them on their guard against those who may try to dissuade them from following Christ.

John wants these believers to understand deeply that Christ is the ultimate reality. Those who belong to God's family will hold to Jesus because God, through Christ, is the one who holds the church. The very Spirit of Christ indwells believers, here called to the anointing they received from Christ.

He charges them to keep what they heard in the beginning as central in their lives—namely, the gospel story. As they seek to continue to honor Christ and live in step with his commands of love and holiness, they will continue to abide in the fellowship of God. And when Christ appears, they will have the joy of being confident and unashamed before him, clothed in his righteousness. They will know the fullness of God's promise, namely, eternal life with him.

And in the meantime, Christ's righteousness will birth more and more righteousness within them—which is one way they will also be able to discern other true followers of Christ.

As you pray, let these words do their work within you. Ask the Holy Spirit for a true understanding of the ultimate centrality of Christ in your life. Thank him for the gift of his anointing. Plead for the power to be steadfast in love and holiness, and to trust in his redemption when you fail. Above all, hope in his coming fullness and in the eternal life that awaits us.

Recommended Closing Prayer

O most merciful Redeemer, Friend, and Brother,
May I know thee more clearly,

Love thee more dearly,
And follow thee more nearly:
For ever and ever. Amen.
(Anglican Church in North America Book of Common Prayer)

Ordinary Time Day 90

KARI WEST

Reflect on 1 John 3:1–3

Call to Prayer

John can barely contain his effusive awe for the love that God has poured over us. The absolute best thing in the world has happened—God has adopted us! God has brought us into his family. God calls us his own. He delights in us as a father delighting in his children. John marvels over this reality. Us—God's kids! That's what we are!

But then he goes on to expound a perhaps even greater, more mysterious truth: We will be like Jesus. Christ will appear in glory, we will see him as he truly is, and we will be like him. We don't know the details of that reality. We don't know the fullness of the humanity that we will be drawn into on that glorious day. And yet, John holds out this marvelous truth to us, surely one that "the angels long to catch a glimpse of," as he tells us at the end of 1 Peter 1:12 (CSB).

What to do with these almost too beautiful realities? Sit with them and invite the Holy Spirit to enlarge your heart to grasp their greatness. Don't let them remain as words on a page or as distant ethereal ideas. They are meant to make your soul swell with gladness, with a deep overflowing joy. And as you hold these truths close to your heart, you will find new and holy desires burgeoning within, pulling you toward that coming glory, full life with our pure and glorious Savior.

Recommended Closing Prayer

> O glorious and blessed God, Father, Son and Holy Spirit,
> thou art mine, and I am thine. So be it. Amen.
> *(Anglican Church in North America Book of Common Prayer)*

Ordinary Time Day 91

KARI WEST

Reflect on 1 John 3:11–18

Call to Prayer

John returns to this theme again and again in this letter. Love is from God; those who love have been born of God. Hatred and murder are from the evil one. Those who remain in hatred remain in death. God has made us alive, and the fruit of that new life is love.

And where do we find the culmination of love? Jesus Christ laid down his life for us. John doesn't construct a thick theological framework. He does not pile one complex truth on another complex truth. Rather, he compels us with simple language, revealing a simple and yet profound reality. The way we know love is by looking to the cross. We see our sinless Savior suffering for our wrongs, bearing the wrath of God, working victory over Satan and all forces of evil, becoming sin for us so that we might become the righteousness of God. We see Christ crucified, the Lamb slain for the life of the world.

Our Jesus did all of this for the joy set before him, the joy of bringing us into the family of God and dwelling with us forever.

Christ walked to Golgotha with us in mind.

So, now we are to live out that same love in our lives, laying those lives down for our brothers and sisters.

As you pray, consider Jesus. See the wounds in his hands and feet, and know he bled for love, for you. Ask the Holy Spirit to show you one way in these coming days that you may live in this same vein of sacrificial love.

Recommended Closing Prayer

O Father, what mercy you've poured on us! O Christ, what depths of love drove you to Calvary! O Spirit, what comfort and guidance you give us! Let us be a humble, grateful, and loving people. By your power and for your glory. Amen.

Ordinary Time Day 92
K A R I W E S T

Reflect on 1 John 4:13–21

Call to Prayer

Jesus has given us his Spirit. He still bears the name Immanuel. He is still God *with* us and is now God dwelling *in* us.

Do you know this incredible gift that God has given to you? Take a moment and dwell on this reality—the God who has strewn the stars in the night sky, who turns the hearts of kings, who pulls rain down from the clouds and grass up from underfoot, who trampled death—this God has taken up residence in you, his child.

This God is before, behind, and within you. This God is at hand when you wake up, when you sleep, when you go out and when you come in, when your thoughts race at three in the morning, when your anger spills over, and when the bitterness beckons and the envy pulls. He is there when you feel far too much and when you can't seem to feel anything.

This God, by his Spirit, will draw you into deeper and deeper fellowship with him, so that you know and rely on his love. This God will make you like Jesus, and his perfect love will continue to drive away your fear, for you have been brought into his family and need fear no punishment, no separation from him.

This God, by his Spirit, will amplify and complete our fumbling attempts to love one another. And in that love for one another, we will know new depths of the love of God.

Pray these truths back to the Spirit of Christ, the very God who indwells you, and find your hope in him.

Recommended Closing Prayer

Our Immanuel, manifest your love in us, we pray. Amen.

Ordinary Time Day 93
KARI WEST

Reflect on 1 John 5:13–15

Call to Prayer

The whole book of 1 John was written so that believers may know they have eternal life in Christ. These words are like a rip in the fabric of the world as we know it, allowing us to peer through and see the deeper realities that are often hidden from our earthbound sight.

The believers who originally received John's words were in house churches strewn around ancient Ephesus. They were facing hostility from the surrounding culture and experiencing upheaval within their communities as some members had recently denied Christ's divinity and left the faith.

It is amid these circumstances that John seeks to lift their gaze to something more lasting: God has poured out lavish love on them, and the Spirit of Christ dwells in them. And their ultimate destiny? Eternal life. Not simply life that lasts forever, but an unimaginably rich, abundant, deeply joyous life in the fullness of God's presence, filling their lives to the brim with the fierce gladness of himself.

We have hints and glimmers of this eternal life now, but we can place our hope fully in God's making good on this promise on the other side of death, when he will pull us up from the grave and into his arms.

Each time we pray, we approach this God. We can rest in the truth that he hears us. If what we ask for will make us more ready for that coming abundance of life, we are given the sure knowledge that we will receive it. Our God will always answer prayers according to his will, and that is a beautiful truth because his will for us is life beyond what we can now hope or imagine.

Ask the Lord what you should pray for "according to his will" (1 John 5:14 NIV). Then ask for a rooted hope in the eternal life promised to each of his children, a treasure trove of his presence to be fully known one day, coming soon.

Recommended Closing Prayer

> Hasten, O Father, the coming of your kingdom; and grant that we your servants, who now live by faith, may with joy behold your Son at his coming in glorious majesty; even Jesus Christ, our only Mediator and Advocate. Amen.
> *(Anglican Church in North America Book of Common Prayer)*

Ordinary Time Day 94

KARI WEST

Reflect on Psalm 113

Call to Prayer

We are the poor, in the dust; we are the needy, living in trash; we are the barren ones, with little to show for our lives.

While these words may or may not describe our outward circumstances, they are the deep true condition of all humanity, of you, your family, your coworkers, and your friends.

Do you know your own neediness, your own poverty, your own barrenness? Perhaps your recent experiences have made these realities inescapable, or perhaps you are still refusing to accept that left to your own, there is little hope for real, rich, overflowing life.

But—hear this even deeper truth—we are not left on our own. We have a King who stoops low and lifts the needy. He takes the poor and sets them among princes. He opens his hand and gives the barren one a family.

He is the life-giver. He is majestic and powerful. He is exalted above all. He deeply desires to meet you in your need, your poverty, and your barrenness—to give you a hope and a future, supply all your needs, and root you more deeply in his blood-bought family.

As you pray, confess how much you need God. Praise him that he bends low to lift up his people. He will not leave us on our own.

Recommended Closing Prayer

> I need Thee every hour,
> In joy or pain;
> Come quickly and abide,
> Or life is vain.
> I need Thee every hour,
> Teach me Thy will;
> And Thy rich promises
> In me fulfill.
> I need Thee every hour,
> Most Holy One;
> Oh, make me Thine indeed,
> Thou blessed Son.
> I need Thee, oh, I need Thee;
> Every hour I need Thee;
> Oh, bless me now, my Savior!
> I come to Thee.
> Amen.
> ("I Need Thee Every Hour" by Annie Sherwood Hawks)

Ordinary Time Day 95

WILLA KANE

Reflect on Isaiah 12

Call to Prayer

"Sing praise-songs to God. He's done it all!" (Isaiah 12:5 MSG). The melody of this message runs from the Old Testament to the New.

God is our strength and our song because he is our salvation. He was angry, and rightly so, when we turned away from him to worship ourselves, to love lesser things. But his anger wasn't forever. He withdrew his anger, and more than that, he moved toward us and brought comfort. What a God! What a Savior!

He brought not just comfort, not just feeling good, but also salvation. He has made us right. In love, he closed the chasm caused by sin. Salvation is perfect love, and perfect love casts out fear.

As you pray, examine your heart and confess any fear that resides within, be it fear that you won't measure up or fear of what the future— or even the next hour—might hold. Let the reality of God's saving love saturate your heart and your soul.

The well of salvation holds springs of living water that we can share as we shout to the nations, telling them what he has done.

Raise the roof; sing your heart out. The greatest—Christ Jesus— lives among you.

God—yes, God—is your strength and my song. Best of all, he is your salvation!

Recommended Closing Prayer

God our Father, whose Son Jesus Christ gives the water of eternal life, may we also thirst for you, the spring of life and source of goodness, through him who is alive and reigns with you and the Holy Spirit, one God, now and forever. Amen.

Ordinary Time Day 89

Reflect on Jude 17–25

Call to Prayer

In this letter, Jude calls himself the brother of James. Throughout the centuries, the church has believed that James is the half-brother or perhaps first cousin of Jesus. If either case is so, then Jude knew Jesus intimately long before he was revealed as the Son of God at the resurrection.

What would it have been like to be close kin with Jesus? When the family quarreled and hurt each other or disagreed about all the things families disagree about, Jesus would not have been involved in the fray. What about Jesus's perfect goodness made Jude marvel?

Jude learned from Jesus what it means to be part of an imperfect family and yet not be caught up in the crisis. He passes on to us the truth he saw Jesus live out: we can mourn and yet give up our outrage that the world is sinful and broken.

Jude invites us to attend to our own lives in God. He urges us to understand that a deepening faith doesn't simply happen; we choose practices that make room for faith to grow. We practice listening to the Spirit and praying alongside him. We choose to stay close to God's love. We put our hope in the mercy that will open the door to eternal life.

Jude calls us to compassion toward fellow Christians. Have mercy on them, he says. Help them; don't judge them.

Finally, Jude shifts our attention beyond our own efforts to the incomparable Jesus. He is the one who keeps us, who is at work in us. He will one day present us with great joy to the Father.

Jude knew the truth: Jesus is not simply an amazing older brother or cousin. Jesus is Jude's Savior, the one he counts on. We too can count on Jesus.

As you pray, thank your Father in heaven that he is the one keeping you. Thank him for the security and joy he constantly offers you.

Recommended Closing Prayer

> O God, you made us in your own image, and you have
> redeemed us through your Son Jesus Christ: Look with
> compassion on the whole human family; take away the
> arrogance and hatred which infect our hearts; break down
> the walls that separate us; unite us in bonds of love; and
> work through our struggle and confusion to accomplish
> your purposes on earth; that, in your good time, all nations
> and races may serve you in harmony around your heavenly
> throne; through Jesus Christ our Lord. Amen.
> *(Anglican Church in North America Book of Common Prayer)*

Ordinary Time Day 90

KARI WEST

Reflect on Romans 1:1–7

Call to Prayer

What comes to mind when you think about the gospel? Is it primarily an
intellectual concept, a list of theological ideas, a rubric for moral living,
or a half-remembered story from your churched childhood?

Do you think of it as what God has done *for us*?

This long-promised reality of the Son of God clothing himself
in humanity, living perfectly, dying sacrificially, and resurrecting in
power—it was all done by God so we could belong to him. We who
hated him, we who ran from him, we who had nothing to offer to our
Creator God, we who would die in our miserable rebellion—now we are
the friends of God.

Why did Christ live, die, and return again to life? Paul knew: So
that God could give us grace and peace.

God did everything for us so that we could be his own.

As you pray, meditate on this passage and ask the Spirit to reveal the deep, personal, intimate love of your Father for you in these words. You are his, and he has moved heaven and earth to make it so.

Recommended Closing Prayer

Father, may you give us the strength to comprehend with all the saints what is the breadth and length and height and depth, and to know the love of Christ that surpasses knowledge, that we may be filled with all the fullness of you. Amen.
(Adapted from Ephesians 3:18–19 NIV)

Ordinary Time Day 97

BILL BOYD

Reflect on Luke 1:26–38

Call to Prayer

All throughout the Bible, angels, when they appear, have to assure those who encounter them that they need not need be afraid. Mary is open to the Lord, willing to receive his message and hold it in her heart. Her response reveals her quiet confidence in the inherent goodness of the Almighty.

How does one cultivate a heart that is open to the Word of the Lord? Luke tells us that Mary was disturbed by the angel's words, but she tried to discern what he meant. She was willing to listen, to consider.

"Willing to listen" would be a fine epitaph for any of us, a succinct summary of a life well lived. The scriptures present God himself as quite willing to listen. The Spirit listens to the groans and utterances of our souls. God listens to the distress of his people in slavery. And to Mary the richest reward is bestowed, the heart-wrenching honor of hearing Christ and then bearing Christ within her, the same honor given this and every day to any and all willing to listen to the Lord.

As you pray, consider Mary's response to the angle Gabriel's annunciation. Ponder these words as one of the finest affirmations of faith. Pray these words as a way to actively practice listening to the Lord.

Recommended Closing Prayer

> My soul glorifies the Lord
> and my spirit rejoices in God my Savior,
> for he has been mindful
> of the humble state of his servant.
> From now on all generations will call me blessed,
> for the Mighty One has done great things for me—
> holy is his name.
> His mercy extends to those who fear him,
> from generation to generation.
> He has performed mighty deeds with his arm;
> he has scattered those who are proud in their inmost thoughts.
> He has brought down rulers from their thrones
> but has lifted up the humble.
> He has filled the hungry with good things
> but has sent the rich away empty.
> He has helped his servant Israel,
> remembering to be merciful
> to Abraham and his descendants forever,
> just as he promised our ancestors.
> Amen.
> *(Luke 1:46–55 NIV)*

Ordinary Time Day 98

WILLA KANE

Reflect on Matthew 20:25–28

Call to Prayer

Does the list of heroes our culture esteems need to change? Instead of sports figures or performers, politicians or CEOs, do we have an opportunity to learn to value and respect those who serve their neighbors at great cost to themselves?

Jesus is the epitome of true greatness; he came not to be served but to serve, and he gave up his life for others.

Christ turns our human understanding of greatness upside down. If we want our lives to look like Jesus's, then we, too, need this great reversal in our thinking about purpose and position. What would Jesus do if he were to walk in the flesh in our world today? Would he head up a large church or work at a rescue shelter? Would we see him on prime-time television, or would he be chatting with the children at the elementary school where he was a teacher? Whether he were a hospital's CEO or a sanitation worker, he would serve the least and the lost.

Is there a way you are being called to let go of narrow self-interest and small ambitions to extend grace beyond the circle of those you know and trust? As we lay down our lives for others, we become conduits of Christ's love to a world that is lost and dying.

Pause to think about those you know who serve selflessly. Thank God for them. Ask Jesus to give you a servant's heart, to fill you with compassion for those around you. Pray that the times we live in would turn us upside down and that we would joyfully give our lives away in service to others, empowered by the Spirit of Christ as we follow his example.

"Whoever wants to be great must become a servant. Whoever wants to be first among you must be your slave. That is what the Son of Man has done: He came to serve, not be served—and then to give away his life in exchange for the many who are held hostage" (Matthew 20:26–28 MSG).

Lord, high and holy, meek and lowly, You have brought me to the valley of vision, where I live in the depths but see You in the heights; hemmed in by mountains of sin I behold Your glory. Let me learn by paradox that the way down is the way up, that to be low is to be high, that the broken heart is the healed heart, that the contrite spirit is the rejoicing spirit, that the repenting soul is the victorious soul, that to have nothing is to possess all, that to bear the cross is to wear the crown, that to give is to receive, that the valley is the place of vision. Lord, in the daytime stars can be seen from deepest wells, and the deeper the wells the brighter Your stars shine; let me find Your light in my darkness, Your life in my death, Your joy in my sorrow, Your grace in my sin, Your riches in my poverty, Your glory in my valley. Amen.

(From *The Valley of Vision*)

Ordinary Time Day 99

SALLY BREEDLOVE

Reflect on Matthew 27:57–75

Call to Prayer

When someone makes a terrible choice, we are flooded with questions. "How could they do that?" we ask in disbelief, anger, or deep hurt. Have you ever wanted to ask Peter, "How could you do this to Jesus?"

Peter had seen Jesus's goodness, his love, and his holy connection to God. How could he have betrayed him into the hands of ruthless men? Did those three years together mean nothing? Was he willing to ignore what he himself had confessed, that this was the Christ? Was he willing to toss aside this new person Jesus had declared him to be—Peter the Rock, not just Simon the fisherman?

In that moment in the courtyard of the high priest, Peter was willing to disregard everything.

Why? Because he was afraid.

We live in a world full of uncertainties and turmoil. And for many of us, anxieties rise up unbidden from within. Ask yourself, "What am I afraid of?" Pay attention to what your own heart says. It's hard to listen to our fears. It's hard to live with the undercurrent of anxiety that runs through so many of our thoughts.

What can we do? Some of our fears may come true. We are not guaranteed safe passage through this life. Peter was eventually arrested and crucified. But many of our fears are the fruit of years of having let our anxious imaginations cut a riverbed into our souls. Through that eroded ravine flows fear after fear after fear.

As you pray, take a stand, perhaps for the umpteenth time, and turn from your fears to the living God. He will never leave you or forsake you. He is all-wise, all-powerful, and all-loving. You are safe in him, no matter what happens. At the end of Peter's life, he found that to be so true for himself that he could face arrest and death without fear.

Recommended Closing Prayer

Offer these words of trust from Martin Luther's hymn up to God as a prayer:

A mighty fortress is our God, a bulwark never failing
Our Helper He, amid the flood of mortal ills prevailing
For still our ancient foe doth seek to work us woe
His craft and pow'r are great, and, armed with cruel hate
On earth is not his equal.
Did we in our own strength confide, our striving would be losing
Were not the right Man on our side, the Man of God's own choosing
Dost ask who that may be? Christ Jesus, it is He
The Lord of hosts His name, from age to age the same
And He must win the battle.
And though this world with devils filled should threaten to undo us
We will not fear, for God hath willed His truth to triumph through us

The Prince of Darkness grim, we tremble not for him
His rage we can endure, for lo, his doom is sure
One little word shall fell him.
That word above all earthly pow'rs, no thanks to them, abideth
The Spirit and the gifts are ours through Him who with us sideth
Let goods and kindred go, this mortal life also
The body they may kill; God's truth abideth still
His kingdom is forever.
("A Mighty Fortress Is Our God" by Martin Luther)

Ordinary Time Day 100

TAMARA HILL MURPHY

Reflect on Luke 18:1–30

Call to Prayer

In case the disciples and the surrounding gathering of people have missed the point, Jesus leaves no space between illustrations in Luke 18. One after another, Jesus offers examples: the persistent widow and the unjust judge, the proud Pharisee and the repentant tax collector, Jesus with the babies and irritated disciples, the rich young ruler trying to cram his overladen camel through the needle's eye of the gospel.

Finally, as if in exasperation, Peter (and isn't it always Peter speaking for the rest of us?) tries to regain some footing, stake some claim as a decent person.

"We have left all we had to follow you!" (Luke 18:28 NIV).

A reminder, in case Jesus had overlooked Peter's efforts to follow.

Yes, exactly. Jesus offers his response without patronizing. Yes, this is the cost of the kingdom. And the reward will be multiplied back with eternal life as a bonus.

As you pray, consider the cast of characters we meet in Luke 18: the widow, the judge, the Pharisee, the tax collector, parents, babies, disciples, and the rich young ruler. What about their various approaches to Jesus feels familiar to you? What questions would you ask for reassurance if you had Peter's boldness? Ask the Spirit to direct you as you ask and wait for God's response.

Recommended Closing Prayer

> Our Father, who art in heaven,
> hallowed be thy Name,
> thy kingdom come,
> thy will be done,
> on earth as it is in heaven.
> Give us this day our daily bread.
> And forgive us our trespasses,
> as we forgive those
> who trespass against us.
> And lead us not into temptation,
> but deliver us from evil.
> For thine is the kingdom,
> and the power, and the glory,
> for ever and ever. Amen.

Ordinary Time Day 101

KARI WEST

Reflect on Matthew 4:23–25

Call to Prayer

The gospels give us picture after picture of the words and works of Jesus. He taught so much, and he entered into our need with miracle after miracle. Yet in these few brief verses, Matthew offers us a rich, succinct encapsulation of the heart of Christ's public ministry. It's as if Matthew wants us to see what Jesus is about before he gets into the details of his narrative.

Take a few moments and reflect on the description of Christ's actions.

He proclaimed the good news of the kingdom, and he healed every disease and every sickness. Let that realization sink in. Every disease. Every sickness. What must have it been like in Galilee in those days with demons cast aside, lame men walking, pain erased, and death cheated?

Why so much healing? That question has many right answers, but one vital answer is this: Christ was setting signposts up all over Galilee. Why eradicate pain? Because pain is an interloper. Why reverse paralysis? Because human beings were meant to dance in joy for the glory of God. Why cast out demons? Because Satan is defeated. Why heal? Because life will trample death.

Because Christ will restore the cosmos. He will rule his good kingdom. He will.

The work is already under way. Perhaps Matthew, in these short verses, is giving us a foretaste of Christ's cosmic undoing of all the world's brokenness and sin.

As you pray, meditate on the works of Christ, culminating in his death and resurrection. Hope in his redemption, his return, and his restoration.

Recommended Closing Prayer

Amen. Come, Lord Jesus.

Ordinary Time Day 102
BILL BOYD

Reflect on Matthew 5:1–11

Call to Prayer

Again and again in our lives with the Lord, we need to reorient ourselves to how very different life in the kingdom of God is from life lived disconnected from God and his rule.

A life with Jesus demands that we understand that "Christianity" is not a creed or set of morals or a religion. No, a life with Jesus is a life where we live as citizens of the kingdom that he has inaugurated, and that kingdom is alive in the midst of the rebellious and broken world we also inhabit. The kingdom does not begin at some later date. It is now. It is a kingdom that transcends the worldly boundaries between heaven and earth. It is a kingdom that places us in our proper place, beholden to the Triune God, who is Love.

As you pray, listen as honestly as you can to Jesus's words about the kingdom recorded in Matthew 5:1–20. Ask yourself, "Am I submitting my thinking, my life, and my heart to these the words from my King? Or have I fallen into the service of another king?"

Then thank God for the ways his kingdom can calm your fears, ease your striving, and clarify your sense of what matters in life.

Recommended Closing Prayer

Lord Jesus, be my King now and forevermore. Amen.

Ordinary Time Day 103

WILLA KANE

Reflect on Matthew 5:3

Call to Prayer

The beatitudes describe a life God blesses. They are not a qualification for salvation—not things to do, but a way to be.

It's fitting that this first beatitude, the foundation for all that follow, deals with the quality of our hearts. It begins a spiritual sequence that leads us down step by step, then up into life in God's kingdom.

There is no entry into this kingdom apart from poverty of spirit, from humility. We must go down in order to go up. How are we to understand this in a world that tells us self-sufficiency, self-confidence, and self-expression are imperative for a successful life?

We have only to look at a holy God and imagine standing before him to understand how small and insignificant we are.

We have only to look at Jesus and contemplate the cross, where he died for us, to turn the tables on our worldly pride, the sin behind all sin.

When we are right-sized and pride is forced to flee, there is room in our hearts for God's Spirit to fill us.

As you pray, contemplate a holy God. Be honest about the pride that infects your heart.

Lift your eyes to the one who wears a crown in heaven because he wore a crown of thorns. This Jesus, who hung on the cross for you, welcomes you into his kingdom, the kingdom of heaven. In true humility, enter in.

Battling pride is a daily chore, something to be fought in the power of the Spirit by acknowledging your need for God and expressing gratitude to him.

Pride wilts in a thankful heart, and humility flourishes in the soil of spiritual disciplines, with prayer being the study of God's Word and worship.

As *THE MESSAGE*'s version of Matthew 5:3 tells us, "You're blessed when you're at the end of your rope. With less of you there is more of God and his rule."

You may feel as if you're at the end of your rope. In God's economy, that's a good place to be. Less of you, more of God. Poor in spirit, rich in the kingdom of heaven. Rejoice.

Recommended Closing Prayer

Father God, I yearn for poverty of spirit so your kingdom can be my forever home. I abhor and turn from pride that closes the door to life with you. Help me in all my doings to put down sin and to humble my pride. Right-size my life so that you might be glorified. In Jesus's name. Amen.

Ordinary Time Day 104

WILLA KANE

Reflect on Matthew 5:4

Call to Prayer

In a season of sadness, we know what it is to mourn and to long for comfort. As Jesus leads us to the next stepping-stone toward life in his kingdom, he invites us to mourn not just the things that are broken in our world, but also what is broken at the center of our hearts.

In the first beatitude, we confront poverty of spirit as the entrance to life in God's kingdom. If poverty of spirit is about understanding God's holiness and humankind's sinfulness, then this second beatitude is about feeling the pain that sinful brokenness brings.

If we let this pain touch us, it will break our hearts just as it breaks the heart of Jesus. Blessedly, as we come to him in sorrow, he comes to us as Comforter. He gives us his Spirit. And his Spirit knows us so intimately, so he knows how to comfort each one of us. It's a provision of grace we can hardly take in.

Listen to Jesus's promise: "And I will pray the Father, and he shall give you another Comforter, that he may abide with you for ever" (John 14:16 KJV).

The word *comfort* means "to strengthen greatly." The apostle Paul embraced this divine exchange offered by the Lord: "My grace is sufficient for you, for my power is made perfect in weakness. Therefore I will boast all the more gladly about my weaknesses, so that Christ's power may rest on me .... For when I am weak, then I am strong" (2 Corinthians 12:9, 12:10 NIV).

In your weakness, in your sadness, open yourself to the comfort, strength, and power of Christ.

A diagnosis of terminal illness causes us to mourn. The diagnosis of sin should do no less. Sin infects and destroys; even small sins in our lives, left unchecked, will germinate, grow, and multiply. Only the gospel can deal with our sin effectively.

As you pray, pause to consider your moral bankruptcy before the

Lord. Let this reality descend down from your mind and settle in your heart. Mourn it.

Push back against a world that tells us grieving sin is repressive and restrictive. Press back against a culture that says, "Don't worry. Be happy."

Jesus doesn't just mourn sin; he also conquers it. And as he does so, he invites us into this upside-down kingdom where those who truly mourn sin will be blessed with the comfort he himself gives.

End your prayer time with thanksgiving. Our Lord does not leave us as mourners. Listen to these promises from scripture. Pray them for yourself and those you love:

- "This is my comfort in my affliction, that your promise gives me life" (Psalm 119:50 ESV).
- "Sing for joy, O heavens, and exult, O earth; break forth, O mountains, into singing! For the Lord has comforted his people and will have compassion on his afflicted" (Isaiah 49:13 ESV).

Recommended Closing Prayer

Father, we confess our sin to you. We confess that we have very far to go in our journey of sanctification. Please forgive us things done and things left undone; forgive us our thoughts, words, and deeds of darkness. Let us know the depth of our sin. And now, Father, strengthen us with your grace and comfort. Let us once again embrace the cross as our place of full and free forgiveness. Give us fresh amazement and fresh gratitude, and let us walk in the light of the gospel. For Jesus's sake and in his name. Amen.

Ordinary Time Day 105

WILLA KANE

Reflect on Matthew 5:5

Call to Prayer

Here, again, is another step toward a life God blesses: meekness. We move from poverty of spirit, to godly mourning, to repentance; this repentance cleanses our hearts so we can be meek.

This is Christ's upside-down kingdom: poverty instead of riches, mourning instead of happiness, meekness instead of control.

The wisdom of the world says that meekness is weakness. But in Jesus's world, the word *meekness* describes what it is like for a wild stallion to be brought into submission by his master. The horse doesn't lose strength as it is tamed, but it learns to wait patiently for direction. Picture a thoroughbred completely still under his rider, until with gentle pressure, his master urges him forward. Imagine yourself, in meekness, looking to the Father, your eyes, heart, and mind focused on him, waiting for a gentle word, a gentle pressure. Meekness does not diminish us. It allows us to forget ourselves as we focus on God.

Look at the world around you. It seems that nothing is given; everything must be seized, asserted, and won. The way to get ahead is to take what you can when you can, to always be ready to define yourself and defend yourself. Fortune favors the bold.

Now consider Jesus, who when falsely accused, convicted, and humiliated, uttered not a word of defense. Consider this Jesus who entered Jerusalem not as a conquering hero on a white stallion but riding on a donkey.

Though he is meek, he still promises an inheritance to those who follow his example.

An inheritance cannot be purchased. It's a gift, something we could never earn or deserve. In meekness, bow before the Lord and receive the inheritance he has planned for you with a thankful heart. When Jesus returns to set up his kingdom on earth, it is the meek who will be there with him. Rejoice.

Father, please give me a right vision of meekness. Let me forsake the pattern of the world in grasping for power and defending what's mine. Let me look to you, trust in you, and wait for you to lead me in paths of righteousness for your name's sake. Amen.

Ordinary Time Day 106

WILLA KANE

Reflect on Matthew 5:6

Call to Prayer

We are praying the beatitudes in order, as each one builds upon the last.

The first four deal with humanity's relationship with God. When we recognize our emptiness without him, we mourn. As we repent of our pride, we become meek.

Once we are emptied of self and the counterfeits the world has on offer, we notice a chasm inside our hearts that cries to be filled. We're hungry and thirsty for something, for someone who will satisfy our longings. We need to be filled.

What are we searching for?

The prophet Isaiah spoke about the remedy we need: "Come, everyone who thirsts, come to the waters; and he who has no money, come, buy and eat! Come, buy wine and milk without money and without price" (Isaiah 55:1 ESV).

The remedy is Jesus, who proclaims blessing on those who hunger and thirst for righteousness. Righteousness—a right relationship with God—is what we need. It comes from being united to Christ through his body and blood, freely given in sacrifice for us. Not a righteousness of our own, but the righteousness of Jesus credited to accounts bankrupted by sin.

Come now, emptied of yourself, to Jesus. Pray to receive this bread of life and living water. Seek satisfaction in him alone.

Hungering and thirsting for righteousness restores our relationship with God and flows out to restored relationships with others. As we become more like Christ, we yearn for righteousness in the whole human family—for freedom, equality, justice, integrity, and honor.

As you pray, consider the broken relationships and institutions around you. How can you, empowered by the Spirit of Christ, be an agent of love? How can you work for justice where there is corruption, freedom where there is captivity, integrity and honor where there is moral bankruptcy?

Our hunger and thirst, unable to be satisfied by anything in this world, point us to another world, the one we were made for. It's God's kingdom, the kingdom of heaven.

Recommended Closing Prayer

> O God, teach me the happy art of
> attending to things temporal
> with a mind on things eternal.
> Send me forth to have compassion.
> Help me to walk as Jesus walked,
> my only Savior and perfect model,
> his mind my inward guest,
> his meekness my covering garb.
> Let my happy place be among the poor in spirit,
> my delight in the gentle ranks of the meek.
> Let me always esteem others better than myself
> and find in true humility
> an heirdom to two worlds.
> (From *The Valley of Vision*)

Ordinary Time Day 107

SALLY BREEDLOVE

Reflect on Matthew 5:7

Call to Prayer

With this fourth beatitude, Jesus continues to turn our presumptions upside down. A life blessed by God, he says, is a life where we offer and receive mercy.

Jesus could have said, "Blessed are those who forgive, for they will know forgiveness." But instead he says, "Blessed are the merciful" (Matthew 5:7 NIV). Why? Two parables can help us here.

In the parable about the sinner and the Pharisee, the sinner stands far off, undone by his sin. He cries out for mercy, not forgiveness. The Pharisee, however, is full of contempt and firmly believes he is better than the sinner.

In another parable, the Good Samaritan turns away from any personal prejudices he may have felt toward the Jews. He rescues a badly wounded Jew lying on the roadside. He doesn't ask the injured man what he'd done wrong. He cleans and wraps up his wounds, takes the man to an inn, and pays for his care. As the lawyer who had questioned Jesus has to admit, the Samaritan was the only one in the story who extended mercy. Mercy cuts through contempt and judgment and invites us to offer forgiveness, kindness, help, and generosity.

What is it like for you when contempt, judgment, and a desire to even the score rise up in you? What is it like for you when you wonder why people can't get their lives together or agree with your beliefs? What is it like for you when someone sins against you?

At the cross, every true judgment God can make about each of us is swallowed up by the mercy of God. If we let God's mercy settle deep in our souls, we will realize that to withhold mercy is to contradict all we say we believe.

Amazingly, the more mercy we offer to others, the more we will understand God's mercy in our lives.

Our world knows so little of mercy. Across racial, economic, and political lines, we fire the artillery of contempt and judgment. Will we own our sin and humble ourselves?

As you pray, ask yourself if you really believe you personally need mercy. Repent of your pride and your contempt toward others. Thank God for the places in your own story where mercy has triumphed. Then speak to God about the ways you judge others and withhold forgiveness and compassion. Ask God to pour his mercy through you to a particular person you struggle with.

Recommended Closing Prayer

O Lord God, help us see how large the mercy is that you have lavished on us. Give us the humility and compassion to lavish mercy on this broken world. Amen.

Ordinary Time Day 108

SALLY BREEDLOVE

Reflect on Matthew 5:8

Call to Prayer

In Matthew 5:8, Jesus tells us that a happy life is one where our purified hearts allow us to see God.

Does seeing God strike you as your highest good? We live in a flattened world where the highest good is social justice, or a certain political party in power, or adherence to good doctrine, or the end of racial tensions, or a better job, or happier relationships, or …

Many of our longings are for good things. But these longings never reach the core of what we need.

We were made for God. David, a man of great ability and passion, wasn't controlled by longing for a place in Saul's government, the respect of his family, safety, to be king himself, or even to build the temple. He confesses his core longing in Psalm 27:4: "I'm asking God for one thing, only one thing: To live with him in his house my whole life long. I'll contemplate his beauty; I'll study at his feet" (MSG).

As we rightly lament a world that is so very broken, it is good for us to pause and realize that nothing in this world will ever be enough. We were made for God.

The path to God is Jesus Christ. His Spirit is our guide, and the hedgerows of faithfulness to scripture and a life of doing justice, loving mercy, and walking humbly with God keep us on the path.

As you pray, examine your own heart. Don't let the following questions lead you to endless introspection or self-condemnation. Listen for the Holy Spirit's voice. He will point out what is amiss and will invite you into life.

- A pure heart is a cleansed heart. Is there a sin or sin pattern you need to confess to God?
- A pure heart is an undivided heart. In the parable of the seed and the sower, the cares of this world, the deceitfulness of riches, and the desire for other things can fill our hearts and choke out our real life. What keeps your heart divided?

Recommended Closing Prayer

Create in me a clean heart, O God, and renew a right spirit within me. For Jesus's sake. Amen.

Ordinary Time Day 109

SALLY BREEDLOVE

Reflect on Matthew 5:9

Call to Prayer

Peacemaking: the costliest of endeavors. At Christ's birth, angels joyfully proclaimed this baby would bring peace. But they didn't disclose the cost of that peace.

Paul does. Colossians 1:20 tells us, "All the broken and dislocated pieces of the universe—people and things, animals and atoms—get properly fixed and fit together in vibrant harmonies, all because of his death, his blood that poured down from the cross" (MSG).

The death of Jesus secured peace. And now, God gives us the work of offering peace to the broken and dislocated places in our world.

What price must we pay? The beatitudes show us the way: a reformed heart; humility to admit our own brokenness; grief as we consider the world's pain and our own complicity in it; surrender to not being in charge; hunger for transformation; submission to living by mercy; the priority of an unpolluted heart over self-interest.

This costly peace with God reshapes us so that the civil war simmering in our hearts is brought under God's kingship. If we locate all that is "wrong with the world" outside ourselves, if we blame a particular group of people, we will not make peace; we will feed conflict.

Learning peace with God and with ourselves frees us to join the work of reconciliation. To make peace, we offer the gospel of Jesus. There is no other path to shalom.

But we are also called to live by the ways of Jesus if we want to be peacemakers. The ways Jesus brought shalom into this world unsettle all of us. He overturned tables in the temple where profits were made by the elite class. He cared for the outcast Syrophoenician woman. He refused to settle an inheritance dispute between brothers. He wore a well-tailored outer garment. He submitted to Pilate's cowardice and the Sanhedrin's murderous hatred. He never spoke against Roman oppression. He refused to conform to the status quo.

If we want to follow Jesus into peacemaking in our world, we must learn from him. If we do so, we will come to look like what we really are, children of the heavenly Father.

Pray for those you know who are broken by the lack of peace in our world. Ask our Lord what needs to happen in you and how you need to be changed so you can become a peacemaker.

Recommended Closing Prayer

O Lord, make me an instrument of your peace no matter the cost.

Ordinary Time Day 110

SALLY BREEDLOVE

Reflect on Matthew 5:10–12

Call to Prayer

At this point, we may find ourselves resisting the beatitudes. How can the happy life be one of persecution, slander, and exclusion? Surely we can agree that a little more humility to admit our own weakness, a little more sadness for the broken places in the world and in our own lives, a little less grasping, a little more compassion, and a little more doing our best to help people get along all make some sort of sense.

But now Jesus raises the stakes. He shifts from talk of a coming kingdom and speaks directly to his listeners. His clarity is unmistakable. If we fully align with Jesus, we will likely end up being opposed and persecuted. When it happens, we will have a great reason to be happy.

This "blessing" seems absurd and scary.

We need to remember: God's people have always been opposed by the world and its systems. At times the two may seem to get along, but eventually, each one of us on earth has to decide which kingdom has our loyalty. If we stand with Christ, we will never be fully accepted or favored by the world.

Do you know the story of the early church? Christians were given a test: Throw a pinch of incense on a Roman altar fire and say aloud, "Caesar is Lord." Then feel free to worship any other god. Defiance meant persecution or even death.

Is our day different? In many places, persecution is deadly. In our world, it's legal, social, educational, and economic harassment, or exclusion. In our world, it's easy just to want to give in. But Jesus encourages us: *Resist going along with the world. Stay in solidarity with me. Endure. I have a reward.*

We need to make sure that we are not being persecuted for our poor work ethic or dishonorable conduct. We need to make sure we are being persecuted for being like Jesus, not for standing on our rights.

As you pray, ask the Lord to make your character above reproach. Ask him to give you an enduring heart of loyalty toward him. Ask for yourself and others true godliness, courage, steadfast faith, and endurance.

Recommended Closing Prayer

Receive these words as a benediction from your heavenly Father:

> You're blessed when your commitment to God provokes persecution. The persecution drives you even deeper into God's kingdom. Not only that—count yourselves blessed every time people put you down or throw you out or speak lies about you to discredit me. What it means is that the truth is too close for comfort and they are uncomfortable. You can be glad when that happens—give a cheer, even!—for though they don't like it, I do! And all heaven applauds. And know that you are in good company. My prophets and witnesses have always gotten into this kind of trouble. Amen.
> *(Matthew 5:10–12 MSG)*

Ordinary Time Day 111
SALLY BREEDLOVE

Reflect on Matthew 5:13

Call to Prayer

The Sermon on the Mount is panoramic teaching. Like the best of guides, pointing out the mountain ranges before a long hike, Christ gives a sweeping view of life in God's kingdom. He shows us the mountains of blessedness this life offers, and he pauses to warn us that we will encounter persecution. Then, stepping onto the trail, he reminds us who we are, not how hard we need to work to become something. He says two simple things: *You are salt. You are light.*

What's so good about being salt?

Jesus's listeners heard three things when he said, "You are the salt of the earth": you're valuable, you're beneficial, and you're essential.

In the ancient world, salt was precious. Sometimes Romans soldiers were paid in salt. Our word *salary* comes from the same root word. Salt was exchanged measure for measure for gold along some ancient trade routes. God instructed the Jews to add salt to their offerings in worship as an additional sacrifice.

Salt was and is useful. It is antiseptic, preserving meat and vegetables from rot. Salt brings out the best. Without salt, eating would only be a duty, something we'd do to assuage hunger and stay alive, but with little pleasure.

Finally, salt is vital. If your body loses too much salt, you die.

Jesus asserts our essential value by calling us salt, but in the same Word, he gives us purpose: Penetrate the world you live in. Change it by your presence. Don't be concerned that you are so few and the world is so large. It only takes a little salt to change things. Your value is in your saltiness, not in becoming like the world you live in.

Be present. Be an agent of change.

We live in a deteriorating, infected, dying culture. Are we willing to be shaken up and poured out for the sake of others? Will we bring practical benefit, joy, and true healing to people around us?

As you pray, pray that God's people will become healing, joy, and life to this world. Pray that day by day you will move toward others as a good gift of salt.

Recommended Closing Prayer

> Almighty God, whose Son our Savior Jesus Christ is the light of the world: Grant that your people, illumined by your Word and Sacraments, may shine with the radiance of Christ's glory, that he may be known, worshiped, and obeyed to the ends of the earth; through Jesus Christ our Lord, who with you and the Holy Spirit lives and reigns, one God, now and for ever. Amen.
>
> *(Anglican Church in North America Book of Common Prayer)*

Ordinary Time Day 112

SALLY BREEDLOVE

Reflect on Matthew 5:14–16

Call to Prayer

We are accustomed to believing we have to do things right and do something significant to matter. But Jesus breaks into our misguided sense of ourselves and calls us salt and light. The sermon is clear: our first calling is to be a certain kind of person—aware of our need and our brokenness, nongrasping, hungry for God, mercy-filled, pure of heart, peacemaking, and willing to be misunderstood and even hated. But that way of being is not a checklist for behavior. It's a call to respond to the mercy of God, the one who knows us fully and loves us completely.

As the rest of Matthew 5–7 unfolds, we learn practically how kingdom people are to live. But first Christ emphasizes our worth to him. So he tells us, *You are the salt of the earth; you are the light of the cosmos* (in the Greek, the word isn't *world*, but *cosmos*).

It's as if Christ is saying, *You are useful, essential. You bring goodness. You make things better. Through who you are, people around you have an opportunity to see God's glory.* We so easily believe that God expects too much from us. But Christ hasn't said "Be the salt; be the light." He has said that you are the salt, that you are the light.

Will you choose to believe such outrageous things about yourself?

Yesterday, we considered the gifts that salt can bring. Now let's ask, what we would be like if we were to take Christ at his word and believe we are light?

As you pray, take a moment to reflect and hold your own heart up to God.

- Do you seek to find your own light, or are you content to reflect the light of Christ?

- Do you trust Christ that the "stand" he puts you on is the best place for your light to shine? Or do you insist on making a platform for yourself?
- Are you committed to a life of doing good, and will you seek to do that good so God is seen; or do you need to be seen?
- Will you ask God to deal with the dark places in your own life and heart so that light, not shadows, spill out to those around you?

Recommended Closing Prayer

Jesus, you are the light of the world; in you is no darkness at all. May I walk with you so that your light shines in me and through me. Make me fully a child of the light. For Christ's sake. Amen.

Ordinary Time Day 113

KARI WEST

Reflect on Matthew 7:7–11

Call to Prayer

In yesterday's reflection, we were reminded that God sees us as salt and light. This passage encourages us to trust the goodness and graciousness of God. This confidence in the love of God should move us to ask, to seek, to knock—to *pray*.

God cares for us with the rich, abiding, all-encompassing love of a father. The human love of a parent for a child is just the barest hint and echo of the kind of love that God possesses for all those who trust in his name. If we comprehend any goodness and provision in the way parents care for their kids, then let that lead us to meditate on the length, width, height, and depth of the love of our heavenly Father. His love far surpasses any human love just as a tsunami surpasses a ripple in the water.

As you pray, contemplate the depth of the Father's love for you. Let his love drive you to seek, to ask, to knock—to know more of him at all costs.

Recommended Closing Prayer

Father, give us the power, together with all your holy people, to grasp how wide, and long, and high, and deep is the love of Christ, and to know this love that surpasses knowledge—that we may be filled to the measure of all your fullness. Amen.

Ordinary Time Day 114
SALLY BREEDLOVE

Reflect on Psalm 100:1–5

Call to Prayer

Gladness is in scarce supply these days. But this psalm says to choose gladness and exuberant joy. Shout out how good things are. Sing joyful songs to God. Come near to him with praise and thanksgiving.

This psalm and Psalm 23 endure as the two most beloved of all psalms. Could it be that at the core of our beings we need to know we are cared for by the Good Shepherd? Could it be that we need deep gladness?

The seriousness and distress of our world lead people to scoff at the idea that joy is meant to have a central place in our lives. But we were made for joy. The work of being changed into the likeness of Jesus is growth toward joy. Paul puts it this way in 2 Corinthians 1:24: "We work with you for your joy" (NIV).

Could it be that the mark of true Christlikeness is not just love and peace but also joy? Could we dare hope that the trajectory of a life of faith is a movement toward greater and greater joy?

We belong to God. He takes care of us. We are safe. He chooses us. We are beloved.

Belongingness, safety, belovedness. If our life with God is our deepest reality, then everything is indeed okay.

Will you let joy find you?

As you pray, let this psalm lead you into joy, thanksgiving, and praise.

Recommended Closing Prayer

> O heavenly Father, you have filled the world with beauty: Open our eyes to behold your gracious hand in all your works; that, rejoicing in your whole creation, we may learn to serve you with gladness; for the sake of him through whom all things were made, your Son Jesus Christ our Lord. Amen.
>
> *(Anglican Church in North America Book of Common Prayer)*

Ordinary Time Day 115

KARI WEST

Reflect on Luke 5:27–32

Call to Prayer

"Follow me" (Luke 5:27 NIV). How succinct and how powerful are Christ's words to Levi.

Tax collectors, corrupt instruments of foreign Roman rule, were universally hated by their fellow Jews for their disloyalty and greed. They wielded the borrowed power of the oppressor to cheat their own people and line their own pockets.

Our Lord holds out this invitation to Levi despite the man's despised job description, despite his dishonest dealings, despite his greed, and despite his disreputability.

In fact, Christ speaks these words *because* of these things and the underlying cause of them. The Great Physician knows these outward symptoms of a decrepit heart. He unapologetically, graciously holds out the remedy: *Follow me.*

The cure is simple: repentance. Jesus calls Levi out of his old sinful ruts and onto a path of discipleship. Levi immediately heeds the call.

But, as a warning to all of us, the Pharisees refuse to acknowledge that such a profound diagnosis of sin could apply to them. "We are well," they maintain. "We have no need of a doctor's care." Rejecting the gracious cure, they are left in their own self-deception, their own decay, their own whitewashed tombs.

By contrast, a life of repentance and renewal fueled by the healing power of the Spirit—like Levi's—spills over into generosity, thankfulness, and celebration.

As you pray, inhabit the place of Levi. Reject the lie of the Pharisees. You are not well. Embrace the reality that sin's infection has spread in you and that there is no thought, word, or deed free of decay.

And now, embrace the cure of the Great Physician. Believe the gospel. Follow hard after Jesus. Leave behind every weight and all entangling sin, and throw a party to celebrate such an elaborate display of grace.

Recommended Closing Prayer

Christ, our healer, let us remember how much we need you. Keep us from believing the lie of our own self-righteousness. Thank you for your shed blood that covers us and empowers us to heed your call of repentance. In your precious and powerful name. Amen.

Ordinary Time Day 116

KARI WEST

Reflect on Luke 6:1–11

Call to Prayer

In this passage, many of the actions stem from need. Christ's disciples were hungry, so they stretched out their hands for grain. David in the Old Testament needed sustenance, so he stretched out his hand for holy bread. The helpless man in the synagogue stretched out his withered hand for healing.

Stretching out our hands is a humble action, one acknowledging our dependence. One of the Sabbath's key lessons is that we need to learn to rely on God. Don't work constantly. Give a day to rest and worship. Recall your creatureliness, your need for respite, your utter lack of self-sufficiency. Recall that God is Lord and that your place is at his feet with outstretched hands, asking for provision and restoration. The Lord of the Sabbath will give you what you need.

Pause a moment and consider the implications of what Christ says about himself. To be the Lord of the Sabbath means that true rest describes the nature of his reign. Christ bids all who are weary to come, lay down their burdens, and find a lighter yoke. We all carry a yoke; no one is free of all burden. However, the yoke of submission to right lordship—the lordship of Christ—is easy and light.

Come and bow before the Lord of the Sabbath. Confess the ways you have again taken up the heavy yoke of self-sufficiency and pride. Confess that your failure to show humility, love, and a desire for true life for your neighbors is the reason you have not been guided into Sabbath living. Confess that you've followed in the paths of the Pharisees and set yourself against the preeminence of Christ.

And now, rejoice! Christ has purchased your future shalom at great cost to himself. Rejoice that he comes with healing in his wings. Rejoice that though we come with hunger and disease, our Lord of Sabbath gives us bread and restoration. Rejoice that his coming kingdom will be full of feasting and rest.

O Christ, as the eyes of servants look to the hand of their master, as the eyes of a maidservant to the hand of her mistress, so our eyes will look to you, O Lord our God, till you have mercy upon us. Bless us and keep us, Lord of the Sabbath. Amen.

Ordinary Time Day 117

KARI WEST

Reflect on Luke 7:1–10

Call to Prayer

What could cause the Maker of the stars to marvel? Christ—he who created all things and who holds all things together, the Son of the Most High God—is there something that can make him wonder?

And if so, would it not be worth all the riches in the world to possess it?

In these verses, we behold a mystery—Jesus marvels at a man's humble faith.

This centurion was a man of some human importance and power. He had soldiers at his command, enough wealth to build the Jewish synagogue, and enough social clout for the Jewish leaders to do him a favor in begging a favor of Christ on his behalf.

Yet this pagan Roman warrior comprehends something that the religious leaders miss. He has the correct assessment of his own worth, and it is the opposite of what the Jewish leaders say of him. He's not worthy for Christ to enter his home. His words echo those of John the Baptist when he said he wasn't worthy to untie the sandals of Jesus.

But with this recognition of Christ's supremacy comes the assurance that Jesus can do great and marvelous works. The centurion understands that while he may have the minor authority to tell his servants what to do, Christ's words—even spoken from afar—can banish death.

It is a supremely precious gift to have this kind of faith—a faith that recognizes one's unworthiness to call on the name of Jesus and yet trusts that he is powerful and gracious to answer one's humble asking.

As you pray, ask for this priceless faith. Ask Christ to help you better comprehend his greatness and your smallness. Ask him, out of his might and love, to listen to your prayer and give you what is best.

Recommended Closing Prayer

Christ, you are so great, and I am so small. I lay my desires before you. I long for the heart to receive whatever it is you give. Amen.

Ordinary Time Day 118

KARI WEST

Reflect on Luke 7:18–23

Call to Prayer

Our faith is not steady.

In the beginning of John's Gospel, we hear John the Baptist bellowing, "Behold, the Lamb of God, who takes away the sin of the world!" (John 1:29 ESV).

A bit later on, in Luke 7:28, Christ says, "Among those born of women none is greater than John" (ESV).

And yet here in these verses, we see John wavering. He sends his disciples to Christ for confirmation. He asks of Jesus, "Are you the one who is to come, or should we expect someone else?" (Luke 7:19 ESV).

Are you familiar with the lingering doubt that John expresses? Do you wrestle with similar misgivings, even if you will not say them aloud?

Jesus, are you truly who you say you are? Are you our Messiah, our rescuer, our Savior? Will you repair the ruined road that leads to friendship with God? Will you keep me until the end? Will you never leave, never forsake? Will you remake the world?

Let this passage teach you. John lays his question at Christ's feet. And Christ answers, *Look around. The blind see, the lame walk, the deaf hear, the lepers dance, and the dead breathe again. And if you aren't offended by me, if you accept my words and my lordship, you will know the very blessing of God.*

Jesus doesn't crush John in his wavering. Instead, Jesus tells John to listen to the shouts of surprise and joy, to see the tears of gladness, to taste these first fruits of his coming reign. Yet in the mystery of his goodness and sovereignty, he does not promise John's release from prison. Instead, he calls him to learn a deeper trust.

The gospels promise a coming kingdom where all disease is undone and where death will be trampled. In this present world, some of that good work is already taking place. But much remains deeply broken. Christ calls to us, "Don't be offended. Trust me."

As you pray, voice your doubts to the Lord, then listen for his invitation to learn a deeper trust. Sit long with the gospels and let Christ's works of grace permeate your imagination and your soul. Hold fast to Jesus.

Recommended Closing Prayer

O Christ, we believe. Help our unbelief. We are bruised reeds and smoldering wicks. Be gracious to us. Give us the courage for honest prayers and the patience to meditate, long and slow, on scripture. Let us consider you, Jesus, and be renewed. Give us the deep faith that holds to you always. Amen.

Ordinary Time Day 119

KARI WEST

Reflect on Luke 7:36–50

Call to Prayer

How much we love Christ will depend in part on how much we own our sinfulness and then forget about ourselves.

This prostitute, knowing that she will face utter contempt from those watching, weeps freely at the feet of Christ, uses her own hair to wipe his feet clean, kisses his feet, and then pours out costly ointment on his skin.

She weeps because she knows her own moral bankruptcy. She kisses and anoints because she knows Christ is worthy of all her adoration. Her actions will arouse the scorn of the other guests. But Jesus's supremacy has freed her from being controlled by the opinions of others and has freed her to worship.

Simon, by contrast, is the exalted center of his own world. He sits in judgment over both the woman and Jesus. He knows this is a sinful woman, and he assumes that Jesus must not be a prophet or else he'd push her away.

Simon is encased in pride, so the faults of others, perceived or real, only reinforce his high view of himself. This woman, however, reveals Simon's self-importance, judgment, and lack of hospitality. Simon withholds honor; he appraises and evaluates, but he doesn't love. The woman humbly gives Christ the adoration he is due.

So it is only the woman who leaves that evening with her sins forgiven and her faith alive.

As you pray, ask God to kill your pride and give you a right understanding of yourself. Ask for the kind of blessed self-forgetfulness that allowed the woman to deny all social convention for the greater good of true worship. Thank Jesus for canceling your massive debt of sin at the cross. Then join this prostitute in the new life of forgiveness and faith.

Father, lift our eyes to you. In the light of your presence, let our pride wilt and our humility flourish. Give us tears of repentance. Let us know you as worthy of any price and any sacrifice. Thank you for free and full forgiveness bought by Jesus. In his most precious name. Amen.

Ordinary Time Day 120

KARI WEST

Reflect on Luke 8:4–15

Call to Prayer

How generative is the Word of God received in a soul ready to listen and obey, and how barren, complicated, and shallow is a life without Christ.

Do you hear both the danger and the promise brimming in these words of Jesus? The parable of the sower is so familiar to us that we are in danger of growing deaf to both its warning and its glory.

Pause and let these divinely chosen images seep into your mind: seed trampled on the ground, devoured by birds; seedlings sprouting up between rock crevices, only to wilt and then die without water; fresh green shoots choked and shredded by encroaching thorns.

These pictures are meant to alarm us. Satan, the evil one, hates life itself. Hardships have power to undo us if we let them. The world, if we are not diligent, will choke and smother our very souls. May we heed the warnings.

But now listen to the last part of this parable: a seed falls into dense, nurturing soil, and over time it grows straight and strong, vibrant and green, until it yields abundant rich fruit.

Indeed, this a life open to the Word of God, one ready to hear, ready to do, and eager to know the Lord. This is a heart where the seeds of scripture are planted deep, where they can flourish into abundance and new life.

As you pray, ask for a heart of tender, attentive receptivity to the Word of God. Ask the Good Sower to plant seeds deeply and to keep the soil rich and ample. Thank him for his good promises.

Recommended Closing Prayer

Create in me a clean heart, O God, and renew a right spirit within me. For Jesus's sake. Amen.

Ordinary Time Day 121

KARI WEST

Reflect on Luke 8:26–39

Call to Prayer

When we neglect listening to the scriptures, we find it easy to remake Christ in our image, as a smaller, less commanding, and more easily explained Savior. Stories like this one help to shake us awake again. We need to remember again and again the true nature of the God-man to whom we pray; we need to see Christ anew in his power, lordship, and great mercy.

Though many people in Luke's Gospel question Christ's authority and Word, the demons do not doubt his identity. They know the far-reaching domain of Christ's rule, and they are powerless to disobey his Word. These demons cannot escape the kingship of Christ or his command. This Jesus is the warrior king in whose name we pray.

Not only is Christ powerful, but also he uses that authority to restore right order, to bring about goodness and life. Demons had wreaked havoc on this man. He enjoyed no community and wore no clothing. He was out of his mind. Tellingly, he took up residence among tombs.

Christ wields his power for the purposes of love. He gives this man back his mind and his life, and seats him at his feet. He overturns the destructive work of Satan and reinstates a taste of shalom. This is the merciful Savior we call on.

As you pray, embrace the power and the mercy of Christ. Sit with these words from Luke's Gospel until they work fresh wonder in your soul at your great and loving Savior.

Recommended Closing Prayer

O Christ, give us eyes to see you, ears to hear you, and hearts to understand you, our Lord and our Redeemer. Amen.

Ordinary Time Day 122
S A L L Y   B R E E D L O V E

Reflect on Luke 8:40–42, 8:49–56

Call to Prayer

Has Jesus taken too long? It certainly seems so. The only daughter of an important family is dying. In a world where big families mean God's blessing, she's all they have. Likely her parents have hoped that she will marry and give them a houseful of grandchildren.

Her father, Jairus, is the ruler of the synagogue, so he has likely been opposed to Jesus. He has heard the conversation among his peers in neighboring towns and knows this would-be Messiah needs to be silenced, perhaps (as is being discussed behind closed doors) even eliminated.

But now Jairus is desperate. He finds Jesus, falls at his feet, and begs him to come to his house and save his daughter.

For some of us, asking for help, even for small things, is hard. But asking for help from someone we look down on, someone we oppose? That's almost impossible. Unless desperation drives us to throw away our pride and beg.

So Jairus does that, but then Jesus gets caught up in an event in the crowd around him. He's delayed. How does that feel to Jairus? Is desperation morphing into anger? into doom? As they finally arrive at his home, Jairus hears the mourners and sees the grief etched on his wife's face. It's too late.

But Jesus says, "Do not fear; only believe, and she [your daughter] will be well" (Luke 8:50 ESV). Then he leads them inside to the child's corpse.

Death is not the end. Jesus pulls her back from death and restores her to her family.

The questions fall to us: Will we humble ourselves before our gracious God and say, "Help me!"? Will we be willing to wait, even when Jesus seems to take too long? Our own circumstances may appear beyond help. The world around us seems to be spinning out of control into chaos and anger and despair. How can we hang on to hope?

As you pray, ask Jesus for the faith to accept his invitation: "Do not fear; only believe" (Luke 8:50 ESV).

We do not know how or when Christ will fulfill his promises. But are we willing to turn to Jesus, to wait with Jesus while he seems to delay, and then to enter in with Jesus to the broken and ruined places of our lives and world?

Recommended Closing Prayer

Christ, please take away our fear. Please enable our belief in you. Amen.

Ordinary Time Day 123
SALLY BREEDLOVE

Reflect on Luke 8:43–48

Call to Prayer

The crowd is pushing Jesus along. Jairus is afraid; his daughter is dying. He's desperate for Jesus to get to his house as quickly as he can. Nothing else matters. Peter also is insistent for them to hurry. You have to wonder, is Peter impressed that the leader of a synagogue is asking for help? It could be quite the opportunity for Jesus.

But in that crowd is a woman with a secret plan. She has been bleeding for twelve years, and seeing doctors hasn't helped. She's almost bankrupt. Her bleeding makes her unclean, isolating her from every part of society. She knows no one wants to be near her, but she presses through the crowd. Perhaps it parts as she comes near. Finally, she manages to touch the tassels on Jesus's garment. Her bleeding stops. Maybe at last she can be free from her bondage of illness and the shame of being unclean, flawed, an outcast.

But then Christ does the most unexpected thing. He knows healing has gone out from his body, and he stops to find out who touched him. Peter wants him to keep moving, but Christ insists: who touched me?

The woman has a choice. Will she step forward and confess why she needed healing? Will she admit what she's done? Will she step into the shame of exposure?

This woman took the first risk by touching Jesus's robe. Now she takes this second risk. She steps forward. She owns the shame of her own story. And Jesus? He calls her "daughter." He declares she belongs in the family. He blesses her with peace.

Can the door to our own freedom possibly be to admit our shame and come face-to-face with Jesus and his mercy?

As you pray, sit with your own story. Do you hide from yourself, from those around you, from God? Do you believe you are fundamentally flawed by things you have done or by what has been done to violate you? Reach out to Jesus. He will not hurry past you. He forgives you; he heals you; he makes you family.

Recommended Closing Prayer

Lord, you know everything about me. You know my shame, my hiding, and my pretense. Forgive the stubborn and resistant ways I keep you at a distance. Heal the broken places in me. Help me to know your mercy. Thank you that you have made me family with you. For Jesus's sake. Amen.

Ordinary Time Day 124
SALLY BREEDLOVE

Reflect on Luke 9:10–17

Call to Prayer

Could it be that the disciples are tired of other people's needs? They urge Jesus to send the crowds away to find food.

But Jesus pushes back. "You give them something to eat" (Luke 9:13 ESV).

Is there sarcasm, or irritated exhaustion, in the disciples' response? It's as if they are asking, *So, you want us to walk to the next village, then buy and bring back enough food for five thousand men and their kids and their wives? What village would have food for five thousand extra people at a moment's notice? You must be kidding, Jesus.*

Christ's only response is to say, "Have them sit down in groups of about fifty each" (Luke 9:14 ESV).

That's a job the disciples can do, tell people where to go and where to sit. But to what end?

While the disciples are busy arranging the crowd, Jesus gathers the small bit of food they have scavenged. Jesus looks upward to heaven and blesses the food before him. Then he begins to break it and give it away, and then break it and give it away, and then break it and give it away, until everyone eats and what is left over is gathered up into twelve baskets.

It never looked like a gigantic buffet on an ocean liner. As the disciples came back to Jesus again and again for another basket of food to distribute, did they ever wonder if the next time there wouldn't be any left?

It was an impossible situation. But somehow the need was met, and leftovers abounded.

We live in a world of impossible needs. Who has the answers? Who has the means? Who can solve the hatred, the contempt, the division, the disease, and the distrust that threatens to consume us? Does Jesus expect any one of us to come up with a large enough answer to set this world right? If we can't do that, what can we do?

Perhaps we need to do what the disciples ended up doing: Keep returning to Jesus, time after time, day after day. Receive from him a basket's worth of wisdom, of love, of patience, of compassion, and of trust. Go give today's provision away and come back again tomorrow.

As you pray, name one or two of the impossible needs that burden your heart and mind. Then hold your hands up to Jesus and ask him to carry what you cannot carry. Ask him to do his perfect will in an "impossible place" in your life.

Recommended Closing Prayer

> Blessed be the Lord,
> who daily bears us up;
> God is our salvation. *Selah*
> Our God is a God of salvation,
> and to God, the Lord, belong
> deliverances from death.
> *(Psalm 68:19–20 ESV)*

Ordinary Time Day 125

SALLY BREEDLOVE

Reflect on Luke 9:18–22

Call to Prayer

Prayer is meant to change us. As we sit with God, we see more clearly how we need to care for those around us. Jesus prays, and then he turns his attention to his disciples and asks them if they understand who he is.

Jesus does what we often do in an important conversation: he asks a less significant question to set the stage for the real question. The first question seems almost casual: "Who do the crowds say I am?" (Luke 9:18 NIV).

The disciples give all sort of answers. Theorizing and reporting is easy. Data and intellectual queries can be simple. Nothing gets personal. Nothing is aimed at the heart.

But then Jesus pivots, and the question confronts his disciples: "Who do you say I am?" (Luke 9:20 NIV).

A world of difference lies between these two questions "Who do they say?" and "Who do you say?" For centuries people have asked, "Who is Jesus?" But only Jesus can look deep into our hearts and ask us: "Who do you say I am?"

Peter answers with insight that the Father in heaven gives him: "God's Messiah" (Luke 9:20 NIV).

What was it like for someone to finally see Jesus for who he really is? Did Christ shout in triumph and praise?

No. Look at what follows. Jesus gives his disciples more information than they can comprehend, telling them he is not the Messiah they have expected: "The Son of Man must suffer many things and be rejected by the elders, the chief priests and the teachers of the law, and he must be killed and on the third day be raised to life" (Luke 9:22 NIV).

What a devastating and confusing reply.

The truth is, Christ never leads us on. He never pretends to be who he isn't. He never glibly promises an easy road. As long as we live in this world, suffering and then glory will be the arc of the story.

Our world is so very broken. We are at odds with each other, within ourselves, with creation, and with God. The suffering in our world comes as no surprise to the God we abandoned. But the God we walked away from has walked into our world. He is indeed the God-man Jesus Christ.

He is the Messiah. After the resurrection, Peter understands: all the suffering we are experiencing will be healed by the suffering Messiah.

As you pray, let Jesus ask you: "Who do you say I am?" What answer rises up in you? Take your heart to Jesus.

Recommended Closing Prayer

> Almighty God, whom truly to know is everlasting life: Grant us so to perfectly know you Son Jesus Christ to be the way, the truth and the life, that we may steadfastly follow his steps in the way that leads to eternal glory, though Jesus Christ your Son our Lord, who lives and

reigns with you, in the unity of the Holy Spirit, one God, for ever and ever. Amen.

(Anglican Church in North America Book of Common Prayer)

Ordinary Time Day 126

SALLY BREEDLOVE

Reflect on Luke 9:23–27

Call to Prayer

Peter has just confessed that Jesus is the Messiah. But Jesus's response is not to explain in detail the great story of his crucifixion, resurrection, ascension, and coming kingdom. Instead, he takes pains to teach his friends that the road of following him can be a hard road.

The disciples are confused. They want to be with Jesus; his authority, his miracles, and his compelling presence cannot be denied. But he keeps driving home his point: if they want to be with him, they must follow him on the path he chooses.

What does it look like to follow Jesus?

It's a life of imitating Christ. His cross was a chosen suffering for the healing of others. How might you need to suffer so that others can be healed?

It's a life where you let go of your own preferences, your privileges, your pride. What would it be like not to insist on having things your way?

It's a life of steadfast loyalty to Jesus, no matter what the world thinks of him. We live in a world where people are fine with personal spiritual beliefs. But Christianity is centered on the real historical Jesus Christ, fully God, fully man, who came into this world to die and rise again so that all people could find salvation in him. In a world where no one is supposed to make a truth claim, holding to the reality of Jesus Christ provokes anger, scorn, and ostracism. Are you willing to stand with him?

If you were Jesus, would you have laid out the cost of following before the disciples experienced Easter morning? Wouldn't it have been smarter to wait until after the resurrection?

Perhaps Christ is asking these first disciples: *Will you follow me by faith, despite your limited understanding? Will you follow me to the cross when it looks like all is lost? Will you follow me even though I will not guarantee you a happy ending to your life on this planet?*

Doesn't he ask us those same questions?

We have to make up our minds about Jesus. Do we expect this world to save us? Jesus unabashedly calls us to follow him. Will we, regardless of the cost?

Pray for Christian people everywhere. Pray we will be loyal to the Son of God no matter the cost.

Recommended Closing Prayer

> Almighty God, whose most dear Son went not up to joy but first he suffered pain, and entered not into glory before he was crucified: Mercifully grant that we, walking in the way of the Cross, may find it none other than the way of life and peace; through Jesus Christ your Son our Lord. Amen.
> *(Anglican Church in North America Book of Common Prayer)*

Ordinary Time Day 127
SALLY BREEDLOVE

Reflect on Luke 9:28–36

Call to Prayer

What was the purpose of the transfiguration? Was it for the three disciples? Was it for us who read the gospels? Was it for Jesus himself?

Imagine what Jesus is facing. He knows the cross lies ahead; he knows his friends do not understand. Judging from what he will pray in the garden of Gethsemane, he knows the cross is an excruciating place of submission. On that mountain as he looks ahead, his Father meets him with encouragement. The transfiguration is, in part, a moment of clarity. He experiences his full glory as the Son, hears his Father's blessing, and receives strength from two faithful men of the past as they discuss what lies ahead for Jesus.

God meets the depth of his Son's human need on that mountain.

The transfiguration is a gift to God's people as well. It reminds us that Jesus has always been the Son of God, that he has never been simply a man. The transfiguration allows us to look past all that seems to be going on and see what is true. Jesus Christ is the eternal Son who shares the Father's glory. And Jesus Christ came to die for our sins.

At the same time, it's good to remember what Peter said about this event years later. In 2 Peter 1:18, he tells us the story of being on the "holy mountain" (ESV). He says the three disciples were "eyewitness of Christ's majesty" (2 Peter 1:16 ESV) and that they saw his glory and heard the voice from heaven proclaiming Jesus as the beloved Son of God.

But we also know these three disciples couldn't hold on to this vision. They came down from the mountain, bickered among themselves, deserted Christ when he was arrested, and despaired when he was crucified. Aware of his own weak and fickle nature, Peter tells us that what we really need is not a vision, but to pay attention to the scripture, the only thing that will sustain us in a dark world.

As you pray, hold in your mind the glory of the risen Christ. His reign will one day bring the shalom we long for. As you pray, ask God for the faithfulness to read the scriptures and follow Jesus day by day.

Recommended Closing Prayer

As you pray, affirm your commitment to a life of reading and heeding the Word of God. Then close your prayers with these words from scripture:

We weren't, you know, just wishing on a star when we laid the facts out before you regarding the powerful return of our Master, Jesus Christ. We were there for the preview! We saw it with our own eyes: Jesus resplendent with light from God the Father as the voice of Majestic Glory spoke: "This is my Son, marked by my love, focus of all my delight." We were there on the holy mountain with him. We heard the voice out of heaven with our very own ears. We couldn't be more sure of

what we saw and heard—God's glory, God's voice. The prophetic Word was confirmed to us. You'll do well to keep focusing on it. It's the one light you have in a dark time as you wait for daybreak and the rising of the Morning Star in your hearts. Amen.
(2 Peter 1:16–19 MSG)

Ordinary Time Day 128

SALLY BREEDLOVE

Reflect on Luke 9:37–43

Call to Prayer

Matthew, Mark, and Luke all tell the story of the transfiguration. Each one follows it with the story of the demon-possessed boy, his desperate father, and the disciples' inadequacy to handle the situation at the foot of the mountain.

Perhaps we need these stories side by side if we are to survive our world. From a mountaintop, a proclamation is made: Jesus is the Son of God whose glory is so brilliant, it blinds. And Jesus is the one who will die.

Meanwhile, "down in the valley," the world is helpless in the face of evil's destructive power. But Jesus enters our broken world. He's not simply the Glorified One adored by all of heaven. He is not simply our "future Savior."

He is also the Lord who enters into the argument taking place at the foot of the mountain. He is the one who pays attention to the father's needs as well, asking him to tell the story of his son's sickness. And he is the one who looks at his disciples and sighs, saying, "You don't have to be faithless and useless as you live in this world!"

Are we like those disciples?

Faithless people quit turning to Jesus. They don't count on him; they don't listen to him. They go their own way and try to make life work on their own terms.

Twisted people are no longer "true." Twistedness makes something become useless, like a twisted ruler, a twisted nail, or a twisted tire. Twisted things were designed for good purposes, but they are out of alignment. They make things worse, not better.

In his grace, Christ comes to faithless and twisted people like the disciples, like us, to heal them and to love them.

As you consider this story, what do you most want to hold in your heart as you pray?

Do you feel anguish for someone you love who cannot find healing?

Do you despair as you see the arguing and ineffectiveness all around you?

Are you bound by evil and sin?

Do you fear you are being destroyed by your own choices and by what other people have done to you?

In Mark's version of this story, the father cries out: "I believe; help my unbelief!" (Mark 9:24 ESV). In your own words, call out to Jesus with whatever faith you have. He will supply the rest.

Recommended Closing Prayer

> Almighty God, whose Son took upon himself the afflictions
> of your people: Regard with your tender compassion those
> suffering from anxiety, depression, or mental illness bear
> their sorrows and their cares; supply all their needs; help
> them to put their whole trust and confidence in you; and
> restore them to strength of mind and cheerfulness of spirit;
> through Jesus Christ our Lord. Amen.
> *(Anglican Church in North America Book of Common Prayer)*

Ordinary Time Day 129

MARYRACHEL BOYD

Reflect on Psalm 143:1–2, 143:5–8

Call to Prayer

Psalm 143 begins with a deep cry for mercy. As our awareness of our sin increases, our awareness of the cross's significance has the opportunity to increase as well. We begin to see how our sins create bigger and bigger gaps in our relationship with the Lord and with other people. The writer of Psalm 143 describes the type of awareness that can come to us by the grace of God when we know without a doubt how badly we need mercy.

Feelings of anxiety can intertwine with our increased awareness of sin. But the gospel promises us that we can always turn in confession and repentance to our Savior. The psalmist is writing long before the Incarnation, but he models this posture of penitence and prayer. He models the hope we can cling to that God will indeed be merciful to us.

How beautiful that we are known by one who steadfastly loves us, who, when we reject him, remains with arms outstretched, eager for us to be eager for him.

As you pray, how is it with your own soul? Will you ask God to give you a humble and contrite heart? Join with the psalmist in crying out to God.

Recommended Closing Prayer

> Let the morning bring me word of your unfailing love
> for I have put my trust in you.
> *(Psalm 143:8 NIV)*

Ordinary Time Day 130
MADISON PERRY

Reflect on Luke 9:46–50

Call to Prayer

A group of Jesus's disciples have been arguing over a burning question. It's obvious who the greatest of the whole group is—Jesus. But what about among his followers? Who is the greatest among them?

Jesus's followers are apparently multiplying far outside the boundaries of their little group (Luke 9:49–50). A hierarchy seems to be breaking out in the group, as Peter and John were chosen from among them to hike with Jesus up the Mount of Transfiguration and witness the glory of God (Luke 9:28–46). So, how could Jesus's disciples make sure their commitment to him wouldn't be overlooked in his coming kingdom?

Jesus's disciples do not trust that God will simply provide for them, bless them, and fill them with boundless joy and contentment. No, there has to be a secret, a way to get ahead and make sure things will go well for them. They believe the blessings of God are scarce.

To teach them, Jesus introduces them to a young child. Jesus's disciples wished that they had all been present to receive Moses and Elijah on the Mount of Transfiguration. But would they be willing to receive a small child, an image-bearer of the living God? The disciples wanted to understand the secrets of heaven and earth and find the secret path to greatness. But would they learn the most difficult lesson of all, a lesson any child could teach them?

Jesus perceives the reasoning of our hearts. He knows the desires that haunt us and drive us.

What has been driving you lately? What threatens to overtake you?

One of the greatest battles in the Christian life is to allow God to put you exactly where you need to be to live forever and to trust him to give you exactly what you need in order to gain infinite joy. God's gifts are on a completely different scale of magnitude from the paltry earnings and accumulations that characterize our days. Status in God's kingdom is unfathomable from an earthly perspective. Now is the time for our schemes and selfish ambitions to be unseated and for us to see that in loving one another we are receiving the greatest gift there is.

Call to mind God's promises to you. He will never leave you or forsake you. He has made you for eternal life. Now tell God about the burdens you have been carrying, the tasks you have given yourself to make yourself great. Ask the Lord to help you to shoulder every load you have been given to carry. Now ask God whom he has called you to receive in love and ask him to give you the strength and courage to receive that person (or those people) in love.

Recommended Closing Prayer

> Most holy God, the source of all good desires, all right judgments, and all just works: Give to us, your servants, that peace which the world cannot give, so that our minds may be fixed on the doing of your will, and that we, being delivered from the fear of all enemies, may live in peace and quietness; through the mercies of Christ Jesus our Savior. Amen.
>
> *(Anglican Church in North America Book of Common Prayer)*

Ordinary Time Day 131

SALLY BREEDLOVE

Reflect on Luke 9:51, Philippians 3:12–14, and Hebrews 12:22–24a

Call to Prayer

The Incarnation has made the invisible visible: God is present with us. We don't have to make an arduous journey to find him. Christ and his kingdom are here now. As his people, we are the temple of the living God. There's no need to fear how things will turn out. The guaranteed ending of our story is full joy, a joy that increases as eternity unfolds.

At the same time, our life with God is a journey of walking toward and working out what is already true. We are not passive recipients of God's grace. God invites us to be active participants in his grace. Our faith is meant to mirror Jesus's. He knew he was headed toward a premature death by crucifixion. He also knew he would be raised from the dead. His death was not the abyss of unrecoverable despair. Yes, it had to be entered into, but he kept his eye on the joy that lay beyond.

As Christians, we know God is sovereign and his kingdom will prevail, but for now, along with the rest of the world, we have to walk it out, day by day.

As you pray, ask God to galvanize your courage. In prayer, remind yourself of the future you have in Jesus Christ. Often what stalls us on this journey is insisting that life work out on our own terms and work out fast. Ask forgiveness for those stubborn places. Pray that your courage and hope will infect those around you who are discouraged.

Recommended Closing Prayer

O Father God, give us eyes to see what lies beyond this world, hearts that know the Spirit's guiding, and pilgrim's feet to follow Jesus. Amen.

Ordinary Time Day 132

MADISON PERRY

Reflect on Luke 9:57–62

Call to Prayer

Jesus has given Israel the chance to encounter him and follow him. He has opened to them a portion of the earth-shattering glories of the good news—healing, wisdom, justice, and life. And now he turns his face to Jerusalem.

When Jesus first called his followers, he was an unknown itinerant, a man from the wilderness possessing no human authority.

But by the power and authority of the Holy Spirit, he now has a reputation and a large following. At the beginning of his public ministry, people joined him out of curiosity, personal ambition, or utter desperation. But now, as his rejection and crucifixion loom large, it will become obvious that the way of Jesus is inextricably bound to death. There will be no path forward for Israel, the known world, or the entire cosmos that fails to reckon with our sin and death. *The time for casual following is over.*

What brings you to Jesus? Do you come out of routine or old habits? Do you come to him in utter desperation? Regardless, what are you prepared to give up for the life Jesus has for you?

The gospels all lead us on a journey. Most often we begin following Jesus at the most casually appealing level. It is only when we are farther down the road that we come to see what it means to choose to follow him to the end.

Mercifully, by the time we are asked to choose Jesus fully, we have come to see through all the other petty agendas and temporary fixes that would threaten our loyalty to him. At first, having a reputation for being a sensible person didn't seem like something to give up. At the end, the perception of other people is nothing compared to the eternal love of the Triune God. At first, following Christ might not have seemed to threaten our old routines and relationships. But in the end, the entirety of our very lives pales in comparison to the weight of glory present in the face of Jesus Christ.

There is no way forward for Jesus that does not involve suffering for our sins. There is no moving forward for us in him that does not involve laying down everything and giving him permission to tell us what to do next. Rest assured: he will be with you to the end, and forever after that.

Come to Jesus and offer him everything. Ask him to help you see through any lies or idols that would distract you from discipleship to him. In that place of surrender, ask him for eternal life and for the patience to wait for his kingdom to come on earth as it is in heaven.

Recommended Closing Prayer

> Almighty God, whose most dear Son went not up to joy but first he suffered pain, and entered not into glory before he was crucified: Mercifully grant that we, walking in the way of the cross, may find it none other than the way of life and peace; through the same thy Son Jesus Christ our Lord. Amen.
>
> *(Anglican Church in North America Book of Common Prayer)*

Ordinary Time Day 133

MADISON PERRY

Reflect on Luke 10:25–37

Call to Prayer

"What shall I do to inherit eternal life?" (Luke 10:25 ESV).

It is easy to forget that the parable of the Good Samaritan follows on the heels of this decisively important question.

The lawyer whose questions provoke the telling of the parable seems bent on finding out the exact minimum requirement for attaining eternal life.

Jesus allows Old Testament revelation to answer the lawyer's question: eternal life depends on living a life characterized by an active and overwhelming love for God and a corresponding love for our neighbor, who is made in God's image. These commandments are not satisfied with a onetime action; they urge us to live lives centered on God, where our every thought and deed reflect God's love.

But the lawyer isn't satisfied; he wants to tease out the bottom-line requirements, so he focuses on the command to love our neighbor as ourselves. "So who exactly is my neighbor?" he asks.

For the lawyer, the commandment to love one's neighbor is an impossible burden. In one sense, everyone is potentially our neighbor. With this in mind, how impossible would it be to attain eternal life?! So many people to care about.

So Jesus tells the story we have heard many times. The Samaritan passerby rescues a half-dead ethnic enemy who has already been passed over by religious leaders. He cleanses him with wine and oil, ministers to his needs, and brings him to safety.

The lawyer's question was about the outer limit of who we have to care for. Surely we don't have to care for *everyone*.

But Jesus asks different question: "Which of these three, do you think, proved to be a neighbor to the man who fell among the robbers?" (Luke 10:36 ESV). Who chose the privilege of being a neighbor?

Jesus doesn't say that the two religious leaders neglected to care for a known neighbor. He instead points out that the Samaritan, in loving and caring for a stranger, gained a neighbor and exemplified the path of mercy, leading to eternal life.

The desolate life apart from God is a life with no neighbors, with no one whom you love as you love yourself. But the grace-filled eternal life of God leads you to discover all kinds of neighbors whom you get to care for.

One path sees love as a scarce resource and strangers as potential burdens (and by no means neighbors). The other path sees love as a place to experience eternal life, where strangers are opportunities to wisely but extravagantly model the love God has for you.

Take time to praise the Lord for his neighborly love for you. Yes, he is your Creator and Redeemer. And he has also drawn near to you as a neighbor would. Ask God which people are the neighbors whom you have been called to love next. Ask God to help you see his image in them. Ask God to give you the strength and generosity to care for them. Thank Jesus Christ for the magnificent gift of eternal life and the great adventure of following him.

Recommended Closing Prayer

> Set us free, O God, from the bondage of our sins, and give us the liberty of that abundant life which you have made known to us in your Son our Savior Jesus Christ; who lives and reigns with you, in the unity of the Holy Spirit, one God, now and for ever. Amen.
> *(Anglican Church in North America Book of Common Prayer)*

Ordinary Time Day 134

MADISON PERRY

Reflect on Luke 10:38–42

Call to Prayer

Consider the famous story of Mary and Martha. This passage follows the parable of the Good Samaritan, where we see Jesus encouraging us to experience eternal life by loving other people. In the story of Mary and Martha, we see what happens when that service becomes a distraction.

Martha hosts Jesus at her house. She works as hard as she can, scurrying about, absorbed in her preparations. Her sister Mary sits at Jesus's feet and listens to his teaching. Martha goes to Jesus and almost demands that he make Mary help her. Jesus ought to have pity on her; she's been left "to serve alone" (Luke 10:40 ESV). Martha thinks Mary is the cause of her problems, but Jesus sees the burdens she is carrying; he tells her she is "anxious and troubled about many things" (Luke 10:41 ESV).

How many times are we driven by the unconscious goals and thoughts of our imaginations? We still carry the impulses given to us by parents and friends, teachers and bosses, entertainers and media celebrities. We are haunted by contradictory impulses, all the while judging ourselves for failing to meet impossible standards.

When have you recently felt like Martha—anxious and troubled about many things? Note that Jesus doesn't articulate Mary's issues. Sometimes getting to the bottom of them isn't as important as getting something else right.

Jesus cuts in: "One thing is necessary. Mary has chosen the good portion, which will not be taken away from her" (Luke 10:42 ESV).

There is a way out of being in bondage to multiple masters. There is a path to clarity and single-minded devotion. But you have to choose it.

Does that sound too easy? If you could just choose the good, you would, right?

Well, what if choosing the good meant sitting at Jesus's feet and listening to his Word? Would you choose it then? What if it meant giving up control? Would you still want it? What if it made you look silly or put you at odds with people who want you to be busy doing more tangible work?

Truly, we cannot escape diminishment. We will all die one day and will be forced to give up everything we have clung to. But this truth, this goodness, cannot be taken away.

Choose the good. Choose Christ. Hear him call your name in love. Listen to him direct your path. Choose the good; it will not be taken from you.

Recommended Closing Prayer

> Almighty and everlasting God, you govern all things both in heaven and on earth: Mercifully hear the supplications of your people, and in our time grant us your peace; through Jesus Christ our Lord, who lives and reigns with you and the Holy Spirit, one God, for ever and ever. Amen.
> *(Anglican Church in North America Book of Common Prayer)*

Ordinary Time Day 135

MADISON PERRY

Reflect on Luke 11:1–13

Call to Prayer

"Lord, teach us to pray" (Luke 11:1 ESV).

Jesus teaches his friends to pray. First, he gives them a series of God-focused petitions. Then he invites us to ponder the nature of prayer itself. What unites these sections is the invitation to become the kind of people who pray frequently, without ceasing and without feeling embarrassed. As Jesus knows, we will never outgrow our dependence on God.

Why don't we know how to pray? Perhaps the real problem is that we don't want to have to keep asking God. Maybe, in our sinful state, what we want is for God to give us enough to sustain us without our having to ask again for a while, so we don't have to keep dragging ourselves before him.

Perhaps you think, *If only God could empower me to just take care of myself and get what I want for myself.* But remember, God loves you so much that he will never make you autonomous. It is significant that the only self-oriented request of Jesus's model prayer is for *daily* bread, just enough for the day.

And what is the greatest thing we could ever ask God for?

"If you then, who are evil, know how to give good gifts to your children, how much more will the heavenly Father give the Holy Spirit to those who ask him!" (Luke 11:13 ESV).

This is almost a dare from Jesus to us to think bigger about God's generosity, far beyond our desires for glory, earthly wisdom, or material provision. God wants to give us his very self. And in the end, in order to fulfill this request, Jesus will die and ascend that he may send his Spirit, the Comforter, into our hearts.

It is a good thing that we are perpetually unsatisfied with all this world has to offer. That is a signal that we need to ask for something greater from God. Ask Jesus to fill your heart with his Spirit, to bring you into communion with his Father. Then the Triune God will never take his eyes off you. His strong arms will always shelter you; his love will be to you "better than wine" (Song of Solomon 1:2 ESV).

There is so much at stake every day and in every prayer. Ask for the Holy Spirit and he will be given to you; seek and ye will find; knock and the door will be opened unto you. Choose what is good and it will never be taken from you.

Recommended Closing Prayer

Our Father who art in heaven, hallowed be thy name. Thy kingdom come, thy will be done on earth as it is in heaven. Give us this day our daily bread, and forgive us our trespasses as we forgive those who trespass against us. And lead us not into temptation, but deliver us from evil. For thine is the kingdom, and the power, and the glory, forever and ever. Amen.

Ordinary Time Day 136

MARYRACHEL BOYD

Reflect on Psalm 135:5–7

Call to Prayer

To call God the Greatest One, the one who is above all others, means we are choosing to submit to his majesty. Submission in the context of scripture is beautiful and safe. We are not at the whim of an unpredictable king or ruthless ruler. Our King's sovereignty is just and gracious. At times we don't understand or see clearly his design or direction, but we can trust wholeheartedly that, as Romans 8:28 declares, "for those who love God all things work together for good, for those who are called according to his purpose" (ESV).

In the stories of the Old Testament, his greatness is made evident on earth, in the seas, and in all the deep. Think back to the story of creation, to the story of Jonah, to the Israelites crossing the Red Sea as they escape the Egyptians. Consider the New Testament: Jesus's calming storms, making blind eyes see, and raising the dead.

In each account, our human frailty and insufficiency is on display, and so is the greatness of God. And yet, Jesus himself came in human frailty, living a life of submission to the Father's will. We are called to full submission just as Christ was. We are safe and we can take comfort, for we are submitting to the one who took on a lowly body, who experienced the shame of human weakness. He knows us, he cares for us, and he will not put us to shame.

Recommended Closing Prayer

Lord God, Lamb of God, you take away the sins of the world. Have mercy on us. You are seated at the right hand of the Father: receive our prayer. For you alone are the Holy One, you alone are the Lord, You alone are the Most High, Jesus Christ, with the Holy Spirit, in the glory of God the Father. Amen.

Ordinary Time Day 137

KARI WEST

Reflect on Psalm 135:13–18

Call to Prayer

You become like that which you worship. This portion of the psalm poses a simple yet profound question to us: will we trust in the everlasting name of the Lord and trust that his renown will endure throughout all of eternity, or will we turn to a smaller idol, hoping in a lesser reality, and in that worship slowly lose our humanity?

This psalmist presents to us a horrifying image, and it's meant to awaken us from spiritual slumber. You can become a person with unseeing eyes, unhearing ears, and a mouth without breath. God is the one who first breathed life into his image-bearers; if we turn from this source of life and attempt to find another fount of identity or wholeness, we'll die.

But the opposite is also true, which is why passages like this offer promises as well as warnings. When we turn toward God as the source for our life, when we take the words of the psalmist on our own lips and proclaim the praise of our everlasting compassionate God, we become *more* human. We inch closer to the image of Jesus, the only full human being who has ever walked the face of the earth.

As you pray, ask the Lord to reveal what you're tempted to worship instead of him. Confess your idolatry and ask him to lead you farther on the path of real humanity through embracing him as the source of all life and goodness.

Your name, Lord, endures forever; your renown, Lord, through all generations. You will vindicate your people and have compassion on your servants. Amen.
(Adapted from Psalm 135:13–14 NIV)

Ordinary Time Day 138

MADISON PERRY

Reflect on Luke 11:33–36

Call to Prayer

It is easy to neglect Jesus's words—they are so counterintuitive that they can be hard to understand and even harder to live out. In truth, his thoughts are not our thoughts. But thankfully, as we mediate on his words day by day, the truth we need from our God will become clearer.

Jesus speaks about our eyes in an unexpected way. He calls them "the lamp of the body" (Luke 11:34 NIV). If our eye is healthy, so will our body be healthy. We will have no darkness within at all. So, how can our eyes be lamps?

An ancient way of understanding how perception works can help us with Jesus's words. People in centuries past believed that our eyes help to form the world that we see. We don't just "take it in." Instead, we actively sort and filter reality according to the patterns we care about and understand. (In more familiar Christian language, we receive the world around us through the eyes of our heart.)

For example, when looking into a crowd for a familiar face, the eyes of our heart filter out unfamiliar faces until they focus on the person we love. In the same way, if we have dropped coins in the grass, the eyes of our heart help us skim over hundreds of green blades until we find what we have lost. The eyes of the heart do help to create the world that we live within, and we do see things through the lens of what we love.

This is why two people can look out at the same scene and perceive it completely differently.

When we love the wrong things, it often leads to tragic consequences. God's Word loses its central place in our hearts. Instead, we see the world through darkened eyes that will fixate on what benefits us most and what we can most easily control.

Praise the Lord that we have had the opportunity of receiving his Word into our hearts. There is no greater privilege than to be saved from our darkened vision. Praise the Lord that he has rescued us with a light that is capable of displacing our pride and unfathomable darkness.

Consider any competing visions of value you are tempted to embrace—greed, lust, pride. Turn your eyes upon Jesus and ask him never to leave the center of your vision.

Recommended Closing Prayer

> Be Thou my Vision, O Lord of my heart
> Naught be all else to me, save that Thou art
> Thou my best Thought, by day or by night
> Waking or sleeping, Thy presence my light.
> Be Thou my Wisdom, and Thou my true Word
> I ever with Thee and Thou with me, Lord
> Thou my great Father, I Thy true son
> Thou in me dwelling, and I with Thee one.
> Riches I heed not, nor man's empty praise
> Thou mine Inheritance, now and always
> Thou and Thou only, first in my heart
> High King of Heaven, my Treasure Thou art.
> High King of Heaven, my victory won
> May I reach Heaven's joys, O bright Heav'n's Sun
> Heart of my own heart, whate'er befall
> Still be my Vision, O Ruler of all.
> ("Be Thou My Vision," lyrics translated by Mary E. Byrne and Eleanor Hull)

Ordinary Time Day 139

Reflect on Luke 12:1–3

Call to Prayer

Imagine this: a crowd of people have gathered around Jesus, thousands in such close proximity that they are nearly trampling one another. They are eager to catch a glimpse of the man who is rumored to be the new king of Israel, God's Chosen One who will free them and usher in a new age of judgment and prosperity.

In the background, politics and power are at work. Jesus has begun to encounter significant opposition from Pharisees. The current leaders of Israel are seeking to find a way to kill him. They claim to worship Israel's God, but they are mostly interested in perpetuating their religious system and their position in the world. They are closed off to what God is doing in Jesus. They are a little bit of "leaven" that will corrupt the whole loaf.

But Jesus doesn't simply say the Pharisees are bad, wrong leaders. Something specific about them is deadly and toxic. Jesus pulls no punches: "Beware of the leaven of the Pharisees, which is hypocrisy" (Luke 12:2 ESV).

The Pharisees are different people in public than they are in private. They manage to appear respectful of Jesus in public, while they scoff and plot against him behind closed doors. They present as God-fearing in public, but they are power-preserving in private.

O that they would simply have the humility of Nicodemus. He was able to approach Jesus in private and have his heart and life changed (John 3).

How can we take Jesus's warning to heart? We need to decide if we will seek Jesus earnestly with complete willingness to lay aside everything and follow him.

If Jesus were to approach you today as he did his first disciples, what would you do? Would you ask him to come back again in a month? What would you have to give up to be ready?

Our faith will never rise higher than our humility. There is no more courageous or truthful way to see ourselves than as people in complete need of Jesus. If we but had eyes to see Jesus and to see ourselves, we would be more than ready to follow him at every moment. Then the humble faith that comes from submitting to Jesus would eventually leaven and pervade our whole lives.

Meet Jesus Christ in prayer. Humble yourself before him and thank him for his love. Express your willingness to follow him, and ask him to lead you. Ask him if there is anything you need to leave behind or anyone you need to move toward in love and help.

Recommended Closing Prayer

> O Lord and Master of my life, give me not the spirit of sloth, despair, lust for power and idle talk. But grant unto me, thy servant, a spirit of chastity humility, patience and love. Yea, O Lord and King, grant me to see mine own faults and not to judge my brother or sister. For you are blessed now and forever. Amen.
> *(Lenten Prayer of Saint Ephrem)*

Ordinary Time Day 140

KARI WEST

Reflect on Luke 12:4–7

Call to Prayer

"Do not fear those who kill the body" (Luke 12:4 ESV). Christ gives this command as the shadow of Golgotha looms large, as those who will torture and kill the body of Jesus conspire behind closed doors. The power of those who can kill the body will soon be on full display on a hill outside Jerusalem.

In light of what is to come, Christ knows that his listeners need a reorientation of their fears. He tells them: Don't fear people whose power ends at death. Fear a holy God who has the power to cast souls into hell. He repeats himself: fear this powerful God!

But he doesn't leave them there. He goes on to say that this God, mighty Ruler of all, never forgets a sparrow. This God, with all creation at his feet, knows the number of hairs on your head. Fear God, and yet you are of great value to the Father, so fear not.

And because Jesus didn't fear those who kill the body, because he feared a holy God who would cast unrepentant souls into hell, because he shared his Father's deep love for his people, lost in sin, Christ bled out on that hill outside Jerusalem. So that we might fear God, and fear not.

As you pray, ponder the power, the holiness, and the love of God. Let these truths make you brave in a world full of lesser realities.

Recommended Closing Prayer

> O Lord, command what you will and give what you command. *(Saint Augustine)*

Ordinary Time Day 141
KARI WEST

Reflect on Psalm 15:1–6

Call to Prayer

Is the opening question of this psalm one that you ask? Is it the reason you seek to live a godly life? The psalmist isn't interested in the best way to get by in life. He's not seeking for the right steps to make it to the top of a social, professional, or religious ladder. He's not seeking the character traits needed to be successful and healthy. No, he asks a much deeper, much more profound, much more interesting question than that: how can we live near God?

God is who we were made for and who we need; God is the source of life; God is the fountain of joy; and God is the wellspring of everlasting delight. Our souls were intricately crafted to know the unknowable riches of God. How can we get near God?

Pause and reflect. How often is being close to God your true desire? What is revealed by the choices you make for your life?

The psalmist goes on to list manifold qualities of godliness: living blamelessly, practicing righteousness, acknowledging truth, actively loving others, honoring goodness, and being honest.

But the first and most important quality? Asking that first question. Knowing that the goal is relationship with the mysterious, everlasting, almighty God, the lover of your soul.

As you pray, ask to know afresh that you were made for life with God. Ask to know that life apart from him is ultimate misery. Thank Christ that he has lived the only perfect life and died so that we might become the righteousness of God in him. Ask for strength to walk in a manner pleasing to him.

Recommended Closing Prayer

God, create in me a clean heart that desires you above all things. Give me a love for all you say, which is good. Draw me to you. Amen.

Ordinary Time Day 142

KARI WEST

Reflect on Luke 12:8–12

Call to Prayer

There is no solely private faith in Jesus. He does not give us the option of honoring him in solitude and denying him in public. Belief in Christ is an all-encompassing reality spilling over into our public personas, our daily conversations, and all our outward living.

Consider here the staggering reward that Jesus holds out to us for faithful witness: he will acknowledge us before the angels of God. He offers us even today a seal of approval, a banner of friendship. There is no better thing.

Yet here too we have a grave warning from Jesus—faith that doesn't overflow into public confession is not true faith. And those without true saving faith in Jesus cannot have his approval or his friendship.

Public faith doesn't mean perfect faith. We know from the story of Peter's denial of Jesus that believers will falter and fail in their witness of the Lord, and Christ does hold out forgiveness and restoration for us in all our failings. But don't let the warning miss its mark. Faith that consistently denies Christ publicly isn't of the Spirit. Jesus's words here must have their full weight.

Yet graciously, Jesus offers us an encouragement after his words of warning. He tells us that the Spirit will give us the words to speak at the right time. We can rest in the reality that Christ will give us what we need to do the things he tells us to do. The Holy Spirit will be our teacher. We must simply walk in obedience to Christ's commands.

Recommended Closing Prayer

Holy Spirit, please give us the words we need to honor Christ. Grant us boldness, trust, and humility. In the precious name of Jesus. Amen.

Ordinary Time Day 143

KARI WEST

Reflect on Luke 12:13–21

Call to Prayer

What is the posture of your heart when you hear a command from Jesus? Is it resentment? dismissal? weariness? Does it feel like just another task for your to-do list?

Will you pause and consider afresh who speaks these words to you, so that you can see them anew for all their strange and lovely potency? Christ wove each of us together and designed the deepest intricacies of our beings. He knows what our hearts, minds, and bodies need so we can grow into full humanity. He wants us to regain our birthright that we lost in the garden. His commands are some of the most solemn secrets of our flourishing: live like *this*, for I made the world and your soul like *this*.

"One's life does not consist in the abundance of his possessions" (Luke 12:15 ESV). We hear the story of a rich man who poured all his energy into safeguarding all his stuff and now believes he has secured happiness for his soul.

Jesus tells us, No! That is the path of the fool. The human soul was made for better things than money.

Learn instead a life of generosity, a way of being rich toward God and his creatures, and you will find a richness welling up within you, something more lasting and more satisfying. And when your soul will be required of you by the Father, you won't hear a chilling rebuke like the one in this parable, but instead the words brimming with love and joy: *well done.*

Recommended Closing Prayer

O Christ, let us know and trust your words as a lamp for our feet, a light for our path, a feast laid out before us, and a spring of water welling up to eternal life. In your precious name. Amen.

Ordinary Time Day 144
KARI WEST

Reflect on Luke 12:22–34

Call to Prayer

Anxiety can feel like a constant weight in your life, dragging on your heart as you move through your days. *What if I lose my job? What if I lose my home? Will my children learn well in school this year? What if my parents get sick? Will life ever feel safe and hopeful?*

What does Christ tell us to do in the midst of this torrent of anxious thoughts? Consider the ravens. God feeds them, though they don't store up provisions for themselves; and he loves you more than he loves them. Consider the lilies. God clothes them with splendor, though their lives are so brief; and he loves you more than he loves them. Christ leans down close, takes us by the hand, and gently reminds us that we have a good Father who will feed us and clothe us.

Life is more than food, Jesus says. Seek the kingdom and find glory that will never fail. The Lord forged our hearts to be filled with richer fare. Instead of chewing on worry after worry after worry, Jesus urges us to remember the loving providence of God, and then to live a life of generosity. And as we trust in God's provision and act on that trust by openhanded living, we will store up for ourselves a treasure trove in the heavens.

As you pray, bring your anxiety to the Lord because he cares for you. Confess your knee-jerk reaction of self-sufficiency. Ponder the ravens and the lilies, and ask God for a fresh awareness of his lavish, loving, perfectly timed provision for you, his cherished child.

Recommended Closing Prayer

God, thank you that you array the lilies in splendor and that you feed the ravens from your abundant storehouses. Thank you that it is your good pleasure to give us the kingdom. Give us hearts of trust in you. For Jesus's sake. Amen.

Ordinary Time Day 145

KARI WEST

Reflect on Luke 12:35-40

Call to Prayer

If you love Christ, you'll want him back.

The men in this story are intently awaiting the return of their beloved master. They are straining their ears for the sound of that familiar knock. They can't wait to throw open the door and welcome him home. They don't know how many more long hours of the night they will have to endure before his return, but they are ready for him.

Jesus says the Master will come back in joy, don a servant's garb, and bid those faithful followers to recline at the table, where he will serve them a feast. The parable promises a greater, almost outrageous honor that no one could have expected.

The Son of Man is like the master of the house, but he's also like a thief in the night. No one knows when he's coming. Of course, no one would leave their home if a thief were coming to steal their possessions. So in the same way, keep watch. Christ will return at an hour we do not expect.

As you pray, ask the Lord for keen ears and a longing heart. Ask that you would be like a servant who strains to hear the sound of the beloved master coming home to stay. Ask for readiness, no matter the hour, for Christ's joyful return.

Recommended Closing Prayer

Amen. Come, Lord Jesus.

Ordinary Time Day 146

KARI WEST

Reflect on Luke 12:57–59

Call to Prayer

Jesus never shies away from telling his listeners the truth. Here he warns them: *Judgment is coming. You have the chance now to be reconciled. Take it! If you don't, you will pay the full penalty.*

Can you feel the tension in this short story? There's not much time left. The accused and the accuser are on their way to trial. Each step brings them closer and closer to court. If they reach the judge and the sentencing, there will be no hope of escape for the accused.

It's a loving act to warn a person when they are running out of time. The truth is, without Jesus, we stand rightly accused before God. Romans tells us clearly that the wages of sin is death. If we do not seek reconciliation by trusting in the work of Christ, then we will know the judgment of God.

Christ utters this story as he nears the end of his life. Within the warning is a promise: We don't have to be dragged before the judge, hopeless as we face sentencing. The free gift of God is eternal life in Jesus Christ our Lord. Through his blood, Jesus has made a way for our reconciliation.

As you pray, heed his urgent warning and embrace the life Jesus offers through faith. Believe in Christ and know the warm embrace of the Father, our just and merciful Judge.

Recommended Closing Prayer

Christ, thank you that you came to set the captives free. Thank you that because of your shed blood on our behalf, we can know mercy instead of judgment. In your precious name. Amen.

Ordinary Time Day 147

KARI WEST

Reflect on Luke 13:10–17

Call to Prayer

Can you imagine what life would have been like for this woman before she encountered Jesus? For eighteen years, day in and day out, she had not been able to stand up straight. She had been bent over, her gaze fixed down.

In our natural state, we are largely unable to look outward toward others or upward toward God. We live in a constant state of navel-gazing.

After eighteen years of her suffering, Jesus lays gentle hands on this woman's twisted body, and she raises up her head to see the Savior of the world. It's no wonder that the first thing she does is glorify the Lord, her healer.

But the leader of the synagogue, curved in on himself, rebukes Jesus for his miraculous, gracious act of healing. Rather than join the woman in praise of God, he calls wrong what is manifestly right.

Jesus, in turn, rebukes this religious leader for his blindness and lack of compassion and for not recognizing God's great work: in Christ, he has lifted up a bent head to gaze upon the goodness of Jesus, so that his people glorify his name.

As you pray, ask the Lord to do this work in your own heart. Ask that your eyes would be lifted up and trained on Jesus so that you may glorify your Lord.

Recommended Closing Prayer

Father, fix our eyes on Jesus, the founder and perfecter of our faith, who for the joy that was set before him endured the cross, despising the shame, and is seated at the right side of your throne. Amen.

Ordinary Time Day 148
NATHAN BAXTER

Reflect on Luke 13:18–21

Call to Prayer

If anyone could have confidence to define the kingdom of God, surely it was Jesus. Yet the Son of Man stands with us to ask, to wonder, and to reckon. Jesus invites us into contemplative comparisons.

Insight grows through comparisons gently explored. Slowly, we see and test ways the more familiar might connect with the less familiar, how the small and simple might imply the larger and more complex.

Jesus starts us with a seed—familiar to the listening farmers and spice market shoppers. Perhaps it's not familiar to us. The mustard seed is tiny, as small as the period at the end of this sentence.

Can you see it? Something so small requires of us a season-spanning patience and trust. The harvest that might come of this tiny kernel of life will not be like the wheat or barley. This shrub will take time to mature before it can support perching birds, before it can yield abundant spice year by year. Yet patience and trust will see it. The seed taken is planted and grows.

How many people bake their own bread? And of those who do, how many bake enough to feed fifty or sixty people for several days? Yet even such an industrious baker must work and then wait. Here we have another contemplative comparison inviting patience and trust. The yeast taken is mixed and worked all through the dough.

Are you daunted or inspired by small and subtle things? Are you discouraged or enlivened by everyday patience and trust? To what shall you liken the kingdom of God so that you too may wonder with Jesus?

As you pray, consider what seems to be too small and insignificant to be of value. Take a moment and pray for eyes to see a small piece of evidence that God is present in this broken world and in the challenges you are facing. Hold that "mustard seed" up to your Father and give him thanks.

Recommended Closing Prayer

> O God, without whose beauty and goodness our souls are unfed, without whose truth our reason withers: Consecrate our lives to your will, giving us such purity of heart, such depth of faith, and such steadfastness of purpose, that in time we may come to think your own thoughts after you; through Jesus Christ our Savior. Amen.
> (*Anglican Church in North America Book of Common Prayer*)

Ordinary Time Day 149

NATHAN BAXTER

Reflect on Luke 13:31–35

Call to Prayer

In a swirling storm of rising polarization, Jesus says, "I will reach my goal" (Luke 13:32 NIV). It's a saying that heartens and humbles.

Earlier in this chapter in Luke, people eagerly seek Jesus's opinion on horrific current events. Instead of giving them a sound bite and a political alignment, he calls attention to God's strange providence, even in awful circumstances. And he calls his listeners to repentance. His answer makes it hard for anyone to claim him as a partisan ally.

"I will reach my goal" (Luke 13:32 NIV).

Later on a Sabbath day, Jesus heals a woman who, for eighteen years, had been "bent over and could not straighten up at all" (Luke 13:11 NIV). His action exposes the hypocrisy of some, and others are impressed by the miracle. Instead of capitalizing on the favor of some, Jesus tells two parables that invite us to ponder what the kingdom is really like.

"I will reach my goal" (Luke 13:32 NIV).

As Jesus continues his steady journey to Jerusalem, people want his opinion on yet another controversy: "Lord, are only a few people going to be saved?" (Luke 13:23 NIV). Again, he does as much to provoke as to pacify as he offers a perplexing response. Again, Jesus refuses to fit into others' agendas.

In this swirling storm of rising polarization, some Pharisees come to Jesus, saying, "Leave this place and go somewhere else. Herod wants to kill you" (Luke 13:31 NIV). Undaunted, Jesus replies in such a way that seems to confuse rather than clarify.

Whose side is Jesus on? What's his main agenda? What stirs his anger and his anguish? What guides his pace and grounds his purpose? What makes him able to assert, "I will reach my goal"? Could anyone even have fathomed that goal if he'd stated it outright? His close friends don't understand, even when he tells them plainly.

"None of the rulers of this age understood it, for if they had, they would not have crucified the Lord of glory" (1 Corinthians 2:8 NIV).

In a swirling storm of rising polarization, Jesus said, "I will reach my goal."

It's a saying that can hearten us. Jesus will follow through on all God's promises. "For no matter how many promises God has made, they are 'Yes' in Christ. And so through him the 'Amen' is spoken by us to the glory of God" (2 Corinthians 1:20 NIV).

It's also a saying that can humble us. "Whom did the Lord consult to enlighten him, and who taught him the right way? (Isaiah 40:14a NIV).

As you pray, bring the concern or conflict weighing on your heart into the wisdom and refuge of Jesus. Remind yourself of a promise from God's Word that will steady and encourage your heart. Thank your Father God for what that promise means to you.

Recommended Closing Prayer

> Our God, in whom we trust: Strengthen us not to regard overmuch who is for us or who is against us, but to see to it that we be with you in everything we do. Amen.
> *(Thomas à Kempis)*

Ordinary Time Day 150

SALLY BREEDLOVE

Reflect on Psalm 4:3–5

Call to Prayer

We may miss the opportunity the turbulence of our time offers us. In an age of endless ways to connect, endless things to blog about, endless things to read online, endless movies, and endless phone calls with people we love, we may miss or resist the invitation right in front of us.

Could it be we are ignoring (or bolting shut) the door that would lead us into silence and stillness? We could take the chance to sit and be still at some point in the twenty-four hours that each day offers. We could be undistracted and quiet and ponder the mystery that God is always present.

We could give our own souls room to speak the prayers we would pray if we were entirely honest. We could have enough space to find out what we really want to say to each other. And we could find that silence is not emptiness, not a terrifying loneliness. We could discover, if we linger in silence, that it is brimming over with the presence of the good and beautiful God.

What do you really want?

Will you choose to stop for ten minutes or even an hour and observe silence each day? Will you make space to be with your own soul and to seek the Triune God, who is always present even when our hurried and distracted lives tell us otherwise?

Be still; be silent. Let there be spaces that aren't filled with connecting, with internet information, or with words.

Pray for yourself. Are there places where God is calling you to simply stop and be with him? Pray for those who are lonely and terrified of being alone. Pray they will know the goodness of God, who is always present.

Recommended Closing Prayer

King of kings and Lord of lords, our striving, searching, and toil brings us back to where we started today: in your hands and sheltered by you. We praise you, who are everywhere present, filling all things. Protect the physicians and caretakers who tend to the sick. And open the mouths of your people that we may be able to sing your praises and lift up the hurting. Grant us peaceful sleep tonight, the hope and faith to do your will tomorrow, and life without end in your kingdom. Amen.

Ordinary Time Day 151

NATHAN BAXTER

Reflect on Luke 14:7–11

Call to Prayer

Don't you love how Jesus meddles?

Here Jesus is a guest "in the house of a prominent Pharisee" and "he was being carefully watched" (Luke 14:1 NIV). It's a Sabbath day, and one of the guests is suffering. Jesus confronts the unspoken prejudice against healing on the Sabbath. Other guests "had nothing to say" (Luke 14:6 NIV).

Then Jesus, the one being carefully watched, reveals his own observational talent. Predinner mingling and conversation has been revealing the status alignments and ambitions, the thick yet subtle dynamics of up and down, inside and outside, center and margin. Horizons of honor beckon some and dishearten others. Jesus meddles by pushing those horizons far beyond where any strategy for reciprocal bettering might easily lead.

What do we hear in the punch line of Jesus's parable? "For all those who exalt themselves will be humbled, and those who humble themselves will be exalted" (Luke 14:11 NIV). Do we hear a subtler means for calculating self-promotion? Do we hear thick irony that meddles with the whole game of status-seeking?

Do we hear the heart of God from the lips of the Son of Man? Might a whole world of upside-down honor be entered through a doorway of humility?

As you pray, confess where you seek to secure or promote your own place and position. Look at Jesus, who lived the upside-down life of choosing the lowest place to serve in obedient love. Ask him to give you a heart that serves more deeply.

Recommended Closing Prayer

O God, of your goodness, give me yourself, for you are enough for me. I can ask for nothing less that is completely

to your honor, and if I do ask anything less, I shall always be in want. Only in you I have all. Amen.
(Julian of Norwich)

Ordinary Time Day 152
N A T H A N   B A X T E R

Reflect on Luke 14:15–24

Call to Prayer

We look forward to a time of fullness, freedom, and satisfaction. How willingly we say, "Blessed is the one who will eat at the feast in the kingdom of God" (Luke 14:15 NIV). We entertain such hopes for many reasons.

Perhaps like the one who said it to Jesus, we're uncomfortable with the social situation we're in, and we look forward, not so much to the kingdom of God, but to something less awkward, less painful, and less fraught with conflict.

Perhaps like some who followed Jesus, we have a sense of the kingdom. We desire the feast, but we hesitate to "sit down and count the cost" (Luke 14:28 ESV).

Perhaps like the outcasts of Jesus's day—and those of our own day—we dream of a feast to distract us from our desolation. We dream of a distant future, yet we remain resigned to the lived prospect of never tasting a crumb.

But what if the feast were to show up? Would we go in, sit down, and eat?

"But they all alike began to make excuses" (Luke 14:18 NIV). What holds our affections so much that we can't quite stomach the thought of leaving it behind?

"What you have commanded has been done, and there is still room" (Luke 14:22). Why was there still room? The world is full of poor, crippled, blind, and lame people. Surely, they will choose the banquet?

Or can people's heart resignations become so habitual that they can't stomach the thought of venturing forth in faith and hope?

No one misses out for lack of invitation. No one misses out because of insufficient clarity, urgency, or assistance.

"Blessed is the one who will eat at the feast in the kingdom of God" (Luke 14:15 NIV).

Will we have the stomach to go in, sit down, and eat?

As you pray, consider your own heart. Are you eager for the banquet? Are you willing to lay aside whatever you need to let go of to join Jesus in his joyful kingdom?

Recommended Closing Prayer

> O God, grant that we may desire you, and desiring you seek you, and seeking you find you, and finding you be satisfied in you for ever. Amen.
> *(Francis Xavier)*

Ordinary Time Day 153

KARI WEST

Reflect on Psalm 10:12–18

Call to Prayer

The psalmist uses God's character as his basis to plead for God to act.

Why? In this psalm, we learn the wicked are killing the innocent. They lurk like lions to attack the vulnerable. They deceive, they scoff, and they use and abuse others. They treat God's beloved image-bearers as trash to be discarded at their whim. They believe God will not demand an account; they live as though God does not see or does not care.

The psalmist doesn't cave in to despair when faced with this grim reality. Instead, he takes these experiences to God and demands that

God not be silent. He even asks why God is far away and why he hides. We understand his questions: in our lives God can also appear distant.

But the psalmist ultimately refuses to give in to his doubts. He continues to petition God for his action, and he gives us this anchoring image of our Father: God himself sees each wrong and each grief. God is not far away, even when circumstances suggest it. He *sees* each moment of injustice, of abuse, of trouble, and of pain. He sees, and he takes it into his own hands. He helps the weak, the vulnerable, the fatherless, and the widow.

It can be hard to believe that. It was hard for the psalmist to believe, and it is hard for us today. And yet, the end of this psalm will hold true. God will listen to and strengthen his people; he will work justice for the oppressed. Evil will not have the last word. Our God is King forever.

Come before the Lord with honesty. Do you believe he is silent or far off? Do you believe nothing in the world will ever change? Pray this psalm to the Lord and ask for his action. Thank him for the justice done at the cross, pray for a heart of humility, and ask that his name would be glorified in all the earth. Pray that his kingdom would come and his perfect will would be done.

Recommended Closing Prayer

> You, Lord, hear the desire of the afflicted;
> you encourage them, and you listen to their cry,
> defending the fatherless and the oppressed,
> so that mere earthly mortals
> will never again strike terror.
> Amen.
> *(Psalm 10:17–18 NIV)*

Ordinary Time Day 154

KARI WEST

Reflect on Luke 14:25–33

Call to Prayer

We are quick to mitigate the words of Jesus. We desire to sidestep difficult, uncomfortable passages like this one where he commands us to hate our families and ourselves and to take up a symbol of cursed, horrific torture.

If this feels harsh to us in our current cultural context, how much harsher might it have felt to the largely Jewish audience of Jesus's day who honored and prized family so highly? Who knew the words of the Old Testament "Anyone hung on a tree is under God's curse" (Deuteronomy 21:23 CSB), and who perhaps had witnessed the horrendous spectacle of Roman crucifixion?

It is good to consider the whole teaching of scripture and to understand that Christ is not actually commanding hatred of ourselves and our brothers and sisters. In other passages, Jesus clearly says that the whole law and the prophets can be summed up in the first two commandments, namely, to love God and love our neighbor. At the same time, we cannot let these words lose their shock value. Christ purposefully chose these statements to shake us from comfort and lethargy, where we don't really believe that following Christ need inconvenience us greatly.

Because Jesus does mean what he says: the cost of following him may be so vast, the love required of us in obedience so great, that by comparison, our earthly loves will look like hatred. And those who desire to know him must follow him "outside the camp" (Hebrews 13:13 ESV) and share in his sufferings. Do not be deceived: the cost of discipleship is real and greater than we like to believe.

And yet, know the mercy of God in Christ's words. He desires to work in us a lifetime habit of relinquishing ourselves to him. In God's economy, nothing freely given over to him will ever be lost. In the laying down of our lives, as seeds dying in the earth, we will find more life and fullness, as beloved disciples of Jesus, than we could ever dream possible. We will be as new shoots of the new humanity growing up to be like him.

As you pray, meditate on the cost of discipleship and ask for fresh faith to follow Jesus wherever he may lead you.

Recommended Closing Prayer

Jesus, let us count the cost of discipleship and find your friendship worthy of any sacrifice. Give us pure hearts and right affections. Enable us to live lives of faithfulness, for that is a work that only your Spirit can do in us. In your precious name and by your blood we pray. Amen.

Ordinary Time Day 155

KARI WEST

Reflect on Luke 15:1–10

Call to Prayer

Pause and consider a beautiful truth in this passage: if you have repented of your sin, it means that Jesus has lovingly, urgently, and carefully sought after you as a gentle shepherd for a lost sheep, as a woman for a precious coin. Christ has placed you upon his shoulders and brought you back to his fold. Though perhaps you couldn't hear them, shouts of joy rang out through the heavenly realms as you turned from death to life.

Rejoice over the fact that Christ came to welcome sinners and eat with those unworthy of him. If he hadn't, none of us could claim his friendship. Don't be like the Pharisees, who drew lines between themselves and the rest of broken, sinful humanity and who criticized Jesus for his indiscriminate call to repentance and faith. Jesus desired all to be saved.

As you pray, consider the miracle of your own conversion.

Ponder these beautiful pictures of Christ's searching of and specific care for you. See in your own faith the undeserved, pressing, rescuing love of the Good Shepherd. Confess any pride or selfishness that would regard another human being as less worthy of our Savior's attention.

Recommended Closing Prayer

Jesus, thank you for not leaving us as sheep wandering or coins forgotten. Thank you for the grace of repentance. Let us see your abiding love in our salvation. For your sake. Amen.

Ordinary Time Day 156

KARI WEST

Reflect on Luke 15:11–32

Call to Prayer

The words we hear most often are words we may begin not to hear at all. Repetition and familiarity can wear down the sharp meaning in a story, like a stone worn smooth in a riverbed. That's the danger we face when we hear the parable of the prodigal son.

Will you pause and try to rehear these words as if you'd never come upon this tale before? Can you imagine the searing pain of the father as he watches his son steal away? Can you feel the younger son's pangs of hunger and his despair as he contemplates the pig slop? Can you see the tears brimming in his eyes as his father embraces him again? Can you sense the festering anger of the older brother, roiling in his stomach, as he hears the echoes of feasting and laughter?

Among a myriad of other things, this story shows us that we are born with hungry souls and that the desires we have for fulfillment, pleasure, and freedom can lead us to the most desperate and terrible places. Our hearts are like broken compasses that no longer recall true north, so they fail us again and again. Whether these hearts lead us to open rebellion and sinful living or to quiet self-righteousness and teeming hatred of our repentant brother, we all need the reorienting words of our Father.

As you pray, contemplate which words you need to hear. Do you need to know again the Father's loud shout of joy in your salvation, that you were lost and now are found? that he delights in you, his child? Do you need to hear afresh his call to you to abandon your hatred, rejoice that all God has is yours in Jesus, and join him in his lavish invitation to others?

Recommended Closing Prayer

Father in heaven, please give us ears to hear anew these familiar words. Let us know your grace, both in your call to renewed repentance and in your words of joy over your children returned. For Jesus's sake. Amen.

Ordinary Time Day 157

KARI WEST

Reflect on Luke 16:1–9

Call to Prayer

This is one of the parables of Jesus where we don't see the end coming. We read along, expecting the dishonest manager to get what's coming to him for his double dealings, but instead, he is commended for his shrewdness. What are we to make of this?

The twist at the end should make us pause and consider. It is meant to surprise us and to drive us back to reread and reexamine the story. Here we see the manager commended because he knew how to take care of himself, and he uses his master's "worldly wealth" to build friendships and forgive the debts of others in the community.

The focus is not on whether or not the manager was honest, but on the fact that he used his intelligence to its highest potential. And Jesus calls his followers to follow this example, using our wits as well as we can, though for a higher purpose than the manager. Christ calls us to have the same kind of desperate, directed focus so that we might "live, really live, and not complacently just get by on good behavior" (Luke 16:8 MSG).

As you pray, ask the Lord to reveal ways that you've been half-hearted in your obedience. Ask for renewed desire to use your all—intelligence, strategy, and will—to follow him.

Recommended Closing Prayer

O Christ, please give us the power to love you with all our hearts, all our minds, all our souls, and all our strength. For your sake and in your name. Amen.

Ordinary Time Day 158

KARI WEST

Reflect on Luke 16:10–13

Call to Prayer

What comes to your mind when you think about true riches?

In this passage, Christ doesn't say to be careful with money because money is precious and a great source of power and comfort. We're not commanded to faithfulness with our finances as if presented with a chest of diamonds, sapphires, and rubies and told to keep them safe.

No, instead Christ asks us, do you want to be entrusted with a real trove of riches all your own? Hold to God as your Master and let faithful dealings with money train you to see a much richer source of goodness on the horizon.

It's as if Jesus holds out money and says, *Be faithful and honest with this small plaything. Let your love of God be displayed and deepened in handling this toy well, without letting it become too important to you. Then one day, you'll be grown up enough to possess the true treasure, the friendship of God.*

Don't get caught up in serving money. There is something so much better, so much deeper, and so much richer to care about. Hold fast to God and trust that a life of seeking him will one day open onto wide vistas of joy and peace, rooted in his love and care.

Recommended Closing Prayer

God, keep us from the love of money. Turn our eyes to the better Master, our hope and our salvation. For Jesus's sake. Amen.

Ordinary Time Day 159

KARI WEST

Reflect on Psalm 7:10–17

Call to Prayer

We like to meditate on a God of love more than on one of justice. We like to consider forgiveness and mercy, and we might feel uncomfortable reading passages like this one. Here we see a God who sharpens his sword and strings his bow, readying deadly weapons to wield against those who love evil and perpetrate injustice.

But the psalmist takes refuge in the justice of God. He calls God a shield because God saves the upright in heart and will ultimately destroy those who persist in opposing his goodness with open rebellion.

When we witness widespread injustice, when we encounter evil men and women thriving, when we see the innocent trodden down and the wicked plotting more destruction, we need a deep, weighty belief in God's commitment to justice and goodness so we don't despair. We need to contemplate these images of God and take them up as our shields against hopelessness in a dark world.

And in God's righteousness, we need to have the right kind of fear before him. Not one that cowers, but one that takes our own sin and his holiness seriously. God is opposed to the wicked, including the wickedness lurking in our own hearts. Though we are made upright through Christ and are being made upright by the Sprit, we are far from perfect. God's holiness should draw us to awe of him, confession to him, gratitude for Jesus, and humility toward others.

As you pray, reflect on the justice of God. Do you need to see God's justice as a banner of hope, as his commitment to righting a wrong world in his good time? Do you need to grasp his righteousness as a warning to your own wayward heart? Ask the Lord to use his Word and his Spirit to convict, change, and strength you.

Recommended Closing Prayer

O Father, thank you that you will bring about justice in the world. Let us remember your holiness. Thank you, Christ, that by your blood we are made righteous. Give us hearts that trust you and hope in you above all things. Amen.

Ordinary Time Day 160

SALLY BREEDLOVE

Reflect on Luke 16:19–31

Call to Prayer

This story begs the question: are we convinced by scripture and by Christ's resurrection? Not simply giving intellectual assent to these things (since, after all, demons do that), but possessing the kind of conviction that seeps into our hearts and our bones, changing our affections, our habits, and our whole lives.

This is a terrifying parable, no doubt. A man who lived wholly opposed to the upside-down values of the kingdom of God dies and finds himself in torment. But don't miss the fact that Christ gives this story to us as a gift, a warning: *This need never happen.* Repent, embrace the scriptures, offer your life to God, and ask for a new heart of careful attention to the needy, the broken, and the poor.

As you pray, confess your hope in the one who did return from the dead—more than that, who crushed death underfoot—so that we could truly be changed. Ask the Spirit to convict you of selfishness and the idol of comfort. Ask for God's heart of love and care for the least of these.

Recommended Closing Prayer

O Christ, who trampled death, we ask you again to work in us the life of the kingdom. Let us be your hands and feet; let us portray your love to a hurting and needy world. Walk with us and work through us your good and perfect will. Thank you that you are now and always Immanuel, God with us. In your most precious name. Amen.

Ordinary Time Day 161
SALLY BREEDLOVE

Reflect on Luke 17:1–6

Call to Prayer

If you want to follow Jesus, at times you'll find yourself objecting to what he says. You'd prefer to gloss over the things you find too difficult.

Resist that urge. Listen to Christ.

He calls us to learn to love as he loves. That means admitting our sin is never just about ourselves; it always hurts others. So, be willing to ask yourself: Where do I fall short? Is it in my contempt of others? my indifference to the suffering around me? my greed? my private indulgence of secret choices? my settled bitterness? my sense of entitlement? my anger? We all need to see that our sin damages those around us. We all need God's forgiveness.

Then Jesus asks a difficult thing. He directs us to care deeply about the sinful choices of others. But instead of judging or fighting back, we are to go to our brother or sister and rebuke him or her. *Rebuke* means to help set things right. Rebuking is not condemning, judging, or shaming someone. It's caring enough to help a person have a freer heart. A wise rebuke says, "I love you; I long for you to know blessing."

This impossibly hard passage asks even more from us. It asks us to keep forgiving others even if they keep sinning against us or if the memories of what they did keep rising up in us.

Rather than ignoring or explaining away what Jesus has said, the disciples cry out—"Increase our faith!" (Luke 17:6 NIV).

And Jesus's response? He says it's not more faith we need. Even a little is enough. What we need is the willingness to use the faith we have to simply obey him.

We live in a broken, divided, and angry world. What if we, what if all Christians, decided to live into these words from Jesus?

What if we cared more about protecting the little ones in our world than having our own way? What if we took a serious look at our own lives? What if we loved those we know in the family of God so much that we risked speaking into their lives? What if we believed that every grudge we secretly harbor must be done away with?

If we were to live into Jesus's words, who knows what could happen?

As you pray, take Jesus's words to heart and ask him for the strength to follow and obey.

Recommended Closing Prayer

O Lord Christ, teach me to love like you love. Amen.

Ordinary Time Day 162

Reflect on Luke 17:8–10

Call to Prayer

What is Jesus after? Isn't it enough to just do our duty? Does Christ expect us to exceed expectations in all we do, or is there something else he wants from us?

If we say we want to follow Christ, we become his servants for life. That's what the apostle Paul means when he calls himself a bond servant of Jesus. To join Paul is to make that same lifetime commitment. Christ is always the Master, always the leader, and we are his followers.

But in the passage, Jesus seems to ask for something else. What would that be? Think about other relationships that involve duty. Parents have a duty to provide for and train their children. Children have a duty to respect and obey their parents. Friends have a duty to be loyal and fair. Husbands and wives have a duty to be faithful and kind and to serve each other. But in all these relationships, we are never satisfied with someone just doing his or her duty toward us. What is the more we want? Isn't it love? Isn't it friendship?

Parents long for their children to grow up to be abiding companions through life—and we grieve when it isn't so. A well-married couple doesn't just keep up their half of the marriage; they offer each other friendship year after year.

And Jesus, at that last Passover, says, "No longer do I call you servants ... but I have called you friends" (John 15:15 ESV). Jesus desires a life of love together with us. Love includes duty—we are obligated to each other at some level in almost every relationship. But doing our duty is never enough in relationships that are important to us. We all long for love and friendship from those dear to us, not just dutiful behavior.

As you go to pray, ask yourself: "Have I made your relationship with Jesus too small?" He offers you love and friendship, as well as the opportunity to follow and obey. Will you receive his offer and learn to love him and enjoy his companionship?

O Lord my God.
Teach my heart this day,
where and how to find you.
You have made me and re-made me,
and you have bestowed on me all the good things I possess,
and still I do not know you.
I have not yet done that for which I was made.
Teach me to seek you,
for I cannot seek you unless you teach me,
or find you unless you show yourself to me.
Let me seek you in my desire;
let me desire you in my seeking.
Let me find you by loving you;
let me love you when I find you.
Amen.
(Prayer of Saint Anselm)

Ordinary Time Day 163

S A L L Y   B R E E D L O V E

Reflect on Luke 17:11–19

Call to Prayer

The apostle Paul is clear: We all have an inborn problem called ingratitude. The nine lepers are not the only ones. He writes, "For [God's] invisible attributes, namely, his eternal power and divine nature, have been clearly perceived, ever since the creation of the world, in the things that have been made. So [human beings] are without excuse. For although they knew God, they did not honor him as God or give thanks to him, but they became futile in their thinking, and their foolish hearts were darkened" (Romans 1:20–21 ESV).

Back to the lepers. If you were embittered in your leprosy, then you would believe healing is only what you deserve. So why say thank you? If you were lost in despair over your helpless situation, then perhaps you would be skeptical of any healing and afraid it wouldn't last. Bitterness, fear, and despair rarely the open the door to gratitude, no matter how great the blessing.

The grateful man in the story is a Samaritan. He knows what it is like to be an outcast for his ethnicity as well as for his disease. The other nine were healed by the broad generosity of God, like rain that falls on the just and the unjust.

But when the Samaritan goes back to say thank you, Jesus tells him, "Your faith has made you well" (Luke 17:19 ESV). Gratitude opened the door into a relationship with Jesus, the healing we all need.

If you fear you don't have enough faith or the right kind of faith, if you fear you are an outcast or that your problems are too much, will you turn from your questions and ask God for his help? Then thank him for what he gives you.

Our world is full of sorrow, violence, confusion, division. But still, there is a lot to say thank you for. Gratitude puts us on a road that leads to Jesus. As you pray, say thank you to God for at least ten specific things.

Recommended Closing Prayer

Lord, I want to say thank you for the good things I have just listed. As James reminds me in his letter, "Every desirable and beneficial gift comes out of heaven. The gifts are rivers of light cascading down from the Father of Light" (James 1:17 MSG). Praise you for your good gifts. Amen.

Ordinary Time Day 164

SALLY BREEDLOVE

Reflect on Luke 17:20–37

Call to Prayer

How will things turn out? Will we ever be happy or secure, as we long to be?

What is Jesus's wisdom to us as we think about the future?

In this passage from Luke 17, Jesus addresses the Pharisees and the disciples. What he says to them seems the opposite of what we would think each group needed to hear.

He tells the Pharisees that they are looking for the wrong thing. The kingdom of God is already among them, and it is not about power. If we look for the wrong thing, we will rarely find the right thing. Perhaps we are more like the Pharisees than we'd like to believe. We want a God who shows up to fix things and make things right. But Christ says his rule in this world is already taking place in subtle ways. If we pay attention, we'll learn how to recognize his work and to trust the way he does things.

He tells the disciples that endurance is hard. They will long to see him come in power, but the world will seem to move along the way it always has. He warns them that they are in danger of being blinded by the everyday realities of work and weddings, eating and drinking. Like Lot's wife, we can lose our hope that a better world lies beyond this one. (Lot's wife perished because she couldn't let go of the life she had enjoyed in Sodom. Even as her sinful city was being destroyed, she looked back with longing.)

Like the Pharisees and the disciples, we are too often blind to the clear evidence that God is inviting us to join him in his kingdom work. We need to ask ourselves if we are consumed with maintaining our lifestyle instead.

We have no guarantees about the future, do we? Are we ready, Jesus asks, for his return?

As you pray, ask Jesus to make you ready for your own death or for his coming. Ask him to help you see that you have kingdom work to do today.

Recommended Closing Prayer

Lord, your kingdom come, your will be done on earth as it is in heaven. In Jesus's name. Amen.

Ordinary Time Day 165
SALLY BREEDLOVE

Reflect on Luke 18:1–8

Call to Prayer

We are taught not to beg. Polite people don't demand. We are told to be patient and to take care of ourselves. In this parable, what does it mean to be like the persistent widow who bothered the judge until he gave in?

Perhaps a clue lies in Jesus's question in Luke 18:8: "When the Son of God comes will he find faith on earth?" (NIV). The word *faith* can also be translated as "faithfulness." Perhaps Jesus is asking, *When I return, will I see faithfulness in my people?*

What is faithfulness? At its core, it is a persistent waiting and trusting, waiting and trusting, waiting and trusting. Faithfulness leads to tested hope. Jesus's first question in this parable is almost rhetorical: "And will not God bring about justice for his chosen ones, who cry out to him day and night?" (Luke 18:7 NIV). The answer is, "Of course! A good God will give justice."

The second question is not at all rhetorical; it is pointed directly at us. When the Son of man returns, will he find faithful people who keep turning to God? who keep expecting him to be the good and beautiful God he is?

We need to know the answers to both questions. Do we believe God is good and that, like a good father, he longs to hear our hearts cry out to him? Or have we made him out to be a harsh Judge whom we have to badger?

The second question turns us back to examine our own hearts: Will we persist in asking for what we need? Will we wait for God to answer? Will we choose faithfulness to our God and Savior, no matter how long the wait?

As you pray, ask the Lord to strengthen the hearts of his people so we may stay faithful to him. Pray especially for any people you know who are struggling to faithfully follow Jesus.

Recommended Closing Prayer

> Most Loving Father, you will us to give you thanks for all things, to dread nothing but the loss of you, and to cast all our care on the One who cares for us. Preserve us from faithless fears and worldly anxieties and grant that no clouds of this mortal life may hide from us the light of that love which is immortal, and which you manifested unto us in your Son, Jesus Christ our Lord. Amen.
> *(Anglican Church in North America Book of Common Prayer)*

Ordinary Time Day 166

SALLY BREEDLOVE

Reflect on Luke 18:9–14

Call to Prayer

Jesus told this parable for those who "trusted in themselves that they were righteous and treated others with contempt" (Luke 18:9 ESV). He gives it to us to reshape the way we see ourselves and other people.

Perhaps you are a fairly good person. You do your best. You're reasonably honest and kind. You know you aren't perfect, but your intentions are good. If you wonder about God, you assume he knows how hard you're trying and that he's reasonably happy with you.

But Christ calls this trusting oneself instead of God.

The Bible makes it clear—no one is good enough. We've all fallen short of God's holiness. Our personal goodness, love, commitment to justice, or purity is a useless thing when held up to the light of God. It's like having twenty-seven cents in your pocket when what you really need is one million dollars.

True Christ followers know they aren't good enough. They're thankful they have a Savior who died for their sins and who gives them new life in his name.

But if we do a full stop at this point, we haven't listened to the whole parable.

Jesus also told the parable for those who looked at others with contempt. Does Christ have your full attention now? What person hasn't muttered in his or her own heart, if not aloud, "Well, I know I'm not perfect, but at least I'm better than _____." We fill in the blank with a certain type of people or the name of a particular person. We judge those around us by what news outlets they listen to, whom they voted for, how they are raising their children, their ideas about God, their T-shirt logo, their tattoos, or their five-hundred-dollar shoes.

It's okay to deeply disagree with someone about their choices, their beliefs, or their values. But when you turn contemptuous toward the other person's differences, you are wrong. You are no better than anyone else.

As you pray, be honest. Do you trust you are "good enough"? Do you justify yourself by how hard you try or how good your intentions are? Don't spend your life defending yourself; trust Christ to save you.

Then ask yourself: whom do you think you're better than? Our hearts all have ranking systems; we rarely see ourselves as bottom-rung people. Repent of your pride. Pray for the mercy of God to teach you mercy toward others.

Recommended Closing Prayer

Lord have mercy. Christ have mercy. Lord have mercy on me. Amen.

Ordinary Time Day 167

SALLY BREEDLOVE

Reflect on Luke 18:15–17

Call to Prayer

The stories in Luke 18 and 19 are the last encounters between Jesus and ordinary people recorded for us. These encounters reveal the heart of Christ. They remind us that humility, not accomplishment, is required to enter the kingdom.

"Now they were bringing even infants to him that he might touch them" (Luke 18:15 ESV). They "were bringing" means it was a recurring event for people to bring their babies to Jesus. Why? The love of Jesus drew them.

In Jesus's day, an important rabbi would never concern himself with little children. But Jesus welcomes the young even as his disciples rebuke their parents. He says, "Let the children come to me, and do not hinder them, for to such belongs the kingdom of God" (Luke 18:16 ESV).

Even as the sands of time empty through an hourglass on his way to the cross, Jesus has time for children. He himself is humble of heart, so he stops to teach. The lesson? Those who are humble, helplessly dependent, without a list of accomplishments or an impressive resume, are welcome in his kingdom. The kingdom belongs to them.

Jesus tells us not only to come as a child, trusting and dependent, but also to receive as a child. Picture the way a child receives a gift—not in cautious consideration of what he deserves, but with exuberance, joy, and delight. Children receive what they are given. They trust the giver and the gift.

How does your own heart see Christ? Trust is confidence in the reliability of someone or something. Do you trust the Giver and the gift? Let go of anything else you're trusting in for entrance to the kingdom, for membership in God's family.

Pray. Acknowledge your helpless dependence on Christ. Let his love draw you in. With open hands and an open heart—in faith, with joy—trust him as your Savior. Receive with gratitude and delight the gift of grace. Enter the kingdom as a little child.

Recommended Closing Prayer

> Gentle Jesus, meek and mild,
> Look upon a little child,
> Pity my simplicity,
> Suffer me to come to thee.
> Fain I would to thee be brought,
> Gracious Lord, forbid it not;
> In the Kingdom of thy grace
> Give a little child a place.
> Loving Jesus, gentle Lamb,
> In thy gracious hands I am;
> Make me, Saviour, what thou art,
> Live thyself within my heart.
> ("Gentle Jesus, Meek and Mild" by Charles Wesley)

Ordinary Time Day 168

WILLA KANE

Reflect on Luke 18:18–30

Call to Prayer

It's no coincidence that this passage follows the story about childlike faith as the requirement to enter the kingdom of God.

The man in this story appears to have everything—wealth, an outwardly righteous life, respect, and prestige. But he realizes he lacks something. "What must I do to inherit eternal life?" he asks. He thinks there has to be something he can do to enter the kingdom, some way he can measure up.

He approaches Jesus as a "good teacher" but not as Lord.

He is wrong about himself, he is wrong about Jesus, and he is wrong about life.

In love, Jesus puts his finger on the young man's errors. Entering the kingdom is not about looking good or being good. The only way in is on bended knee, like a little child. It requires absolute allegiance to God, the only one who is good, loving him with one's heart, soul, and mind. No substitute gods or idols.

Instead of entering the kingdom in joy with a promise of eternal riches, this young man grasps earthly wealth and leaves in sorrow.

Jesus knows what is competing for your affections. As you pray, ask the Spirit to show you. Turn and accept anew the grace Christ offers. Choose eternal riches, not the poverty of worldly gain.

Recommended Closing Prayer

> O God, you have prepared for those who love you such good things as surpass our understanding: Pour into our hearts such love towards you, that we, loving you in all things and above all things, may obtain your promises, which exceed all that we can desire; through Jesus Christ our Lord, who lives and reigns with you and the Holy Spirit, one God, for ever and ever.
> Amen.
> *(Anglican Church in North America Book of Common Prayer)*

Ordinary Time Day 169
WILLA KANE

Reflect on Luke 19:1–10

Call to Prayer

Zacchaeus is not a cute little man who climbed a tree to see Jesus, but a crooked tax collector, chief among those who defrauded his neighbors to become rich. A known sinner, he is despised. He has fallen to the bottom rung of society by dishonestly climbing the ladder of success. If you lived in Jericho, you'd have written him off.

Jesus is on the way through Jericho to Passover in Jerusalem, where he will be the Passover Lamb.

But before he reaches Jerusalem to suffer and die, his larger mission is on view as he calls to Zacchaeus. Jesus has not written him off but is drawing him in.

The Son of Man came to seek and to save the lost.

This is the gospel: Jesus to the rescue. It's why he came.

The story of Zacchaeus is powerful in its message and position. Following encounters with a blind beggar trapped in poverty and a rich young ruler trapped by his wealth, this is the last personal encounter we see before the Passion Week begins to unfold.

The disciples have asked, "Who can be saved?" (Luke 18:26 ESV). Encounters with these people give the answer. Those to be saved acknowledge they are lost. They turn to Jesus.

Your sin is not a barrier to Christ's seeking you; it's what beckons him. Jesus came to seek Zacchaeus, a sinner, and he came to seek you, a sinner. He came to save Zacchaeus, a sinner, and he came to save you, a sinner. He is the friend of sinners. His love is directed toward sinners.

When Jesus, not counting equality with God as a thing to be grasped intersects with the humble and contrite heart of a sinner. Divine love takes root and changes lives.

Pray. Acknowledge your sin before Christ. Thank him that he came to seek and to save. Open your heart to the God who sees you and knows you. In humility, receive his forgiveness and let divine love change you.

Recommended Closing Prayer

> O God, whose Son Jesus Christ is the Good Shepherd of your people: Grant that, when we hear his voice, we may know him who calls us each by name, and follow where he leads; who, with you and the Holy Spirit, lives and reigns, one God, for ever and ever. Amen.
>
> *(Anglican Church in North America Book of Common Prayer)*

Ordinary Time Day 170

WILLA KANE

Reflect on Luke 19:11–27

Call to Prayer

The encounters we've considered in Luke 18 and 19 lead us to the lesson of this parable: humility is required for stewardship.

A humble Savior entrusts his followers with capital to invest. That sacred deposit is primarily the gospel, but it is also our lives, our influence, our time, our resources, and our talents.

Until Jesus returns, we are responsible to use all these things under his lordship and for his glory. Humble servants steward these gifts, and they will be rewarded for doing so. Enemies of Christ will be punished.

Enemies of Christ aren't always openly hostile. They can be politely indifferent or casually irresponsible with gifts of grace.

Take inventory of the trust account Christ has put in your hands. On days that are difficult, is the deposit he has given you working hard for his benefit? How are you investing the gifts he has given? Are you indifferent or irresponsible with opportunities to share the gospel? Have you ignored the gift of salvation?

As you pray, ask Jesus to guide you into faithful, trustworthy stewardship of all he's given. Confess where you've fallen short, and in humility, embrace with joy the role of a servant in the kingdom of God.

Recommended Closing Prayer

> Almighty God, whose loving hand *hath* given us all that we possess: Grant us grace that we may honor *thee* with our substance, and, remembering the account which we must one day give, may be faithful stewards of *thy* bounty, through Jesus Christ our Lord. Amen.
> *(Anglican Church in North America Book of Common Prayer)*

Ordinary Time Day 171

ABIGAIL HULL WHITEHOUSE

Reflect on Luke 19:29–48

Call to Prayer

Our reading from Luke 19, including Jesus's triumphal entry, seems a little out of step with Ordinary Time and more fitting for Lent—the season contemplating Christ's death that precedes Easter. But the words of warning we find in verses 41–44 speak well into the call to faithful following that is the hallmark of Ordinary Time.

Seated on a lowly donkey, like his mother before him, Christ looks over the city of Jerusalem and weeps. He says, "Would that you, even you, had known on this day the things that make for peace! But now they are hidden from your eyes" (Luke 19:42 ESV). We sense a deep sadness in Jesus concerning how they have missed him and his time of visitation. If only they had seen! If only they had heard! If only their hearts had been open enough to receive the presence of God in their midst! But, tragically, "the things that make for peace" (Luke 19:42 ESV)—Christ himself and the meaning of his sacrificial death—are hidden from their eyes.

Like the city of Jerusalem, we, too, can become blind to the very presence of God in our midst. Caught up in the swirl and burden of our day-to-day lives, we forget that God is in the room here with us, *watching* and *waiting* to be recognized and invited in, waiting to be praised.

Take a moment to center yourself in God's loving presence and let the frustrations and stresses (and all that you did or did not accomplish) fade away. Perhaps imagine gathering all the tasks, concerns, worries, and questions up in your mind and setting them aside.

Now invite the Prince of Peace to come in a powerful and personal way. Repent of the ways that you've become distracted by lesser things, and ask God for *eyes to see* and a *heart to praise*. Be honest with him about the areas where you've struggled today, and trust that he will draw close to you as you draw close to him in this time of prayer (James 4:8).

Recommended Closing Prayer

I hand over to your care, Lord, my soul and my body, my mind and my thoughts, my prayers and my hopes, my health and my work, my life and my death, my parents and my family, my friends and my neighbors, and my country and all humankind. Today and always, I offer this time, and all that I am, to you. Consecrate my life, and give me the grace to seek you first. Amen. (Adapted from *Saint Benedict's Prayer Book*)

Ordinary Time Day 172
ELIZABETH GATEWOOD

Reflect on Mark 15:1–15

Call to Prayer

Ours is a world of being quick to speak, slow to listen, and quick to become angry. Our agile typing thumbs condition our minds and hearts to carefully craft and protect our image and our positions.

What, then, do we do with this Jesus who stands before the state and religious authorities of his day and remains silent? Why does he refuse to defend himself? Why doesn't he take credit for his righteous life and deny the false charges leveled against him? Why does he allow Barabbas to be released without putting up a fight, trading his own freedom for that of a rabble-rouser?

Wouldn't it be more effective to *say* something, to prove himself, to show a mighty miracle that would convert the most powerful people of his day? Wouldn't it have been a benefit to the gospel to set the record straight about who he was, to remain alive?

Our imaginations can scarcely grasp a power that empties itself for love. And yet this Jesus, the one who stands silent before the mocking accusations of the religious and political powers of his day, invites us to take his path.

As you pray, hold in your mind the image of the silent, meek Christ:

God-man and powerful beyond all measure, but weak by choice for the sake of the world.

Recommended Closing Prayer

Lord, we are quick to speak and quick to become angry. We cannot imagine a power that empties itself for love. We cannot imagine refusing to defend ourselves and prove our position and righteousness. Please help us. Show us the way of Jesus, who invites us by the power of the Holy Spirit to take his way of meekness. Amen.

Ordinary Time Day 173

MATT HOEHN

Reflect on Galatians 3:25–27

Call to Prayer

While what we wear may seem to be an inconsequential topic, the apostle Paul maintains that clothing is crucially significant for the Christian.

In Galatians 3:25–27, Paul isn't so concerned with *what* one wears: togas, or tunics, or trousers (which were actually highly unfashionable in his day). He's much more concerned with *who* one wears: namely, Jesus Christ himself.

Paul says that being baptized *into* Christ necessarily entails clothing yourself *with* Christ. Baptism means undergoing a symbolic death to the old age of the law, sin, and death in order to rise to life as a member of God's family and a participant in new creation. When we rise from the waters of baptism, we no longer wear the old self of our former sinful flesh; rather, we have been clothed with Christ.

What does it actually mean to be clothed with Christ?

It means *protection*. The Lord is our shield (Psalm 33:20), and he hides us in the shadow of his wings (Psalm 17:8), even though the world at our doorstep seems threatening.

It means *witness*. The good news of the gospel is on display as we exhibit the fruit of the Spirit to the watching world: "love, joy, peace, patience, kindness, goodness, faithfulness, gentleness, and self-control" (Galatians 5:22–23 ESV).

It means *loving embrace*. Regardless of the future, nothing "in all creation will be able to separate us from the love of God in Christ Jesus our Lord" (Romans 8:39 ESV).

Even though our world has overwhelming issues, our spiritual clothing with Christ is a reminder of our status as God's beloved children, adopted into his family. It is an assurance of our eternal inheritance with him. This clothing never changes, never wears out, and never goes out of fashion.

As you pray, ask that God would remind you of the incredible assurances that accompany being clothed with Christ. Ask that those who are fearful will be comforted by the protection and loving embrace of our Father.

Recommended Closing Prayer

Father, help 7me to trust in you and to root my life in you today. When the things of this world threaten to overwhelm me, give me your peace. As the news cycle continues to constantly change, remind me that you never change. Clothe me with Christ so that I may experience your loving embrace today. Amen.

Ordinary Time Day 174

MADISON PERRY

Reflect on 2 Thessalonians 2:16, 3:16

Call to Prayer

The World Wide Web is indeed taking up more and more space in the conversations around us. Your inbox is likely cluttered with missives from pastors, politicians, and academic leaders, as well as every business that has access to your email address. But all this communication is so very different from the communication that flows from the scriptures.

The impulse in 1 and 2 Thessalonians is quite different. These letters were to those whom Paul dearly loved, a community who had received the gospel in joy and became a good community. However, now they are suffering under persecution. Many have died.

How would you advise them? More important, how would you pray for them?

Paul's prayers here are simple. He reminds his dear friends of God's love, which has given them eternal salvation and now can bring comfort and consolation. Further, his prayer reminds them of the hope they have in God. They can be hopeful that just as God's grace prevailed over Jesus's death and led to his resurrection, so grace will prevail over their own suffering and possible deaths.

What does hope look like during times like this? Paul talks of being established in work and word—that is, for the Thessalonians to continue doing their daily work and speaking their regular words, to go on doing the regular things that may well be powerless to directly stop trials and tribulation.

You may find yourself lacking hope. Perhaps you have never faced the hard places in life as you are facing them now. You have tried to live and plan well, but nothing you have done is a fortress of protection.

Yet, you can be hopeful. Our hope is not that our structures, memories, and descendants will outlast every sea change. Our hope has nothing to do with our competence or calculations. It isn't derived from the greatness of our cities or the wisdom of our experts. Our hope is built on nothing less than Jesus's blood and righteousness. The salvation of our God will prevail, even if it is with us now as a whisper and a sense of comfort and love.

Therefore, even when faced with seemingly impossible challenges, we can go on doing our daily work. We can go on caring for others and ourselves, praying, keeping the flowers watered, making the next meal, and doing the dishes. We do our daily work because of the eternally significant work God is doing through it. He is establishing us and sinking our roots ever deeper into his grace and love. He is glorifying himself and creating quiet testimonies of his beauty that will lead others home as well.

Pray against despair. Pray for relief for those who suffer. Ask God if there are others who face hopelessness. Be willing to tell them of your cause for hope. Trust that God is at work, and surrender yourself to him anew.

Recommended Closing Prayer

Lord Jesus Christ and God our Father, you who have loved us and given us everlasting consolation and good hope by grace, please comfort our hearts and establish us in every good work and word. Our Lord of peace, please give us peace always in every way. Lord, be with us. Amen. *(Adapted from 2 Thessalonians 2:16, 3:16 NKJV)*

Ordinary Time Day 175

S A L L Y   B R E E D L O V E

Reflect on Matthew 13:44

Call to Prayer

The kingdom of heaven is like treasure hidden in a field that a man found and covered up. Then in his joy, he goes and sells all that he has and buys that field.

The kingdom of heaven is Matthew's focus as he writes his biography of Jesus. The bottom line is that Jesus is King of the cosmos.

The kingdom of heaven is present now, in this world, wherever people recognize and follow Christ as King.

That's important to remember. Life can be impossibly hard; it disappoints and confuses us. Every one of us has wondered, *If God is King, why doesn't he fix things now?! What must he be like if he lets such terrible things happen?* We might wonder if there is a really is a God.

Interestingly, Jesus doesn't defend or explain God's kingdom. Instead, he paints pictures to help us recognize that God's kingdom is real, even in a still-broken world. It's like a field full of plump grain alongside invasive weeds. It seems tiny, like a seed or speck of yeast that you can hardly see, but in fact, it is living and growing. It looks like a hodgepodge of people, and we wonder who really belongs. It is a like a treasure hidden in an ordinary field, but we have to buy the whole property to get it. It's like an exquisite luminous pearl for which we've searched our whole lives, yet when we find it, it will cost us everything we have.

We think the question is: "Where is God's kingdom is in this world of conflict, confusion, and economic pain?" But Jesus's question is different. He wants to know if we are paying attention and are willing to pay the price.

Indeed, are we seeing only weeds and missing the good grain? Do we see the world as nothing more than a muddy, uncultivated mess? Are we disappointed because the church seems unfixable, or do we trust that God will sort it out in the end? Does gaining the kingdom feel like too much work, too costly?

Are we too bored, too sure of ourselves, too hurt, too angry, or too exhausted to recognize the treasure that can be ours if we trust that God really is at work, let Christ be King, and search for the signs that God still reigns on earth.

As you pray, ask God to open your eyes to his work in the world. Then, commit yourself again to acknowledging Christ as your King. Commit yourself to the work he wants to do in you. Commit yourself to the work he wants to do through you. Count the cost, pay the price, and pray.

Recommended Closing Prayer

> Our Father in heaven,
> hallowed be your name.
> Your kingdom come,

your will be done,
on earth as it is in heaven.
(Matthew 6:9–10 NIV)

Ordinary Time Day 176
SALLY BREEDLOVE

Reflect on Malachi 4:5–6

Call to Prayer

What would we see if we were to really see our children?

Jesus saw children as a gift. He said they're the example of what it means to trust God. He liked being around kids.

As many children as adults were resurrected in the scripture. That's something worth pondering.

The gist of the book of Proverbs is that the work of adults is to teach children to be wise. That means parents need to learn wisdom for themselves.

The Shema, the heart of what it means to follow after God according to the Old Testament, gives parents their marching orders. Parents are to teach their children to love God and to know his Word.

"Hear, O Israel: The Lord our God, the Lord is one. You shall love the Lord your God with all your heart and with all your soul and with all your might. And these words that I command you today shall be on your heart. You shall teach them diligently to your children, and shall talk of them when you sit in your house, and when you walk by the way, and when you lie down, and when you rise" (Deuteronomy 6:4–7 ESV).

Pray for yourself as a parent. How have you been called to grow up? No one comes close to being a perfect parent. You may be weighed down with a sense of your inadequacies and failures. Will you receive God's mercy and accept how human you are? Even as a parent, you are God's child. Let him father you.

Your heart may ache for the broken mess your family is in. Pray for those you love and for your own heart.

If you are a grandparent, a neighbor, an aunt or uncle, or a friend, ask God to show you how you can do good for a particular child. Pray for children who are isolated, in danger, unhappy, or facing neglect and need. Pray the Lord gives you something you can do to help.

Recommended Closing Prayer

O Lord, Jesus taught us to love one another and showed us what love looks like. For those of us who are living with family and friends, please give us an extra measure of love for the people we have been placed with. May the heart of parents be turned to their children and away from hollow ambitions. May spouses be given patience and affection for one another. For those of us who are living alone, help us to be patient and to remain in prayer. Please give all of us who are lonely friendship with other people and, above all, the companionship of your Son by the power of the Holy Spirit. Join us all together into the body Christ, and let us hear the words you spoke to him at the river Jordan—that we are beloved by you. Amen.

Ordinary Time Day 177
ELIZABETH GATEWOOD

Reflect on Matthew 14:11, 14:13, 14:19–20

Call to Prayer

At his banquet, Herod serves up the grotesque. He had wanted to avoid killing John the Baptist so as not to arouse the anger of the people who considered John a prophet. But caught in the web of an adulterous relationship with his sister-in-law and a swaggering promise, Herod keeps his words to impress his guests. He serves up John's head on a platter. His narcissism, violence, and insecurity leap from the pages of scripture. We have seen his type. We have been invited to his banquet. Though its pleasures rarely last beyond the morning, its destruction endures.

Jesus invites us to a different sort of banquet. In grief over the beheading of his cousin John, Jesus goes away. He doesn't compete for attention, sponge up influence, or grab power; he seeks solitude. But the people follow him anyway. The multitudes pursue Jesus because they are hungry—hungry for this person who empties his power and takes the form of a servant. After literally following after him on their feet, they are hungry for food.

Jesus's banquet is an unexpected feast in the wilderness. At his banquet, Jesus serves real food and real teaching. There is abundance for all. Jesus himself is the feast.

As you pray, consider where you are feasting on the fare of destruction instead of on the nourishing banquet of Christ.

Recommended Closing Prayer

Father, Son, and Holy Spirit, so often we are enticed by the banquets served up by our world, banquets of showy power, cheap entertainment, and grotesque spectacle. Yet you invite us to taste the simple fare of your body and blood, broken for us. Let us hunger for this banquet that will transform us and enliven us. Thank you that through this banquet, you unite us to yourself and your body, the church. Amen.

Ordinary Time Day 178

ELIZABETH GATEWOOD

Reflect on Matthew 15:3, 15:6, 15:10

Call to Prayer

"Have you washed your hands before dinner?"

The Pharisees ask a version of that same question to Jesus: "Why didn't your disciples wash their hands before dinner?" They end up in deep waters, in a theological debate with Jesus. Jesus is not worried about germ transmission; he is worried about hearts rotting.

The disease that the Pharisees have isn't one transmitted by touching the wrong surfaces; it is a disease that has originated in their hearts. It is the disease of spiritual idolatry. They have begun worshipping their tradition and have ceased to be in relationship with the living God. Jesus goes so far as to say that their tradition-worship has nullified the Word of God. As it turns out, holiness is not about having the right soap or the right washing process.

Perhaps we are sometimes like the Pharisees, trying to become holy from the outside in, through tired and idolatrous traditions or misguided spiritual rituals and practices.

What is the answer? How do we root out the evil thoughts that defile us? Jesus wants people to turn their attention to the heart, to be holy and clean from the inside out. But how do we become holy and clean from the inside out?

Jesus introduces plant imagery in this passage, noting that the weeds of tradition-worshippers will be uprooted, but the plants lovingly planted and tended by the Father will remain. The way to be holy and fruitful is to be a vine planted by the Father, connected to the Son, and nourished and enlivened by the Holy Spirit. This was beyond what the Pharisees could imagine; yet for us, the invitation is clear. We bear fruit by remaining in Christ.

As you pray, consider where you are captured by religious or social convention and how these things might be blocking you from relating to the Triune God.

Recommended Closing Prayer

Father, Son, and Holy Spirit, so often we squabble among ourselves about the right ways to do things. We might worship tradition or eschew it, and in either case, we often miss you. Yet you are in our midst, showing us how to be clean from the inside out and inviting us to a relationship with the living God. Please lovingly graft us to Jesus Christ, the True Vine. Amen.

Ordinary Time Day 179

ELIZABETH GATEWOOD

Reflect on Matthew 15:30, 15:32, 15:36

Call to Prayer

Jesus had a big agenda: to usher in salvation for the healing and redemption of the world. But Jesus attends to the small things right in front of him—the mute, the crippled, the lame, and the blind.

He also attends to the hungry. He has a mass of people in front of him, hungry for bread and for something they can't quite put their fingers on.

Jesus doesn't give them a comprehensive explanation or a sign from heaven, despite their desiring one. Jesus offers them presence, healing, compassion, and nourishment. Ultimately, he offers them himself.

It is Ordinary Time. And indeed, perhaps your days feel way too ordinary. They are filled with tedious, repetitive, seemingly insignificant tasks: slogging through emails, changing diapers, waiting in carpool lines, serving meals, navigating bureaucracy, or managing small tasks that seem disconnected from a meaningful whole. Perhaps you long to do work of importance, to move the needle toward achieving personal goals, or to heal the systemic and personal ills and injustices of your community.

As you pray, consider what you might learn from Jesus, very God and very human, who takes time to attend to the physical people and things in front of him. Consider where you may be missing the invitation to attend to things in your life. What do you begrudge because it feels beneath you? With whom do you become impatient because your agenda is interrupted?

Recommended Closing Prayer

Heavenly Father, we want to be important. We passionately care about certain issues, businesses, subjects, places, and people. And we have been told that we can make a difference. Yet you show us a way of meekness. Your agenda isn't fulfilled by executing a strategic plan but by loving and attending to the things in front of you. Refine our attention. Give us humility to attend to the things that you have placed in front of us. Amen.

Ordinary Time Day 180

ELIZABETH GATEWOOD

Reflect on Matthew 16:16, 16:20, 16:24

Call to Prayer

In the course of Jesus's ministry, people struggle to understand who he is and what he is about. The disciples and the Pharisees are constantly attempting to tame Jesus and fashion him to fit their categories. Jesus continually resists this.

Yet Peter gets it. He doesn't seek to explain Jesus; he simply proclaims him: "You are the Christ" (Matthew 16:16 ESV). Our understanding of God comes not from slotting him into our existing categories for deity, but from revelation.

Even after this earth-shattering proclamation, Jesus desires hiddenness. Perhaps he doesn't want throngs of people following him for the wrong reasons, projecting their agendas and hopes onto him. And even after his moment of clarity, Peter gets things wrong. He rebukes Jesus when Jesus predicts his own death. But Jesus is quick to make clear to his disciples that following this Messiah means sacrifice, not glory. It means God's masterful plan, not human agendas.

As you pray, remember that you are in the presence of the living God. Take a moment to be still before God.

Recommended Closing Prayer

Father, Son, and Holy Spirit, you are the living God. We confess that so often we approach you with our own agendas and plans. We slot you into our categories of "deity" and decline your invitation for relationship with the living God. Forgive us. Let our idolatry and our agendas for you fade away. Let us joyfully proclaim, "You are the Christ, the Son of God." And give us the courage to follow Jesus Christ, who takes us not on a path of glory but on a path to the cross. Amen.

Ordinary Time Day 181

MADISON PERRY

Reflect on Psalm 23

Call to Prayer

Psalm 23 opens up for us a vista of blessing, but the doorway to that goodness means giving up control of our lives. When we pray Psalm 23, we again center on God's ways and God's leading. To pray this psalm, we must acknowledge that we are but sheep.

Throughout the gospels, Jesus and his disciples proclaim that the kingdom of God is near. It is good news that the kingdom of God is near because in this kingdom, we can be mere sheep who receive rest, sustenance, and protection.

This psalm doesn't promise a pain-free existence; it takes us from verdant pasture through the shadow of death, from God's comfort and salvation to a table set in the midst of our enemies. But ultimately, we will receive these promises: we will be anointed with the Holy Spirit, our cup of life will overflow, goodness and mercy will follow us all the days of our life, and we will dwell in the house of the Lord forever.

Begin your prayers in humility, as a sheep looking to your shepherd. Acknowledge your dependence on his hand. Ask that Christ's will would be done in your life now and forever. Finally, let your requests give way to hope; thank God for his salvation; and express your wish to dwell in his house forever.

Recommended Closing Prayer

O God, whose Son Jesus is the good shepherd of your people: Grant that when we hear his voice we may know him who calls us each by name, and follow where he leads;

who, with you and the Holy Spirit, lives and reigns, one
God, for ever and ever.
Amen.
(Anglican Church in North America Book of Common Prayer)

Ordinary Time Day 182
MADISON PERRY

Reflect on Hebrews 1:1–4

Call to Prayer

Hundreds of years ago, people aspired to master all fields of knowledge.
They would study philosophy alongside biology, astronomy alongside
poetry, business alongside music. A mature mind would be able to hold
a working knowledge of most areas of learning.

Today, we live in an infinitely more complex world. Everywhere we
turn, we are out of our depth; very few people can explain how water
treatment works, how a person falls in love, or why the gold standard
in currency matters.

The writer of the letter to the Hebrews asserts something very
striking—Jesus Christ is at the heart of the universe. When it is all
said and done, all matters practical and beautiful are summed up in
him. You can contemplate nothing richer than the words and person of
Jesus Christ. Through the Son and in the Spirit, God the Father created
everything. The Son's power upholds the universe.

This should move us to worship and to love. If the God we love is
upholding everything, then every person and every dimension of this
reality is deserving of our steady and affectionate attention.

Praise God—Father, Son, and Holy Spirit. Lift up the name of
Jesus Christ where you are, calling to mind the breadth and depth of
his reign. Ask that God would protect your heart from worshipping
any false gods. Ask that God would enliven your heart so that you

will love every square inch of his creation and every person made in his image.

Recommended Closing Prayer

Christ, we praise you as the radiance of the glory of God. We praise you for your infinite attentive power that holds the universe together. Grant us the grace to see you as you truly are, to live in awe of you, and to rest in your miraculous love for us, your blood-bought people. Amen.

Ordinary Time Day 183

MADISON PERRY

Reflect on Hebrews 2:1–4

Call to Prayer

The writer of Hebrews raises a hard possibility: we may neglect the great salvation offered in Christ and drift away from it. King David's great declaration in Psalm 51:12 has a similar sense of urgency and clarity: "Restore to me the joy of your salvation" (ESV).

The remedy to this danger? This passage in Hebrews is straightforward in what it recommends that we do: "pay much closer attention to what we have heard" (Hebrews 2:1 ESV).

How do we pay close attention? The book of Hebrews is a long meditation on the person and work of Jesus Christ. It is extremely prayerful, as the author is frequently pausing to examine one or another psalm of praise.

Is prayer a nourishing activity for you? Are you feasting on your salvation in prayer?

Return to the Author of your salvation, the perfecter of your faith. Even where you are weak, if you acknowledge him, his faithfulness will overcome your faltering. If you have lost sight of the radiance of

God's glory in the face of Christ, ask him to reveal himself. If you have forgotten your need of a Savior and are losing an appetite for salvation, confess this as well. Be patient if the growth of your faith is slow. Be humble and grateful as you begin to taste new life.

Recommended Closing Prayer

> Have mercy on me, O God,
> according to your steadfast love;
> according to your abundant mercy
> blot out my transgressions.
> Wash me thoroughly from my iniquity,
> and cleanse me from my sin!
> Amen.
> *(Psalm 51:1–2, ESV)*

Ordinary Time Day 184

MATT HOEHN

Reflect on Hebrews 3:12–14

Call to Prayer

Have you ever gone through a prolonged season of being unable to exercise according to your normal pattern? During such times, muscle groups that have taken years to develop can atrophy quickly.

In today's scripture reading, the author of Hebrews gives us a stark warning against allowing our most important muscle, the heart, to atrophy. The neglect of the heart leads to the direst of all outcomes: "fall[ing] away from the living God" (Hebrews 3:12 ESV).

The atrophy of the heart isn't a passive process as it is in other muscle groups. A corrosive agent actively fuels this process: "the deceitfulness of sin" (Hebrews 3:13 ESV). The heart has no neutral gear; it is always either being strengthened in the faith or withering under the effects of unchecked sin.

How can we fight this atrophy of the heart? The answer is counterintuitive. It is not to work on our hearts harder or to apply some new technique to them; rather, it is to "hold our original confidence firm to the end" (Hebrews 3:14 ESV). The confidence referred to is the confidence of faith—faith in what Christ has done on our behalf in his perfect incarnate life, his atoning death, and his resurrection to the right hand of the Father. It is not confidence in our own innate capacity to repair our hearts. Remembering what Christ has done for us and holding on to faith are the exercises that keep our hearts from atrophying.

We're not isolated and alone in this. We must "exhort one another" (Hebrews 3:13 ESV) in this process through being our brother or sister's keeper, by sharpening others, and by being sharpened by them. Self-exertion is futile when it comes to strengthening our hearts. Remembering Christ, holding fast to him, and joining in Christ-centered community is the regimen for a healthy heart.

As you pray, open your heart to God. Ask him to strengthen you in the virtues of faith and perseverance, and invite him in to work in any areas where your heart is directed to something other than him.

Recommended Closing Prayer

Heavenly Father, strengthen my faith in your Son Jesus Christ. Help my unbelief, and soften my heart in areas where it's hardened. Grant me the ability to persevere to the end, that I may enter the joy of your presence in the company of all the saints. Amen.

Ordinary Time Day 185

Reflect on Hebrews 4:12–13

Call to Prayer

When you imagine being cut or pierced by a sharp object, what's the first image that comes to your mind? Surely it's not a pleasant one. Whether it's the minor paper cut you received last week or that slice on your finger you got while chopping vegetables, the thought of a cut from a sharp object leads to recoil and squeamishness.

But there is a notable exception to this desire to recoil. If you've ever badly broken a bone or had a serious internal condition, you'll know the experience of undergoing surgery firsthand. In this instance, the cut of the surgeon's blade is desired; it's an act of compassionate care in repairing what is broken or excising what is unhealthy inside us.

According to the author of Hebrews, God's Word is like a spiritual form of surgery. When we spend time communing with God by reading his Word, scripture operates on us as an active surgical blade: it makes an incision into the hardness of our hearts, it renews and repairs what is broken inside them, and it cuts out the unhealthy growth of sin and disordered desires. We do not simply read the Bible; God's Word also reads us by "discerning the thoughts and intentions of the heart," leading to repentance and communion with the Father.

As you bow your head, let the Word of God give direction to the words you offer back to God in prayer.

Recommended Closing Prayer

Heavenly Father, thank you for revealing yourself to us. Thank you for making yourself known to us through your Word. Enable me to allow scripture to do its proper work on my heart, and strengthen my desire to spend time in it. Amen.

Ordinary Time Day 186

MATT HOEHN

Reflect on Hebrews 4:15–16

Call to Prayer

Loneliness can be one of the most despair-inducing of all experiences. The feeling of isolation, the sense that *no one could possibly understand what I'm going through,* is among the most difficult lived realities of the human condition. That feeling of being without connection to others is sometimes related to besetting sin patterns. We feel the pain of our loneliness as our shame plagues us. "If anyone knew about my struggle with _____, they would recoil from me. I'd be exposed and devastated." So, we choose isolation; it's the price we pay to keep parts of our lives hidden.

The Lord God sees all. He knows everything about us, even the things we hide. The good news of the gospel is that he doesn't look on our besetting sin patterns and recoil from us or reject us out of disgust. Actually, the precise opposite is true: he sent his Son to us out of love, to assume our human nature, to become familiar with our condition, and to redeem us by his perfect incarnate life, atoning death, and victorious resurrection.

We don't have a God who is removed from our fears, our temptations, and our feelings of isolation. We have a God who took on human flesh to calm our fears, to experience our temptations, and thereby to bring us out of the darkness of isolation and into the light of truth.

Because of Jesus, we can draw near to God, not with fearful trepidation, but with confidence in the goodness of his grace and in the efficacy of his abundant mercy to forgive.

As you pray, invite the Lord to enter into the hidden, isolating parts of your heart. Meditate on the incarnate humanity of Jesus Christ, who knows temptation firsthand and sympathizes with your struggle. Repent of your sinfulness, draw near to his grace, and receive his mercy.

Recommended Closing Prayer

Father, you know everything about me. Hiding from you is futile. Please meet me in my brokenness and bring me out of darkness and into light. Thank you for your Son, who understands the human struggle, and who was tempted as I am yet lived a perfect life. Amen.

Ordinary Time Day 187

MATT HOEHN

Reflect on Hebrews 6:19–20

Call to Prayer

As you come to pray, do you feel that God is distant from you? Many Christians have a relatively easy time grasping God's grandeur, power, and transcendence. But for many, it's God's intimate closeness that's so difficult to believe. It can be challenging to trust that God knit us together in the womb, knows the number of hairs on our heads, and cares deeply for our individual fears, questions, and life circumstances.

This scripture reminds us that God, who created galaxies by the breath of his mouth, is the very God who sent his Son Jesus to assume our full humanity. The curtain that once reminded God's people of their sinfulness and inability to be in the presence of God's holiness has been torn in two by the atoning death of Jesus. Christ went behind this curtain and now leads us in victorious procession after him, through this curtain, into the welcoming presence and loving embrace of the Father. He is truly "a forerunner on our behalf" (Hebrews 6:20 ESV), leading us where only he himself could bring us.

If God feels distant, impersonal, or inaccessible to you, be reminded that God is not far off: you have been brought near to him through the blood of Christ. As you pray, hold to the truth that God knows you, loves you, and cares for you deeply and personally. Even during challenging times, even amid a dark night of the soul, you may hold on to this "sure and steadfast anchor ... of hope" (Hebrews 6:19 ESV).

Recommended Closing Prayer

Father, help me know that you are near. Give me a greater sense of your intimate presence, your ever-present grace, and your tangible love. Help me not only to worship you in your majesty but also to walk alongside you daily. Amen.

Ordinary Time Day 188

MATT HOEHN

Reflect on Hebrews 7:26–29

Call to Prayer

In this passage, the author of Hebrews provides us with a litany of reasons to praise the name of the risen Lord Jesus. He is the true "high priest" and is "holy, innocent, unstained, separated from sinners, and exalted above the heavens" (Hebrews 7:26 ESV). Jesus now sits enthroned at the right hand of the Father, and he is worthy of all our praise. He has "been made perfect forever" (Hebrews 7:28 ESV).

As we reflect on the person and work of Jesus, we must not let his ascendant glory obscure the means by which he was exalted to this glory.

In proving himself to be the true High Priest, Jesus was condemned to an unjust death by the corrupt high priest of his day.

Though perfectly holy, he took on human form among the unholiness of the human race.

Though "unstained" by the sin of this world and thus "separated from sinners" (Hebrews 7:26 ESV), he was despised in his day for his notorious reputation as "a friend of tax collectors and sinners" (Matthew 11:19 ESV), leading to his being stained by the blood of the cross.

Before he was "exalted above the heavens" (Hebrews 7:26 ESV), Jesus was first suspended underneath the heavens on a gruesome tree, then deposited lifeless below the earth in a tomb.

As you pray, focus on the victory of the true High Priest, who intercedes at the right hand of the Father on your behalf, drawing you into his presence. As you do so, be reminded of the cost Jesus paid in order to do this. Lift your heart to the Father in gratitude.

Recommended Closing Prayer

Father, thank you for your Son Jesus, who was brought low that I might be brought on high into your presence for eternity. Thank you for his sacrifice for me. Help me to honor the name of Jesus and to love and serve you each day. Amen.

Ordinary Time Day 189
MARYMAC HOEHN

Reflect on Hebrews 8:10–12

Call to Prayer

Do you *love* God's law? Do you long for it to be written on your heart? So often when we think of God's law, we think of rules and regulations. It can be tempting to think of God's law as a guidebook for how to win his favor or to think of God as a demanding Judge, watching us and assessing how well we obey the rules. Why would anyone want a list of rules engraved on their heart—at the center of their being?

The author offers us insight in Hebrews 8:11: "For they shall all know me" (ESV). God reveals himself to us *through his law*. He does not give us rules to follow for the sake of laying out rules, but he uses his law to teach us what he is like.

Psalm 119:103–104 provides us additional understanding: "How sweet are your words to my taste, sweeter than honey to my mouth! Through your precepts I get understanding: therefore, I hate every false way" (ESV). The law of God is sweet—it offers us knowledge of the law's Creator, and it helps us to live a life in accordance with his *best* for us.

So often we think of the law as being like broccoli or spinach. We eat it because it's good for us, but it's not the most enjoyable experience. Yet in scripture we are offered a very different picture of the law: it is honey. It is sweet, delicious, and enjoyable. Why? Because the law is God's gift to us. How gracious of our Creator to show us how to best live the lives he has given us in the world that he created! Through his law we can come to know God. God makes himself known to every one of us, from the least to the greatest.

We will all fall short of full obedience. How gracious is our God? Not only does he engrave his law, which is sweeter than honey, on our frail human hearts, but also, at great cost to himself, he offers us mercy when we fail to obey and when we choose sin over obedience. As you pray, may your heart be moved to worship, to gratitude, and to affection for God as you reflect on his law and his grace to you through his law.

Recommended Closing Prayer

Heavenly Father, thank you for your law. Thank you for choosing to write it on our broken human hearts. You are very gracious to reveal yourself to us, and, Lord, we long to know you. Would you continue to work in our hearts? Help us to love your Word and to follow you faithfully. And reveal more of yourself to us. Thank you for showing us mercy through Christ's sacrifice on our behalf. Amen.

Ordinary Time Day 190
MARYMAC HOEHN

Reflect on Hebrews 9:11–14

Call to Prayer

"He entered the Most Holy Place once for all by his own blood, thus obtaining eternal redemption" (Hebrews 9:12 NIV).

Once for all. What a beautiful reminder to the guilty heart that

Christ has paid the price for our sin in a onetime sacrifice—a sacrifice that does not have to be continually repeated.

In our lives with God, we may find it hard at times to take this beautiful truth to heart. We find ourselves ruminating on moments of failure and trapped in feelings of shame. Hebrews 9 offers us a sweet reminder that Christ has fully paid for our sin in a onetime sacrifice that has sanctified us and purified our consciences.

It can be tempting to continue punishing ourselves and to dwell in shame. But God wants so much more for his people! He has purified us and redeemed us through Christ.

What do we do with this gracious gift? We "serve the living God" (Hebrews 9:14 NIV). Christ sets our consciences free from shame and empowers us to serve God with unblemished hearts. Rather than sitting in guilt, we are called to walk forward, empowered by God to love and serve him!

How do we serve God? One way we can serve him well is to forgive each other. Not only should we refrain from fishing in our own sea, but also we must not fish for the sins of others. When we forgive someone, we leave the way the person has hurt us in that sea instead of bringing it up over and over again. Christ's sacrifice *once for all* was for us and for the person who has hurt us. May we accept his forgiveness, and may we extend forgiveness to those around us.

As you come before the Lord in prayer, remember God's great act of mercy toward you. Ask him for the power to forgive others as you have been forgiven. Praise him for his grace.

Recommended Closing Prayer

Jesus, thank you for offering yourself as a sacrifice *once for all*. Help me to live in light of this truth. Set me free from guilt and shame, and empower me to serve you. Lord, teach me how to forgive those who have wronged me. Amen.

Ordinary Time Day 191

SALLY BREEDLOVE

Reflect on Hebrews 12:1–3, 12:11

Call to Prayer

It is true that none of us signed up for the impossibly hard things that happen to us, but we still find ourselves in painful places at many points in our life. What do we do? We all hold responsibilities when life is hard. We are still called to live ordered and humble lives, to do our work well, to care for those around us, and to seek justice for all. All humans are rightly being asked to do these things regardless of whether or not they have faith in the Lord Jesus Christ.

But do we who worship Jesus have a different calling in this time? You may want to read all of Hebrews 12 as you ponder this question.

We are called to follow Jesus, who endured all the way to the cross. And we are called to live in hope. The present distress will not have the last word. As we follow Jesus, we will begin to see more and more clearly where we are headed. Ahead of us down the road is the kingdom of joy, where Jesus sits at the right hand of God. We can be realistic about the sufferings we are called to endure alongside Jesus in the present moment and also be energized as we walk toward a joyful eternal future.

As you pray, ask God to make you a follower who endures. Ask him to give you faith to see the kingdom that lies ahead and breaks in even now.

Recommended Closing Prayer

Visit this place, O Lord, and drive far from it all snares of the enemy; let your holy angels dwell with us to preserve us in peace; and let your blessing be upon us always; through Jesus Christ our Lord. Amen.

Lighten our darkness, we beseech you, O Lord; and by your great mercy defend us from all perils and dangers of this night; for the love of your only Son, our Savior Jesus Christ. Amen.

Be present, O merciful God, and protect us through the hours of this night, so that we who are wearied by the changes and chances of this life may rest in your eternal changelessness; through Jesus Christ our Lord.
Amen.
(Anglican Church in North America Book of Common Prayer)

Ordinary Time Day 192
SALLY BREEDLOVE

Reflect on Hebrews 12:18–29

Call to Prayer

Hebrews was written to Christians who were struggling to continue to believe and follow after Jesus. Instead of coddling these dispirited people, the writer paints a large picture of the beauty of Jesus and all that lies ahead for us who believe. He reminds us that the call to live a faithful life is a serious one. Hebrews never "dumbs down" the cost of discipleship and never takes the focus off Jesus.

Could it be that this writer is speaking directly to our time? Yes, his words are meant for all generations, but our world is awash with a choose-what-you-want-to-believe-about-Jesus discipleship. We live in a time when so much is being shaken to the core and when sin everywhere is being exposed. Will we be faithful, holy people? Ordinary Time reminds us again and again that this is indeed what discipleship is about.

The desire of the writer of Hebrews is to call out the best in us, not to make our lives more difficult. He calls us to life, to Jesus, to grace, to an unshakable kingdom, to a coming celebration. Throngs of festive angels and believing people are gathering, and we are invited to join them.

So what do we do in turbulent times like ours?

Run to Jesus.

Will we believe what he has promised? Beyond all the destruction, disease, and division of our day, the unshakable kingdom awaits us. Yes, be sober. God is fire; God is on a housecleaning mission. But beyond the sifting and the shaking that is taking place lies the beautiful city. If you pay close attention, you will hear, see, and smell the first hints of a huge party, the marriage feast of the Lamb. Have you said yes to your invitation?

As you pray, say yes to the Triune God. You are walking toward the party where Jesus is the exalted Bridegroom. He awaits the arrival of his bride, the church. Will you let him make you beautiful so you are eager to join that party in that city?

Recommended Closing Prayer

> O God, the King of glory, you have exalted your only Son Jesus Christ with great triumph to your kingdom in heaven: Do not leave us comfortless, but send us your Holy Spirit to strengthen us, and exalt us to that place where our Savior Christ has gone before; who lives and reigns with you and the Holy Spirit, one God, in glory everlasting. Amen. *(Anglican Church in North America Book of Common Prayer)*

Ordinary Time Day 193

SALLY BREEDLOVE

Reflect on Hebrews 13

Call to Prayer

Hebrews 13 contains a vast number of instructions. In only twenty-five verses, the writer will step on all our toes.

Listen to the breadth of his instruction: Offer a startling level of hospitality, even to people you don't know. Identify with prisoners and victims of abuse. Live by and within God's plan for sex: it's a gift for covenant marriage between a wife and a husband. Give up your greed that insists on acquiring more and more things. Appreciate and imitate your pastor.

He goes on: Don't be led away from solid truth. Join Jesus in the outsider world. Give up your obsession with being an insider to any group. Get a job and work hard. Share. Help build the unity and peace of the church; don't destroy it with your constant critiques. Pray for others, not just for yourself.

After this catalogue of commands, the writer says, "I've kept it as brief as possible; I haven't piled on a lot of extras" (Hebrews 13:22 MSG).

We might want to reply, "You've got to be kidding. If I live like this, I won't fit in anywhere. I'll be seen as too conservative, too liberal, too supportive of the establishment, too supportive of the disenfranchised, too judgmental, and too dismissive of the values of people whose esteem I really want."

Look at the passage again. Yes, the writer gives us many instructions for living a with-God life, but he assures us that Jesus is the one who will always be faithful, and he promises us that his grace is the only good ground for life.

A holy life isn't a duty; it's a joy. It's the pathway to deep intimacy with the Father. We practice living like Jesus because it puts us in sync with Jesus, the one who has loved us first.

As you pray, will you speak aloud to God some ways your life needs to change? Will you thank God that Jesus is the one who puts you together and provides for you? You are not on your own in this world.

Recommended Closing Prayer

> Look upon us, O Lord,
> and let all the darkness of our souls
> vanish before the beams of thy brightness.
> Fill us with holy love,
> and open to us the treasures of thy wisdom.
> *(Saint Augustine)*

Ordinary Time Day 194

Reflect on James 1

Call to Prayer

Life is a major challenge. We encounter difficulties that threaten to swamp us. We find ourselves confused in the midst of the haves and have-nots. We hear the whisper of evil thoughts within our own hearts. "Give in," they say. "This is the way to life."

We forget to listen, we speak hastily, and then our anger makes things worse. We study God's Word, but then we're off running our own lives, forgetting what we read just hours before. We parade a spiritual persona and forget to show compassion to the hurting people right under our noses.

So, what is James's point as he puts his finger on issues that create havoc in our lives? Is following Christ as complicated as running through the checklist on a huge airplane before takeoff? Is the Christian life a convoluted endeavor with way too many particulars to get "just right"?

If so, then it's an exhausting self-improvement program.

But what if the Christian life is a far more beautiful and joy-filled endeavor? Listen to James 1:21: "In simple humility, let our gardener, God, landscape you with the Word, making a salvation-garden of your life" (MSG). Gardens emerge over time. They change season by season. New plants are added and weeds are pulled out over and over again. Differences abound: cool shade, bright sunshine, spots of color, and quiet places with subtle variations. No two gardens are identical. The gardener always works with the givens of a particular site. But that same gardener, with time and work, can transform a littered, wasted place into a place of great beauty. We are not asked to be the gardener, but we can be receptive soil.

Do you demand to be the foreman of a construction site and force your life to have a certain look? Or will you let the Gardener garden your life?

As you pray, submit to the givens of your life—your gifting or lack of gifting, your opportunities or lack of opportunities, the things out of your control. Give God both space and time to work in the soil of your life. Ask him to transform you into a salvation garden.

Recommended Closing Prayer

> Almighty God, you alone can bring into order the unruly wills and affections of sinners: Grant your people grace to love what you command and desire what you promise; that, among the swift and varied changes of this world, our hearts may surely there be fixed where true joys are to be found; through Jesus Christ our Lord, who lives and reigns with you and the Holy Spirit, one God, now and forever. Amen.
>
> *(Anglican Church in North America Book of Common Prayer)*

Ordinary Time Day 195
SALLY BREEDLOVE

Reflect on James 2:1–13

Call to Prayer

Could any rule set us free? Our world insists that the best life is one where nobody tells anyone what to do.

But think about it. If I am hurt or diminished by what you want, then are we really on a path that leads to freedom and joy for everyone?

But it's also true that we could never come up with enough laws to protect us from each other. As this passage reminds us that even in our playing favorites, deciding who belongs and who should be excluded, makes us hurtful people who cannot be trusted.

The command to love God and to love others as we love ourselves is the only law that covers everything.

But what is love? Our world uses the idea of love to justify so many things that aren't love. Love is not doing what we want to do, but learning to be like Jesus. He always loved, and his love was always life-giving, unhypocritical, holy, sacrificial. It always built up those who received it. His love never damaged other people's souls or bodies. His love also spoke the truth, and it fiercely opposed all sorts of evil and hypocrisy. Ultimately his love triumphed in the most devastating event in history: the death of the beloved Son of God on the cross.

As you pray, sit with your own life this past day and past week. Where have you loved like Jesus loves? Where have you fallen short? Confess to Jesus what your lack of love has done to those around you. Ask him to teach you to love as he loves.

Recommended Closing Prayer

O Triune God, teach me to love as you love. In the name of Jesus Christ. Amen.

Ordinary Time Day 196

SALLY BREEDLOVE

Reflect on James 2:14–26

Call to Prayer

James won't let us get away with anything, will he? He says that hard times help us, that the rich are no more important than the poor, and that we can't blame our sin on situations beyond our control. He tells us to lead with our ears, not our mouths, and to get our tempers under control. He declares we are to be people of compassion. He says we set ourselves against God if we favor the rich.

Now in this passage, he expands on a point from chapter 1: listening to God's Word, knowing it, and even saying we believe it is not the same thing as receiving it into our hearts and obeying it.

To make his point, he gives us three examples: demons, the patriarch Abraham, and Rahab the harlot.

Demons accept that God is God—but it doesn't change them. Solid doctrine without worship and obedience is frightening. It's the path of demons.

The faith of Abraham was not something he could simply hold in his head or heart. It had to make itself known. Real faith is never simply a private or intellectual position. Because his faith was real, Abraham had to obey and choose sacrificial worship.

The harlot Rahab who lived in Jericho was not a Jew, but she believed, and that belief propelled her. She risked hiding the Jewish spies when her house was searched, and she put her safety and future in the hands of God. Faith involves risk and a deep obedience. It takes us past what we can see and count on.

As you pray, ask yourself if your faith summons you to worship and obedience. Does your faith ask you to believe God even when to follow him looks like the path to pain and loss? Does your faith ever take you to risky places?

Are there choices you could make that would increase the ways you live by faith? What are they? What will you choose to live by a living faith in the living God? Pray!

Recommended Closing Prayer

> O Lord, who hast mercy upon all, take away from me my sins,
> and mercifully kindle in me the fire of thy Holy Spirit.
> Take away from me the heart of stone,
> and give me a heart of flesh,
> a heart to love and adore thee,
> a heart to delight in thee,
> to follow and to enjoy thee,
> for Christ's sake.
> *(Ambrose of Milan)*

Ordinary Time Day 197

SALLY BREEDLOVE

Reflect on James 3

Call to Prayer

James says our tongues have the power to destroy. They set forests on fires; they offer up polluted water; they are like wild beasts tearing people to shreds. It can't go on like this, James says. But what is the hope? He has already said the tongue is impossible to fully train.

But instead of taping our mouths shut, James invites us to cultivate wise and humble hearts. Without humility, we are lost. Our need to protect, promote, and present ourselves in a certain way never leads to real friendship or community.

We also need real wisdom. Life is confusing. Mercifully, James tells us what wisdom looks like. It never tries to be impressive, and it never pits people against each other. Instead, it looks like holiness and decency. Wisdom is steady. Wisdom is kind. It is usually a quiet presence, not a pushy opinion.

In a world like ours that is fractious, angry, and accusatory, what would it be like to live by humility? What would it look like to become a woman or man (or boy or girl) of wisdom? How would being humble and wise deepen your ability to love? Is real community even possible without humility and wisdom?

As you pray, ask God to make you both wise and humble.

Recommended Closing Prayer

> O God, without whose beauty and goodness our souls are unfed, without whose truth our reason withers: Consecrate our lives to your will, giving us such purity of heart, such depth of faith, and such steadfastness of purpose that in time we may come to think your own thoughts after you; through Jesus Christ our Lord.
> Amen.
> *(Anglican Church in North America Book of Common Prayer)*

Ordinary Time Day 198

KARI WEST

Reflect on Zechariah 10:6–9

Call to Prayer

Exile is not the end.

God's promises to gather his people back from the ends of the earth pervade the scriptures. He will do it because of his great compassion, his great faithfulness, his great love. He will do it because he desires to make the hearts of his children glad, as glad as with wine.

God will whistle for us and gather us in, all those he has redeemed and called by name. In the far countries, we will remember the Lord.

This passage was a specific promise to the people of Israel, scattered because of their sin and rebellion. And yet it's also a promise for those of us from all the nations whom God has redeemed and brought into his family. The gathering-in has begun, and Christ has flung wide the door to the sheep pen through his death and resurrection, but the job is not yet complete. A sense of not-at-homeness haunts us all, ever since our first parents were flung out of the Garden.

As you pray, take heart. God will gather you. God will make your heart glad. God will cause you to remember him in all the far places of your soul. He will draw you to himself, and you will live.

Recommended Closing Prayer

God, you are our homeland. Thank you for your promise not to leave us alone on foreign soil. We praise you for your compassion and your great love for all your people. Strengthen us. For Christ's sake and for the glory of your name. Amen.

Ordinary Time Day 199

KARI WEST

Reflect on Matthew 22:34–40

Call to Prayer

Here again we have a religious leader testing Christ. But this time, Jesus gives a direct answer to his question, though it was not asked out of a desire to understand. You can almost picture this man asking his question and then sitting back, arms folded, ready to weigh Christ's response and judge his character accordingly.

But Jesus offers an answer that has sifted souls for centuries. He lays two commandments at the feet of this teacher, so simple and yet profound enough that we will never delve the depths of these few words: "Love God with all you are, and love your neighbor likewise."

As you come to pray, what stirs in you as you read these two greatest of commandments? Do they simply slip out of your sight and mind, too well-worn by familiarity for you to grasp their profundity? Ask the Lord for fresh insight into these commands.

Do they stir up guilt or perhaps desperation within you? How could you ever love God with all your heart, soul, mind, and strength? How could you ever bend out of your own inward navel-gazing long enough to love your neighbor?

Take your feelings of inadequacy to the Lord, and with Saint Augustine pray that God will command what he will and grant what he commands.

Most of all, come to Christ and thank him that he has fulfilled these two vast, paramount commandments. He has loved the Lord with everything, and he has loved all his neighbors perfectly, including you. Come and partake of his righteousness through the free gift of salvation.

Recommended Closing Prayer

Thank you, Christ, that you will love us to the end. Work in us, Holy Spirit, that we may love as we have been loved. Amen.

Ordinary Time Day 200

KARI WEST

Reflect on Psalm 89:20–29

Call to Prayer

Why should we care about a poem about a long-dead king from a far-distant time?

Scholars understand King David of the Old Testament as a forerunner of Christ. Psalms like these—though truly a promise to David—find their ultimate fulfillment in Jesus. He will be the most exalted of the Kings of the earth, his covenant will never fail, and his line and his throne will be established throughout all the ages.

This is a beautiful and important psalm because Christ's victory is our victory. Christ's supremacy and exaltation are what our hearts desire in their redeemed, inmost places. Here God promises that what we most long for will come to pass—the everlasting reign of King Jesus. Nothing will stop God's plan from unfolding in the fullness of time.

Even now we share in Christ's righteousness; how the Lord sees his Son is how he sees all his people. God promises his faithful love will always be with Christ, so we can know his faithful love is with us. We are his beloved ones, hidden in Jesus.

As you pray, meditate on the surety of Christ's present and coming kingdom, his present and coming kingship. Ask the Lord for specific ways Christ's supremacy can encourage you to live faithfully and joyfully as you wait. And above all, rest in God's forever love for you, his child.

Recommended Closing Prayer

God, we praise you that Christ's reign will stretch throughout eternity and that your covenant with us, bought by his blood, will never fail. Strengthen us and sustain us. Amen.

Ordinary Time Day 201

Reflect on Psalm 131

Call to Prayer

Do you know what it's like to be held by God?

Here the psalmist likens his soul to a weaned child at rest in the arms of its mother. His soul is *held*—cradled in the arms of God—and in that place of perfect security, the psalmist is at rest. His soul is weaned from the need to strive, control, fix, or finish. There is no anxious energy here, no pushing past limits, and no drive to achieve or be recognized. Rather, the psalmist acknowledges that there is much "too great and too marvelous" (Psalm 131:1 ESV) for him—much that he cannot conceive of or contain—and he is content with his humble capacity and place. He has released the need to be anything other than who he is, and he has surrendered completely to the arms of his Father.

The psalmist gives us a picture of the daily invitation at the heart of Christian discipleship: to come to God exactly as we are, acknowledge where we have fallen short or taken on too much, and rest in the hands of the one who holds us and the world.

As you settle into prayer, become aware of all that you are carrying and how the weight of it registers in your body, heart, and mind. Is there anything you need to release to the Lord in order to rest more fully in his loving presence? Invite the Holy Spirit to guide you through this process of repentance and surrender. Be gentle with yourself as you acknowledge places where you have resisted God's grace, tried to control things, or willfully chosen your own way.

Then take a moment to read through Psalm 131 again. Imagine surrendering all that you are carrying and then crawling into the arms of your loving Father. Rest like an infant in his embrace, and let yourself be held. Take as much time as you need in this place of childlike surrender before finishing your time of prayer.

Recommended Closing Prayer

Gracious Father, make my heart like a weaned child—content and at rest. Help me to loosen my grasp on the things of this world and to find my security in you alone. Show me what I was meant to carry and what you are asking me now to release. Help me to trust you in all areas of my life and to walk humbly with you as your beloved child. In Jesus's precious and powerful name. Amen.

Ordinary Time Day 202

SALLY BREEDLOVE

Reflect on Revelation 22:6–21

Call to Prayer

Everything is going to be all right. What strange words to write or to read in a world like ours. Could it possibly be true that we are headed home, headed to a city brimming with life, where our thirst for we-are-not-sure-quite-what is finally satisfied, where there is nothing we have to earn, because grace supplies what we have tried so hard to achieve on our own?

In this present moment, the gates have not yet been flung open to that city where all will be well. We are mired in a world of conflict. But John encourages us. Despite the brokenness and the rebellion all around us, even as "evildoer[s] still do evil, and the filthy [will] still be filthy" (Revelation 22:11 ESV), God's people are to seek to be like Jesus. We are called to be people of whom it is said, "The righteous still do right, and the holy [will] still be holy" (Revelation 22:11 ESV).

How do we keep our focus as we wait for something to finally make things better on this earth? Can we have any assurance that the future will eliminate the pandemics of sickness, evil, injustice, and brokenness that plague our world? Is there a way to live in hope?

Jesus spans the arch of history, making sense of God's work in this world. He is the "Alpha and the Omega … the Root and the Offspring of David, and the bright Morning Star" (Revelation 22:13, 22:16 NIV). He will one day judge evil and cast it into the abyss. The new city he is fashioning—that uncorrupt, incorruptible place—will be ready. We'll be welcomed home.

Turn to Jesus; he will take you home to God. As you pray, pray with the whole church, and with the Spirit, "Come, Lord Jesus" (Revelation 22:20 NIV).

Recommended Closing Prayer

Hasten, O Father, the coming of your kingdom; and grant that we your servants, who now live by faith, may with joy behold your Son at his coming in glorious majesty; even Jesus Christ, our only Mediator and Advocate. Amen.
(Anglican Church in North America Book of Common Prayer)

Afterword

STEPHEN A. MACCHIA

My first introduction to Lectio Divina (also known as Contemplative Bible Reading) was at a spiritual formation conference twenty years ago. But it seems like only yesterday given how memorable the experience was for all of us in the room.

The facilitator was gracious, poised, and confident. Step by step, he led the room full of hungry pilgrims into the presence of God. First, we sat in silence for what felt like a forever pause. Then, he read the short passage oh so slowly. Each word was graciously vocalized and pronounced with clarity. Emphasis was placed appropriately on each and every word. It was as if we'd never heard or seen the text before. The room was hushed in palpable stillness. The Spirit was leading us by the hand one syllable at a time.

Silence a second time. A rich and abundant opportunity to reflect. Holding the verses, one delicate word at a time. Noticing the phrase or word that caught our attention. Reviewing it, observing it, interviewing why it had landed so obviously in our mind's eye. We asked God to reveal his Word to us in a fresh way, as if we'd never heard it before.

Step by step, we traveled together the Lectio journey ...

- from that initial silence to still our hearts and receive God's Word (*silencio*);
- into a sacred reading of the text (*lectio*);
- then into deep meditation on the single word or phrase that leapt off the page and into our hearts (*meditatio*);
- followed by a prayerful response to the present work of God (*oratio*);
- with some additional listening and noticing of the Word taking root in our souls (*contemplatio*);
- and, ultimately, entering into the transformation of our inner being and our relationship with God (*incarnatio*), mostly focusing on the Word and how it has nourished and strengthened our souls.

It was a sweet experience. Led by the Spirit, focused on the Word, facilitated by a trusted companion, we were opened up to a new world of prayerful encounter with the living God.

When Lectio Divina becomes prayer, then you know you've touched a nerve the Spirit is inviting you to consider. There's a fresh wind of God's Spirit when one genuinely receives the living Word. It's profoundly good for the soul.

As I practice Lectio Divina today, I imagine myself alive more than five hundred years ago, immediately prior to the Protestant Reformation and the discovery of the printing press. I place myself in the public square or the sanctuary of a village church. The "learned" one holds a parchment in his hands. He reads it for the gathered ones. We hang on every word. We say "Read it again," and he does so. The repetitive reading of the scriptures causes them to come alive at the hearing. We have no written manuscript, just the ears of our hearts, gently inclined toward the Word.

If we were alive at that time, we'd be sitting on the edges of our seats, attentive to the invitation of God to receive the seed of his Word and allow it to enter the goodness of our souls' soil. Let it rest there and become a new planting. The fruit will be a hundredfold if we leave it alone to be rooted within, destined to restore and renew us from the inside out. May it be so today as it was so long ago.

You are blessed to be holding this resource in your hands. May the words of your mouth and the meditations of your heart be inspired by the Word and then multiplied in your soul and in your service to others. Sit on the edge of your seat and receive what God has in store for you. Like you've never heard the Word before. Such joy.

Acknowledgments

On the Eighth Day has been the work of friends—coming from a cross section of people, organizations, and churches—who hope in the power of scripture-focused prayer and hunger for the growth of God's church. This prayer guide would not be in print without Willa Kane's gift of faith and generosity and her ability to call people to action; Madison Perry's leadership, vision, and energy; Sally Breedlove's depth of spiritual insight and writing ability; and Kari West's love for scripture and the written word.

The project of scriptural invitations to prayer began as a daily email to friends around the world from Willa Kane, Sally Breedlove, and Madison Perry, relying chiefly on the lifetime of scriptural reflection of Sally, who wrote the majority of the first hundred calls to prayer. Kari West joined the team early on, bringing her gifts of editing and writing. This volume represents invitations to prayer written mainly by Sally and Kari, though a significant number were written by Madison and Willa and by many other generous, gifted guest writers.

Francis Capitanio from the American Anglican Council gave significant creative direction, from the book title to the seasonal ordering, writing several entries along the way. Other writers include Phil Ashey, Nathan Baxter, Bill Boyd, MaryRachel Boyd, Steven A. Breedlove, Steven E. Breedlove, Elizabeth Gatewood, Art Going, Gayle Heaslip, MaryMac Hoehn, Matt Hoehn, Tamara Hill Murphy, Brandon Walsh, Abigail Hull Whitehouse, and Andrew Williams. Steven E. Breedlove also provided the rich introduction to the Christian year and the introductions to each season. Ken Boa kindly wrote the foreword, and Stephen A. Macchia graciously provided the afterword. The North Carolina Study Center, a Christian study center based in Chapel Hill, North Carolina, devoted organizational assistance to bless the global church.

About the Authors

Sally Breedlove is an author, spiritual director and the co-founder of JourneyMates. She serves alongside her husband, Steve, a Bishop in the Anglican Church of North America. They are the glad parents of five married children and 16 grandchildren.

Willa Kane is a trustee for the American Anglican Council, trustee emeritus for the Anglican Relief and Development Fund and a founding member of Holy Trinity Anglican Church in Raleigh. She and her husband, John, have four married children and 11 grandchildren. They live in Raleigh, NC and Sea Island, GA.

Madison Perry is the Executive Director of the North Carolina Study Center. He also is an ordained priest in the Diocese of the Carolinas (ACNA). Madison and his wife, Pamela, live in Durham, NC, and have six children.

Kari West has worked in the nonprofit world for the past nine years in a variety of roles. She enjoys literature, creative writing, and exploring the intersection of faith and art. Kari lives in Apex, NC, with her husband, Jason, and two daughters, Eliana and Riley.